Psychodynamics for Consultants and Managers

Psychodynamics for Consultants and Managers

From Understanding to Leading Meaningful Change

Leopold Vansina and Marie-Jeanne Vansina-Cobbaert

With contributions from
Gilles Amado and Sandra Schruijer

A John Wiley & Sons, Ltd., Publication

Other Wiley Editorial Offices

John Wiley & Sons Inc., 111 River Street, Hoboken, NJ 07030, USA

Jossey-Bass, 989 Market Street, San Francisco, CA 94103-1741, USA

Wiley-VCH Verlag GmbH, Boschstr. 12, D-69469 Weinheim, Germany

John Wiley & Sons Australia Ltd, 42 McDougall Street, Milton, Queensland 4064, Australia

John Wiley & Sons (Asia) Pte Ltd, 2 Clementi Loop #02-01, Jin Xing Distripark, Singapore 129809

John Wiley & Sons Canada Ltd, 6045 Freemont Blvd, Mississauga, ONT, L5R 4J3, Canada

Wiley also publishes its books in a variety of electronic formats. Some content that appears in print may not be available in electronic books.

Library of Congress Cataloging-in-Publication Data

Vansina, Leopold.
   Psychodynamics : for consultants and managers / Leopold Vansina and Marie-Jeanne Vansina-Cobbaert ; with contributions from Gilles Amado and Sandra Schruijer.
      p. cm.
   Includes bibliographical references and index.
   ISBN 978-0-470-77931-6 (alk. paper)
   1. Organizational behavior.   2. Organizational effectiveness–Psychological aspects.
3. Organizational sociology.   I. Vansina-Cobbaert, Marie-Jeanne.   II. Amado, Gilles, 1945-
III. Schruijer, Sandra.   IV. Title.
   HD58.7.V365 2008
   158.7024′658–dc22

               2008017091

British Library Cataloguing in Publication Data

A catalogue record for this book is available from the British Library

ISBN-13   978-0-470-77931-6 (hbk)

Typeset in 11/13pt Times by Aptara Inc., New Delhi, India

This book is printed on acid-free paper responsibly manufactured from sustainable forestry in which at least two trees are planted for each one used for paper production.

Contents

About the Authors

Leopold Vansina, PhD. in psychology, is Professor emeritus of the Catholic University of Leuven and Université Catholique de Louvain-la-Neuve, Belgium, where he taught, on a part-time basis, Organisational Behaviour, Issues in International Organisations, and Consulting. After a year of study at Yale University and the University of Michigan, he started his post-graduate training in psychoanalysis at the Belgian Psychoanalytic Society with the intention of becoming an organisation consultant. He founded I.O.D. Leuven, an international, interdisciplinary institute active in consulting, research and training, which he managed for 25 years. Currently, he continues his professional activities from the Professional Development Institute, Ltd. His writings have been published in various journals and books. He is member of the Academy of Management, and the International Association of Applied Psychology. E-mail: Leopold.vansina@skynet.be

Marie-Jeanne Vansina-Cobbaert, PhD. in psychology is a retired, full member of the Belgian Psychoanalytic Society, The European Psychoanalytic Federation and the International Psychoanalytic Association. She conducted a nine-year research study at the University of Leuven on S. Freud's psychoanalytic work. Subsequently she became a senior member of the International Institute for Organisational and Social Development (I.O.D. Leuven) where she worked as a group consultant in management development programmes and as a researcher. The last 15 years of her career, she worked at the University Mental Hospital as a psychoanalytic group therapist, and as consultant and supervisor in the post-graduate programme for psychoanalytic therapists. Currently, she is an active member of the Professional Development Institute, Ltd. She is the author of a book, several articles and chapters in the domain of psychoanalysis, group dynamics and organisation development. E-mail: cobbaert.mj@skynet.be

Contributors

Gilles Amado, Psy. Dr. is Professor of Organisational Psychosociology at the HEC School of Management, Paris, a consultant and an action researcher. He is a founding member of the International Society for the Psychoanalytic Study of Organisations, co-editor-in-chief of the *Nouvelle Revue de Psychosociologie*, and a member of the French Society for Psychoanalytic Group Psychotherapy. E-mail: amado@hec.fr

Sandra Schruijer is Professor of Organisation Sciences at the Utrecht School of Governance, University of Utrecht and Professor of Organisational Psychology at TiasNimbas Business School, Tilburg University, both in the Netherlands. Her research involves the psychological dynamics of conflict and collaboration between organisations. Sandra heads Professional Development International, an institute that organises professional development programmes and consults organisations and managers with respect to collaboration and large-scale change. Sandra is editor of the *Journal of Community and Applied Social Psychology*. She has developed a special interest in cultural history and also holds a doctoral degree in History. E-mail: Schruijer@yahoo.com

Acknowledgements

We wrote this book based on the many years of practice that both of us had. With appreciation we recognise that our practice and the book would have been quite different without having had our many tutors and mentors. They did not only teach, but were always questioning their own work and assumptions, always looking at the influence of changing conditions and at the need to adapt their theory and practice. Their enthusiasm was such that it became infectious, and we shall always be thankful for catching their 'viruses'.

Apart from that, the book is also the result of many, often-heated discussions we have had with colleagues and students, including those who disagreed with or even opposed some of our viewpoints.

If we finally decided to write, it was largely due to repeated, strong insistence from colleagues and students, who listened to our talks or took part in our International Professional Development Programme, seminars or supervisions. Now that a large part of the work is done we are very grateful for their encouragement, even if at times it became a bit pushy.

Our gratefulness certainly includes the people and organisations that allowed us to use the work we did together, either as illustrations or as cases. And we surely wish to thank those who read our manuscript or parts thereof, and suggested different kinds of important improvements in the text.

General Introduction

Some twenty-five years ago, while I was doing some work at the dinner table, my wife, Marie-Jeanne, sitting in front of the fireplace, called my attention: "Leopold, here is something that is worth remembering!" She read me a passage from Roy Schafer's book. "I think it was Sartre who said somewhere that experience usually consists of somebody's repeating the same error over a long enough period to feel entitled to claim absolute authority for doing things in that faulty way" (1983, p. 287). The tone in which she read this phrase made it clear that she wanted me to reflect on it as much as it made her think about her work. I didn't learn the phrase by heart, but it left an imprint in my mind that stayed with me and still tickles my critical thinking about standard practices as well as my own work as a consultant. In this book we wish to share with you our thinking and experiences in the somewhat obscure field of psychodynamics. The major share of publications on psychodynamics are either written by Group Relations consultants who have moved into work in organisations, or venture into explaining macro relations and phenomena in society based on psychoanalytic theory. We present a book that intends to further professional development and inspire organisation consultants and managers. We take you beyond the field of simply applying group relations to groups in organisations and beyond process consulting or Organisation Development into the richer domain of assisting clients to create conditions that on the one hand, change the dynamics of the system studied in a more lasting way and on the other hand, provide conditions for human development.

We have two aims. The first one is, as already stated, educational. Psychodynamics may be defined as an approach by which consultants or managers endeavour to gain a good enough understanding of what is happening or not happening in a social system and why in order to take effective action (or inaction) to improve the functioning of that system in a more lasting way, while offering opportunities for psychic development of the people in it. Psychodynamics is still, since its definition by Freud (1915), a broad, largely vague concept. Therefore, we attempt to clarify it by describing it successively as an '*evolving body of knowledge*'; a '*perspective*' or a way of looking at the world around us; a form of '*inquiry*', and a way of '*taking action*' based on a good enough understanding of the system in its context. These four angles create a pretty good picture of what the psychodynamic approach can bring to organisational and community life and of the inevitable, personal involvement of the manager or consultant in this work. But, psychodynamics is closely associated with psychoanalysis. This is partly due to its original definition by Freud, but it is even more related to the fact that psychodynamics does not only deal with conscious but also with unconscious factors that play a role in organisational behaviour and performance. Therefore, we would like to inform and take you with us in understanding the essence of psychoanalytic thinking and foremost, in the understanding of the essential principles of psychoanalytic work. This basis is fundamental to move into distinguishing psychodynamics from psychoanalysis from which it largely developed.

The realities of organisational life are, however, too complex and too evolving to be grasped by psychodynamics alone. In order to gain a good enough understanding for taking action on them, we bring to bear different frames and methods from various disciplinary perspectives. Furthermore, we, as consultants and managers, become engaged with these complex realities with changing and partly overlapping modes of consciousness: apprehensive, reflective, experiencing, and participative thinking and responsive acting (see Chapter 9 in Part Two). The shifting modes, frames, perspectives and methods are not purely the outcome of rational processes. Our intuitive capabilities and creative processes also play an important part in bringing them about. Four projects, different in nature and setting, are described in detail to illustrate the psychodynamic approach at work (see Part Three).

The second aim of the book may, at first sight, be of less interest for the practice of consultants or managers. It reflects our scientific interest in clarifying concepts and working principles, in critical reflections on standard practices to encourage further thinking, study and validation. However, by no means do we intend to provide the practitioner with a more extended vocabulary for the practice. In fact, all along the way we encourage managers and consultants to use common, comprehensible language in their work. The clarifications of concepts only serve to encourage people to explore further some phenomena to enhance their understanding of what may be going on at a certain time, in a certain setting to take proper action: inquiry, interventions or creating conditions to bring the system to a more effective and satisfying level of functioning.

At various points, the book will inevitably be a source of happy and unhappy learning as Lyman Ketchum and Eric Trist (1992) categorise learning experiences. Happy learning is basically additive, an extension or a refinement of things we already know. It makes us feel good. Unhappy learning is different. It involves a confrontation with oneself, the values, beliefs, theories and models that one uses to work with, but which are now being challenged by the thinking and practices of others, in this case the authors. These confrontations may lead to a kind of learning that questions the very beliefs, values and models that we hold. In order to generate genuine learning of this sort, it must lead to a revision of ourselves, and to a process of unlearning. Unhappy learning of this kind may even challenge parts of our identity, which entails stress or makes us at the very least feel somewhat uncomfortable.

Before we discuss basic notions in and principles of psychoanalytic work, we would like to present a simple case to introduce the psychodynamic practice. The case raises various questions: How did the consultant spot a possible underlying conflict? How did he time his intervention? How did he combine and manage technical advice on restructuring with a self-reflective task? Why did he formulate that reflective question in an indirect way? How did it become possible to discuss delicate issues with the manager present? These questions or issues and many more will be directly and indirectly covered in the book.

Leopold Vansina and Marie-Jeanne Vansina-Cobbaert
Leuven, May 2007

REFERENCES

Freud, S. (1915). The Unconscious. In: *Standard Ed.*, **14**. London: The Hogarth Press.
Ketchum, L.D. & Trist, E. (1992). *All Teams Are Not Created Equal: How Employee Empowerment Really Works*. London: Sage Publications.
Schafer, R. (1993). *The Analytic Attitude*. London: Karnac. First published in 1983 by Hogarth Press Ltd.

A CASE TO INTRODUCE THE PRACTICE

An international chemical firm wanted to centralise all the purchasing departments of its 10 business units into one, new Purchasing Centre. The Centre would be responsible for establishing frame contracts with a range of preferential suppliers, and for evaluating their reliability. The business units would then have direct computer links with these suppliers enabling them to purchase directly from the suppliers within these frame contracts. James, the new Purchasing Director was in charge of recruiting suitable people from the business units, and training them for the new jobs while the various purchasing departments in the business units continued to operate. Since there were too many people working in purchasing some personnel had to be outsourced, others had to be made redundant through early retirement.

I was called in to assist James in making this 'eighteen-month project' successful. The major challenge was to synchronise the various change efforts of building the Purchasing Centre, downsizing the 10 existing purchase departments, and establishing a new software programme (SAP) while keeping the business units in full operation without any interruption. At the same time, these changes were to be introduced with care and due consideration for the people, all in line with the spirit of the company's personnel policy.

A steering group was formed which consisted of the ten personnel managers of the business units, the project manager of ITC, James, the new Purchasing Director and myself. A 'network plan' was carefully set up, specifying the various contributions and the timing of the change efforts. The plan was presented to and agreed by the business units at a special meeting at corporate level and subsequently negotiated with the unions. First, lists were to be made of people to be transferred to the Centre, to remain in the business units, to be outsourced or to be made redundant. When a rough estimation could be made of the number of persons to be outsourced and/or made

---

redundant, a social programme was to be developed and negotiated with the unions. Second, all purchasing personnel were to be individually informed about their future and about the timing of the change in their status. These changes would come in waves; yet, the persons would be asked to stay on until the work itself was properly taken over by the Centre. The special training of the people for the Centre would take place as soon as everyone had been informed and the hard- and software were available. Everything appeared to be under control until James went on sickness leave with serious heart problems. When he came back to work, he could, at the start, only work part-time and he had to stop smoking. The network plan was adjusted and everyone in the steering group witnessed his struggle to stop smoking his cigars. Shortly after his return to work, I sensed an increase in tension at our regular meetings. Paying more attention to the changes in tension and the content under review, I observed more reservations in coming to an agreement on the lists of persons that had to be outsourced or made redundant. I assumed, but could not verify, that the increased tensions were largely due to the change in the content of the work. As long as we were involved in the network planning, getting the numbers right and designing an appropriate social plan, the personnel managers were less confronted with real persons. Now, we had begun to make the four lists of persons to be transferred to the Centre, to remain in the downsized departments, to be outsourced or to be made redundant. The future of the persons on these last two lists seemed to stir up much greater concern and uncertainty amongst the personnel managers. The lists contained names of employees they had known for years and the decisions were clear-cut: in or out of the company. Delays surfaced in some business units more than in others. Some personnel managers explained these deviations as being due to the business unit management's difficulties with the agreed network plan. James became frustrated and started opening the following meetings with a progress follow-up during which he wanted to know "How many (employees) had been thrown over the fence?" This particular way of talking triggered some irritation amongst the personnel managers, but not one person made a comment. Something was going on beneath the surface that hindered effective work. It was maybe something that escaped their awareness, or something they did not dare to talk about. Yet, I was not sure *what* it was. Knowing about James' heart problems, I suggested taking some time out during which each member in the steering group should write down on a piece of paper what gave meaning to their current work. When everyone had finished I asked each member to read aloud their answer. The personnel managers found meaning in the old personnel policy to care for the employees, to provide reasonable career prospects and so on. James' answer was clearly different: "To meet the agreed time schedule". In the ensuing discussions, the members could express, although with difficulty, how much they felt that James was only concerned about the schedule and did not pay any attention to their concerns about outsourcing or laying off concrete persons; persons they had known for some years and who had given them their confidence. "Throwing persons over the fence" conflicted with the values they had in working with their employees. The employees were persons, not objects. It seemed that in an unconscious way, a split had taken place between meeting the time schedule and dealing with downsizing in a human way. This split was expressed in terms of the normal conflict between *building* the new Purchasing Centre and *downsizing* the purchasing departments: James stood for the new business and they, the personnel managers, had to deal with the stresses and strains of breaking up relations with employees. For whatever reason, building and downsizing, although intrinsically related, had become split and became perceived as unrelated: it became the excitement of building versus the pain of breaking up relations.

Some other issues emerged: the business unit managers were accountable for their profits and losses and were seen as caring for *keeping the business going*, while James had been pictured as working for his new *career* in the Purchasing Centre, as if these two were also unrelated. In other words the issues of the steering group had already spread outside its boundaries into the wider organisation. The personnel managers had taken them into the business units, where images also developed about the persons involved in the project.

The time-out created an opportunity to voice concerns, perceptions and feelings that either could not be talked about during the progress reports, or may have been there at an unconscious level. Exploring why this had been so revealed a more delicate issue that affected me also, namely a concern for James' health.

Before his sickness leave the members felt more free to point to some critical issues, or voice their concerns and reservations. Now, they felt they had to hold back and swallow their own feelings in order not to raise tensions within him. Although plausible as an explanation, it may equally be that James' heart problem provided them with a handy, additional reason not to speak about their internal conflicts. Left without a place to voice and work through these internal conflicts, they felt alone and had looked for support from some of their managers in the business units. The normal competing priorities between *building* a new Centre, *downsizing* the departments and *keeping the business in operation* had become split up and incarnated in respectively James' work, the task of the personnel managers and the business unit managers. During the discussions these three major tasks, which were competing for attention, could be brought together and seen as interdependent. The group members came to face their internal conflicts and tensions and found courage and care in carrying out their stressful tasks.

Why James had become more sensitive and defensive about stress was not discussed. It may have been his heart condition and/or his impatience to regain the lost time, or something else, we don't know. What we did find out was that the other members of the steering group made, consciously or unconsciously, an effort to spare him. Most important, however, was the experience that time-out had created some kind of safe haven that allowed the members to reveal their concerns and talk through some pent-up feelings about the workplace and subsequently pick up their stressful work. This experience led to the decision to reserve from that session onward and on a regular basis some time for reflection on our work together. I volunteered to chair these review sessions.

The Purchasing Centre and the new way of working were introduced without significant delay and without work stoppages.

I have brought this life project up front at the very beginning of our book to stir your interest as a consultant or manager in this special approach, by which in a vast project one can zoom in to inquire into seemingly, insignificant events that may reveal some underlying processes that erode effective work and could lead to other serious problems. The sources of the issues in the steering group may have been unconscious to the members, and in that case, direct questions would most likely not have led to valid answers. Yet, the experiences of the workplace might most likely have led to a split up of tasks as if they were unrelated, while in fact they were not. Or, one may have been conscious about some attempts to spare James, because of his heart condition, but one could not talk about these concerns openly. Conditions needed to be created to make it possible. This approach to sensing and observing, to inquiring and creating conditions for dealing with organisational issues and underlying unconscious/non-conscious processes we call *psychodynamic*.

PART ONE

A Psychoanalytic Perspective on Groups and Organisations

Introduction

Marie-Jeanne Vansina-Cobbaert

As already stated in the General Introduction, a psychodynamic view on groups and organisations looks at *all* possible factors – conscious and unconscious – that influence group and organisational behaviour and structures. In as far as psychodynamics is interested in the way unconscious elements affect groups and organisations, it relies heavily on psychoanalytic thinking, because the core of psychoanalytic thinking and practice concerns the influence of what is called 'the dynamic unconscious' on human experiences, motivations, choices and actions. Consequently, elements of psychoanalytic theory and practice occupy a central place in the psychodynamic view on groups and organisations. For this reason the first part of the book explains and illustrates some of the basic psychoanalytic notions and work perspectives that are relevant for looking at and working with group and organisational features as well as problems.

Often, when one starts to talk about psychoanalysis to a non-analytical audience, one elicits a triple reaction. At one extreme one sees an over-enthusiastic group of people, ready, able, and all too willing to apply psychoanalytic notions or make interpretations whenever possible. At the other extreme one finds the over-critical ones. Some of those throw their arms into the air and try to convince you that to talk about something unconscious is plainly stupid.

"Whatever is unconscious you can't possibly know" is their credo, "so let it be!" Another section of the over-critical group just sigh, shake their heads in disbelief for they cannot understand that people who look quite normal and at times even seem to say interesting things, expect something worthwhile from psychoanalysis. They are convinced it is only about 'digging into your past', about sexuality or about the relationship with your mother. What good could that do for improving group or organisational functioning? Then there is also a middle group, composed of individuals who are interested but cautious. They listen thoughtfully, with a critical ear, but are always willing to learn something new that might be useful for solving their problems. This third group may indeed leave with new perspectives. The others hold a rather distorted view of what psychoanalytic thinking is all about. For one thing, the *unconscious as a system* is far from inaccessible; on the contrary. To a very large extent it is almost constantly trying to make itself known. The only problem is that one has to learn to understand its 'languages'. Moreover, psychoanalysis is not about applying concepts, and it is not about distinct, limited experiences or needs and desires that belong to our past. It is about discovering – through exploration – the meaning of whatever occurs in a specific, emotional, relational context that evolves in an actual field of tensions.

The *unconscious as a system* or the *dynamic unconscious* represents a very special and wonderful aspect of mental life. It is a complex, and continually active psychological system; a combination of contents, structures and processes that were either never clearly conscious or disappeared from consciousness due to several influences that will be discussed in the following chapters.

Over time, and depending on the author or the school s/he belonged to, different concepts are used to refer to this part of our psychodynamic, mental functioning. Freud (1915) used the expression "primary process thinking" to indicate the typical thought processes that belong to the *unconscious as a system* (the Ucs.). People like Klein or Isaacs and Kleinians in general, preferred the notion of phantasy as distinct from 'fantasy'[1] (Hinshelwood, 1989). Bion – although he belonged to the Kleinian group – used notions

---

[1] Today, the term phantasy is sometimes replaced by 'phantasm', a choice which in my view is not really adequate because 'phantasy' refers to a psychological process as well as to its content, while 'phantasm' refers primarily to content. I will elaborate upon this notion as well as upon its relation to fantasy in Chapter 1.

like: dream-thoughts, dreams, myths, pre-conceptions and conceptions (not concepts, those belong to another level of mental functioning) (1967). Finally, Meltzer (1984), also a Kleinian, introduced the notion of dream-life.

The different notions stress different characteristics of the unconscious dynamic processes; be it their origin in time and their energetic charge (Freud), their emotional, relational, imaginary bases (most Kleinians), or their typical developmental processes that provide the foundations of later forms of scientific conceptual and even mathematical thinking (Bion).

Personally I prefer the notions 'phantasy' and 'dream-life' because they express better than the others the originality, the imaginary richness, complexity and motivational power of the unconscious part of our inner world, and its indirect accessibility. Besides, 'dream-life' accentuates the continuous, uninterrupted activity and development of that part of our mental functioning. It is not only something that belongs to our past, it is just as active and important right now and all through our life; moreover, it is not only active during sleep, but also during waking life although we are not directly aware of it. Still, whatever notion we use, it always refers to a part of mental life (of an individual, a group or an organisation), which is omnipresent. Without our being aware of it, it has an influence on the way we experience our world and try to organise and live in it. It directs our sense making. It has an influence on what we fear or seek; on what we love or hate, try to attain or achieve, and on what we try to avoid. It directs our moods, and it plays a role in the development of our character. It underlies our conception of possible projects and futures.

Yet, although I prefer 'phantasy' and 'dream-life', for the sake of simplicity, I will often use Freud's letter word 'Ucs.' when I refer to the unconscious as a dynamic system in general terms.

Originally psychoanalysis was only interested in individuals. At first it had absolutely nothing to do with groups and organisations. Yet, if one looks at psychoanalysis as a body of knowledge that grew out of the attempt to assist people in overcoming their psychic difficulties and suffering, one may immediately wonder if such a body of knowledge might not be of interest in the context of some of the difficulties that occur in organisations. One reason for this could be that people are an important asset of organisations. Another reason might be that most organisational problems make people suffer. A third and important reason however could be that psychoanalysis – apart from looking at contents that form the bases for problems and at structures and processes that cause problems – has developed a way of finding out about specific factors that underlie difficulties, as well as a way to overcome them and enhance new, healthy development, including more pleasure and creativity.

Indeed, at a certain moment some pioneering analysts (like W. Bion, H. Bridger, E. Jaques, I. Menzies-Lyth) started to work with groups and organisations from a psychoanalytic perspective, in order to understand what was going on and to promote development and change. They, together with their colleagues and followers (e.g. E. Miller, K. Rice, E. Trist), approached groups and organisations as 'unknown others' whom they were going to discover and become acquainted with. On the basis of that work, they developed some specific concepts that fitted the specific phenomena they encountered. Think of Bion's *basic assumptions* (1961), which were later on, supplemented by Lawrence, Bain and Gould (1966) as well as by Turquet (1974). Think also of Jaques' (1955) and later Menzies-Lyth's *social defences* (1961), of Janis' *group think* (1982), of Harvey's *paradoxes* (1988), and of Vansina's *dominant logics* (1998).[2]

I suppose that some people who are familiar with Freud's writings, will argue that he himself – before those pioneers – already applied some of his notions to group, mass and cultural phenomena (1921, 1929). And this is absolutely true; but I am not so sure that Freud is a good example for what we are supposed to do whenever we *work in* organisations with the difficulties they actually face. What Freud did was to *imagine* certain social developments or *study* certain events, which he tried to understand by *applying*, from behind his desk, *concepts he had developed in another context*. This never helped to solve any of the problems he addressed.

One of the most striking examples of the way Freud sometimes worked occurred when he was over his ears in the doldrums of the young International Psychoanalytic Society. At that time he tried his very best to keep his key followers from 'killing' each other in their fight over the presidency of the young Society and over their influence on publications; but apparently he did not attempt to explore and understand the nature of what was going on. During that period Freud wrote *Totem and Taboo* (1913), and explained the origin of social and cultural institutions as the result of a gang of brothers conspiring

---

[2] The different concepts shall be developed in several of the following chapters.

to kill their father in order to get at his women. Although it probably never was Freud's conscious intention, this story deflected attention from the hatred between the brothers to their hatred of the father. The basis for that hatred was supposed to be the frustration of sexual desire. In other words, rather than facing the problems in the real situation, Freud addressed and explained an imagined situation in terms he was familiar with: terms of the Oedipal relationship and the Oedipus complex, while the disturbing relationships among his followers (his 'sons', the 'brothers' of his own days), seemed to be based on a complex combination of factors involving at least some ethnic and religious elements, some envy and jealousy, the need for power and glory, the need to be recognised by him as the most important one. Thus, when it comes to groups or organisations, it seems to me that – in the context of *Totem and Taboo* – Freud is at best a good example of what we had better avoid: applying psychoanalytic notions to social phenomena from our office seat, or explaining an imagined version of (past) human reality in well known theoretical concepts, rather than staying with the day to day realities, and exploring and discovering the meaning of a complex, frightening and maybe painful experience.[3]

Personally I have never doubted that psychoanalysis could provide important assistance to the exploration and solution of some of the problems that organisations struggle with. What amazes me time and again when I read the literature concerned with that field, or when I attend colloquia, is the way in which psychoanalytic knowledge is put to use. Some consultants seem to forget that there are essential differences between a developing individual on one side, and a developing group or organisation on the other. For instance, psychoanalytic concepts (such as id, ego and superego or paranoid-schizoid and depressive position), which refer to the psychological structure and development of an individual in a specific type of family setting, are not as such transferable to group or organisational situations. Group and organisational phenomena that resemble those structures may occur, but they are of different origin, have different meaning, and will need a different approach whenever they become a source of problems.

It alarms me just as much when I hear a consultant describe a complex, puzzling situation and hear him/her ask: "How could we understand this?" and

---

[3] In this context Gilles Amado very rightly remarked that my criticism concerning *Totem and Taboo* does not exclude the fact that – especially through some of his later writings – Freud opened the avenue to the exploration of unconscious processes that form and/or infiltrate social phenomena.

then hear him/her answer: "Psychoanalysis provides us with some concepts that can help". Whereupon s/he 'applies' (in the most literal sense of the word; almost like sticking a label onto the situation) the psychoanalytic notions that s/he thinks fit the situation. It looks as if those consultants think that a study becomes psychoanalytic just by 'using the proper words'. I would say that in both instances the important and unique contribution that psychoanalytic thinking might provide for the understanding of group and organisational situations is completely lost. The only thing left is a misuse of psychoanalytic notions to create an illusion of understanding that is misleading to the groups and organisations concerned, because it never includes an understanding that creates the possibility of overcoming or solving the problems at hand. The reason is that *the whys and the hows* of group and organisational problems differ completely from those that form the basis of individual difficulties. And without an understanding of those whys and hows, there is no possibility for adequate, long-term solutions.

What then is this important and unique contribution that psychoanalysis might provide? I can very well imagine that, on hearing this question, some sceptics might smile somewhat mockingly. For it has been said many times, many ways: "Psychoanalysis as such does not exist. The only thing psychoanalysts have in common is an office and a couch."

I can assure you, it is really not that bad. When it comes to their *working perspective*, psychoanalysts share some important, interdependent basic interests and convictions about what they work with, about how to do that, and about the purpose of their interventions.

The first thing we share is our interest in, and even enthusiasm about the content, the functioning and the extensive influence of the *dynamic unconscious system* on all aspects of human life.

The second element is our conviction *that psychoanalysis is about discovering meaning in a specific, actual situation, rather than about applying theoretical notions to human phenomena*. It is about discovering the wonderful world of unconscious mental content and processes; about the way this world came into being, develops and relates to other levels of mental functioning. But, when at work, it is above all about discovering which unconscious elements play(ed) a role in an actual situation we are confronted with. It is about discovering the unconscious factors involved in why and how something came into existence, about the unconscious meaning some features of the actual situation have and about the function(s) they fulfil. At work we do not talk in abstract, general, theoretical terms about possibilities. What we do is try to find out what is happening at this moment for this person, group or organisation, and how this is related to factors in their specific history and actual situation of which they are not fully aware. Moreover, this 'finding out' is not something analysts do on their own, or in discussion with colleagues. They do it in constant interaction with the people involved.

A third idea that we share is that such a discovery is only possible if it starts over and over again *from a position of not knowing*, and is based to a large extent on our own emotional reading of the situation we are in; a reading which is possible only in the context of an intimate, emotional relationship with the 'total situation' wherein a problem occurs.

Next is the idea that our work is directed at the *creation of conditions that facilitate change*. Depending on the wishes and possibilities of the client, such changes can include the heightened unity of functioning of a system, as well as the increase of co-operation between people and systems. The changes can mean a better awareness, understanding and acceptance of problems and pain as unavoidable aspects of living. They may raise the tolerance for frustration and the acceptance of dependency. Simultaneously they may enhance the capacity for creative problem solving, and bring a deepened joy about positive experiences and successes – even if those are only minor ones.

Finally, there is the conviction (maybe not as explicitly shared as the previous ones) that an important result of our work is a *contribution to the development of the dynamic unconscious as a system*. This means that by doing the work of finding out together with the people involved in the issues at hand, we alleviate some of the primitive anxieties that this system contains, even without ever touching those directly through interpretation. As a consequence, we not only facilitate the interaction of the dynamic unconscious system with the system conscious/pre-conscious[4], but we also increase a person's (a group's and even an organisation's) 'feeling at ease' with what life may bring, and with the

---

[4] The notion 'pre-conscious' refers to that part of the system 'conscious' which, at times, can be called 'unconscious' but only in a descriptive way, because it can be reached at any time just by paying attention to its contents.

capacity for taking care of whatever may be needed at a certain time, including the help of others.

I strongly believe that the most important thing *psychoanalysis has to offer* to the understanding and development of organisations is *this working perspective, not its theoretical concepts*. And even this perspective has to be adapted to the specificity of the organisational realities. Consultants working from such a perspective might then develop concepts that arise from the reality they work with, exactly as the pioneers tried to do. How such a working perspective can be put into practice, will become visible through the many illustrations that follow throughout the book.

Yet, even at its best, psychoanalysis can provide only a restricted contribution to the understanding and development of organisations. The psychoanalytic perspective represents only a part of the wider psychodynamic one. Moreover, groups and organisations are influenced by political, social, economical, ideological, structural, technical, and other factors. Most of those are constantly changing and interacting with psychodynamic factors.

I will write about the way in which psychoanalysis could be used more extensively and effectively to the benefit of groups and organisations, and how its way of looking at certain phenomena could become more accessible and beneficial to non-analytic consultants and managers in the context of their day-to-day work. In order to do this, I will tackle five main subjects in the next chapters. First, I will evoke our original, primary, basic form of mental functioning. Secondly, I will describe and illustrate some of the ways in which the primary form of mental functioning 'talks' to us after it has disappeared from consciousness, and I will describe some of the ways in which we become emotionally involved in the work we do. Thirdly, I explore important, supportive process structures. Then I move to the field of group and organisational defensive and protective structures. Finally, I will explore a form of creativity that is important in group and organisational life.

REFERENCES

Bion, W. (1961). *Experiences in Groups*. New York: Basic Books.
Bion, W. (1967). A Theory of Thinking. In: *Second Thoughts*. London: Heinemann.
Freud, S. (1913). Totem and Taboo. In: *Standard Ed.*, **13**. London: The Hogarth Press.

Freud, S. (1915). The Unconscious. In: *Standard Ed.*, **14**. London: The Hogarth Press.

Freud, S. (1921). Group Psychology and Analysis of the Ego. In: *Standard Ed.*, **18**. London: The Hogarth Press.

Freud, S. (1929). Civilisation and its Discontents. In: *Standard Ed.*, **21**. London: The Hogarth Press.

Harvey, J. (1988). *The Abilene Paradox*. Lexington, Mass.: Lexington Books.

Hinshelwood, R.D. (1989). *A Dictionary of Kleinian Thought*. London: Free Association Books.

Janis, I.L. (1982). *Groupthink*. Boston: Houghton Mifflin Co.

Jaques, E. (1955). Social systems as a defence against persecutory and depressive anxiety. In: M. Klein, P. Heimann & R.E. Money-Kyrle (Eds), *New directions in psychoanalysis*. New York: Basic Books, 478–498.

Lawrence, W.G., Bain, A. & Gould, L.J. (1966). The Fifth Basic Assumption. *Free Associations*, **6** (37).

Meltzer, D. (1984). *Dream Life*. Perthshire: Clunie Press.

Menzies-Lyth, I. (1961). The functioning of social systems as a defence against anxiety. *Human Relations*, **13**, 95–121.

Turquet, P.M. (1974). Leadership: the individual and the group. In: A.D. Colman & M.H. Geller (Eds) (1985). *Group Relations Reader 2*. Washington DC.: A.K. Rice Institute, 71–88.

Vansina, L. (1998). The individual in organisations: Rediscovered or lost forever? *European J. of Work and Organisational Psychol.*, **7**, 3, 265–282.

CHAPTER 1

Original, Primary Mental Processes

Marie-Jeanne Vansina-Cobbaert

The 'dynamic unconscious as a system' (the Ucs.) develops out of our original, primary mental processes. Quite a lot of people still seem to think that this system is but a sort of garbage can for our mental life. They think of it as the collection of all their ugly, unacceptable infantile sexual or aggressive desires, which – because of the anxiety they generated – were pushed out of consciousness. And of course, such elements can be part of that 'dynamic unconscious'. Moreover, this is not a totally unimportant part, because it can form the basis for some of our psychic problems; but that part is not involved when we talk about the relevance of psychoanalytic thinking for the understanding of groups and organisations. I would even say that it is a part that should never be touched in the context of work with groups (with the exception of psychoanalytic therapy groups) and organisations.

Primary mental processes are partly present from the time before we are born. They slowly develop until we are around seven years old, after which they give the impression of fading away in favour of a very different kind of mental functioning called 'secondary process thinking' or, in common language: logic, scientific thinking. It takes at least until the end of puberty to firmly establish this second form of mental functioning – but our original 'primary process' way of thinking does not really disappear, it is only sort of pushed behind its highly valued counterpart. From then on it becomes less directly visible. Yet, it stays active, continues to develop and to influence our way of being and operating.

Most interesting, however, is the fact that the hidden, basic mental processes not only have an impact on individual, but just as well on group and organisational life. In a certain way and to a certain extent, one could say that apart from individuals, groups and organisations also have a dynamic unconscious that penetrates their preferences, choices and ways of operating. We do not really know how this dynamic unconscious world of groups and organisations comes into being, nor do we know how it develops over time. The only possibility we have is to 'see it at work'; meaning that some observable group and organisational phenomena become understandable if we suppose the existence of such an unconscious inner world, and are able to reveal its impact in a given situation, which then becomes changeable. It is this feature that makes understanding primary process thinking so interesting in the context of consulting for groups and organisations.

The simplest way to look at our basic form of mental functioning is to define it as 'non-logic thinking'. It includes perceiving, experiencing, meaning attribution or sense making, motivation and communication. It is a form of thinking that starts well before we acquire verbal language. Consequently, at first, images dominate over words. We have reason to believe that this form of thinking is based on an association of images, and that, originally, it becomes visible only in behavioural reactions.[1] When words become part of the picture, they may at first be used in their literal or 'pictorial' sense, exactly as in dreams.[2]

---

[1] Those who are interested in the origins of this form of 'thinking' as it becomes visible during pregnancy, I would refer to the magnificent book by Piontelli (1992).

[2] It is interesting to see how other fields of study, like for instance philosophy and religion, talk about similar phenomena – be it only in adults – using opposite terms. Referring to adult forms of primary process thinking, they use the term 'secondary language'. On the other hand, what we would call 'secondary process thinking', they refer to as 'primary language'. Whenever this 'primary language' (for us meaning 'secondary process thinking') is equated with 'conceptual thinking' it comes a bit closer to psychoanalytic theory, but it is still not really the same. Moreover, primary and secondary processes are ways of 'thinking'. Basically they represent different ways of giving meaning to experiences; only later on do they give rise to different types of language. This will be explored further in the following chapters.

ILLUSTRATIONS

When I illustrate how the Ucs. functions, I often start with stories about young children because that is where it all begins and where it is relatively easy to see what I am talking about. This way it also becomes possible for me to show how these primitive ways of 'thinking' develop. Only further on will I introduce some vignettes from group or organisational contexts. How to use this way of looking when working with complex organisational problems is illustrated in Parts Two and Three.

Let me start with some observations about a pre-verbal child. Imagine a nice and warm early summer afternoon at a poolside. I walk on the lawn with my granddaughter, who is barely one year old, when her parents and their friends decide to go in for a swim. As the adults are sure that the water-loving girl will be eager to join in, I pull a bit further away from the pool, and talk to her about "mummy and daddy going in for a swim", something that she has not seen before. She looks interested at the grown-ups as they appear in bathing suits. She points at them, and babbles away laughingly until everyone has entered the water. At that moment she grabs one of my legs and slightly shaking she starts whining. A bit lost at her unexpected reaction, I pick her up, try to comfort her, talking softly, inquiring, and stroking her back. But she holds on to me, hiding her face in my neck. As she slightly relaxes her grip, and acts as if willing to take a peak, I take a step closer to the pool. Instantly she grabs me even tighter and continues to hide her face in my neck. I pull back again, and sit myself down on the grass while holding her in my lap. As I sit there, looking at the swimmers, still trying to calm her down by slow, somewhat enthusiastic talk about mummy, daddy, and the others, enjoying themselves in the water, I begin to realise that all I see in that pool is a group of laughing, talking heads. I start wondering: when my granddaughter stands on the grass, her head is at about the same height as mine when sitting; could it be that, when she saw those 'heads floating on the water', she 'thought' that the people had lost their bodies? In order to check my supposition, I call my daughter, and ask her to step out. Hesitantly, visibly unclear about my reasons, she does so. With explicit pleasure I tell the little girl: "Look, mummy is back!" While holding onto me, she ventures to look up, and immediately, without a moment's hesitation and with a joyful cry, she runs to her mother who picks her up, sharing in the pleasure. As soon as I reach them, my daughter, still uncertain about what has happened, returns to the pool, while her daughter and I sit down at the edge. From our new seats it is possible for the girl to see the whole bodies floating and moving around. She laughs, claps her hands, and starts a 'song', moving her body to the rhythmic sounds she produces. For the rest of the afternoon the pleasure abounds!

Was I right to suppose that my granddaughter reacted with intense anxiety because, in her 'view', once you are in a swimming pool, your head detaches from your body, and your body just disappears? I can't know for sure. It is no more than my understanding of the total situation we were in together.

It happens, especially if an incident occurred repeatedly, that children remember their anxiety, and what it was all about. I had an acquaintance who remembered very well how, as a young child, she would get wild with anxiety whenever she had a stuffed nose. She could not tell her mother why, because she lacked the necessary verbal capacity. Regularly, the mother got fed up with her daughter's anxious insistence on getting help with blowing, and even cleaning out her nose. The situation became a source of constant, and to some extent hopeless struggle between mother and child, until, at a later age, the little girl was able to explain. In connection with the knowledge that worms can eat away on wood until it crumbles, she had imagined that, if the 'worms'[3] were not taken out of her nose in time, they would eat the insides of her head, and it would come apart.

Once children possess sufficient verbal capacity, most of them tell us about their ways of looking at the world. Mothers, and especially kindergarten teachers, are able to produce many examples of the sort. From such examples it becomes clear that this primary form of thinking results, at least partly, from the way a child 'explains' its observations or experiences to itself. It is also based on the fact that to a child everything that moves or looks even a bit like a human or an animal is thought to be alive, holding thoughts and intentions.

When my daughter was somewhere around four she received a pair of orange-red pyjamas with little hearts on the front-top, as a Christmas present. She became wildly enthusiastic about it, and thought that she should be allowed to wear it just as well to kindergarten as to bed. During that same period I was trying to teach her that, when undressing at night, it is much more efficient if you put your clothes nicely in a little heap on a bedroom chair, than when you drop them along the way between the living room and your bedroom. She agreed that this sounded like a wise idea, but added that she might forget about it anyhow. A couple of months later, we went for a walk. Part of the way

---

[3] In Dutch the childish word for hardened nasal mucus is 'worms'.

followed a ridge from where we had a panoramic view over the valley and the sky above. It was one of those beautiful early spring days during which the sun goes down rather early, and becomes a well-lined orange-red sphere in a plain greyish-blue sky. As my daughter looks over the valley, and notices the sun, she says with a combination of conviction and excitement: "Look mummy, the sun already put on its pyjamas!" and then, with a pensive nod of the head, and talking more to herself than to me, she adds: "It must have put its beams on a chair . . . ".

From the time children have mastered an understandable level of verbal expression, and until they are in primary school, one can hear them explain experiences in ways that adults would seldom think of. A kindergarten teacher told me once about a little girl in her care that, for the first time, saw a little boy take a pee. After visible amazement, the girl became very enthusiastic and asked the little guy: "Did your mummy sew this on to you?" The boy looked a bit puzzled, but could not provide an answer. Maybe he never wondered who 'put together' his body, or he never associated mothers with sewing, or whatever.

Once, one of our own boys came home from kindergarten and told me proudly that there was a new girl in his class, and that now she was his best friend, and did I know her name? Of course I did not, I told him. Her name was Wettilly, he said, and in a sort of reassuring voice, mixed with a touch of amazement he added: "But she is not wet you know". It took me a few seconds before I grasped what he was saying. I laughed, gave him a kiss, and confirmed with pleasure how good it can feel to find a new friend, and that for sure she was not wet.

Apparently, if we call this form of basic mental functioning 'unconscious', it does not mean that we never experience(d) it, or never knew about it. It only points to the fact that it is part of a thought system that, originally – in babies and pre-verbal children – functions in a way that we can hardly imagine. Then, as verbal expression increases, it develops into something that we know about and understand. Yet – except in art and in some types of humour – it does not become integrated into our adult, secondary, conscious, and so-called 'rational' thought processes. Superficially it looks as if it disappears completely. In fact, as I already indicated, it continues to be active and to develop all through our adult life.

In as far as we refer to these primary thought processes as 'phantasy', the ph is intended to differentiate it explicitly from fantasy. At times, phantasy may be the unrecognised source of an ongoing fantasy. The development of the fantasy itself, however, is at all times fully conscious, and a completely different thought process. We choose to start it, and can interrupt it willingly although not always easily. In addition, fantasy fulfils a specific developmental and/or protective function. Phantasies just happen to us, exactly like dreams. That is the reason why they may be referred to as 'dream-thoughts'. Like dreams they use homonyms interchangeably, or they use surprising combinations of images and words. As dreams often do, phantasies also function as a kind of trial to understand, to explain, and to give meaning.

STEPWISE TRANSFORMATIONS

As said: our primary way of thinking disappears over time in favour of logic, scientific (secondary process) thinking, which is highly valued in our western civilisation. And it is certainly true that we have a lot to thank it for. Yet, if we explore a bit under the surface, it looks as if our original way of mental functioning often has positive, creative influence on our much praised logic thinking. This is possible because primary thinking is never lost. It only sort of goes 'underground' from where – without interruption – it influences what happens 'above-ground'. It is this active, but largely hidden part of our mental life that Meltzer referred to as 'dream-life' (1984), thereby stressing the fact that this section of our mental life is not only active during sleep, but equally during our daily waking life (I shall illustrate this in a moment). From the moment our primary thought processes become unconscious, it is as if we live simultaneously on two levels, in two different worlds. I like to say that the only Atlantis that ever existed, and still exists, can be found in our own inner world. Moreover, it constantly sends its 'messengers' into our 'above-water' world. The problem is that we either don't see them or that we don't understand the 'languages' they use (Vansina-Cobbaert, 1993).

Before I explain and produce some vignettes concerning those 'languages', let me illustrate a few occasions where a sort of mixture of phantasmatic and logic thinking becomes visible.

Remember the little girl of the 'floating heads? When she was almost three she got a brother, and for a long time she was very interested in pregnant mothers. One day, when she is a little over four, and comes to visit, she tells me right away, and very proudly, that when she grows up, she will become a lady (not simply a woman), and that when she is a lady, she too will be able to grow a baby in her tummy. She explicitly stresses her own decision, as if it is all her own doing. I nod: "Yes, sure". Without interruption she continues: "And you know what, grandma, then you too can be in my tummy. Will this make you happy?" Here things become a bit trickier. So I answer somewhat more carefully: "Well, I feel happy already, when you propose this, because I think that it means that you love me very much". By then she is sitting on my lap, and I receive an enthusiastic smack. Hereafter, but with a slight hesitation and a somewhat seductive smile, she wonders: "Could I maybe be in your tummy too then?" Here I waver. Until this moment the little girl is completely immersed in her phantasmatic world. Still, her slight hesitation together with her seductive smile seem like signs of the fact that she could be ready, yet ambivalent, about leaving the phantasmatic in favour of what we like to call 'the real world'. As I do not want to rush this delicate developmental process, I draw out my "We-e-e-ll", while I think about the best way to formulate somewhat more 'realistic' possibilities. But before I have a chance to go on, she fills in. Her eyes reduced to small splits, and her face full of wrinkles, as if it is costing her an intense effort, she asks: "But it is not possible, is it? We can't go back, can we?" I hold her, and nod with a smile and a sigh, for this is indeed a big leap she has taken, a big leap into the world of logic, realistic, scientific or simply: 'down to earth' thinking. "Yes," I continue, "this is absolutely true. Once we are out we can never get back into somebody's tummy. But I don't mind you know. In the beginning it might be pleasant in there, we can float around in the water like in a comfortably warm swimming pool, but, towards the end, when we become bigger, the place gets rather tight. We have to stay curled-up all the time, and the only thing we can still enjoy is to suck our thumb. Now, as we are out, we can talk together, we can play, we can learn all kinds of things, and we can be pleased with each other." "Yes", she says with conviction, "Yes! Come, let us go out and play", as if, for the first time, she feels sure about the fact that life in the outside world is by far preferable over a stay in a narrow tummy, even if it belongs to mummy or grandma.

A few months later she added the last chapter to that part of her story. I heard it from her mother. By then the girl was almost five. One day she asked her mother if she had a baby growing in her tummy. When the mother answered: "No, not right now", the girl immediately advised: "Then ask daddy to put one in. I think it would be nice if we got a new baby". Somewhat surprised the mother wondered: "Who told you about daddy?" Whereupon the girl explained with conviction: "Nobody told me. I thought, if you are my mummy because I grew in your tummy, then daddy must be my daddy because he put me in there!'"

Well, all by herself, she had moved nicely in the direction of 'logic' insights. On her own, she even reproduced one of the original, primitive 'scientific' explanations of fertilisation. The only task left for the mother, was to fine-tune her daughter's version of the 'facts of life'.

REFERENCES

Melzer, D. (1984). *Dream Life*. Perthshire: Clunie Press.
Piontelli, A. (1992). From Fetus to Child. London & New York: Tavistock/Routledge.
Vansina-Cobbaert, M.J. (1993). Per-agir (Acting-through). *Rev. Belge de Psychanal.*, **23**, 13–30.

CHAPTER 2

Languages From Another World

Marie-Jeanne Vansina-Cobbaert

Although we may be very right in valuing our capacity for logical, scientific thinking, we should not underestimate the importance of our buried 'underground treasure'. I will try to show how it can be a source of valuable information, wise decisions, creative thinking and the like.

In fact, the whole field of artistic expression originates from this part of our mental functioning. The problem is that the unconscious dynamic system (the Ucs.) does not reveal itself easily. This feature of the system is not related to what psychoanalytic theory refers to as id and ego resistances. For those are connected to repressed material. The problem I am talking about here is related to the fact that the unconscious uses several 'languages', which we don't understand readily. We can learn about those languages but we never really know them. Moreover, they can be used separately or in combination, and the meaning of what they communicate becomes clear only in the context of the total situation in which they are used.

At least by name, some of those 'languages' became rather popular as, for example, the language of spontaneous associations, of all kinds of errors and wit, of images, dreams and myths. But there is also the language of actions, which is often looked upon with some suspicion by psychoanalysts. Then comes the language of characteristics of relationships, to which belongs the less well known one: the language of personal experiences we may go through in our role as consultants.

I'll restrict my discussion to the languages of images, actions and relations, which are the most important ones in the context of understanding groups and organisations.[1]

THE LANGUAGE OF IMAGES

At times, under specific conditions, the language of images seems rather easy to grasp. It may be understood almost right away when the images pop up unexpectedly during waking life, or reach us through mediation of a dream, in the context of an intensive, stressful involvement in a research project. Think for instance of the way F.H.C. Circk and J.D. Watson came to the idea of the double helix structure of DNA; remember the simple dream of a snake biting its own tail that suggested the circular structure of benzene to F. Kekulé.

Usually though, accidental images and certainly dream-messages or myths, are much more complex, because they often use a rebus-like combination of images which stand for words, while sometimes words stand for images; on top of that, the words may combine into sentences that sound either like logic, understandable, or more like weird or magic parts of a conversation. Yet, with some 'work', or a little assistance, they might be revealing and helpful.

I shall use two different illustrations of this kind of more complicated but 'wise' dreams.

---

[1] I am sure that at this point some of you might remark that relatively early in his theorising, Freud too had begun to think of the Ucs. as expressing itself in different ways. And indeed he had. He even spoke of the Ucs. as communicating and co-operating with the system conscious/preconscious (1915). But to him this was only intended to facilitate the satisfaction of the primary impulses and repressed wishes the Ucs. contains. Due to this creation of 'derivatives' of primary or repressed impulses, we get to know some of the contents and processes of the Ucs. It was seen as an interesting secondary gain, not as an intention of the system. In this context 'communication' does not mean 'to tell, to make known' in order to enhance the unity of (our psychic) functioning. Therefore I do not think that Freud would have said that the Ucs. made use of 'languages'.

The first one occurs during a psychoanalysis that has been going on for a little over two years. For some weeks now, the woman analysand has been talking about the possibility of terminating our collaboration. She feels well, the problems that brought her to analysis have disappeared, and she has made some wished-for changes in her way of living. In this context she has a dream, which she experiences as important. In the dream she is reading an illustrated book about diving. Each page shows a picture of a person who jumps from a diving board, and underneath is a written text explaining the important features of the jump. After a set of pages, there is one which says: "If you suppose that now you are able to dive, then look at the next page". This next page shows a person in mid-air between the diving board and the water, and along her back a tangent touches her head, her buttocks and her heels. Under the picture, the text says: "Only if you can dive like this, can you really dive!"

The analysand understands that the dream is telling something about the analysis, because the images of 'diving', as well as the one about a train or a boat journey, have been around before. Apparently the dream indicates that she still has something to do or to learn; that she needs to link up some parts, or bring some things in line. But which parts? What does it mean 'to link up', or to bring 'in line'?

Associations reveal rather easily the meaning of the 'back of the head' and of the 'heels'. The first stands for her 'mathematics knot' that represents her love for abstract, scientific thinking. The heels become associated with the Achilles tendon: an illusion of invulnerability, of being untouchable, yet extremely sensitive in a restricted area. She further relates the vulnerability to some narcissistic aspects of her personality. But the buttocks don't seem to fit anywhere in the picture that starts to surface. It is only, when a couple of sessions later and in another context, the analysand talks about the fact that she always thinks of her unconscious as residing in her tummy, that the buttocks come back to mind, and appear as hiding the 'doorway' to her unconscious. So there we are! The work that still needs to be done is to put her love of abstract thinking in line or in accordance with what she experiences as a primitive, creative, yet slightly wild part of herself, and with her narcissistic vulnerability.

After this revelation the women continued in analysis for some time. The surprising thing however, is that it looks as if in this situation, the messenger of Atlantis presents himself as the wise adviser on the possibility for further psychological development.

A second revealing dream illustrates the capacity of the 'hidden system' to pick up, understand, and tell us about cues that belong to the external world, but have escaped our conscious observation, a fact that indicates even better than the previous illustration, how the primary thought system is still active even during waking life.

Imagine a young woman. She gave up the job she loved, because her family had to move to another part of the country. She found a new employment but she misses her previous work and work setting. One day, to her great pleasure, she discovers that there is a vacancy in a firm similar to the one she left. She applies for the job and is accepted. She is overjoyed, and describes her experience as: "It feels like coming home". The job resembles the one she had before, and the head of the department, a nice man, showed her around and explained to her everything she needed to know in order to start. But when she starts – a couple of months later – she has the shock of her life. For this nice man apparently showed her only the nice part of the situation; and in her enthusiasm she had not probed any further. The department head had omitted to mention all the unfinished business and the problems her predecessor left behind, and kept silent about the frictions between the department she was going to work in and some of the other departments in the organisation.

The moment this young woman is confronted with the reality of her new situation, she remembers a dream, which she had in the context of the job interview. At the time she paid little attention to it. Now it strikes her as connected. She dreamt that she went back to the village where she was born, and bought herself an apartment based on the nice façade of the house, on the beautiful entrance hall, and on the spacious, bright living room. When she moves into the apartment, she discovers that the rooms behind the living room are filled with rubble that the previous owners have left behind, and she realises that it will take her quite a bit of time to clean up the place and make it fit for pleasant living.

It is as if the hidden/primary functioning part of this woman's mind had registered some elements present in the new job situation that escaped her conscious perception, and then tried to tell her about it, by producing this beautiful 'tell-tale' dream. This communicative quality of the Ucs. provides the basis for phenomena such as those Lawrence refers to as 'social dreaming' (1998). Of course one can wonder why the young woman was not able to listen to her dream when it occurred; and we can be relatively sure that the dream is also telling her something about her own state of mind at the time. But that is not what concerns us here. The important part for us now, is to see that the Ucs. can pick up information in the external world that escapes our conscious attention, and then 'tell' us about it.[2]

What this woman picked up, without being aware of, was consciously known to the people in the department where she went to work. But the unconscious system can just as well pick up information that is only present at some unconscious level in the organisation or parts thereof, although it may have an impact on their functioning, structure and performance.

THE LANGUAGE OF ACTIONS

Two different aspects of action may at times be very revealing. One is the way in which people carry out their specific task(s). The other is the symbolic action that may occur in work systems, in management and project teams or in 'learning groups' (also referred to as 'Study or Search Groups').

Task Performance

Let me try to illustrate how the way in which people go about their task can be the key to understanding the basis of a dragging conflict that occurred in a department of a psychiatric hospital.

The department was known for its good results demonstrated by the fact that, after discharge, former patients managed to stay out of the hospital, found work – although the economic situation was rather bad – and started satisfying, stable relationships. Simultaneously, again and again frictions and conflicts developed between nurses and therapists within the staff group. A consultant to the staff explained that such conflicts often occur in teams that work with a severe borderline population, because the heavy, dominating splitting mechanisms that characterise those patients, get transferred to the staff who have to live and work with them.

This is a clear illustration of 'application' of psychoanalytic concepts. What the consultant said is indeed possible. But we do not know if it applies in

---

[2] An elaborate discussion of the relationship between 'Atlantis' and dreams can be found in: Vansina-Cobbaert, 1992.

this situation unless we do the hard work of finding out. And even if we know *what* happens, we still have to find out *why* and/or *how* this is possible, in order to *create an opportunity for change*. Only if we can discover and understand something about the fields of tensions and anxieties that lurk behind the observable phenomenon, does development become possible.

But let us return to the psychiatric department. One of the first things that became clear during staff meetings, was that the frictions were in fact between the nursing staff and the psychoanalytic group therapists, while the other therapists were sort of hanging in-between those two groups, and kept as much as possible out of the squabbles. The complaints of the nursing group were essentially that their work was not valued and that they were always blamed for what went wrong. The complaints of the psychoanalytic therapists were that the nursing staff isolated themselves too much, and made too many and in fact 'wild' interpretations. By interpretations they meant that nurses would sometimes say things like: "Aren't you projecting this or that onto so or so?" or, "It seems to me that you're seeing your father in him".

An observable characteristic of the nursing group was that in their unofficial contacts, there was often quite a bit of ridicule of psychoanalytic thinking and notions. Yet, when I talked with them about their work, I met a group of dedicated people who seemed to be doing a difficult and stressful job. They had an amount of individual contact with residents, trying to prevent destructive behaviour (overeating and vomiting, cutting or burning themselves, committing suicide), or trying to help them explore a complex situation and find a constructive way of coping. They also assisted the group of residents they were associated with, in doing their household chores or in preparing some special activities. With that same group they led a meeting three times a week for half an hour, to discuss how things were going. Here I assumed without asking, that those meetings were review meetings. It was only after I attended some community meetings that I started to wonder. As I asked for more precise information, I found out that indeed *all* meetings were conducted as if they were psychoanalytic group therapy sessions. I also discovered that residents also had a hard time seeing the difference between group meetings and psychoanalytic group therapy sessions, or between their daily department meeting and the weekly community meeting, apart from the difference in length, frequency and attending staff.

When all this came to the fore, it became clear that although at a conscious level there was criticism and even ridicule of certain aspects of the psychoanalytic approach that prevailed in the department at that time, on an unconscious level there was the generalised idea that psychoanalytic group therapy was really the only valuable thing to do. This was revealed through the way the nursing staff went about part of their work, trying to make it look like psychoanalytic therapy. Further exploration revealed that this unconscious 'idea' was based upon the impression that the supervisor treated the psychoanalytic group therapists with special respect, as if their work was much more important than that of other therapists and nurses. Simultaneously it became obvious that the feelings of dissatisfaction, frustration and irritation that prevailed amongst the nursing staff, were not so much related to their impression that their work was not valued, but were the consequence of the fact that they were trying to do something they were not trained for, while an important part of the tasks that were specifically theirs, was omitted.

Once we got that far, and over a period of time, a lot could be changed (rather than 'labelled') to the satisfaction of the whole staff and to the benefit of the residents. Each group of therapists started to perform their own specific tasks, which simultaneously initiated, supplemented or rounded off the tasks of the others. After a while, and depending on the type of task, the nursing staff felt free enough to perform it in settings that differed completely from those one would use for psychoanalytic therapy. Some reviews, for example, would be done during a coffee break; some planning at the breakfast table, and so forth.

Later on, we also understood that the tendency of the nurses to isolate themselves was not due to the so-called 'conflict'. It proved to be related to the way their work was organised in shifts, which necessitated extensive briefings between shifts. It was also a consequence of their need to protect themselves from even more complexity, during periods when destructive actions from patients were a constant threat.[3]

Symbolic Actions

In the following situation the action reveals the image the group has about itself, without any one member being aware of this image or of the fact that they are expressing it.

---

[3] In Vansina-Cobbaert (2005) I devote a whole chapter to the discussion of the development of that department.

Imagine a group of 12 active, ambitious, and quite aggressive young managers who take part in a seven-day residential seminar on group and inter-group dynamics. We have reached Saturday morning, and start the last 'learning group' session. The night before, most of the work concerned a woman participant who up until then had participated actively in whatever happened in the seminar situation, but had been very reticent about her own difficulties in the back home work situation. Then, on the last night, she opened up, and told a rather sad story. One of the men in the group was more sensitive to her problems than the others, and managed to phrase in a direct but concerned way some of the issues she seemed to be avoiding.

On Saturday they start by rounding off the work of the night before, and then, after a short pause, they begin to talk about going home; about how long it seems since they left, although those seven days went by so quickly; about how they are going to share their experience with colleagues and family; about how they will be different in their work or at home. At that moment one of the men who had told that stress situations always disturb his stomach, says: "Oh boy, such thoughts are enough for my stomach to turn upside down". The man who sits next to him asks: "Would you like me to get you a glass of water?" Whereupon another man says: "Oh, a glass of water; I saw that they were preparing the wine for the farewell dinner, can't we get a glass of wine?" He looks around the group, and in a thoughtful way the others nod: "Yes, we probably could". The 'water-man' and the 'wine-man' get up and leave the room quietly together, while the others go on talking about going home. After a short moment the two men return; the water-man holding a glass; the wine-man holding a bottle of red wine and a corkscrew. The glass has the form of a chalice, and is normally used for a very good Belgian cloister beer. Both men, standing up, listen to the group that is still continuing, while the wine-man has some difficulty unscrewing the bottle. When he finally succeeds, the group quietens down while he pours some wine in the glass that is still held by the water-man. The water-man hands the glass to the man with the stomach problems who accepts it, hesitates, and then hands it over to the woman saying: "Here, have a drink; maybe you need it even more than I do". The woman, visibly surprised, hesitates in turn, then gets up and offers the glass to the man who was so sensitive to her difficulties and says: "For you, and thank you". That man too hesitates, gets up and hands the glass to me with the words: "You drink first. Without your help we would never have been able to achieve what we did". And there I am, with little time to decide if I'm going to put that glass down and say something, or if I'm going to drink. Drinking means that I take part in an ongoing action, which, for a psychoanalyst, is certainly not one's first choice. Yet, I decide to drink. I do it on the basis of the mood the group is in (a quiet, reflective mood that contains affection and respect, a mixture also of gladness and sadness), but also because it seems to me that there is a story in the process of being told, and I would certainly like to hear it to the end. Thus I drink and hand the glass to the person sitting on my right (herewith of course, and maybe regretfully, I introduce a pattern). He drinks too, and hands the glass to the one sitting next to him. And so on. While this happens, the wine-man, still holding the bottle, moves behind the seats, following the glass, and in between two participants, and before the glass is empty, he fills it up. Finally he also drinks; puts the glass and the bottle which still contain wine, on the table and says contentedly: "There, and we have some left". And I answer: "Yes, maybe to take home". Then I say something about the way in which, through their gestures, they seem to be telling how they have experienced the past week. How, after some hesitation (now expressed in connection with getting the wine) and some wrestling (now visible in handling screw and cork), they have managed to 'change water into wine'; and how they have been trying to see to it that there would be enough for everyone, and also some left to take back and to share with others.

A thoughtful silence follows. Then they remember their mixed feelings at the start, the painful fights that occurred in the first part of the week, how and why things had changed afterwards. They also wonder in what way they are going to share some of their experiences with those who stayed home, while doing this without damaging, overstepping, transgressing the intimacy, privacy of other members and of the group.

When we try to understand the meaning of actions, we often have to rely on the *emotional quality* of the situation and *the way it affects us*. Actions that are similar to the ones I just described could very well be used to erase disappointments and express some wishes that were not fulfilled. But then the mood of the group and my reaction to it would have been different. There might have been some nervous, noisy laughter, while I might have felt rather depressed or irritated, or might have felt the tendency to flee. There might have been an element of excess and a feeling of something 'too good to be true'. Or the action might have been introduced by one or two participants while the others seemed absent or half-dead; and so on.

This illustrates once more the importance of our being part of the situation we have to understand, because our own emotional experience can be crucial for that understanding. Of course, what happened in that group tells a lot more than what I expressed in my intervention. The way the glass is passed on in the beginning, could express the recognition of individual similarities and differences, and the recognition of their real dependence on me. Or maybe it is just some uneasiness about daring to be the first to drink at such a special moment. We could suppose that there is also the recognition of the fact that men do not live by words alone; that sometimes one also needs a supportive or comforting gesture. They seem to make use of some of the most elementary phantasms that we carry within ourselves: the image namely that whatever you love and want to keep, you have to swallow or eat. Finally, there is the experience of something sacred, something that has to be protected and cherished, as can occur at important moments of transition in our lives, and seems present in the group's mood and in symbols that make me think of a combination of the biblical stories of the Wedding in Canaan and the Last Supper. But all this is only supposition. In order to be sure I should have shared those impressions with the group, and I should have listened to their reactions, and maybe some very different meanings would have emerged. Meanings I had not imagined. But most surely, if I had intervened in such a way I would have spoiled the special beneficial effect of the mythical elements that were actualised in the action. Moreover, it would have looked as if I asked them to start all over again, as if their previous work had not been enough. I always agreed with what Joseph Campbell once said about myths (Flowers, 1988), and which is just as true about fairytales: you do not need to analyse/explain them in order to release their positive influence on psychic development. On the contrary, explaining can sometimes prevent the benefit from occurring. For myths and fairytales, exactly like dreams, can produce a direct, beneficial influence without the need for interpretations. This suggests that not only does the Ucs. possess its own languages, but that it is able to understand us, and initiate change, if we manage to express ourselves in the same languages.[4] This does not mean that interpretation or explanation is counterproductive; as often, it depends on the total situation. In the context of a psychoanalytic session, dream interpretation may be very fruitful. Yet, whenever myths were presented as reality – as sometimes happens in religious contexts – explanation of their phantasmatic origin and hidden messages becomes unavoidable at a certain moment, otherwise people will feel cheated or abused.

The illustrations I used show that we never grasp the meaning of something unless we take into account the *total situation* in which it occurs, and until we explore our impression extensively with the people involved. The dynamic

[4] For a more elaborate view on the subject, consult: Vansina-Cobbaert, 1993.

unconscious does not reveal itself readily or easily. Its contents are transferred and thereby indirectly expressed in the totality of an actual situation. Here, the notion of transference[5] exceeds by far its original classic meaning.

THE LANGUAGE OF RELATIONS

The language of relations as well as that of our personal perceptions and experiences (in as far as they are part of close, emotional relations), are not only very important in the context of consulting, training and managing, they are also especially misleading and difficult to learn.

One could easily say that the most fundamental element, the basis for all psychoanalytic work, be it with individuals, persons in roles, groups or organisations, is emotional relations – sometimes partly or even exclusively expressed in behaviour – that can be thought and talked about. This means that to work as an analyst, or from a psychoanalytic perspective, is only possible if one has, over a longer period, a direct contact with the system one is working for or with. Thus, making interpretations about problem situations or interactions or even a dream, without having been part of the context wherein those occurred or were told, and without interactive associative exploration of the proposed interpretations, reduces those to 'wild interpretations', which, at best, reach the level of mere theoretical suppositions.

Spread over a period of about 50 years, psychoanalysts described a group of peculiar phenomena in the interactions between people, which were apparently determined by our primary way of mental functioning. The phenomena – which are in fact complicated psychological processes – were conceptualised as: transference, counter-transference and projective identification.

The concepts are inter-related, and their meaning has developed over time. All of them refer to emotional, interpersonal relations that occupy a prominent place in all types of psychoanalytically oriented work. But they are not by far restricted to psychoanalytic work relations alone. On the contrary, the phenomena they refer to are part and parcel of our daily life. It is just that in psychoanalytically inspired work, and especially in psychoanalysis proper, due to the context and the attitude of the analyst or the consultant, these phenomena become more easily visible and accessible. Most important of all:

[5] See the following section on the enlarged notion of transference.

analytic situations allow for their exploration; they can be thought about, and talked about, and eventually they may be worked through.

I would like to strongly stress that I do not discuss those concepts in view of *applying* them to specific situations. As far as I am concerned, people at work can even forget all about those strange and maybe impressive words, as long as they recognise the phenomena, are able to explore the dynamics that feed them, and then – if necessary, wished for, and possible – move towards change.

Transference

Transference is the oldest of the three concepts. It was introduced by Freud in one of his early publications, and it referred to the fact that in a psychoanalytic situation, a past emotional experience that is related to an important figure in a person's life, becomes expressed in (is transferred to) the relationship with the analyst. For some time Freud thought of this phenomenon as an annoying, hindering factor. Only slowly did it dawn on him that this was one of the ways the unconscious system expressed and tried to satisfy a socially unacceptable, repressed desire, and that he was not going to resolve the problem through a rational argument with his patient; the reason being that the original wish and feelings had vanished from the patient's conscious mind, while the unconsciously functioning part was, and always is, completely insensitive to logical argumentation.

It is this original meaning of the notion of transference that became popular and is still used quite often in groups and organisational contexts. People seem to accept automatically that feelings and/or behaviour that were once part of a person's relationship with his parents are transferred to authority figures, while behaviour and/or feelings related to siblings may become expressed in relationships with colleagues. And this might indeed be the case. But in order to know for sure you would need a lot of extra information; and even then you would not be able to do anything about it, exactly as Freud was unable to, with the help of rational argumentation. Also, if a person explicitly says things like: "I just hate (love) my boss, he is a bastard (concerned, caring person) exactly like my father". This has nothing to do with transference. It could be a simple truth: the recognition of a real resemblance. If it were a question of transference, the person would not be able to make the connection. Moreover, in a transference relation, what the person consciously remembers is often different from what becomes visible in the actual situation. For instance, you might see a person who is always, and a priori, suspicious about the good intentions of authority figures, while he tells you about his absolutely trustworthy parents. Experiences can indeed be kept in the Ucs. by means of *the overemphasis of the opposite*. Thus this *might* be transference. Yet it could be somebody who indeed had trustworthy parents, but who (e.g. in the context of reorganisations) found out the hard way, that management is not very trustworthy; but then, he would most likely be able to tell you about the experiences that made him become suspicious. Anyhow, the important thing is to realise that one never understands immediately and on one's own. There is always a need for exploration together with the people involved in order to reach an insight that might lead to real change.

But if this is all so complicated, so difficult to trace, and anyhow almost unusable outside a therapeutic context, what is the utility of talking about it here? Well, the concept of transference has developed over time, and it is the new meaning of transference, which is interesting for the understanding of groups and organisations. Two factors contributed towards that development. The first one was the insight that the contents of transference are not always by far experiences connected to persons as a whole. What becomes transferred are often experiences or reactions related to certain functions that people do or don't perform for us, such as: caretaker, admirer, playmate, feeder, protector, lover, teacher and others.

The second, and for use in groups or organisations a far more important factor, was the understanding that the subject of transference, is something (a need, a wish, an anxiety, a knowledge, or an experience) that is *now* present in our inner world, although it may have connections with past experiences or past phantasies. This means that – without our awareness or conscious intention – our *actual inner world* becomes visible in (is transferred to) *the totality of the actual situation* (Joseph, 1985). Experience showed that this is not only valid for the actual inner world of individuals but also of groups, while the expression does not only happen through what is said, but also by means of actions, by the way people go about their task, and most often by a combination of both: words and behaviour.

It is this larger notion of transference that is important for work with groups and organisations. It means that groups/teams (through the way they relate to each other and to their job) can 'tell' us about experiences, even about 'thoughts' and phantasies, *related to the actual situation they are in,* and of which they are not consciously aware. Think of the situations I described and discussed earlier, concerning the mental hospital and the 'wine drinkers'. Another example may make it even clearer. It concerns a group that I worked with over a longer period of time, which means that at times we interrupted the sessions because I was going on vacation. The session I would like to present is the one before I leave for a period of three weeks. The group is working hard, and as happens more often in this type of 'last session', they sort of try to pick up and round off 'left-overs' of previous sessions. Doing exactly that, they make meaningful connections between experiences of different members; they associate, elaborate and do some delicate interpretative work. The mood is agreeable; active but without any overtones. And there is almost no need for me to intervene. After a while, I observe how pleased I feel with what is going on, while I wish that things would work out this way, more often. The only thing that seems to be lacking is some elaboration of the approaching end. There have been no more than some fleeting references to it. They work as if they could go on like this forever.

When there is about a quarter of an hour left, and I have the feeling that we have reached a point of rest, I say that it is as if, through their hard and efficient way of working, to which I needed to contribute only very little, they had not only tried to finish whatever lay in waiting, but that in this way maybe they had also shown me and themselves that there is really no reason to be concerned about the coming break, because they are quite capable of doing the necessary work without my help. After a short pause I add that maybe, in this way, they are also trying to give me a sort of going-away present, so that I shall remember them with pleasure, and will be glad to come back after my vacation. In association with my long intervention, they elaborate on some of the moments, when there were indeed vague images of my vacation present at 'the back of their minds', and what this might have meant.

In my opinion, my intervention referred to the wishes and hopes that were present in the group's 'Atlantis'. I inferred them from what was said and the way it was said, in combination with my own emotional reactions in the situation. But whenever I talk about unconscious contents or processes I use expressions like 'as if' and 'maybe', to make clear that I am not really sure, don't really know what is going on. I want them to understand that the only possibility for me is to suppose, and then for us to explore together if what I say could make sense. Depending on the situation, I may explicitly mention the elements on which I base my intervention, talking in terms of, for example, "If I hear/see this and that ... I wonder if" or "If I hear/see I start thinking about ... ". In doing so I reveal to the people I work with that

I do not possess some special 'sixth sense' they lack; that on the contrary, whatever I say is based on things that they too can see or hear or experience emotionally, while the observations as well as the conclusions I make, are always open to further associative elaboration, exploration and discussion. Sometimes my intervention is not based on clear 'facts' or experiences that I would be able to name, but only on a vague apprehension of the total situation I am in, and then I try to express that. I may say, for example, that something I can't really put my finger on, but which seems present in the way they talk or behave towards each other and me, gives me the impression that they are hesitating about something, or feel ill at ease ... or whatever. In doing so I try to open up the associative and explorative capacities of the group with a view to understanding what is going on. All too often I am confronted with the exactness of the remark made by one of my tutors: "Never forget that your patient, client or group are the only ones who *really* know!"

In the case of the mental hospital it was important to understand the unconscious element that revealed the real bases for the continuing conflict, in order for resolution and development to become possible. But in the case of the 'wine drinkers' and the 'going-away present' there is no problem to be solved; there is no need for change; those groups are working just fine. Interpretation is probably not even needed in order for the integrative effect of what happens, to occur. The integration might come about in a similar way, as dreams are able to fulfil several integrative functions independent of interpretation! Here, revealing the underlying unconscious story or motivation of what happens provides the added pleasure of understanding, maybe it contributes to the self-knowledge of the people involved, and it provides an additional element in learning about group processes.

Counter-transference

As the term indicates, counter-transference is the counterpart of transference. It refers to the emotional responses of the analyst, consultant or coach to their clients, and of managers to their co-workers.

The notion came into use some years after that of transference had been introduced. Originally – and for quite some time – counter-transference too was seen as an annoying hindrance for good therapeutic work. In those days, analysts were not supposed to have emotional reactions towards their analysands. They were presumed to be benevolent, neutral listeners who assisted their clients in bringing the part of the Ucs. that was the result of repression, back to consciousness, thus gaining insight into the cause of their problems, and creating the possibility of a solution to them. If an analyst experienced some emotional reactions to an analysand, this was viewed as a sign of the insufficiency of his/her personal analysis, which meant that s/he needed at least to do a bit of extra self-analysis, start an extra period of supervision, or even an additional period of analysis. But of course, as you probably can imagine, in those days, analysts almost never experienced counter-transference feelings!

And then came a brave woman. Paula Heimann was her name. While exposing her personal experiences, she dared to contradict her own, by then already famous and respected teacher, Melanie Klein, as well as Sigmund Freud himself. She stated that in fact psychoanalysts have all kinds of feelings towards their analysands, and that some of these can – unknowingly – be induced by the analysand, and used by the analyst to understand the person s/he works with.

Herewith, counter-transference – as transference before – had been transformed from a hindering element to one that could be an important expedient in analysis. Since then, three different forms of emotional reactions on the part of the analyst have been distinguished:

- Those which are indeed a sign of personal problems in the analyst, and which might need some assistance from a colleague;

- Those that are an expression of the empathic qualities of the analyst who senses the mood of the analysand or the fluctuating sphere of a session, and is able to use this to the benefit of the analysand;

- Those that the patient – unconsciously – induces in the analyst, thereby revealing an aspect of himself that belongs to the Ucs.[6]

Would you be surprised to hear that ever since, emotional reactions towards patients abound in psychoanalysts? With fervent enthusiasm some talk about and explain what they refer to as 'my counter-transference'. Of course this explanation never refers to the first category.

[6] For a longer discussion of the subject, consult: Vansina-Cobbaert, 1991.

A couple of years after Heimann's publication (1950), and in order to distinguish clearly and explicitly between the first and third type of counter-transference, Klein introduced the term 'projective identification' to refer to that third form of emotional reaction.[7] The second form is sometimes designated as 'normal projective identification'. Personally I would keep the term 'empathy' because in my view it refers to a psychological process that differs in several ways from projective identification. I'll come back to this shortly. Klein disliked the new way of looking at things, because she was all too much aware of the complexity of this difficult notion, and of the way it could be misused by analysts to provide a fast explanation, or to cover up their personal problems. And right she was! It seems to me that projective identification became one of the very important but simultaneously badly misused, if not abused, notions around. Maybe even much more so in so-called 'applied psychoanalysis' than in psychoanalysis proper.

Projective Identification

As with transference and counter-transference, projective identification is a *fully* unconscious process through which one tries to inject a part of the self into someone else, while one is neither aware of that part nor of the intention to get rid of it. The process is often classified as a defence mechanism, which at times it certainly is; yet not always. And anyway, it is much more a 'process' than a 'mechanism'. It can be used defensively, for example when it is employed as a way to get rid of some parts of the self that one does not like or is afraid of. If the process is used – in the context of envious feelings – to destroy in the other person qualities one would very much like to possess, but feels unable to develop, then the defensive character is more complex, and not immediately clear. The same is true when projective identification is used to put likeable, valuable parts of the self into another person, in order to protect those parts from one's own destructiveness. But apart from these, and sometimes in combination with them, there is the very important fact that *projective identification is always a means of communication*. It is one of the important 'languages' of primary process thinking. Moreover, once in a while

---

[7] It is often said that Klein introduced the notion of projective identification in 1948 (two years before the publication of Heimann's article). In fact this did not happen until 1952 when the notion was added to a new publication of the text of 1948 (cf. Vansina-Cobbaert, 1991).

I saw it used as an unconscious way of finding out how 'the receiver' would handle a difficult situation.[8]

The idea has been put forward that 'projection' and 'projective identification' refer to the same phenomena. Projection is then supposed to indicate the process, while projective identification is the term that points to the phantasy (Sohn, 1985). Personally I see projective identification as different from projection. This is already apparent in the language we use. Of projective identification we say that it is *into* the object. When it comes to projection we talk about *onto* the object. But there is more to it than that.

- In the case of projection one explicitly names the projected element. A person might say for instance: "Well, I don't really like her, I think she is jealous" and the person might even add some examples of that jealousy, while you, as a listener, might be a bit amazed because you think that the examples could easily be explained differently, or you believe you see more signs of jealousy in the person who talks than in the one who is talked about.

- The object onto which one projects, can be a person or a group one has no direct relations with, or has never even met.

- The receivers of the projection may react irritatedly or angrily because they feel accused, but they do not *become* whatever is put onto them. Inverted: although the person who projects is not aware of the fact that s/he possesses the projected properties him/herself, others will be able to detect them. They have only disappeared from the awareness of the projector.

When it comes to projective identification, the situation is in many ways different.

- Here, the projected part – it might be more exact to talk about 'ejected part' – is never named. It is the *way* a person behaves or talks about something – that might even have no direct connection with the ejected part – that injects this part into the receiver. Thus, there is no talk about jealousy or destructiveness, or worthlessness, or whatever, but the person who is talked to, will start feeling that way. And s/he might even be wondering about what happens, because by nature s/he is not prone to the feeling s/he experiences.

---

[8] For an extensive discussion of the subject in the context of psychoanalysis, see: Vansina-Cobbaert, 1991.

- This means that projective identification is only possible in situations where people are in *direct contact* with each other. The more emotionally intense that relationship is, the easier it becomes for projective identification to occur. From the time a baby is born, it becomes one of the important primary processes it uses to communicate with its mother, certainly during the first months of life. Until their children have acquired a workable level of verbalisation mothers seem especially sensitive to this form of communication. It is also a process that is often at work in couples, and in therapeutic situations. All too easily people seem to forget that we talk about a phenomenon that can work both ways. Children can become depositories of the projective identifications of their parents; patients can carry ejected parts of their therapists. And of course it is a process that occurs in groups, teams, between colleagues or between managers and their subordinates.

- Contrary to projection, when projective identification is at work the receiver *becomes* what is put into him/her. S/he is depressed, or angry, or confused, or feels stupid, or something else. Simultaneously – and also different from what happens in projection – the part that is put into the receiver is not recognisable in the personality of the ejector. It is only when the receiver disappears, or if s/he changes (e.g. with the help of therapy), that the previously ejected part may become observable in the person where it originally belonged.

- Projective identification occurs most likely into a person who is sensitive to the ejected part.

A real danger, and one that Klein was extremely concerned about, is that some people who know about projective identification seem to have a tendency to jump all too quickly to conclusions; especially when their experience is, in one way or another, unpleasant they tend to decide right away that it must be an experience that they carry for X or Y. In fact, it takes a good deal of difficult personal reflection and a great deal of exploration – together with the people involved – of the situation wherein the experience occurred, before one can draw any conclusions.

Let me tell how I came to understand more about this important notion and the realities it refers to.

Many years ago I was co-consulting under the supervision of Ronald Markillie, a British psychoanalyst, who worked regularly as a consultant in training programmes on group and inter-group dynamics. We had been doing a 'learning group', and I had been quiet all through the second part of the session. During the break, I told Ron how I had felt dead tired and incapable of saying anything. We talked about my experience, and after a while he said: "Well, if you feel like that in a group, when you had a good night sleep, and you did not drink too much wine at lunchtime, then you can almost be sure that there is a subtle form of fight going on in the group you are working with, and you will have to try and find out".

To me this was a revelation that later on affected all of my work. In those days I could not have imagined that it is possible that something which is going on at an unconscious level in a group, could be communicated to me by way of a very personal experience occurring in my body: I became dead tired. Neither could I have imagined that I could make use of such an experience, although *only on condition* that I did some finding out first. To start with, I had to do some finding out about myself: did I sleep badly? Had I been drinking too much wine? If not, then I had some finding out to do about the group. For if indeed it looked like a communication, what was it all about? Was it a fight? What was the fighting about? What was the anxiety behind the fight? A lot of questions one will have to answer in a consultative relation with the group.

Since then, I have told this story many times, because it had such an important influence on my understanding of this complex process and on the possibilities of its use.

What worries me today is that people seem to forget that in order to find out if an experience is induced, one has quite a bit of work to do; work that is often more difficult than finding out if one had a good night sleep or didn't drink too much wine. Especially when experiences or actions are unpleasant or condonable, individuals and groups seem to ascribe the origin of these experiences and actions light-heartedly to others. They will say things like: "I carry the sorrow; I express the anger for the whole group"; or, "Our team carries the feelings of incompetence for its leader"; or, "The participants are acting out the problems of the staff". And of course things like that do happen, but we don't know what is going on in the situation we are in, unless we – together with the client – do some hard explorative work first. If we don't, we abuse an important concept, and we mislead or even confuse our clients.

'Finding out together' does not mean that we start by just telling the people involved what we experience, and connect it to what we *suppose* is happening.

Such demeanour would be completely improper analytical work. It would have been unthinkable that I might have said something like: "I have felt dead tired for some time now, thus there must be some subtle form of fight going on in this group". Such an intervention would focus the attention of the group on something that happened to me, as if the group is responsible for my experience and for finding out what it is about. I am solely responsible for finding out why something is happening to me; while my task is to help the group find out what happens with them, or what happens between them and me. Moreover, I would have made a connection based exclusively on theoretical notions. In order to assist a group in exploring what might be going on, I need to point to some 'facts' which are present and that they too can see, hear or experience. Finally, as always, it is not enough to be sure that indeed there might be a phenomenon going on that in theoretical discussions or in writing, one would call 'projective identification'. In order for change to become possible, one needs an idea of *how* it is possible and especially *why* it is happening. This is essential in all forms of psychoanalytic work: knowing *what,* is never enough. It needs to be supplemented by *how* and especially by *why.* Asking these questions to the people involved, is almost never adequate, because they can only tell you what they are *consciously* aware of, while some of the answers may only be available at the level of primary process thinking. Those can be revealed only with the help of 'messages from Atlantis' be it through the way the work is organised, through images that are around or through typical relationships, spontaneous associations, the use of some unexpected words, some hasty remarks that are not picked up, and the like. Listening to those, and again exploring them together with the participants, belongs to the central tasks of the therapist or consultant.

The interventions I made in the case of the 'wine drinkers' and of the 'going-away present' were to an important extent based on my own feelings in the situation. Would I think of those as being the result of projective identification? No, I would not. Looking at the situations from the perspective of the group, I would say that both are forms of transference of the inner world of the group to the total situation they create. From my own perspective I would talk about an *emphatic* reaction. And, as I already announced, I would not classify empathy as the normal form of projective identification. In my opinion those are two different psychological processes. What happens in the case of empathy is what one could describe as 'being in touch with the *explicit* emotionality of the group', or as 'sensing the actual mood the group is in'. This could happen when you enter a room filled with people and think: "Brrr, what an amount of tension is hanging around here; what a stressful situation!", and you start feeling stressed yourself, while you wonder what this could be about. Or you meet some people and immediately sense that they are in a pleasant mood, and you start to feel pleased too, maybe asking them what is happening, what they are so enthusiastic about. But all the time there is not a moment of doubt that you are picking up something that is present 'out there'. Moreover, the people too know about the mood they are in, although they are not aware of what their way of working expresses indirectly. This 'out there' is not present in the case of projective identification – at least not until some difficult and often time-consuming explorations have been going on. The experience at the start is a very personal one: *I* am dead tired! It may even look as if you are the only one! What you experience may at first seem completely absent from the situation you are in, while the experience might stay with you even after you have left the situation wherein it started. On the other hand, once it becomes clear what is happening, you will feel relieved, as if delivered from a burden.

I hope that by now my account has made it clear that primary process thinking should not be equated with the rubbish dump of mental functioning. On the contrary, Ucs. processes, which often form the background of our daily activities, can play an important role in the working through and in the integration of experiences, as well as in the understanding and adaptation of maladaptive organisational processes and structures.

PUTTING THE INFORMATION FROM 'ATLANTIS' TO USE

Originally psychoanalysts thought that the only thing they had to do was to make the unconscious conscious. In this context 'the unconscious' was largely equated with the so-called 'repressed', which was seen as the basis for psychic problems. That the unconscious as a system contained much more than whatever got repressed was very well known but did not seem important then in the context of therapeutic work.

But we should not forget that those terms are part of individual analysis. Moreover, this way of thinking belongs to a period wherein we looked at psychological functioning with a rather mechanical paradigm, while we believed in the absolute supremacy of rational thinking, and thus over-valued the consciously functioning part of our mind. By now, we look at the mind as an organic system, and in this context we accentuate much more the development of co-operation between two forms of psychological functioning which both hold specific, valuable, and non-reducible characteristics. Today, our central field of work is the unconscious yet dynamic part of the 'internal world', be it of an individual, a group or an organisation, as it becomes indirectly visible in verbal expressions, images and in actions, as well as in the context of relationships and of task performance.

For organisations it is certainly valid to know that whenever unconscious elements are a source of dysfunction, bringing them to awareness is one of the possible first steps towards development and change. But it is just as important to know that in doing so, we apparently, simultaneously create directly important changes in some of the regions of the Ucs. It looks as if *just by going through the process* of exploring the conscious and unconscious background of problems, the *phantasmatic functioning* part of our mind develops and becomes richer. Changes in ways of thinking and in behaviour create the impression that previously unconscious contents gained access more easily to the pre-conscious/conscious system, while some primitive, unconscious anxieties seem to have lost their impact, even without having been made conscious. Moreover, taking part in this kind of work seems to increase a person's self-esteem, while increasing trust in his/her creative powers and in his/her capacity for reparation.

At least two important factors form the basis for those direct developments in the unconscious system. One is the way we phrase our interventions. The other is the development of certain specific characteristics of work groups or teams.

If we want to understand the Ucs., we have to understand its 'languages'. That is for sure. But it also looks as if we directly stimulate the development of that system if, in our interventions, we ourselves also make use of those 'languages'. It is as if the Ucs. not only 'speaks' but also 'understands' its own languages, even if our 'fluency' is only limited. Herewith I do not mean that we need to introduce some special 'imagination' or 'dream sessions'. The changes seem to come about very naturally whenever, in our interventions, we use the images, symbols, stories or myths that are part of the way a work system expresses itself.

Similar developments are also stimulated in groups, which, through their work, have acquired the following – partly overlapping – characteristics:

- A search mentality (a mentality of open exploration of work-related issues, including the honest expression of one's personal opinions and stance), that ranks above a mentality of knowing and judging.

- A capacity to contain, and process through thinking, intense emotionality, while distinguishing between aggression and passionate involvement (vehemence). Quite a few people mistake the intensive emotional reactions that often go together with vehemence, for aggression, and they withdraw from the relation with discomfort or even fear. Yet, vehemence is an expression of positive involvement. It is a life-enhancing factor, while aggression always contains an element of destruction. If a group is not capable of making that distinction, it loses its liveliness and enthusiasm. It becomes lame and tame, and creative development comes to a halt.

- A capacity to contain deviant ways of thinking while questioning and non-aggressive confronting prevails. This means that there is neither passive submitting to deviant elements (often expressed as 'anything goes'), nor isolating them. It also means that deviations do not lead to the 'explosion' of the group.

- The presence of mutual concern and, if necessary, a natural tendency towards sincere willingness to repair (make good) what went sour by intentional or non-intentional interactions.

- The presence of honesty and the absence of manipulation.

In groups that show these characteristics, members are allowed to know an important part of each other's inner world. This enables them to see how their fellow human beings experience and interpret 'reality'. It facilitates insight into the hard work and patience required for understanding and change to occur, and in the necessity to provide emotional support for each other during such periods. Such groups are more creative in most of their endeavours. They seem to enhance mental health in their membership, are sensitive to the underlying reasons for problems, and seem to have a positive influence on other parts of the organisation they belong to.

All this together promotes effectiveness, and the pleasure people find in their work, which is of course as important for the persons concerned as for the organisations. For the consultant it means becoming familiar and feeling at ease with the use of 'the languages of the Ucs.', which includes the capacity of exploring one's own emotional reactions in a given situation as well as the capacity to tolerate the unpleasant and sometimes even scary experience of not knowing. Finally it requires knowledge of group dynamics and sufficient experience in explorative group work in order to create the possibility for the above mentioned group characteristics to develop.

Apart from the above, some of the basic technical rules applied in individual analysis have been adapted for use whenever a psychoanalytic perspective is chosen for working within organisations. It seems to me that today's psycho-analytic technique puts the emphasis on three essential rules. The first one is: listen with free-floating attention. The second one urges us to work with the here-and-now situation in its totality, while keeping ears and even eyes wide open to the ongoing process. The third one stresses the importance of understanding and interpreting the unrecognised desires and anxieties, as well as the fields of tensions that give rise to defensive movements.

Both Menzies-Lyth and Bion have rephrased these rules in a way that makes them more suitable for work in group and organisational contexts. First of all, rather than talking about 'free-floating attention' they talk about working with 'equally divided attention'. To Bion (1970) this means that the attention is moving between the two levels at which work goes on: one being the level of the work-group mode (dominated by secondary process or logic thinking), the second one being the level of the basic assumption modes (dominated by primary process or phantasmatic thinking).[9]

With a slightly different emphasis, Menzies-Lyth (1989) says that we pay attention to the level of the unconscious world in as far as it hinders the per-formance of the primary task[10] and becomes expressed in conscious feelings, thoughts and the discourse of the people concerned or in the structure and in the way of functioning of groups and organisations.

But 'equally divided attention' does not mean 'equally divided interventions'. Depending upon our *mandate*, we might only intervene at the level of the un-conscious processes, and maybe even talk about some of those processes that do not hinder an ongoing task; for example, when we are as consultants in a 'learning group'. Here, the participants are together in order to learn

---

[9] Bion's views on small groups are discussed extensively in Chapter ***.
[10] The primary task is a heuristic and not a normative concept referring to the task an organisation or part thereof has to work on in order to survive.

about group processes in general, and to learn about differences between processes that might be hindering or helpful depending on the objectives and circumstances that prevail. In other situations, however, we might intervene almost exclusively at the level of the work-group mode; using interventions concerning the Ucs. level only when it blocks the ongoing task. At such a moment we may call for 'time out' to explore the hindering factors; thereby concentrating our interventions concerning unconscious processes within the 'time out'. This may happen, for example, in the context of assisting a client with a restructuring process or with a strategy definition. On other occasions we might decide not to reveal the influence of unconscious elements, but instead try to create conditions or situations that allow for anxieties, doubts and uncertainties to become tolerable, and for creative forces to return or to develop. Sometimes we may choose to advise that some processes or organisational structures be changed in a way that might take away the negative influence of the unconscious processes, without the need for revealing them (Jaques, 1989).

If we put all this together, we are left with quite a complex task, for we have to pay attention to what is going on at the conscious level while paying attention to what is revealed at the unconscious level, simultaneously being attentive to our personal experience of the total situation, and sorting out with what, when and how to intervene, either verbally or through influencing structures and/or processes.

Over the years, an interesting development occurred in relation to this idea of 'influencing structure and/or processes'. At first – think, for example, of Menzies-Lyth first hospital studies – in work with group and organisational problems, the emphasis was on identifying defences (in fact: defensive reactions and structures) and the anxieties, fields of tensions, that lurked behind them. Later on, the accent was more on detecting the consequences of inadequate holding and containment, and improving or creating it, whenever possible.[11]

Menzies-Lyth and Bion also talk about: "working from a position of cultivated ignorance or negative capability"; a position that Bion (1970) specified as a position of "eschewing or suspending memory, desire, understanding, and sense impressions". Bion's surprising, at first sight controversial and for psychoanalysts even defiant formulation, is essentially a way of stressing that

---

[11] I shall discuss the phenomena of holding and containment in the next chapter.

our attention has to be in the here-and-now situation in its totality. Our most important task is 'to be with' the client and with the ongoing process in the actual situation, following the thoughts, the emotional movements and the moods that prevail. As such, *allowing* for things to happen and *for meaning to emerge.*

The possibility that sense impressions hinder access to elements that cannot be sensed (except by analogy) is an idea that Bion puts forward in the context of individual analysis. We should not forget, however, that in groups and organisations, the situation is somewhat different. There, 'what is visible' is not only valuable, sometimes it's the only cue we get to start from, in order to identify the unconscious factors which play a part in the actual difficulties.

Memory is related to the past, and can hinder us in discovering what is going on right now. Only memories that come up associatively can throw some light on an emerging meaning. One could say for instance that it is only when we can forget about the fact that a team has been working together for several years that we will be able to 'see' that they act as if they have never met before.

Desire on the other hand, is connected to the future. Desire for change or fast improvements can get in the way of just 'being with' the client in the actual situation, taking the time needed for meaning to develop; an attitude which of course is difficult to sustain when working under time pressure. And finally: 'understanding' in the sense of 'working with a theory in mind', prevents us from discovering what is going on that might not fit our theory.

In this context, 'emergent meaning' is a very important notion. It is distinct from meaning that we give or attribute. It is also different from understanding. Understanding as well as meaning attribution refers to an active and more cognitive involvement. It is something that we *do*, and that surpasses the here-and-now. Meaning attribution is political when imposed, while understanding is something that can become shared for further exploration. Emerging meaning just happens; it evolves 'before our eyes', sometimes to our surprise. It is something that we can witness in the here-and-now, but we don't make or give it. We can try to put words to it and share it. Moreover, 'fully emerged meaning' includes a 'why'; it reveals the need and/or the anxieties, fears or tension fields behind an occurrence. Concepts and theory belong to the domain of understanding, at best they come after meaning has emerged in the here-and-now, and they are only suitable for scientific discussions or publications.

The application in practice of the above cited work principles will be extensively illustrated in Part Three. But let me stress now already, and in fact once more because it can never be said loud and often enough: questions such as 'What is the meaning of X in terms of Freudian, Bionian, Lacanian, or Y's theory?' are absolutely useless and even a hindrance in a work context. When at work, the only important thing is to understand the meaning of X in the context of *this* person or *this* group of people, doing *this* work, having *those* responsibilities in *that* organisation, *today*. This meaning will never become clear through thought activity alone. It will reveal itself through the stories told, the images used, the ways people react to each other, to the consultant and his/her interventions; it may express itself through the way people go about doing their job or through some structural features; it can reveal itself through some of the emotional experiences of the consultant. But whatever comes to the fore will have to be explored again and again with the people involved, before the central meaning of something has a chance to 'evolve before our eyes'.

REFERENCES

Bion, W. (1970). *Attention and Interpretation.* London: Tavistock.
Flowers, B.S. (Ed.) (1988). *Joseph Campbell, The Power of Myth*, with B. Moyers. New York: Doubleday.
Freud, S. (1915). The Unconscious. In: *Standard Ed.*, **14**. London: The Hogarth Press.
Heimann, P. (1950). On Counter-transference. *Intern. J. Psycho-Anal.*, **31**, 81–84.
Jaques, E. (1989). Requisite Organisation. Harlington, VA.: Cason Hall.
Joseph, B. (1985). Transference: the total situation. *Intern. J. Psycho-Anal.*, **66**, 447–454.
Lawrence, W.G. (Ed.) (1998). *Social Dreaming and Work.* London: Karnac.
Menzies-Lyth, E. (1989). *The Dynamics of the Social. Selected Essays*, Vol. II. London: Free Association Books.
Sohn, L. (1985). Narcissistic formation, projective identification, and the formation of the identificate. *Intern. J. Psycho-Anal.*, **66**, 201–213.
Vansina-Cobbaert, M.J. (1991). L'identification projective, une tour de Babel. *Rev. Belge de Psychanal.*, **18**, 59–69.

Vansina-Cobbaert, M.J. (1992). Atlantis et les rêves. *Rev. Belge de Psychanal.*, **21**, 65–88.
Vansina-Cobbaert, M.J. (1993). Per-agir (Acting-through). *Rev. Belge de Psychanal.*, **23**, 13–32.
Vansina-Cobbaert, M.J. (2005). A Therapeutic Community: a space for multiple transitional change. In: G. Amado & L. Vansina (Eds), *The Transitional Approach in Action*. London: Karnac.

CHAPTER 3

Supportive 'Process Structures'

Marie-Jeanne Vansina-Cobbaert

The process structures that I intend to present are meant to be supportive towards meaningful change. They designate conditions, activities, and ways of doing; ways we can use to enable and support a developmental process in a chosen direction. I shall describe and illustrate three such developmental, healthy processes.[1] They are referred to as holding, containment and transitional phenomena. The first two are concerned with things people do for or to us. The third activity demands our own participation.

It may look as if I am moving into the field of psychoanalytic jargon, and maybe some readers were already wondering about such a possibility when I wrote about the languages of relations. This is certainly not my intention. I use some 'labels' explicitly for two reasons. The first one is that you will often find labels in texts about psychoanalytic studies of organisations, without a clear definition of what they refer to. The second reason is that, sometimes, using a label can make it easy to talk about important and complex phenomena without reverting over and over again to long descriptions. But, as stated before, in order to do sound work in organisational settings, there is no need

---

[1] In Chapter 6 a further distinction will be made between 'process structures' and 'facilitating structures'.

to be able to *apply* these concepts to specific situations. The important thing is to recognise, and be able to handle the *phenomena* they refer to. I worked in this way for several years with the experience that R. Markillie helped me to understand[2] before I realised that, in psychoanalytic theory, the experience I got trapped in, was referred to as 'projective identification'. Markillie had not used the term, he only talked about things that can happen, and about how to explore and work with them. Knowing the sophisticated word certainly did not change the difficulties in the work!

HOLDING AND CONTAINMENT

Often, the notions of holding and containment are used interchangeably. Yet, although there is some overlap in their meaning, they are not identical. Holding is a concept that was introduced by Winnicott during the mid-50s. Winnicott, being a paediatrician as well as a psychoanalyst, wrote a lot about mother–child, and parent–child relationships. This is the context wherein the idea of 'holding' was introduced (1955). Fundamentally it refers to the way a mother provides her baby with a feeling of safety and being loved, through the way she holds it in her arms, and goes about her daily care. At the start it creates a sort of continuation of intra-uterine life, and a soft transition to life in the outside world. Good-enough holding is viewed as providing the basis for the development of a sense of wholeness, stability, safety, and being a person distinct from others. It is often said – and Winnicott contributed to this view – that holding is predominantly *external* and *sensuous*. To a large extent this is true. In holding, the accent is on the interplay of the bodies of mother and child, and on the meaning this interplay can have for the child. It is about handling a baby, and protecting it from over-stimulation. But I am sure that mothers who read this, are already thinking of the fact that while taking care of their babies and young children, they also did quite a bit of talking. They talked in order to express their love, friendliness, pleasure, enjoyment, concern, and enthusiasm. They talked to calm down an over-excited child, or to reassure a visibly anxious baby. Would all that talking be referred to as sensual? It might. Young children don't understand what we say. They 'tune into the music of the words', which is – at least at first sight – a sensual reaction. Yet, if the tuning in by the baby means being influenced by the quiet, calm, reassuring voice of mother, in a way that the anxious or scarred baby calms down, for example, takes over the peaceful trust of its mother, then the

---

[2] See Chapter 2, paragraph on projective identification.

difference with containment becomes extremely vague. Also the notion of the mother 'psychologically holding-the-baby-in-mind' while taking care of its physical needs comes very close to the notion of containment.

Winnicott sees the mother's holding function as supplemented and eventually taken over first by the family, then by the environment, and finally by society.

Containment is a notion, which developed within the Kleinian group of psychoanalytic thought. It is directly linked to the idea of projective identification: in order for projective identification to occur, there has to be a containing element. Bion (1962) seems to be the one who contributed most to the development of the notion. He described the mother as the original container. Over time social groups to which the individual belongs, take over her function. In contrast to holding, containing is seen as a purely *internal, psychological* process. Holding refers to something one does with/for a *person*. 'To contain' is something one does for certain psychological *features of a person*; mostly features that the ejector experiences as unpleasant, dangerous, destructive and anxiety provoking.

Although the notion 'containment' developed in association with projective identification, its use is not restricted to the occurrence of this process. Containment can be just as necessary for experiences that are consciously present; especially so if they include intense, overwhelming emotionality.

The developmental importance of containment depends on several conditions. The container has to recognise him/herself in that function. S/he needs an adequate sense of what s/he contains, is not excessively disturbed by it, and can hold the contents for as long as necessary for the ejector to be able to take it back. Moreover s/he has to be able to understand the experience of both ejector and container, while restricting him/herself to the expression of the experience of the ejector and his/her motives. If containment is part of a process of projective identification, the first step of 'recognising oneself in that function' becomes extra difficult, because, at least at the start, the container is not conscious of the fact that s/he is used as such.[3]

Today, probably more so than when the notion of container was introduced, the term easily evokes the image of a large, square, hard metal reservoir, while one of the important features of the living, psychological container is its flexible

---

[3] See also the paragraph on projective identification pp. 44–47.

suppleness, its adaptability to changing situations and conditions. Expressed in simple terms, one could say that an efficient container is someone who manages to stay calm under stressful conditions, while the people who are emotionally upset or anxious can feel his/her honest concern and orientation towards solving the difficulties at hand.

Let me try to describe an event that illustrates the difference and the overlap of both holding and containment.

Imagine a situation where a father, a mother and a baby come home after shopping. The baby has become very hungry, and screams uncontrollably. Mother picks the little one out of his chair, and in the meantime father has already opened the front door. In the kitchen, while warming the milk, the mother does not put her child safely in its crib or in an armchair. She keeps the hollering baby in her arms, and calmly, in a soothing voice, she talks to him. While stroking his back, she tells him that everything is perfectly under control; that his feeding is on the way, and that very soon all those painful, scaring pangs in his stomach will disappear. When mother sits down with the feed, father comes in. He has already put the frozen stuff they bought in the freezer and the meat in the refrigerator. He picks up the ringing phone. "No," he answers, "my wife is not available right now; maybe in half an hour; could you call back?"

Here, the mother is mostly *holding* the baby; especially so when she does not put him down somewhere while preparing the feed. A very young child, when left alone in a scary situation becomes panicky, because it cannot yet imagine that help will be around in time. The panic reaction can become visible in the fact that sometimes, when finally feeding comes, for a while, the baby will be unable to start eating. It will continue to holler, and even turn its face away from the feed, as if mother and bottle became a source of pain and danger. By keeping the baby in her arms the mother prevents this from happening. It is as if she creates in her child the feeling of being safely 'held together'. But I would say that the mother is *containing* her baby when she starts talking in a calm voice, which can transfer the feeling that she is at ease, that she is sure that there is absolutely nothing to worry about because she is around and taking care. Only through the psychological action of calmly, soothingly talking, is she able to pass on to her child the feeling that his actual experience is not going to destroy him. That she will see to it that, in a minute, he recovers into a satisfied, happy baby. By acting as container for her child's anxiety, the mother is also paving the way for the development of self-containment in her baby. Some of the steps in such development may become visible in a similar situation with a slightly older child. Such a child can already visibly recognise its warming bottle. When a mother talks calmly to such a screaming child in her arms, the screaming will calm down to a slight whimper, while the child looks from the bottle to the mother and back, as if trying to urge her on a bit. If, in comparable situations, a mother often loses her calm and becomes anxious herself, or if she misjudges the bases of anxiety in her child, she may be the source of psychological problems in her baby because not only does she deprive her child from the containment that he badly needs, but on top of that she adds her own anxiety to his.

The father in the given situation does a perfect job of providing a 'holding environment'. Sometimes this is referred to as: 'holding the mother who is holding the baby'. He opens the front door, while his wife picks up the baby, which allows her to start the needed task as fast as possible. Subsequently he sees to it that she has nothing else to worry about: frozen items are in the freezer, perishable ones in the refrigerator, and the person on the telephone is kept at bay. He allows for his wife to have their baby as her sole concern.

Now, back to groups and organisations. I would say that an experienced surgical team at work in a surgical theatre comes close to perfect holding and containment. Holding in as far as they have maximum protection against disturbing intrusions from outside the operating room, while each participant knows his/her personal task in the overall procedure; containment, because each member of the team has been trained to a high level of self-containment of anxiety under stress. And if something unexpected should happen, there is little chance of panic because some of the leading members, or just the head surgeon, will decide on the necessary action, thereby absorbing – containing – the upsurge of anxiety in the rest of the team. It is a situation comparable to that of an experienced combat team, which when under dangerous, enemy fire, will automatically, without questioning follow the orders of the commander. Those who acted as 'containers' may have to blow off some steam afterwards, but during the intervention, the team will not 'fall apart', for they are confident in their capacity for survival, because they know from experience that they are capable of absorbing unforeseen difficulties and responsibilities without collapsing.

In actual work situations holding and containing are almost always intertwined. And this is perfectly all right. The important thing is to see to it that they are available, especially when the work is dangerous and stressful. An efficient form of co-operation between the two occurs when the presence of a holding environment allows for containment to be sustained, or to develop; one could say: creating an organisational variant of the family described above.

Something like this occurred in an organisation which was planning to carry out some rather extensive re-structuring. As soon as the workforce heard about it, their imagination ran wild. All sorts of stories about the worst possible consequences started to circulate. They talked about massive lay-offs, more complex, stressful responsibilities, a different organisation of the shifts, and so on. The moment the negative fantasies reached the general manager, he did not panic, neither did he deny the forthcoming changes, nor did he act as if there was nothing to worry about. Instead, together with the personnel manager, he organised a meeting to talk directly to all the employees. He explained what the re-organisation was about; how many jobs would be lost; how the redundancies would be decided, adding that these decisions would be announced in time. Moreover, he and the personnel manager explained what kind of support the company planned to provide in order to help relocate workers who might wish so; how redundancy fees would be calculated and paid in consultation with the unions, and how they intended to provide training on the job for those whose tasks and responsibilities would change. Finally they assured the people that the organisation of shifts was not in question.

All this can be seen as the installation of an elaborate holding environment. Yet, in as far as the informers stayed calm and were seemingly honest, they certainly absorbed part of the tensions and anger that were around and thus already provided some containment. When they continued to stay calm, and gave elaborate answers – also telling what they did not yet know for sure – to the many, at times aggressive, defiant questions that came their way, they were providing all the containment that was possible during that stage of developments. More of it, and in other forms, became possible once the lay-offs and job re-allocations were known. But then the containment was directed at individuals and small groups, as it was tailored to the specific experiences and needs of the people involved.

At the level of groups and organisations it is important to avoid the possibility that persons or structures that are supposed to provide holding and containing, themselves become a source of uncertainty or stress. One of the worst examples of such a situation that I have ever encountered was an organisation where employees were never sure that, when returning after sick leave or vacation, their job or their office would not have changed, or even disappeared. This did not mean that they were laid-off; it only meant that they were re-assigned to another department, or received new responsibilities, which might include having a new office also, or continuing without one.

Sometimes, group and organisational problems are a consequence of the fact that authority figures, instead of absorbing part of the organisational stress and providing sufficient safety for work to continue, create their own unpleasant experiences of being inadequate, unsuccessful, and the like, into their team. On the other hand, it may happen that managers or leaders 'export' successes into the company or into their teams. This can be a way of doing away with feelings of inadequacy that exist at a deeper personal level. A negative consequence thereof is that it becomes difficult for the organisation, the team or the managers, to hold on to experienced failures in order to learn from them.

It can be relatively easy for a manager to detect that his team is ejecting some of its painful, unpleasant, anxiety provoking feelings and experiences into him/her. And anyhow it belongs to his/her responsibilities to take those on, and work with them to the benefit of team development, and if possible to the benefit of the personal development of the members, and of him/herself. On the other hand, without the help of a consultant, it is extremely difficult for a team to work through the problems of a manager who uses them as a container for his/her own difficulties. Consultants too have a demanding and complex task. They are supposed to be able to contain the anxiety, anger, depression, excitation ... that is present, in order for the work that needs to be done, to continue. Simultaneously they need to contain their own stress and anxiety about facing an angry, demanding, passive, depressive, over-excited, or whatever group, and they need to contain their own anxiety about not immediately understanding the complexity of the problem, nor a road to solution. Finally, they have to be able to distinguish between the experience that is originally theirs and the part that they take over from the people they work with.

Would it not be fantastic if organisations, when selecting and appointing someone in a managerial or consultative function, could and would also take into account his/her talent to recognise, accept, and work with his/her capacity for containing? Such a choice would undoubtedly install a continuous form of team building, as well as favour the psychological development of the team members.

TRANSITIONAL PHENOMENA

Long before Winnicott started his theories about transitional phenomena, mothers knew about the importance of different sorts of soft objects in the context of soothing their young children. They were also aware of the fact that those objects somehow had an influence on the healthy psychological development of those children.

Not only mothers, but some organisations as well have, in the context of change processes, used some activities that years later were labelled and theorised as 'transitional change'. This provides a very good example of the fact that we do not necessarily need 'the words' in order to work with the realities, while in reverse, 'possessing the words' does not always mean that we know how to handle the realities they are supposed to cover.

From 1951 onward Winnicott described and theorised a rather wide group of transitional phenomena with the help of concepts such as: transitional object, transitional space, potential space, intermediate space, a resting place, play, a place for play and/or cultural experience.

The best-known transitional objects are the classic soft toys that mothers provide for their young children in order to comfort or reassure them. They often acquire an exceptional position among a child's toys and are especially needed at bedtime or more generally at times of change, frustration and loss. In fact, children always choose their own transitional objects from what mothers provide intentionally or from objects that are available in their surroundings. Such personal choices become visible when a child selects a piece of coloured – and shapeless – soft cloth, or an object with a special smell, rather than one of the nice, often expensive, animal figures that adults offer.

The notion 'transitional' refers to the fact that the objects help a person to move from one way of being to a more appropriate, necessary or wished-for one. For a child this could mean going from anxious excitation to quiet satisfaction or going from wakefulness to sleep, from being with other people in the light to being alone in the dark, or it may also refer to slower and much more complicated developments as for instance the move from the experience of being fused with a mother figure, to the experience of oneself as separate and different from mother and from other persons.

I suppose that this already indicates the importance of transitional phenomena in the context of organisational development and change.

Transitional phenomena are the many ways in which transitional objects may be used or treated. They belong to the field of 'doing', but the change they aim at is at the level of 'being'. Moreover, if the process makes use of an object, this object – contrary to most objects psychoanalytic theory is concerned with – becomes unimportant as soon as the change process is completed. There is no feeling of loss, nor is the object internalised. It just loses its meaning. It might be remembered with pleasure. It might be picked up again later on, and adapted to new situations that include a need for development, but in-between it has no value whatsoever. The essential thing is that it helps us to realise a passage that is almost always concerned with reconciling our inner world with the external reality or vice versa. Winnicott was the first analyst who designated this task as central to the course of psychic development, and as an important source of creativity.

But what we refer to as a 'transitional object' does not have to be an object in the narrow sense of the word. It can also be a tune, a saying, a poem or a ritual. Such a ritual developed in our family in the course of a period of several years, during which my husband was often absent for a whole week, and returned only on Saturday afternoon. In trying to make the rather complicated transition from 'widowhood' to married state, and from a single parent to a two-parent family, a set of activities came into being. It started with my husband and I taking a sauna late in the afternoon. Afterwards, and together with the children, we had an extended dinner, always using the same ingredients and the same way of preparing. There was a large T-bone steak that my husband, with assistance and the necessary comments of the children, grilled on an open fire, while I prepared a salad. The whole 'ceremony' provided ample time for all the events of the week to be told and thought about, and thus for re-establishing a feeling of belonging together and sharing an important part of each other's life experiences. Over time this stable ritual acquired a special extra value for the youngest of our sons, when he wrestled with the difficult task of distinguishing between the days of the week. As soon as his daddy started to grill, he would look up with a large, happy smile, and in a self-confident voice that was never there during the rest of the week he would state: "Mummy, today is Saturday!" No doubt about it, that one he got right from the start!

Similar rituals are often present in organisations, even without us being aware of them. Their importance becomes clear only when for one reason or another they get lost. When I worked as a group analyst in a mental hospital, I often started a group at 9 a.m. On those days I came in a bit after 8.30, took care of some practical, administrative chores, and then, shortly before 9, I went to 'our kitchen' for a cup of tea. Apparently some of my colleagues from other departments held similar habits. We would be together quietly for about five minutes, using words sparingly, sipping our hot brew, and then off to a hard day's work. It went on like that for several years. Then one day, the hospital management decided that from then on the only coffee breaks would be between 10 and 10.30 a.m., and between 3 and 3.30 p.m. Only during those periods would coffee and tea be available. I could not believe that such a decision had been made for the totality of the many different functions that were around. Moreover, and a bit to my own surprise, I not only felt irritated, I felt completely lost. So did my colleagues. After a couple of days I found out that the most important reason for my vexation was not that we were never free during those official coffee breaks, it was the fact that our morning ritual became impossible. But it was only at the moment I lost my 'passage ritual' that its meaning and its importance surfaced. Fortunately enough, we had an understanding and wise head of personnel, who had experience with therapy groups in mental hospitals. After some explanations and explorations, we were able to return to our early morning habit, while the mid-morning and afternoon breaks were reshuffled a bit too. For sure, it was a relief!

In organisations, transitional phenomena and especially transitional structures are most in need during restructuring or reorganisations. Not only because those situations are of a transitional kind, but because transitional structures are meant to facilitate the harmonisation of the inner world and the external reality. Although this task – as Winnicott rightly stresses – is an important, continuous assignment for human beings, the need for such harmonising is at its highest during organisational change processe. At the time Winnicott was writing, he could not have guessed how important this part of his insights and thinking would become for organisations. In the context of change processes, at best, organisations provide some holding and containment. Sometimes there will be specific additional job training. But almost always the not so easy task of harmonisation, of bringing together and working through anxieties, fears, fantasies, hopes and wishes, with objective, but sometimes complex, intricate facts, will be entirely left in the care of the individual employee. Yet, transitional objects and structures can be provided together with holding and containment. The only problem is that in contrast with holding and containment, a transitional task necessitates action from the side of the employees themselves. They need to be able to explore actively and explicitly that part of their inner world that concerns their experiences of the work situation; and they need to do this in relation to what happens in their changing environment, and to the many consequences this might entail for them and their families. They also need to find the time and space to 'play around' with possible scenarios – still in the virtual world – on how to navigate through the hectic period of transition, and on how to prepare best for the new situation ahead. If the process of harmonising the inner world with the external realities in the context of sufficient holding and containment works out well, it may provide the basis for enthusiastic and creative work in the new organisational setting.[4]

REFERENCES

Bion, W. (1962). A theory of thinking. *Int. J. Psycho-Anal.*, **43**, 306–310.

Winnicott, D. (1951). Transitional objects and transitional phenomena. In: *Collected Papers: Through Pediatrics to Psycho-Analysis* (1958). London: Tavistock Publications.

Winnicott, D. (1955). Group influence and the maladjusted child. In: C. Winnicott, R. Shepherd & M. Davis (Eds), *Deprivation and Delinquency* (1958). London: Tavistock Publications.

---

[4] An extensive discussion of a combination of different supportive structures used in the context of a complex change project is provided in Part Three.

CHAPTER 4

Defensive Processes and Behaviour

Marie-Jeanne Vansina-Cobbaert and Leopold Vansina

Defensive processes and behaviour are broader notions than the psychoanalytic one of defence mechanisms. The latter provides the ground on which the other concepts have been built.

INDIVIDUAL DEFENCE MECHANISMS

The notion of defence mechanism refers to a specific group of automatic reactions by the individual's dynamic unconscious system, to anxiety. Sometimes one may also find them cited as reactions to shame and guilt. This is a consequence of the fact that both shame and guilt are viewed as complex human experiences that develop out of basic, primary anxiety. In its connection with defence mechanisms, anxiety is distinct from fear, which should not be thought of as a mild form of anxiety.

Fear is one of those notions that received very little attention in psychoanalysis. Sometimes it is referred to as 'objective anxiety', while anxiety is then defined as 'irrational fear'. It seems to me that we might view anxiety as a basic emotion evoked by a primary functioning mental system[1], whenever

[1] See Chapter 1.

it experiences something as dangerous. If, in such circumstances, holding, containment and/or a suitable transitional object are not available, a defensive mechanism will automatically take over as a form of flight in the face of what is experienced as an uncontrollable danger. Fear could then be defined as the emotional reaction to danger of a mental system that has developed at least a minimal level of secondary processes. A tendency to flee would then automatically surface, but would not necessarily, automatically be followed. Curiosity might for instance be able to overrule the inclination to flee.

In psychoanalytic publications you'll find between 9 and 15 defence mechanisms, depending on how they are clustered (e.g. idealisation may be put together with splitting and denial, projection may be too; reaction-formation can be seen as a form of reversal, think, for example, of exhibitionism turning into voyeurism, sadism into masochism). Publications in the field of Organisation Development often refer to many more defence mechanisms. This happens because, under the heading 'defence mechanisms' or 'social defences', authors add some quite different psychological mechanisms that serve a protective purpose, sometimes even some important developmental processes that can be used defensively. It is important to distinguish between those different processes because, the way of handling defensive behaviour will be different depending on how and what process is active.

We will not discuss the different defence mechanisms separately. The important thing is to remember that they function *automatically* and *unconsciously* as a reaction to *anxiety*. A person is not aware of the fact that s/he uses one of those mechanisms. S/he has no choice. It is even possible that the anxiety that provoked the reaction did not become fully conscious. Thus, to say: "I tried very hard, and it took me a long time before I was able to repress those feelings", makes no sense. Repression is not achieved by trying to ban something from awareness. We can decide to *suppress* something, and that may indeed take some time and sustained effort, but we can never try to *repress* something. Either it happens without our being aware of it, or it does not occur at all. If something succumbs to repression, it becomes inaccessible to memory – it can neither be thought nor talked about – without a difficult effort, the help of 'the languages of Atlantis', or sometimes even of a specialist. Whatever becomes suppressed, can be remembered, thought or talked about. This only depends on self-reflection and conscious elaboration, which is for the person to decide.

If you try to explore the existence of a defence mechanism, you will meet at least with some sort of amazement and disbelief, and most likely with some opposition, which is called *resistance* to insight. People will say things like: "You are crazy; you talk nonsense; you don't understand me ... ". But, if you work in an organisation or an institution as a manager or a consultant, you are not even supposed to touch those *individual defensive mechanisms*. They belong to the private life of the individual. You can sometimes try to advise a person to seek help for some of his/her ways of reacting that create great difficulties within the work situation. But that's it.

Yet, you may have some positive, *indirect influence* on individual defence mechanisms in operation. They often loosen up when people have the possibility to belong to, and work in a group that has the characteristics that we mentioned earlier, in the paragraph on 'putting the information of Atlantis to use'. Groups with this kind of characteristics will use defensive processes rather sparingly, and the ones that are used will be more easily accessible. Consultants and managers can assist workgroups in developing such characteristics, which are beneficial to the individuals, and also to the task-oriented functioning of the group.

Apart from the known, classic defence mechanisms, all kinds of *developmental* processes can, at times, be used for defensive purposes. Yet, it does not mean that they are defence mechanisms. This may for instance happen with processes such as symbolisation, fantasy, and identification.

Symbolisation is one of the most important developmental processes that exist. One of its finest and complex expressions results in amongst others our capacity for verbal interaction. But, it also becomes regularly abused for defensive purposes. For instance: instead of talking with the intention to express our experiences, feelings or thoughts, we may speak in order to make some important facts disappear from attention; to prevent others from saying something; to make it difficult for others to think ... for example, deflecting from a difficult issue.

The same goes for 'fantasy'. Fantasy (contrary to 'phantasy') is a conscious process that can help us to prepare in thought, for a forthcoming, difficult situation. It can help us to survive in painful circumstances over which we have no control, like being in jail, or being tortured. It can alleviate some unpleasant experiences related to illness and treatment. Sometimes it can even provide a cure. But you can also use fantasy/imagination to do away with a painful or scary reality that is largely under your own control. You can for instance imagine all the fantastic things you are going to do during the coming vacation, instead of studying that awful course of statistics that you hate and might flunk, and then of course flunk it!

Identification is a third enormously important developmental process. If we can say that we only become human in a human environment, this is largely a consequence of identifications. Even the process of symbolisation is partly based on identification with people around us. Yet, if identification is triggered by anxiety, it may operate as a defence mechanism, and then the result can lead to disaster. This is, for example, the case when identification occurs with an aggressor. When a person, a group, or even a people take over the characteristics of the one or those that mistreated them over a long period (and this happens without their being consciously aware of it!), they may become worse than their abusers. The positive comments about their kidnappers, by people who were taken hostage during a long period, are but a mild example of such an occurrence.

The result of defensive use of a developmental process is a *rigid* structure, while the adaptive use of this process creates a *flexible* structure. This becomes very visible through the different ways in which conscience can develop. If it is the result of an identification, based on love, admiration, and 'wanting to be like' a person or a group, the result is a righteous, yet mild structure, that is capable of forgiveness and consolation. If conscience develops out of anxiety, through identification with the aggressor, it becomes rigidly harsh and de-manding, oriented only towards punishment, most prominent self-punishment in one form or another. A similar over-strict conscience can also develop in an attempt to protect oneself from an over-indulgent or seducing parent.

When a developmental process is used defensively, it is *not always* triggered by anxiety, and it is *not always* an unconscious process that operates auto-matically. It can be related to the need for influence and power, and can be used with conscious intentions. Illustrations are: lying, or talking to prevent the discussion of an important but delicate subject.

DEFENCE MECHANISMS IN GROUPS

With his theory on small groups, Bion (1961) made the first attempt at iden-tifying group specific defence mechanisms. The phenomena he described occur in groups only when 3 conditions are simultaneously present: the group is small (8 to 15 participants), its task is delicate (it contains some real or imagined dangers), and participants are interdependent (there is no formal leader) for successful task accomplishment. Whenever such conditions are present, groups may operate efficiently in what is called the 'work group mode'. This means that the group members explore the task(s) at hand, and allocate the necessary sub-tasks to different participants in function of their natural talents and acquired expertise; expected difficulties are explored; progress and unforeseen problems are discussed, and work-related emotional experiences are talked about, and, in as far as is possible, taken care of. But sometimes, and apparently without awareness, group members move to another type of functioning that Bion labelled 'basic assumption mode'. This is a defensive move groups make when trying to get rid of vague, not clearly conscious, yet threatening pressures or anxieties. The experienced dangers are mostly related to the destruction or annihilation of the individual or the group.

In Bion's thinking, basic assumptions belong to the world of 'phantasies'. Thus, they express our primary ways of giving meaning to the phenomenon of groups to which we belong. They are the images that we all harbour about what groups are, what purpose they serve and how they function. They are 'phantasies' we are all intimately familiar with from our early childhood when we were born and grew up in families and in other groups. These 'phantasies' emerge, without awareness, when the group is confronted with various kinds of tensions. At such moments group members may start behaving *as if* the group is gathered with a different goal in mind than task accomplishment.

Bion identified three of these 'as-if' goals. Under the basic assumption *dependency*, the members behave as if the group merely exists for someone to take care of its members. Such a person is experienced as someone who knows everything, is able to do and understand everything – even without words. The dominant emotional climate is one of *helplessness*, powerlessness and utter dependence on a person or a method, put forward as a danger-control authority or device. Under the basic assumption of '*fight-flight*' people behave as if the raison d'être of the group resides in fighting an imminent danger or enemy, or fleeing from it. The emotional climate is characterised by *over activity* and *urgency* without any reflection. In the basic assumption of *pairing* (sub-grouping) members act as if the group has gathered to await a miracle, or the arrival of a 'messiah' who will change everything to the better. The group's emotional climate is one of *hope*, of *euphoria* that is completely disconnected from its real achievements.

We only refer to 'dependency', 'fight-flight', and 'pairing' or 'sub-grouping' when the realities of the group in its context don't justify, nor warrant these types of behaviour or emotional climate.

General characteristics of 'as-if' functioning are the loss of touch with reality and thus the absence of reality testing. People talk in generalisations that remain vague, anonymous and un-testable. The distinction between individuals disappears, together with the notion of time and history. The thinking is rather magical, while control and submission to group norms gain extreme importance. Frustrations are barely tolerated, and feelings and actions are overemphasised to the detriment of thinking, reflecting and exploring the internal and external realities. People behave as if what is happening is relevant for task accomplishment, yet without ever verifying the correctness of that stand. Finally, the leader is ascribed unreal emotions, desires and power.

Since Bion's work, two other basic assumptions have been identified. Under the basic assumption of '*one-ness*' (Turquet, 1974, p. 375) "members seek to join in a powerful union with an omnipotent force, unobtainably high, to surrender self for passive participation, and thereby feel existence, well-being and wholeness". The individual self fuses with the group. By contrast, under the fifth basic assumption: "*me-ness*", (Lawrence, Bain & Gould, 1966) people behave as if the group has no reality, neither exists, nor can really exist, because "the only reality to be considered and taken into account, is that of the individual. It is the culture of selfishness in which individuals appear to be only conscious of their own personal boundaries, which they believe have to be protected from any incursion by others. The nature of the transactions is instrumental, for there is no room for affect, which could be dangerous because one would not know where feelings might lead" (Lawrence, 2000, p. 100). The overriding anxiety is that the individual will disappear in the group.

Probably more specific patterns of as-if behaviour than the current five can and will be identified. However, to remember their names is not important for the practitioner. What is relevant for the praxis is (a) to pay attention to the presence of as-if behaviour, (b) to explore its relationship to assumed fields of tensions, (c) subsequently, to share this understanding with the group, and (d) if found correct, take action to bring the tensions within the range of tolerance.

Summarising, we may conclude that fields of tensions trigger anxieties and basic assumption behaviour which is unconscious. Thus, the as-if behaviour in and of the group is not pretence. Group members experience it as genuinely related to the task(s) at hand, although there may be some vague feelings of uneasiness present in some of the members. These feelings may then provide the start for some explorations that lead the group back to a workgroup mode of operating. Basic assumption behaviour disappears when the causal tensions and anxieties are removed or made tolerable, exactly as with individual defences.

SOCIAL DEFENCES

Elliot Jaques (1955) was the first to identify some social defences in an industrial organisation. Later, Isabel Menzies (1961) explained a variety of standard practices in general hospitals as social defences against 'anxieties' emerging from the work itself. Both of them were psychoanalysts who started to study and deal with organisational problems. While trying to understand what was going on, they reached the very interesting insight that the primary task[2] is not the only factor responsible for the way an organisation is structured, nor for the way the work is organised and performed. Structure and the way the work is organised, are just as well a consequence of a tendency to protect the members against anxieties that are stirred up by the work.

'Social defences' then, are procedures, processes, structural measures, ways of organising work and/or allocating responsibilities aimed at alleviating work-related tensions that may or may not trigger some primitive anxieties. But using defences in order to 'protect employees against ...' or 'to alleviate tensions or anxieties' does not mean that the tensions and anxieties disappear, they may become less pronounced, more hidden, even for the people who experienced them originally. What may stay on is a vague feeling of discomfort or restlessness, and/or a way of organising and structuring that is rather inadequate or inefficient in view of the tasks that need to be performed. Under such conditions it may for instance happen that patients in a hospital lose their individuality and become 'diseases' or even 'beds' to be taken care of. Nursing becomes just another job. As a consequence the more caring nurses may opt for part-time work, or leave their vocation altogether.

---

[2] The notion of primary task is in essence a heuristic concept defined as the task that an institution or part thereof must, at any time, perform in order to survive (Rice, 1963; Miller, 1993).

Protecting members from the experience of tensions can also have a detrimental influence on the way responsibilities are allocated, and on collaboration within or between teams. It can further impinge on the way supervision is organised, and decisions are made.

In the context of organisations the notion 'anxiety' covers a broader range of experiences than in psychoanalysis proper. It includes for instance all kinds of fears that were at least at some moment, conscious. Some of those fears and the protective measures that they entail, are related to objective dangers. For example: danger of assault in jails or in psychiatric hospitals; danger of contamination when working in hospital departments for contagious diseases, e.g. HIV, tuberculosis; dangers of radioactive contamination in nuclear plants, or the persistent threat of being fired, and the like. Consequently, it is more appropriate to talk about fields of tensions stirred up in the context of carrying out the work than calling them anxieties.

Tensions can take a rather subjective colour, for example, fears about clients and their reactions; fears that are stirred up by the condition the client is in (e.g. terminal patients); thoughts of becoming ashamed, feeling guilty, losing self-esteem or of being made redundant for whatever reason beyond the employee's control. It happens that fear is only indirectly present in a need to avoid some difficult, complex tasks or situations such as conflict within a group, explicit individual differentiation and confrontation in the context of absenteeism, cheating or pilfering. Moreover, some of the defensive processes in organisations do not originate in the need to avoid tensions, fears or objective dangers, but in the need for power and control.

One of the problems with social defence theory is that both Menzies and Jaques made use of the concepts that were known through individual psychoanalysis, while in fact the processes that are active in society and in organisations or institutions are of a different kind. Yet, some practitioners claim that these tensions become somehow and at a deeper level always associated with individual anxieties.

We like to stress the difference between social defences and defensive mechanisms. The sources of discomfort, tension or real dangers don't trigger an *automatic* defensive response. Even when these sources of tension become linked to individual, primitive anxieties or sensitivities they are at the start, mostly, consciously experienced as *disagreeable*. Once these social defences become established as procedures or ways of organising the work, they become socially embedded and remain even when the sources of tensions have been removed. People may not even understand why these measures came about.

SOCIAL REPRESSION

One of the many criticisms directed at Freud's thinking and theories, argues that repression is in fact a social phenomenon. It is learned through social interactions and in particular through language and the activity of conversation (Billig, 1999). In fact, Freud too, as well as some of his followers, sometimes used the notion 'repression' in this very broad sense, referring to a group of processes which might be brought on by anxiety that was stirred in the context of interpersonal relations. Such could be the case when the anxiety was about the possibility of losing a person one felt dependent upon for survival. However, this is not what critics have in mind when they insist on 'repression' being a 'socially based process'. What they mean is that, from the time that we are young children onwards, we sense the emotional climate that is part of social interaction. We feel what can be said and what not; we detect how things are supposed to be expressed and how not; we even get some inkling about subjects that we are not even supposed to think about. And of course, all this is absolutely right. Only, it has nothing to do with 'Freudian repression'. What is talked about under the label 'social repression' is a normal, developmental use of identification and learning. These are processes that can indeed make things disappear from consciousness, without us being clearly aware of the fact that it was ever there. But not at all in the way it happens in the case of Freudian repression. *Social* repression and *suppression* are very important processes by which we adapt our way of talking and acting as a function of what we experience as 'acceptable ways to say/do things' or as 'things one does not mention', at least not directly.

Thus, social repression differs fundamentally from the Freudian notion because:

- The process is not automatically triggered by anxiety, although it might be related to some fear of not being accepted. But it can just as well be the consequence of a wish to be like or to be part of a group or system that one likes, loves and respects; it can also be based on a political stance.

- In adults at least, it starts with some awareness and some conscious intention.

- The process is stretched out in time; there is some learning involved.

- When you talk about the things that seem to have disappeared, you will not meet with resistance but maybe with some awe. People may even be very interested and enjoy the exploration.

In as far as social repression is not an automatic process, but is learned during conversation and/or established through identification, it is a process that is an important part of organisational life. Certain experiences disappear; certain things are not done, not said, even not thought. The sources of tensions, like fears of being cast aside, losing affection, losing chances of promotion, being reprimanded may become forgotten, but may have been known at the time. However, social repression may well last after these sources of tensions have disappeared. Here too, the 'learned' behaviour may have become socially embedded.

Social repression or, more exactly suppression, can become reinforced by observable pressure from group cohesion and/or from a dominant leader (Janis, 1972). This process in group-decision making is known under the classic name: 'groupthink'. Yet, such pressures don't necessarily have to be present in a concrete situation. Individuals or groups can anticipate becoming excluded or losing something valuable if they were to speak their minds freely. Harvey (1974) described this kind of 'defensive phenomena' under the label: the 'Abilene paradox'.

DEFENSIVE STRATEGIES

We use this more general term to refer to a group of defensive processes that are situated in the grey area between non-conscious and conscious behaviour. People behave in a way – without fully realising – that protects them against anticipated loss of self-esteem, shame, and discomfort, or against being held accountable. Over time the functional relevance of these strategies is forgotten. As such they are closely related to social repression or suppression.

Defensive or protective strategies are widely spread in organisational and community life. Argyris (1976, 1985, 2004; Argyris & Schon, 1974) speaks about 'defensive routines', 'defensive reasoning' and 'Model I theory-in-use' that reinforce one another to avoid feared consequences. 'Model I theory-in-use' fuels defensive routines and defensive reasoning by emphasising the following values: (1) be in unilateral control, (2) maximise winning and minimise losing, (3) avoid expressing negative feelings, and (4) act rationally by using defensive reasoning. Beneath the observable behaviour we may be able to detect some fears about uneasiness and/or uncertainty, appearing vulnerable and/or incompetent, and about losing self-esteem. Yet, Argyris calls them variables or 'universal values' that are *learned* and become expressed in three major *action strategies*. These are: (1) to advocate one's position, (2) to evaluate the actions of others and oneself, and (3) to make attributions about other's and one's own interventions without attempts to validate them. "The most important consequences of Model I theory-in-use include misunderstanding, escalating errors, self-sealing processes, and self-fulfilling, counterproductive, self-fuelling processes" (Argyris, 2004, p. 9). In other words they lead to a reduced contact with the whole reality, restrict learning opportunities, and impinge negatively upon organisational effectiveness. In his writings, it appears that the defensive quality of 'defensive routines', 'defensive reasoning' and the 'Model I theory-in-use' escapes *awareness* through forgetting, covering up, and cover up of the covering up and replacement of these core values by good sounding *espoused theories*.

It is difficult to illustrate defensive routines and defensive reasoning by a simple vignette. The 'display' of these processes and their impact become expressed over time in conversations and/or in a text. A rich variety of examples are presented by Argyris (e.g. 1976, 1985, 1992, 2000). They are taken from tape-recorded meetings of managers or consultants, from role-plays and from the study of research publications (2004).

Argyris sees the tendencies to stay in control and to win as *universal values*. We are more inclined to conceive them as tendencies that are partly biological givens and partly learned through interactions with the physical and social world. Without them the human species would not have survived the various unfriendly, even hostile environments they found themselves in. Because they are partly ingrained in our genes these behavioural patterns are easily passed on to the next generation through processes of social interaction and identification. Together they constitute a pattern of responses, partly unconscious, partly non-conscious, so that the mind can focus on more important things. The pattern of responses can stay with us even when the external conditions in which we live render them no longer effective. They become even counterproductive when we move from a competitive to a collaborative mode of interacting.

Defensive routines, as well as defensive strategies can hardly be seen as real defences in the psychoanalytic sense because they seem to be more grounded in *survival* than in avoidance, although the latter is often not far away. In these instances, defensive strategies develop as reactions to tensions that are originally consciously experienced, which is not the case with defence mechanisms. To the extent that defensive strategies operate unconsciously, they are likely to be denied by the actor(s). Furthermore, once defensive strategies, routines and defensive reasoning are installed, they tend to become imbedded in standard procedures or they become hidden in 'the way we do things around here'. They are taken for granted. Like social repression and social defences they may stay on long after the original fields of tensions have gone. Defensive strategies must be brought to awareness before they can be 'unlearned', before persons can be *re-educated* in the use of 'Model II theory', which emphasises inquiry and testing of one's claims, including self-questioning of the foundations of one's sense of confidence in producing effective action. Learning 'Model II theory' implies that one learns to cope with higher levels of tension because of its positive pay-offs and the reassuring experience that these tensions do not lead to panic or chaos. Yet, the tendencies to stay in control and to win can never be completely removed because they are grounded in our genes. Defensive routines reappear if the re-education is not maintained. Critical for managers and consultants is to learn to distinguish under which conditions 'Model I' or 'Model II theory' is likely to be most effective; that in the social world today 'Model II' is more often effective than we are biologically predisposed, and learn to develop a rich response repertoire that is appropriate to deal with a range of changing situations.

Apart from these defensive and protective strategies people are no longer fully aware of, we can be confronted with strategies the user is fully *conscious* of. They are *intentional* and used to avoid embarrassment, or something that is experienced as dangerous or unwanted, but they may equally be aimed at achieving something of value. Deflecting attention, deceiving, lying, filibustering and ingratiation belong to this group. They are not necessarily easier to deal with, but they are less delicate to confront.

WORKING WITH AND THROUGH DEFENCES

The literature on defensive processes and behaviour is complex, and fraught with confusion. But, as we already said in other contexts, here too, one does not need to know all the 'appropriate words' in order to do good work. The important thing is to be able to find out/sort out the *reasons* that lie behind some observable, inadequate behaviour, structures or ways of working, and then see how these 'reasons' could be handled in a more satisfying way.

Defensive processes have a function. They allow individuals and groups to operate at a certain level of effectiveness, although at the expense of being in touch with the whole reality, and thereby losing part of the effectiveness that otherwise would be possible. Therefore, handling them presupposes a *considered judgement* about (a) the relative importance of the observed, (unintended) negative consequences of them in relation to the task and objectives pursuit, (b) one's ability to deal with them in that particular setting, and (c) the legitimacy derived from one's actual role as a manager or consultant in that setting.

(a) Observed negative consequences for task accomplishment and goal attainment.

Managers and consultants often experience defensive processes as *additional inconveniencies* to their work. And indeed, they can be tiring and exhausting. As such one may wish to get rid of them. However, this is not a sufficient reason to take action in order to remove them. The first necessary reflection is *self-reflection* on whatever is triggered off in me by the observed defensive processes and the appropriateness of one's intentions to deal with them. Defensive behaviour tends to trigger defensive reactions, leading to a spiral of ineffective reactions rather than further explorations into the *reasons* behind the 'noticed defensiveness'.

In this context I think of a business unit manager who had just returned from a group relations conference. When he observed the hesitation of one of his managers who was supposed to take charge of his suggested action plan he did not explore the background of the observable hesitation but reacted with a direct interpretative comment, and said: "I see, you are afraid to take responsibility for that plan of action". Such a direct interpretation of the reasons for the observable hesitation is in fact a 'wild interpretation', and thus the expression of a defensive reaction on the part of the business unit manager, rather than a revelation of the supposed defensiveness of his co-worker. The manager went silent. His reservations were not explored and he did not volunteer to express his point of view on the plan. After a while he just complied. The action plan was initiated and further delayed the project. The business unit manager concluded from this incident that the plan was all right but his manager could not take proper responsibility for it; a conclusion, which of course may have been completely wrong.

Frustration and/or irritation about defensiveness do provide a risky basis for handling it. They often lead to inappropriate interventions that further increase cover-up and move whatever defensiveness there was, deeper underground. If we feel no irritation, nor wish to get back in control, we may try to assess what the negative consequences are (or will be) if the defensiveness is left for what it is. If the current task doesn't require that the defensiveness be worked through immediately, one may – if really important – deal with it later in a more appropriate setting or time.

Such a situation occurred while discussing a paper with suggestions to implement the accepted mission of a University parish. The parish minister first deflected the discussion of the University's character by emphasising the importance of building a good parish, and subsequently added: "some statements in the paper are not theologically justified". The author of the paper considered it more appropriate to let the other group members continue with the discussion and to pick the issue up with the minister at a later occasion. In an interpersonal talk, he asked the parish minister to elaborate what statement was theologically incorrect and why. It appeared that in fact theologians are divided on that particular issue, and the position taken in the paper sided with a stance that was *not his own*. In a subsequent meeting, this issue could become clarified in the whole group.

When we are sufficiently clear and honest about our intentions and our assessment of the negative consequences of the observed defensiveness we have to come to an appreciation of our ability to deal with them appropriately. One may accept them as a given, one may take notice of them and try to work around them, or one may act on one's understanding by reducing the assumed causal sources of tensions, when possible. Defensive processes in general are only dealt with as long as and to the extent that they create such negative consequences that effective work is rendered impossible, or that the integrity and/or development of people are at risk.

(b) One's ability to work through the observed defensive processes and (c) one's legitimacy in a particular setting.

In as far as the sources of anxiety activating individual and group defence mechanisms are part of the unconscious as a system (Ucs.), we as managers or consultants are not able to bring these irrational anxieties to awareness. But, even if we could, our role does not legitimise such an intervention. A generalised statement – a bit like pulling a rabbit out of one's hat – that a particular defensiveness is triggered by 'a deeply rooted primitive anxiety' does not help the person/group concerned to gain control over it. It might be completely wrong and anyhow, at best, it may lead to a temporary change in position, but not to a more integrated way of being. Neither does the *labelling* of a defensive process help to learn about the *functions* it may fulfil. More-over, such an intervention sets managers or consultants apart from the others. The ability to make it look as if we would be able to interpret the uncon-scious (Ucs.) directly, becomes coupled with the power position proper to a manager, consultant or employee, thereby modifying the existing social order and reinforcing or even creating other obstacles in the work setting (Curseu, 2007). But maybe worse of all, it would just be a lie! Nobody is capable of interpreting the unconscious (Ucs.) directly.

Whenever we discuss ways of dealing with defensive processes and behaviour, we have to make distinctions between the various kinds of defences. When faced with *individual defence mechanism*, be it in individual contact or in a group setting, the best we can probably do is to draw attention to the 'illogical quality' of the expressed behaviour, and this in very simple wording. In order to deal with behaviour patterns that could be related to splitting, idealisation, or scapegoating, questions like: 'Aren't we making a distinction between these two (entities) as if there are no relations at all between them?' or one could wonder aloud: 'S/he (they) can't be all that bad (good), can s/he (they)?' Sometimes popular folk sayings can be very helpful. For example, projection can be brought to awareness by remembering that: 'We often see the splinter in the eye of the other, and not the beam in our own' or by wondering 'Isn't the pot reproaching the kettle for being black?' Sometimes it is enough to say something like: 'It looks as if we are trying to have the cake, and eat it' in order to make people wonder if indeed, they are trying the impossible and why. With a little *creative* thinking we can build on such statements of popular wisdom or invent our own to make people reflect on the logic behind their behaviour.

In none of these instances one touches directly upon unconscious *anxieties*, one just appeals to the *logic* of the people concerned, to reflect and to enable the discussion to move forward. The persons concerned are not likely to change their inner selves. That isn't the intention either. We move on with the task without giving up our role. In using this type of intervention, it is good to choose them in accordance with the prevailing mood of the person or group, and to phrase them in terms that belong to their own typical way of talking.

Group defence mechanisms like basic assumptions can be dealt with differently. We first draw attention to observable behaviour in the group and/or we may share an impression, a sensed quality of the group climate, for example, the feeling of helplessness, in order to make space for reflection and exploration of possible underlying tensions – emanating from the work setting – that group members try to avoid or alleviate. We may share our sense making of the observed behaviour and the assumed causal field of tension in order to explore whether it also makes sense to the group. Not in an authoritarian way, but as an opening to inquire into the possible tensions emerging from the work. It calls for 'time-out' to reflect and explore with intent to take action to bring these tensions within the range of tolerance, by either bringing them to consciousness (thereby making them less threatening) or by altering the working conditions. Yet, we only explore actual or back-home work conditions and the associated difficulties, and we stay away from the possibly, triggered primitive anxieties.

We would like to stress here the importance of bringing observable data or the manifest content in relation with assumed fears or fields of tension so that everyone can see how our minds work, so that they too can learn from our psychodynamic perspective (Vansina, 2000).

Since *social defences* in the workplace are often expressed in irrational or inefficient procedures, structures of roles, and ways of organising or dividing the work, these inefficiencies may offer a starting point for inquiry into their origin and subsequently for imagining more productive ways to carry out the work. In this process we pay particular attention to the reasons for the resistance that people display to altered work arrangements. Amongst the hesitation to break with tradition, we most often are able to detect the fears, dangers and tensions that one likes to avoid. Once they are identified one can adjust the organisation of the work so that people feel sufficient support to accept them. All this can be checked by organised reviews with the people concerned after the changes have been introduced on an experimental basis.

Thinking through the actions and conditions that are likely to generate undue stress beforehand often enables managers and consultants to create proper conditions for effective work. Let us illustrate this with some examples.

Reorganisation confronts many employees with changes in their working lives. Spontaneously, they develop *negative fantasies* seeing the disastrous consequences for themselves and significant others. Knowing all that, managers or consultants should prepare themselves in advance and figure out as much as possible what the real negative consequences will be, for example, the number of lay-offs, job changes over time. They should also be prepared to give an account of the way they plan to deal with them, for example, what kind of support will be provided, training, and/or financial compensation and how the reorganisation is going to be planned (consultation or not, and with whom) and implemented (incrementally or all at once) *before* they inform their employees as honestly as possible about the whole process.

If the work is likely to generate objective fears or dangers, it is important to inform people about what and how they can gain some control over them. Nuclear power stations and chemical plants have well established procedures and regular training programmes, but in mental or general hospitals, in schools and re-educational institutions tensions, which emerge from the work setting, are often less well thought through. One should think about what *support* could be provided over which the employee has control, without appearing silly. Young nurses for example should not have their first work assignments at night, and if they take the nightshift some personal assistance should be made available.

There is also much to be said in favour of procedures to arrange for coffee, tea and meals away from the tension-generating work setting, in locations that enable informal conversation, consultation and sharing of experiences. L. Klein's study (2005) of a hospital layout and its impact on the opportunities for informal consultation among the anaesthetists provides an interesting example of how the architectural design can build in features to facilitate or hinder social support in stressful work.

These three examples only serve as illustrations of what managers or consultants can do to help social systems cope with tensions proper to the work setting, without reducing the effectiveness. By preference these measures can be taken beforehand, but they can also, as we have indicated, be developed with the people concerned after a joint exploration of encountered social defences.

Social repression and *defensive reasoning* often exist alongside social defences. Certain issues are not discussable or are reasoned away by highlighting only one element or side of the coin. One can only think and talk about the most scary, disastrous things that will happen if these issues are brought to the table, or if the situation is drastically changed. Thereby, people can't think about the positive outcomes that may result from such explorations and actions. Making the issues discussable, by drawing attention to the other side of the coin, brings about more considered judgements and choices. It often stimulates creative thinking.

We know quite a lot about the conditions that lead to groupthink (Janis, 1982). Isolation from outside contacts, homogenous composition of the group, emphasis on group cohesion and a dominant leader emphasising only one alternative action. Many of these can be taken care of before the group meets for problem solving and decision making. We always discourage groups or management teams to decide on important issues (e.g. mergers, acquisitions, strategic management issues) while still at a resort. Instead, we recommend preparing for decision taking, but postpone taking it until they have moved back into their normal work setting and had time to sleep on it.

Defensive behaviour may be less risky to handle than psychic defence mechanisms, but it is often more difficult to detect because it lies hidden in routines, automatic responses and defensive reasoning which have become part of organisational life, or in the so-called 'way we do things over here'. In as far as defensive behaviour is covered up in special ways of reasoning, it becomes undiscussable. Therefore, individual interviews may not be sufficient to put one's finger on the 'irrationality' of particular behaviour patterns, and even less on the underlying fears and tensions. Most often one has to enter the social system, either working in or with the system; one has to listen to the conversations and to observe the interactions in order to get a feel for what it is like to be working in it, what the specific tensions are and how people have learned to cope.

Note, however, that groups that work together, express through their way of working, not only the defences that are present, but also wishes, hopes and concerns of which they have no conscious awareness, although there is *no defence* at work. Remember in this context the 'wine drinkers' and to a large extent also the 'going-away present'.

CONCLUSIONS

The literature on defensive processes and behaviour is complex and fraught with confusion. But, as we said earlier in a similar context: "One does not need to know the 'right words' in order to do good work". Sometimes it is even better not to worry about those 'right words' or 'labels', but just to try to understand the situation we are observing or experiencing.

Defensive processes and behaviour of all sorts are a *regular part* of human life and work. Consequently we may take them as 'normal' phenomena, yet without skipping the important question: 'To what extent are they hindering the work and the development of genuine interpersonal relations in the actual situation?' The answer to this question provides the basis for exploring first the possible relation between the defences that seem to be present and the possible fields of tensions, and then deciding about the appropriateness of doing something about them in the context of our role in the given situation. Creating more appropriate conditions relies maybe more on creative thinking processes than on pure rational thought.

Working on defensive processes and behaviour is important, yet – as we will discuss in the first chapter of Part Two – it may not be the most important part of our task in a psychodynamic approach to consulting and managing.

REFERENCES

Argyris, C. (1976). *Increasing leadership effectiveness*. New York: Wiley-Interscience.

Argyris, C. (1985). *Strategy, change and defensive routines*. New York: Harper Business.

Argyris, C. (1992). *On organizational learning*. Oxford: Blackwell Publishing.

Argyris, C. (2000). *Flawed advice and the management trap*. Oxford: Oxford University Press.

Argyris, C. (2004). *Reasons and rationalisations: The limits to organisational knowledge*. Oxford: Oxford University Press.

Argyris, C. & Schon, D. (1974). *Theory in practice*. San Francisco: Jossey-Bass.

Billig, M. (1999). *Freudian Repression: Conversation Creating the Unconscious*. Cambridge: Cambridge University Press.

Bion, W. (1961). *Experiences in Groups, and other papers*. London: Tavistock Publications.

Curseu, P.L. (2007). Is conflict vernietigend voor vertrouwen of vermindert conflict door vertrouwen. In: S. Prins, S. Schruijer, J. Verboven & K. De Witte (Eds), *Diversiteit en vertrouwen in sociale systemen*. Leuven: Lannoo Campus, 193–208.

Lawrence, W.G., Bain, A. & Gould, L.J. (1996). The fifth basic assumption. In: W.G. Lawrence (2000). *Tongued with fire: Groups in experience*. London: Karnac, 92–119.

Klein, L. (2005). *Working across the gap: The practice of social science in organisations*. London: Karnac.

Harvey, J. (1974). The Abilene paradox: The management of agreement. *Organisational Dynamic;* or *The Abilene Paradox and Other Meditations on Management*. Toronto: Lexington Books.

Janis, I. (1972). *Victims of Groupthink*. Boston: Houghton Mifflin.

Janis, I. (1982). *Groupthink* (second edition). Boston: Houghton Mifflin.

Jaques, E. (1955). Social systems as a defence against persecutory and depressive anxiety. In: M. Klein, P. Heimann & R. Money-Kyrle (Eds), (1957). *New directions in Psycho-Analysis*. New York: Basic Books, 478–498.

Menzies, I.E.P. (1961). The functioning of social systems as a defence against anxiety. *Human Relations*, **13**, 95–121.

Miller, E. (1993). *From Dependency to Autonomy: Studies in Organization and Change*. London: Free Association Press.

Rice, A.K. (1963). *The Enterprise and its Environment*. London: Tavistock Publications.

Turquet, P.M. (1974). Leadership – the individual in the group. In: G.S. Gibbard, J.J. Hartman & R.D. Mann (Eds), *Analysis of groups*. San Francisco: Jossey-Bass.

Vansina, L. (2000). The relevance and perversity of psychodynamic interventions in consulting and action research. *Concepts & Transformation*, **5**, 321–348.

CHAPTER 5

The Capacity for Creative Living and Its Importance in Organisational Life

Marie-Jeanne Vansina-Cobbaert

In general, psychoanalytic theory about creativity is almost exclusively concerned with developmental and psychodynamic factors that influence creativity in the individual artist. That is to say: in people who possess a special talent (Segal, 1991). As such these theories are of little relevance for the day-to-day problems that occur in organisations and need to be handled by common people.

Winnicott, however, talks about a different phenomenon, which he calls "the capacity for creative living". This 'capacity' does not presuppose a special talent. To some extent it is in itself a special talent, but one that belongs to ordinary people, often without them being aware of it. It is precisely this capacity that is relevant in the context of group and organisational functioning.

ORIGINS AND FUNCTIONING OF THE CAPACITY FOR CREATIVE LIVING

Winnicott relates the capacity for creative living to loss and destructiveness, exactly as other psychoanalysts do with artistic creativity. But he does this in a significantly different way. In his opinion the capacity for creative living is not at all the result of a replacement or of an attempt at recreation of what is lost. In Winnicott's view (1982, 1988, 1990), if everything goes well, *we start life as creators*. Or at least we start with the *impression* that we are creators of whatever we need. And it goes well if we start off with a caretaker who is tuned in to our needs. Under this condition it feels as if it is enough for us to need something, to wish for something, for that thing to materialise, including the caretaker. On top of that it will look as if we can handle this 'caretaker-thing' in a ruthless way without him/her being hurt or destroyed.

But, somewhat later in life a second movement has to come about. That same caretaker, thanks to his/her sensitive adaptation to our needs in the context of our growing capacity for tolerating frustration, will bring about the *necessary disillusionment*. In fact this means that s/he will help us *discover* – when we are ready to assume the impact – a whole set of very important things. Amongst others: that the external world is really not our own creation; that it existed long before we did; that for many things we are dependent on others who are more capable than we are; and that all this is OK. We can even contribute-in whatever the caretaker is doing for us, babies. Furthermore we discover that we can have an intense emotional relationship with the caretaker without doing him/her any harm, because this loving person will keep in check the destructive tendencies that are part of human nature and, at times, threaten to overwhelm us. Thus, if everything goes well, 'losing our illusion of omnipotence' looks much more like a very worthwhile gain rather than a loss. Because, instead of holding onto and getting lost in an illusion, we discover a varied, complex and emotionally rich world that includes the pleasure about our original experiences of being a creator.

It is clear to me that the presence of this 'loving person', capable of keeping our destructiveness under control, is crucial to the development I described. The zest for life, sexual drive and destructiveness are things we bring along at birth, but concern and love, that keep those important, basic givens within human limits, only develop in the context of our relations with people whose unselfish love and concern we experience while growing up. But I'll come back to this later.

Thus, the capacity for creative living is embedded in the basic relationship between baby and caretaker, as well as in the way that relationship develops in time, and also in the way aggression and destructiveness are part of it. The combination of three essential elements: (1) permitting us for a while to have the impression that we are able to create our needed world, (2) a sensitive way in helping us to outgrow that illusion, (3) the impression that the vehemence that we put into our actions is not harmful, provides us with a security about our capacity to create what we need, possibly so with the help of others. It also provides us with the security that the intensity with which we attack life situations, won't destroy something meaningful. The capacity for creative living is nothing but the expression of this basic security and of the pleasure in living.

A very essential element in Winnicott's way of looking at creativity is that, through the way this capacity for creative living develops, it includes pleasure and security in the context of intense emotional relationships with other people. This seems to me like a crucial attribute in the context of taking part in transitional change processes (Amado & Ambrose, 2001).

Not only does the capacity for creative living thrive independently from a special talent, it is also less connected to the acquisition of symbolic representation. It does not necessarily lead to special performances or achievements, nor is it exclusively related to solving problems. It is more like a sort of natural movement that adds value, together with a positive attitude or a shared pleasure with others who engage in the same activity. It can be seen as an inner disposition which is present in the way we look at things; in the way we go about our daily chores; in the way we put food on the table or on our plate; in the way we comfort ourselves or others at times of loss and sorrow; in the fact that we understand and accept that in order to reach certain goals, we may need a specific talent that we do not possess; and so on. All this makes the capacity for creative living fairly different from artistic creativity. For that matter, artists are very often people who are in search of this capacity. Then, some of their creations can be seen as repetitive attempts at finding this special way of feeling at ease – or maybe one ought to say 'at peace' – with life in its many forms of joy and pain. I also have the impression that artists who show a capacity for creative living cover a larger range of subjects in their work than artists who are still struggling to find it.

But let me illustrate what I'm talking about. I'll use an example from ordinary life, one from a training situation, and I'll elaborate on problems related to creative living that occur in organisations.

Imagine a young mother with a little girl of about 34 months, at the time her second baby is born. The little girl knew and had been very enthusiastic about the baby developing in her mummy's tummy, until the moment that baby was visible in its hospital bed. Apparently she had imagined a baby as something quite different from this 'misfit' whom she thought ought to stay at the hospital for the doctors to take care of. But of course the baby came home, and the little girl was miserable. She cried hopelessly or became furious because *she* wanted to sleep in the cot; *she* wanted to be bathed in the little tub; *she* wanted to go out in the pram. She even wanted to wear nappies and be breastfed. You can imagine the mother's despair trying to reassure and comfort her daughter. She gave her all sorts of extra attention; explained to her over and over again that she *had* already slept in the cot, bathed in the baby-tub, gone for walks in the pram, and that all this happened a long time ago, when she too had been a tiny baby. All to no avail! After a couple of days and at her wits' end, the mother had an idea. Somehow that mother, without being conscious of it, had sensed that her little girl was not yet capable of imagining herself in the past, so the mother said: "Look here, I'll show you". She got out a photo album and showed the girl all those important moments of the past. After that, whenever the mother did something for the baby, the little girl wanted to look at the pictures. This created a new problem because she could not do it on her own. But the mother had a second helpful idea. She found one of those small, plastic photo books, put the pictures in it, and said to her daughter: "Here, you can keep this, and now you can look at it whenever you like". And that did it! From there on the little girl recovered her happy old self. The picture book replaced her rabbit. She took it with her wherever she went, and it had to be close to her when she went to sleep.

The next time I met the little girl, she had the book tucked under her arm, exactly the way she used to carry her rabbit. There was no time for greetings. Right away she took me by the hand and said: "Come, I have a new book, I'll tell you a story!" And so she did. She told me *her* story. She went on doing that for many months to everyone who was willing to listen.

When the mother told me how the storybook came into being, I listened with pleasure. It provides not only a good example of a mother with a capacity for creative living. It also provides a good example of how her capacity fosters the development of creativity in her child, through assistance in the creation of a new and appropriate transitional object. I can assure you, this mother knows nothing about psychoanalysis or about transitional objects. Yet this is what the photo book became: a new transitional object. Partly still – as the rabbit before – a transitional object between the 'me' and the 'not-me' experience. This was visible in the way the girl introduced her "new book" to me as: "I'll tell you *a* story" as if it was not yet fully her own. But when she told it, she said: "Look, this is *me* in mummy's tummy; and this is *me* in the tiny hospital bed when I was just born" and so on. It was also a transitional object between the 'me' in the here-and-now and the 'me' in the there-and-then. And, towards the end of its usefulness, it provided the transition between the here-and-now and the future. This happened when she added a part to the story without the need for pictures. Then she proudly said that when she is an adult, she too will be able to grow a baby in her tummy. She used that very active expression as if it would be all *her own doing*. Later on she found out all by herself that even in this context she would need the assistance of somebody else. Yet, this discovery did not provoke a disillusion. On the contrary, she seemed pretty pleased with her (be it rather) personal understanding of one of the many wonders in life.[1]

Let me move on to an example taken from a group situation. The group was one out of three, in a seven-day residential in-company-training programme on group dynamics. The programme was made up of a combination of 'learning groups', plenary sessions and some theoretical inputs. In the 'learning groups', the task of the participants was to share work and actual experiences in order to learn from them; the task of the consultant was to share his/her impressions about what was going on in the group, and why. S/he would do this in as far as such interventions might further the learning.

From the start, one of the male participants in one of the groups had trouble expressing himself, and as time went by, he became more quiet and withdrawn. About halfway through the programme, when emotional involvement in the group was rather high, he seemed to be getting into real trouble. It was visible that what people said, did not reach him any longer, while his own interventions became increasingly incoherent. This made the consultant fear that the man might suffer a nervous breakdown, and after some hesitation, the consultant made a very unusual intervention. He said to the group: "It seems to me that we are all rather tired right now, and that we are a bit stuck [both statements were based on shared experiences]. Why don't we stop this session, go out, and play some volleyball together?!" Everybody agreed, and so they did.

The next session and the rest of the programme went without problems. The young man's difficulties had disappeared and he participated in a more

---

[1] A longer version of the last part of this development can be found in Chapter 1 under 'Stepwise transformations'.

active and relaxed way. What in the world made such an unconventional and unexpected intervention work? One important feature was certainly the fact that the proposed activity was not an unusual one, coming out of the blue. It was an activity that was part of the company culture, and that was present on the seminar grounds. The company brought the volleyball equipment along, there was a field ready for play, and participants used to play during free time, although not in their 'learning group' constellation.

A second important factor was probably that the programme itself contained some activities that were partly non-verbal. As such, during one of the plenary sessions, each group was supposed to picture itself and put this into a drawing. These drawings were then put up, discussed during the rest of the plenary session, and they were often referred to and worked through later on in the 'learning groups'.

A third positive influence was certainly the fact that the troubled young man was good at playing volleyball (a factor unknown to the consultant) and found his place in that group-activity without any difficulty. He did a large share of the work and was respected for it by his fellow group members.

Finally I suppose that the different forms of body contact that were part of the game, later on helped to facilitate other forms of contact within the 'learning group'. This is something I have witnessed often in the context of therapeutic programmes in psychiatric hospitals: different forms of body contact that occur in specific therapies facilitate afterwards verbal expression and verbal contact in contact-disturbed individuals. Of course all these explanatory thoughts were the result of explorative thinking afterwards. They were by far not consciously present in the considerations of the consultant when he made his adventurous suggestion.

In organisations the capacity for creative living can have a positive influence on whatever tasks and activities constitute daily life. It forms a constant part of an organisation's success, and it provides the basis for the pleasure that goes with working in it. If problems occur in relation to this natural form of creativity, they are related to the psychological make-up of certain team members or managers.

In organisations as in day-to-day life, the capacity for creative living consists essentially of someone or a group who has an idea or a new way of looking at a situation. This idea or the way of looking will then help to further the development of (preferably) all concerned, the people involved as well as the organisation or parts thereof. Of course, this '*all* concerned' in itself makes it already difficult. But it becomes even more complex because, in the work situation, we have to be able to tolerate that we are not the only creative ones. Others too can come up with good ideas. We have to be able to endure that such ideas may affect our own work or our own position in a way we might not like. We have to be able to elaborate on somebody else's good idea, and thereby make it even better, or move it into the direction of a group idea. Some of us might not like that at all. If some of us tend to look at new ideas the way the little girl looked at the new baby, our only hope is for the team to produce a 'mother' with a capacity for creative living, who will see us through.

If such a 'mother' is not available, or if her attempts at solution of the difficulties are rejected, the psychological make-up of a team member, and even much more so of a manager, can have a long-term, devastating influence on the expression and use of the capacity for creative living in a work-team. Most of the time the negative influence of a team member is less extensive or long lasting than that of a manager, because a team becomes less immobilised by certain characteristics of members then of a manager. In the particular situation I have in mind, it took several months after the manager had left, before the team members fully understood the thought system they had been trapped in, and before the team could regain its capacity for creative living, and manage to restructure its department with the assistance of a newly appointed manager. The problem had not been that the team members had not seen what was happening, or had never said anything about it, it was that they were unable to take any action in accordance with what they perceived.

This experience brought me to the conclusion that the capacity for creative living disappears or is actively destroyed in the following situations:

- If a manager has a tendency to present developing ideas or positive results that are part of his/her team, as his own, while negative outcomes or failures are invariably attributed to others.

- If s/he experiences creative ideas that s/he cannot integrate as his/her own, as destructive to him/herself.

- If s/he is envious or jealous, and especially if s/he does not recognise these feelings in him/herself but attributes them to his/her colleagues or team members.

- If s/he never manages to see that the anger and aggression, which indeed sometimes comes his/her way, is the result of the way s/he acts in a denigrating way towards some of the team members.

The capacity for creative living does not disappear however (at least not immediately) in people who do not mind being robbed of it, as long as they obtain some special favours in exchange. But even then, I have seen it work only temporarily. After a while, the situation becomes so perverted that it explodes. Apparently, over time, these managers become suspicious of those who are willing to abdicate from their own creations. S/he despises or ridicules them behind their backs. S/he starts controlling, changing or disowning the favours s/he granted, and eventually the situation becomes untenable.

DESTRUCTIVENESS IN THE CONTEXT OF CREATIVE LIVING

The final, important influential factor in the context of the development and use of the capacity for creative living is destructiveness and the fact that we feel at ease with it. My point of view in this matter differs quite a bit from Winnicott's. I certainly agree with him when he points to the importance of a mother's reactions to the ruthlessness of her baby (1992). I too am convinced that the impression the baby gets about its mother surviving its ruthlessness unharmed is of great importance. This very experience reassures the baby that the intensity with which it goes about living, is as such not dangerous; that *it can be kept within non-harmful limits*; as such the experience also lays the foundation for the baby's later capacity to distinguish between vehemence and aggression.

It seems to me that Winnicott's views in the context of aggression and destructiveness were often misunderstood by mothers, but also by so-called 'psychoanalytically informed' managers/consultants, and sometimes even by analysts. Some of them seem to think that in order to be 'good enough' they have to stand whatever aggression and destructiveness comes their way, thereby acting as if they are not even touched by it. While in fact 'being able to stand and to survive' means that one is capable of making a distinction between aggression and destructiveness on the one side and vehemence on the other; it also means that one is capable of handling, containing, and controlling the destructive attacks without becoming aggressive or destructive oneself. If on the contrary we act as if we are untouched by what happens, we not only rob the person we work with of an important object for identification, but simultaneously we become inhuman, with all the consequences this might entail, including the provocation of more aggression.

In his later publications Winnicott explicitly emphasises that primary destructiveness is *unintended*, and that it only occurs *at the level of phantasy* (1964). I myself on the contrary, think that our life and development is based on destruction; and I mean *destruction that occurs in reality*. I'm not referring to Freud's notion of 'death instinct' (1921), which never made much sense to me. The notion in itself is of a highly speculative nature, and Freud makes several jumps in the reasoning that leads him to this 'discovery'. Moreover, however, Freud's notion does not refer to a *primary* destructive drive. It was only later on that some authors gave it this meaning. Freud's 'Thanatos' is at the same time similar to and the opposite of 'Eros'. Exactly as Eros, Thanatos is a basic urge, inherent in organic life, *to restore* a previous state of being. Where Thanatos is concerned, this 'previous state' is the inanimate/inorganic state out of which life is supposed to have developed. Thus, in Freud's conceptualisation there is no real primary tendency to destroy. Destructiveness is a derivative of the supposed basic need to move back to our origin. It is the consequence of the fact that Eros manages to put the death instinct – at least to some extent – at the service of its own purpose. Thus, we try as best we can to destroy whatever seems to hinder living.

Contrary to Freud and to Winnicott, I would say that the need to destroy and the pleasure in destroying constitute an essential part of our basic human make-up. I would even say that *we live by the grace of destruction,* and as I already said: I mean destruction *that, from the very beginning, is directed outward, and occurs in reality,* not only in phantasy. If we were not destructive by nature, we would not live!

Saying this, I am first of all talking about our bodies and about physiology. I am talking about the fact that in order to survive and to grow, we have to eat. And eating is one of the most destructive acts you can imagine, as much in what we do, as in what happens to what we take in. It is also the start of one of the most fantastic transformational processes around. Think only that within a couple of hours, our dinner 'has become human', and that whatever part is not fit for transformation, will soon be evacuated. Day in day out we create human life out of the destruction of other types of life. Already at this level destruction and creation are closely linked. Of course, at least at the beginning of life, and from a psychological point of view, this is all completely unintended destruction. Yet, the fact that life is so totally dependent on that destruction cannot but have important consequences. A relationship, which is so vital to life at the physical level, cannot but have its repercussions at the behavioural and psychological level.

And I think that we can observe that. One of the consequences is for instance that, because of the connection between eating and destroying, eating can become very scary and even impossible. All child-analysts know that eating problems in young children are often related to the child's anxiety provoking phantasies about destroying its mother in the act.

Another consequence is that, as with eating, and all life-enhancing activities, destruction is originally and in itself pleasurable, and those who are involved in child rearing know all too well how difficult it can be to help children keep their destructiveness at bay, and to direct it towards activities that are not harmful. Young children enjoy tearing things apart with hands and teeth. From a very young age they love to destroy the towers or cardboard houses we build for them. And from early on we teach them to keep their destructiveness in check, telling them: "Wait! It is not finished yet!" When they can finally have a go at it, their pleasure abounds. It also takes effort and time to teach children that they cannot destroy other people's creations unless they get permission to do so. Very soon they will build their own pieces with blocks or Lego. And with vehement pleasure, they will destroy constructions as soon as they don't want them anymore. Sometimes they only build with the prospect of destroying. I remember from my early teens, how, in groups of three or four, we would build elaborate sandcastles on the beach, about halfway between the low- and the high-tide line. We would spend hours embellishing them with seaweed and shells. We built dams to protect them from the waves. Then we sat down, looked at them, admired them, made some small improvements, and waited. The cheers came when the 'finishing wave' rolled over the top of the structure and made it disappear forever. The next day, if the tides permitted, we started all over again.

I never had the impression that the basis for our pleasure was the knowledge that we could always restart. It seemed to me that the intense satisfaction we experienced was related to a feeling of becoming an integral part of an essential feature of life: the intertwining of creation and untameable destruction. For people living along the coast, the sea expresses this feature better than anything else. It is an inexhaustible source of pleasure, food and life (at least that was what it looked like when I was a child); yet, at times its destructive power is overwhelming.

If as babies, we don't feel safe with our oral vehemence, if mother reacts to it with fear, as if indeed it might destroy her, we may never find the intense pleasure of harmless destruction. Moreover, we may be hesitant to use our capacity for creative living, because we are too uncertain about our capacity to restrain the destructiveness that goes with it. It also looks as if often, on growing up, we lose this pleasure in destroying or in having destroyed something we conceived of, even if it has lost its function. I have no idea why this happens. As we grow older, do we overvalue our achievements? Is their liquidation all too reminiscent of our impending redundancy and death? I don't know, I just wonder. Not only can this natural, pleasurable, primary destructiveness become dissociated from life enhancing situations, it can also develop into or become associated with greed, envy, jealousy and hate, or with the striving for influence and power. One of the consequences is that we start to hinder the expression of the capacity for creative living in others, or we try to steal or to destroy the products of that capacity.

Hate occupies a special position in relation to the capacity for creative living. Although Winnicott is not very explicit about it, he apparently thought that, because of the fact that the first 'not-me' objects appear in the context of the disappearance of the primary illusion that we create our 'needed world', these 'not-me' objects are hated before they are loved (1990). This viewpoint starts from the premise that when we lose our illusion of omnipotence, and find out that for the satisfaction of our needs we are dependent on benevolent others, our first reaction is one of hate directed at those who seem to be richer and more influential than we are, and at whatever escapes our control. It is a viewpoint comparable to what Freud suggested when he talked about the passage from pleasure-ego to reality-ego (1915). I have no doubt that this can happen. There could be many reasons for such a development (e.g. the discovery of dependency and of all the wealth that belongs to somebody else; hate because it becomes clear that mother also shares her riches with others; hate related to objective shortcomings of mother). But I am also quite sure that *if* it happens that hate towards not-me objects develops before love, we are in for a lot of problems. I think that in this instance the capacities for creative living will not develop; at least not right away, and maybe not without some specialist's help. Besides, the persons concerned are in danger of becoming the kind of people that cannot stand the capacity for creative living in others, unless they see the possibility of robbing them of this desired attribute.

As I observe babies and young children, I have the impression that for many of them the disappearance of the primary illusion of omnipotence is *not* a source of hate. On the contrary, it often seems to provide the basis for *amazement* and *wonder*, and to include the start of an inquisitive exploration of the 'real world' and of the influence they may have on it. It is as if, in the surprise expressed in the face of young children, and in their enthusiastic explorations, one can almost 'read' the thought: 'Oh boy, the world is even more wonderful than I could ever have imagined!' I am sure that it is only in the latter context that the capacity for creative living can really develop and flourish.

In organisations the intertwining of destruction and creativity is almost always present in the context of work improvements, organisational change and product/process development projects. Sometimes, but by far not always, both factors are rather well balanced. One of the important challenges is the possibility of finding a creative way of disposing of previously appreciated elements in the work situation that will become redundant or obsolete in the new one.

I have the impression that an important potential for creative living is often lost in organisations; more so in larger than in small ones. At least one of the reasons seems to be the tendency present in larger organisations to standardise rest or relaxation time. Everyone has coffee or a smoke between 10 and 10.30; mutual consultation is only allowed during specific, planned meetings, etc. Of course, some form of control may be necessary, but it is often superfluous when people have the impression that their efforts to improve the work situation are taken seriously and appreciated, and if their proposals are thought through and if necessary mended by colleagues and by the head of department.

People seem to be especially creative in the domain of inventing supportive process structures. It is a domain in which the need for variation is high and standardisation can only be detrimental. This is a consequence of the fact that the kind of holding, containment or possible transitional space and objects that are needed, depend upon the sort of stresses and frustrations that are typical for a certain profession or job in a specific context. What the nursing staff in a psychiatric department for psychotic patients needs is different from what would provide support for the nursing staff in a department that works with severe borderline personalities, which differs again from what could be of help for nurses in an oncology department for children in a general hospital. Moreover, what may be supportive for these different groups of nurses is certainly not identical with what may be needed by the different groups of doctors, psychotherapists or social workers who are active in the same departments. Giving different groups of employees some extra leeway in deciding about the supportive process structures that would best fit their needs at a certain time, can but heighten their work motivation. It would also contribute to their work efficiency and to the pleasure they find in doing it, even if that work remains often stress- and painful.

It leaves no doubt that organisations would benefit if they could select employees on the basis of their capacity for creative living. And it seems to me that it must not be too difficult for psychologists to develop some tests or test-situations in order to detect the presence of such an important attribute in a candidate. Yet, if we can believe Maccoby (2000), in as far as managers are concerned, the actual preferences of organisations seem to go to people with narcissistic personalities. It means that organisations select people who can be creative at times, but who also possess all the 'qualities' that I described above as belonging to managers who, under certain circumstances, destroy the capacity for creative living in their colleagues and fellow-employees.

REFERENCES

Amado, G. & Ambrose, A. (Eds) (2001). *The transitional approach to change.* London: Karnac Books.

Freud, S. (1915). Triebe und triebschicksale. In: *Standard Ed.*, **14**, 117–140. London: The Hogarth Press.

Freud, S. (1921). Jenseits des Lustprinzips. In: *Standard Ed.*, **18**, 69–143. London: The Hogarth Press.

Maccoby, M. (2000). Narcissistic leaders: the incredible pros, the inevitable cons. *Harvard Business Review*, **78**, 1, 79–90.

Segal, H. (1991). *Dream, phantasy and art.* (The New Library of Psychoanalysis, **12**.) London: Tavistock/Routledge.

Winnicott, D. (1964). Roots of aggression. In: C. Winnicott, R. Shepherd & M. Davis (Eds) (1984). *Deprivation and Delinquency.* London: Tavistock, 84–99.

Winnicott, D. (1982). *Playing and reality*. Harmondsworth: Penguin Books.
Winnicott, D. (1988). *Human nature*. London: Free Association Books.
Winnicott, D. (1990). *The maturational process and the facilitating environment*. London: Karnac Books.
Winnicott, D. (1992). *Through paediatrics to psycho-analysis*. London: Karnac Books.

A Psychodynamic Approach

Introduction

Leopold Vansina

Managers and consultants are first introduced to the somewhat confusing domain of psychodynamics. What is important and useful in the psychoanalytic perspective for managers and organisation consultants will be included and discussed in this broader concept.

Part Two consists of five chapters, each dealing with some critical aspects of working with a psychodynamic approach. Although psychoanalytic theory, but foremost its practice, was and still is a rich source of concepts and working principles, the psychodynamic approach must not be confused with psychoanalysis *applied* to groups or organisations.

Psychodynamics refers at the same time to an evolving body of knowledge, a way of looking at work and life in organisations, a form of inquiry leading to a deeper understanding of a system in order to take action, for example, creating conditions for organisational improvement and development (Chapter 6: Psychodynamics: A field of study and an approach).

In Chapter 7: "'Me' in the problem situation", we discuss the personal involvement of the consultant or manager in the social construction of a problem definition as a solid base for further work on a project. Subsequently, we review the other domains of building continuity and terminating a project. In the final section, we explore the impact of transferential processes on the relation between the consultant or manager and their clients while working.

Problem construction is an ongoing process in understanding the often changing, underlying dynamics in our work. The issue of locating the problem in its context and history further complicates that process. In organisations, like in organic systems, one may not look too closely at the location where the pains and difficulties are experienced to work on the causes of the problem. Boards, management and project teams may be too readily taken as the client system, while the real causes may reside in their context and history. Physical and outspoken social boundaries may restrict our conception of the causes or opportunities in dealing with organisational problems. Too permeable system boundaries may prevent the development of appropriate conditions for effective task accomplishment and expose the work system to too much interference from outside. Finally, we review and illustrate the major import and export mechanisms by which issues may be moved from one location to another part of the organisation (Chapter 8: "Groups as the tip of an iceberg: Locating issues in their context").

In Chapter 9: "Being in and working with the 'here-and-now'", we focus on the consultative work itself of consultants and managers. In particular we deal with the alternative mental modes that can be adopted: 'apprehension', 'reflection', 'experiencing' and 'participative thinking' and 'responsive action' and on the changing frames and perspectives we bring to bear on the work in order to collect data and change the dynamics of the system concerned in a more lasting way.

In the final Chapter 10: "The art of reviewing: A cornerstone in organisational learning", we discuss at length the process of organised, retrospective self study in order to learn how to improve the system's functioning in the future. Reviewing is a valuable tool that managers and consultants can use to institutionalise learning from experience. However, reviewing has its own shortcomings proper to retrospective reconstruction, the composition of the work system and its dynamics.

Part Two conveys the complexity of working with a psychodynamic approach to improve the functioning of a social work system in a more enduring way. It is also an attempt to communicate the limitations of our human endeavours as managers and consultants. Yet, we don't see these inevitable limitations as a source of discouragement or resignation, but as an impetus for continual learning and development.

CHAPTER 6

Psychodynamics: A Field of Study and an Approach

Leopold Vansina

In this chapter, we will first distinguish the field of psychoanalysis from that of psychodynamics. Thereafter, we will try to define psychodynamics in a way that is relevant and useful for managers and consultants who are already working with or preparing themselves for working with a psychodynamic approach. Subsequently, we will discuss some conditions that enable personal development before we take a closer look at some, often unnoticed potential benefits of a psychodynamic approach. Finally, in the concluding comments we review briefly the major premises on which psychodynamic work is based, and the relevant personal competences for the practices.

SOME MAJOR DIFFERENCES WITH PSYCHOANALYSIS

Psychodynamics borrows a lot from psychoanalytic theory and practices. This has led to a number of misconceptions wherein the psychodynamic approach, at times, becomes perceived as a deluded form of psychoanalytic practice, or as a more socially acceptable, yet masked form of psychoanalysis. In this confusion, some very important differences, in particular with traditional psychoanalytic thinking, may be passed over or just forgotten. Yet, these differences alter and distinguish both fields of study and are of extreme importance for the practice of consultants and managers.

The Enlarged Notion of the Unconscious – Non-conscious

As extensively discussed in the first part of this book, the psychodynamic approach works with an *enlarged notion of the unconscious* system. This means that apart from its proper typical way of functioning, we are interested in contents that differ from the individual, repressed infantile wishes. Moreover this infantile part in the unconscious is something we never work on. We are concerned with what becomes repressed and suppressed under the influence of groups, social interactions and social defences embedded in work systems.[1] Repression and suppression is an ongoing process, which takes place throughout human life and is part and parcel of all social interactions. It results in 'views' on what may or may not be talked about, on what may or may not be seen and on what is or is not done. It gives rise to 'dominant logics' these are statements of so-called 'common wisdom' that in fact block critical investigation and creative search for alternative courses of action (Vansina, 1998).[2]

In work systems social repression and suppression become visible in defensive processes, or in different types of 'secrets'. And of course they become expressed through the classic pathways that belong to primary process thinking ("l'imaginaire" as it is called by Enriquez, 1997) like images, metaphors, phantasms, mythical stories and fantasies, and in interpersonal/inter-group

---

[1] In the English and German languages, the distinction between 'suppression' and 'repression' is clearly maintained. Also in French, but they use the concept 'repression' for suppression and 'refoulement' for what in English is called repression.

[2] 'Dominant logics' are designed, social constructions of reality expressed in statements that through their rational and logical appeal block critical investigation and the creative explorations of alternatives. They are often launched from a power position to manipulate or channel thinking; later on they may become unknowingly the shared property of groups. For example: 'What is good for the business is good for the economy and good for society!' Or 'To stay competitive in the market we must control wages and salaries!' And 'Steady economic growth is required to secure continued happiness!' Or 'A well developed social welfare state is detrimental to global, economic competition!' And 'People are costs!'

relations and through actions.[3] All this contributes extensively to our ways of envisaging projects, missions, strategies, careers and the future in general. Indeed, human beings tend to fill up with their 'imagination' what is missing or not directly accessible to observation or measurement. Yet, in the psychodynamic practice, much like in good psychoanalytic work, we start as much as possible from observable data and experiences before touching upon possible hidden meaning, expressed in the languages of images, actions and relations, or in defensive behaviour.

The Relevant Past and Sense Making

In a psychodynamic approach, we work predominantly with the *history of a system* and the *recent past* (which is always somewhat constructed, sometimes even fabricated) as they appear or emerge in the 'here-and-now' in the languages of images, actions and relations. The expressions may take a rich variety of forms like repetitive, yet ineffective behaviour, images, myths, assumptions, taken for granted evidence, defensive relations. This attention to the recent past and the history of the system contrasts sharply with *early* psychoanalytic thinking, which was interested in early childhood experiences of the individual, where it located the origin of all 'disturbed behaviour'. Today, however, modern psychoanalysts work with the actual *internal world* as it becomes revealed in the actual relation with the analyst, who eventually endeavours to link this emerging inner world with early phantasies and infantile experiences of the analysand. These latter endeavours to *link* parts of the emerging inner world to childhood experiences and phantasies are not at all proper to psychodynamic work of consultants and managers, how tempting that may be.

Furthermore in psychodynamics, we are much less involved in making *interpretations* of hidden meaning referring to the past, than in sharing, comparing and finding out our *sense-making processes* about observable behaviour in context, about interactions, expressed thoughts and feelings; images and

---

[3] Although a distinction is being made in psychoanalysis between phantasies and fantasies, we do not think it fundamental to maintain that in our further discussions. Consequently, we will use the notion of 'imageries' for the product of imagination regardless of their origin.

about the use made of space and time. Sense making is an *active* process by which pieces of data are brought together into a congruent whole that draws new light and gives meaning to what may appear as unrelated. It often touches more on *invention* than on *discovery* of concealed meaning. Sense making has a 'fragrance' of doubt because other elements may be selected and combined into another congruent whole and a different meaning may emerge in the process. Furthermore, we rely for sense making not just on *words and associations*, typical for traditional psychoanalytic thinking, but on *behaviour* that may reveal the recent 'history' of the system, its impact on the current work behaviour and emerging underlying processes. Relying exclusively on the 'here-and-now' has some severe limitations since we are as human beings inclined to work with what we know. We may forego questioning what we don't know. Therefore it is desirable to explore in advance the organisational context and history of the system: for example, how the client system came into being, how important persons became appointed, how the organising or restructuring processes were organised, how one deals with suppliers, consultants, clients and employees, and how one relates to the outside world: competitors, local and international authorities etc. This knowledge as it *comes back* into our minds, while working in the 'here-and-now', provides us with hints to be further explored as to its *relevance* for the work and the objectives of the study.

Exploring Fields of Tensions and Fears, Not (Primitive) Anxieties

In psychodynamics, we explore assumed and/or experienced *fields of tensions and fears* (the latter are related to a specific situation) and much less anxieties, which – in psychoanalytic theory – are more vague, primitive and part of the unconscious as a dynamic system (Ucs.). As discussed earlier, psychic defence mechanisms and even group (Bion, 1961) and social defences (Jaques, 1955; Menzies, (1959/1988)) have their roots in primitive anxieties triggered by *current fields of tensions*. Yet, in psychodynamics it is sufficient to deal with these *current fields of tensions*. Anyhow 'anxieties' in the psychoanalytic sense of this concept are part of infantile experiences, which we do not touch as consultants or managers. These anxieties, however, may intensify the experienced fears and fields of tension. But bringing the actual field of tensions and fears to awareness is most often sufficient to restore a good enough contact with reality, thereby enabling the resolution of current problems.

The Unit of Study

In psychoanalysis the unit of study is the individual in relation to other persons, the analyst in individual therapy, the group and its members in psychoanalytic group therapy. The other social realities of daily life are only indirectly accessible through subjective accounts of the persons concerned. The way a person relates to these other realities may become reflected in the 'here-and-now'[4] but the individual or the group holds the centre of attention in interpretative work. They are the figure against a vaguely, indirectly known ground. In psychodynamics we work with *social entities* in their *context*: an organisation in its environments, a group or a department in its organisational context, organisational roles within the pattern of roles, or persons in their organisational roles. What we call context here is in part directly accessible and verifiable, and partly constructed by subjective individual experiences and/or the intersubjectivity[5] of the social entity. Most often the manager or consultant shares and becomes part of that same context. Because of the equal attention paid to the social and physical realities and the human subjective experiences and interactions, the term 'socio-analysis' or 'l'analyse psycho-sociologique' as the French call it, is a much more proper notion. The unit of study, or social entity, is always inquired within its context and history. Both are partly real and partly constructed, socially and/or by imagination. It is up to the manager or consultant to sort that out and share the findings with the people concerned.

The Domain of Psychodynamics

The objective of psychoanalysis, as therapy, is to facilitate the occurrence of some intra-psychic changes that result in a feeling of being more at ease with oneself and an ability to find more joy in life. This includes a greater tolerance for life problems and for what was previously, automatically defended against. Life problems become solved in a way that is simultaneously more gratifying to him/herself and more socially acceptable. It also includes the development

---

[4] The 'here-and-now' refers to what is happening or not happening (while it logically should) in the interactions and emerging in relations and images within a social system engaged in whatever task.

[5] Intersubjectivity refers to the shared experience that occurs between interacting human beings (and groups) with reciprocity of mutual influence. We'll come back to discuss this phenomenon more at length, later in this chapter.

of a natural inclination towards self-observation (self-reflection) and wonder. The actions taken in rearranging his/her life are solely his/her initiative. If brought up in the therapeutic setting, they can be explored to increase self-understanding, but the analyst will refrain from suggesting alternative actions. Furthermore, the whole therapeutic process is achieved through the exploration of verbal associations and exchanges and through the working through of the transference and counter-transference relations in the psychoanalytic setting.

In a psychodynamic approach, the work is not restricted to verbal exchanges and relations, but a lot more attention is paid to the 'language of action' *and what the system and the context do to the people in it, in reality or imagined.* Moreover, in a psychodynamic approach, understanding the social entity in context is only a condition for taking appropriate action to bring it to a better level of functioning, while creating conditions that facilitate psychic development. Here, the consultant and manager take an active role. They take action either by creating conditions for development, or directly to improve the functioning of the social entity. A better level of functioning is appreciated on several criteria. Minimally, they include sustainable improvement of performance and the well-being of the actors in the system.

In a psychodynamic approach one works with a set of alternating states of consciousness to understand the situation of the client system in its context and subsequently, based on this understanding to explore in the virtual world actions to be taken in the real world. In the virtual world these actions are appreciated against one's understanding of the situation, the anticipated outcomes and wider implications. Subsequently, the actions taken in the real world are checked by reflective practices and organised reviews against the intended impact on performance and well-being of the person(s) concerned. In psychodynamics one strives to create genuine and more lasting behavioural change, not by adding another cosmetic way of behaving, but by change resulting from *being* differently within a *changed context.*

AN ATTEMPT TO DEFINE PSYCHODYNAMICS

We like to define psychodynamics in a way that makes sense to consultants and managers, while elucidating its relevance for work in organisations. In the praxis we see psychodynamics as an approach by which one endeavours to gain a *good enough understanding* of what is *happening or not happening* in a system in order to take *effective action* (or in-action) to *improve* in a more lasting way the functioning of that system in its environment, while *offering opportunities for psychic development* for the people concerned.

On the basis of years of study and practice as consultants to organisations, we prefer to describe psychodynamics further and more precisely in its four basic and inter-related components. *First*, as an evolving body of knowledge that, *second*, colours and feeds the way in which one looks at oneself and the world and *three*, most importantly, fuels inquiry, and *fourth*, inspires the creation of conditions to facilitate the achievement of organisational objectives and psychic development.

An Evolving Body of Knowledge

It would still be incorrect to define psychodynamics as a fully-fledged discipline. To the extent that it incorporates in its praxis an action-research methodology[6] and borrows concepts – adjusted or not – from other disciplines, it is a field of study in development. Whenever a discipline is under development, it is quite normal and even encouraging that theory and praxis are unsettled; its assumptions and concepts are defined in various ways by different authors and practitioners. In this way, psychodynamics shares several features with the developing psycho-sociology (Enriquez, 1997; Mendel, 1992; Amado, 2007), and 'les sciences cliniques'[7] (Levy, 1997; Lhuilier, 2006) in France. This lack of clarity and the divergence of approaches in the field add uncertainty to that which is already present in the field of work itself. Working within uncertainty, however, is not only proper to developing disciplines, it is part of all scientific endeavours, and inherent to human life itself.

---

[6] Action-Research encourages broad participation of the people concerned in the research process and supports actions leading to a more just or satisfying situation for the stakeholders. Researcher and stakeholders strive to maintain a shared problem definition, co-generate relevant knowledge, use social research techniques and take action. The results are interpreted in the light of what they have learned (Greenwood & Levin, 1998).

[7] Literally translated as 'clinical sciences', yet the concept does not refer to anything pathological, but to a specific way of analysis and action taking in society. 'Clinical sciences' stands for an approach, which puts a greater emphasis on understanding than on mastering or control, more on discovery than on giving evidence.

The purpose of psychodynamics as a field of study is not to generate universal laws or truths, but to enrich the frame of reference of the consultant or manager so that a particular social system can be better understood and the manager or consultant can undertake more appropriate actions. Its application validity rests not in the identification of lawful connections between an issue, its causal factors and/or actions and improved performance, but in increasing the diagnostic and action repertoire of people engaged in qualitative studies, judgement and action taking. Psychodynamics does not lead to simple applications but to *applicable knowledge*. Its basic principles are accessible to most human beings and can be spread within the organisation. Some people, through their make-up are more suited for psychodynamic work than others. Yet, while most people can learn to work with a psychodynamic perspective, acquiring proficiency demands further education and – by preference – should be followed by some scholarly supervision.

The body of knowledge has and is being developed much more from careful reflection on one's practice and from borrowing concepts from other disciplines, than from controlled research. It originated from psychoanalysis, in particular when trained psychoanalysts departed from the established field of psychoanalytic therapy and started working with and investigating social systems. Here, we must mention the early work of Jaques (1955), Menzies-Lith (re-published in her collective papers, 1988, 1989) and Balint (1968). Other analysts from the Tavistock Institute, like Bion (1961) and Turquet (1974) contributed in studying the psychodynamics of small and large groups; while still others like Bridger, Miller, Rice, and Trist (Trist et al., 1990, 1993, 1997) moved beyond *Group Relations* into *Action-Research* and studied *the dynamics of organisation and change*, of *socio-technical systems* and *inter-organisational domains*. In their work, they were much influenced by Lewin's early ideas (1951) favouring action-research and advancing the view that groups should be studied as a whole in relation to its context. But the blending of psychoanalysis and open systems thinking must be largely attributed to the social scientists of the Tavistock Institute in its early years.

In the USA the situation was more complex. Several developments can be distinguished. The first one initiated by psychoanalysts like Fromm (1941), Janis (1958, 1969), and Levinson (2002). A second development found its origin in the thinking and concerns of the German fugitive, Lewin, about democratic leadership. It resulted in a variety of training programmes and studies in group-dynamics (Bradford, Gibb & Benne, 1964). Once these programmes became introduced into organisations, they – together with survey feedback – paved the way for *Organisational Development* (a.o. Bennis, Benne & Chin, 1961; Schein, 1985). Others built on Lewin's conviction that knowledge production should be based on solving real-life problems in a real context. Stimulated by the early work of the Tavistock Institute, they became engaged in '*industrial democracy*' (Pateman, 1970) and further promoted *Action-Research*.

In France where psychoanalysis and Marxist thinking was very much present in the teaching of social scientists, we found a development similar to the one in the UK. From group dynamics (Groupe de dynamique de groupe (Pagès, 1968)) one moved rapidly into '*institutional analysis*' (a.o. Lapassade, 1971) with a focus on the issues of power, and into '*psycho-sociology*' (a.o. Amado, 1980; Enriquez, 1997), and '*les sciences cliniques*' (a.o. Levy, 1997; Pagès et al., 1979, Lhuilier, 2006) where the emphasis is on understanding the *subjective experiences* in organisations. Unfortunately, the differences in languages have severely reduced fruitful exchanges between the French and the Anglo-Saxon social scientists. To complete this brief review, we must mention the pioneering work of Gunnar Hjelholt, a Danish social scientist, who studied group and inter-group dynamics in *mini-societies*, which he created by bringing different social categories (e.g. students, academics, union representatives, drug addicts) temporarily together in a small, rented village (1973). In fact he opened a field of study that would now be part of community psychology.

Social psychologists in Europe contributed valuable insights in social identity (Tajfel, 1982), social identity conflict versus real conflict stemming from mutually wanted but limited resources (the latter studies were pioneered by social scientists: Sherif & Sherif, (1953)). *Experimental social psychology* in the USA and Europe continued to enhance our understanding of group dynamics, influence processes and attitude changes through processes of identification, compliance and internalisation (Kelman, 1958). Much later, *social constructionism* drew attention to the importance of language as a means to repress, suppress, and replace content, as well as to reveal meanings.

When a field of study is so much influenced by various disciplines and approaches, from psychoanalytic theory and practices, from social psychology and organisational development, from open systems theory, sociology and cultural anthropology, it cannot but be confusing and overwhelming to managers and consultants who are not bred in the social sciences. Even social scientists tend to put their emphasis in psychodynamics on those fields of study they feel most comfortable with thereby reducing complexity to a level they can comfortably work with. It would be nice if we could condense the relevant, yet diverse body of knowledge in a manageable way. In our considered opinion this looks like an impossible task. Therefore, we have chosen a selective approach. In Part One, we discussed the key notions and processes from psychoanalytic theory and practice. Some of these will reappear when we define psychodynamics as a perspective and a way of inquiry. In the course of these discussions, we include essential elements of 'les sciences cliniques' and Action-Research. In the subsequent definition of psychodynamics as a way of creating conditions we borrow some valuable ideas from Organisation Development and Action-Research. We will further review some important findings about the social context that enable people to develop. Yet, it remains an impossible task to review all the notions and findings that may become relevant in a psychodynamic approach. The realities the social sciences are dealing with are too complex, changing and influenced by their varying contexts. We are practicing social scientists that continuously learn from the field we are working in, we have a living interest in finding out from our experiences, as we go along, and from reading. In fact the body of knowledge is not knowledge to be simply applied, but it colours and fertilises the way we look at the world and most of all it drives inquiry. This evolving body of knowledge does not hold the forefront of our minds, but stays in the background as a source of hunches about what would be interesting and relevant to explore. Indeed, too much preoccupation with theoretical concepts and empirical findings may pre-structure what we see and study, at the expense of finding out what is really going on in a particular socio-technical system with its own economical and/or social objectives. We want to avoid, in other words, that the evolving body of knowledge *becomes taken as a* form of a cookbook for the *applications* of concepts or the creation of conditions, whereby *inquiry becomes pre-empted* and replaced by sheer *structural* interventions, or by wild psychoanalytic interpretations and blind applications of findings that don't solve any problems, but categorise behaviour, 'typologise' human beings or turn them into averages.

Psychodynamics as a Perspective

The way of listening to the languages of images, actions and relations and of looking at verbal interactions, activities and other forms of behavioural expressions is grounded in psychoanalytic thinking. One pays attention to how ideas and expressions become connected or disconnected in a particular context to reveal meaning, a meaning or the 'music' behind the interactions that may call for further explorations or attention. It is a way of listening to and looking at the flow of interactions, hesitations or abrupt changes of content, the quality of silences and the qualitative features of the emotional climate. One does this to sense the congruence or incongruence between the manifest (what is said and done) and the latent (what is left out, concealed or not done, not talked about although common sense) in order to get a feel for its possible underlying significance. The assumption behind the perspective is that human interactions are related or disconnected through meaning. Human beings are not isolated entities but are constantly created and recreated "at the interface of reciprocally interacting worlds of experience" (Stolorow, Atwood & Branchaft, 1994, p. x). The 'product' of these human interactions is called 'intersubjectivity'. The process, amongst others, makes it possible that members of a social system, in interaction, become *like-minded*.

The phenomenon of 'like-mindedness' in groups has drawn the attention of social scientists from different fields. Some have approached it from the cognitive perspective. Cognition, one argues, is *socially situated* and "every cognitive act must be viewed as a specific response to a specific set of circumstances" (Resnick, 1993, p. 4). The group does not have a brain of its own, but the members in shared circumstances and through verbal and non-verbal interactions, develop a communality or conformity that looks like a 'group mind' with its own emotional and dynamic properties. Many theorists, also cognitive psychologists, have come to accept the existence of a group mind, but are still exploring the different ways in which it is formed (a.o. McClure, 1990). A first explanation of collective cognition is that inter-individual homogeneity in shared beliefs, scripts and shared interpretation of the world is promoted by the tendency to achieve consensuality and convergence in groups of individuals working closely together (Moscovici & Doise, 1994). Although this way of looking at a like-mindedness is valuable for the praxis, it is somewhat too general and a little simplistic since individuals construct and process knowledge independently of one another and are therefore unlikely to hold exactly the same views on issues and their interpretations, while sharing the same framing of issues. Furthermore it underestimates the importance of the *context dependency* of thinking and acting. A second more refined explanation suggests that individuals do not share the same beliefs, attitudes and views to produce consensuality, but they do share *core elements*. Individual differences tend to converge incrementally towards the dominant view through interaction and political influence. The resulting overlap of information may only give rise to a transitory artefact, and members may later diverge in their memory of what was agreed and what was not. Other researchers shifted the emphasis from collective cognition towards the actors. They posit that collective action may be more the outcome from core communality between the social actors than from homogeneity in cognition.

These studies shed a complementary light on the psychodynamic perspective of looking at phenomena of 'groupthink' in boards, management teams and policy-making bodies (Janis & Mann, 1977; Janis, 1982, 1992). It further moderates the overemphasis in the perspective of the 'group-as-a-whole', since any person may have a role in generating the group reality, but the entire group reality can never reside in any one person (Johnson, 2004). It also gives additional credit to the interplay between individual members and group phenomena described by Redl (1942) and underlined by Sutherland (1985/1990).

The psychodynamic perspective incorporates a way of listening whereby one tries *to understand* the subjective experience beyond the *used vocabulary*. Clients may either find no proper words to communicate a particular experience, or the experience itself is still in a state that does not yet allow for conceptualisation. Bollas (1987) refers to this state of an experience as the *unthought known*. In both instances, the client uses popular concepts or an existing vocabulary by which the original and intended message becomes mis-communicated. For example, the established board of an international bank called upon a business school to organise a conference on 'decision making' as if over the years they had not been taking effective decisions. After further explorations it appeared that changes in the crossroads of financial transactions had created inefficiencies in their organisational structure, hindering proper decision making. The request for lectures on decision making was their way of expressing an experience of losing ground in managing the bank under changed conditions.

It would be wrong, however, to restrict the psychodynamic perspective to just paying attention to the 'languages' of images, actions and relations, as if these exist in a vacuum, without any relation to the actual context in which they take place. Such a misunderstanding would inevitably open the road for 'psychologising'. In order to avoid this trap the unit of study is conceived as an open system in interaction with its environment. Both the unit of study and its environment are engaged in realities that can be described along social, physical, technological, economical and political dimensions. These distinguishable, but non-exhaustive aspects of the realities of real life create conditions and opportunities that impact on the behaviour of the unit of study. These conditions and opportunities are to be taken into account in the psychodynamic perspective. It does not mean that one ought to be an expert in all these fields, but that one holds enough interest in understanding these aspects to grasp the realities in which the 'languages' of images, actions and relations emerge and reveal their meanings. Yet, one implication stands out: the psychodynamic perspective in itself is not sufficient for dealing with all managerial or organisational issues. It remains a necessary but often not a sufficient perspective.

The relevance of a psychodynamic perspective for managers and consultants comes to light in four important ways. First of all the perspective expresses itself in *self-reflection*. It is not just a matter of looking at what is happening or not happening in the system under study, but also of being attentive to what the system does to oneself: its various ways of 'talking back' to one's presence and actions. Without self-reflection one can hardly understand the 'language' of relations in which one may be involved. Second, the psychodynamic perspective enables managers and consultants to choose actions from their repertoire on the basis of a more profound *understanding of the situation* at a given time. It helps them to create conditions and select methods that facilitate the system to achieve task accomplishment. For example, when the government broke its tradition of subsidising the activities of an engineering firm, we found an unusual degree of difficulties amongst its managers in coping with the resulting uncertainties. They now had to face drastic re-structuring in order to survive the increasing international competition. Yet, they were unable to see alternatives to meet the now uncertain future. So we suggested *playing* with all kinds of half-baked ideas to simply match the price level of their major competitor. We did that during a couple of meetings until we became sufficiently confident to start exploring seriously the relevance and feasibility of the ideas. Third, the perspective with its emphasis on being attentive and listening expresses a genuine attempt of managers and consultants to understand the people in the system, their *subjective experiences and affective lives in the work situation*. Last but not least, the psychodynamic perspective generates impressions, feelings and hunches that require further exploration before they can become acceptable as data. In other words, the perspective *fuels inquiry and reality testing*. These endeavours include some sharing of one's current understanding, which in turn enables the persons concerned to become equally involved in exploring the underlying dynamics and in taking actions.

Psychodynamics as a Form of Inquiry

In psychodynamics we are interested in discovering *why* a social system behaves, as it appears to behave. Consultants without a psychodynamic perspective may equally be exploring the causal texture of a work system. For example, consultants in total quality management are trained in asking the famous 'five whys?' when confronted with mistakes, and deviations from the expected. Each answer of why it happens is followed by a subsequent exploration of why until, usually after five attempts, one arrives at the primary cause(s). Or, they may fall back on other methods like statistical analysis and video recordings to identify the disturbing factors beneath the observed problems. However, their interest is not so much in discovering the *meaning* of particular behaviour, but to move directly to the removal of the causal factors. Although this approach is interesting and useful, in psychodynamics there is recognition that people, and social systems may not be able *to give valid answers* to direct questions like the 'five whys?' First, because the 'whys' in psychodynamics are to understand the meaning a particular setting, activity, or an object has for the human beings concerned. The meaning may not be directly accessible in factual answers. The group or person may not be able to give an answer because s/he *simply does not know* (since the reasons may reside in 'Atlantis'). But, the answers may become revealed indirectly in experiences, emerging images and in behavioural patterns. The particular meaning in other words is deduced from behaviour and needs to be further validated by inquiry and data. Furthermore, the deduced meaning can't be validated by an empathic 'yes' or 'no' from the person or group concerned. Such a quick empathic answer most often serves to stop further thinking and exploration. Only in subsequent elaboration can one get a sense of its validity. Second, the person(s) concerned may at a certain level know the answer but s/he is *afraid* to tell it. Either because it may sound *silly* (anticipated loss of self-esteem), or the real reasons may not be stated because of *social pressures*, and an honest answer may reveal what must be kept *concealed*. For example, some secondary gains derived from a problematic situation may become exposed or one may discredit a person in need of protection. Obtaining a valid answer may therefore take quite some time, demanding continuing attention and explorations to notice what may not be seen or said. Often, another person from outside the system, with another way of looking is needed to get to the concealed truth.

An example may illustrate what is meant by psychodynamic inquiry. In a building firm, we spent a day with its architects, engineers, electricians and other professionals, in total around 60 employees, to make an inventory of experienced problems at work. Towards the end of the day, I got the feeling that there was not much energy in the discussion. So I asked whether they had heard anything new during the day. After a silence, someone said: "No, we've known about these problems for years!" Then I asked them why nothing had been done to solve them. Another silence set in. Unfortunately, we ran out of time. So we ended the meeting with a kind of contract to think about it and to discuss their ideas at the next meeting. When a few days later, we met with the management team, one senior manager said: "You were right when you told them that they don't seem to learn from their experiences. This is exactly what another consultant told us, about three years ago". Again I questioned why? Yet, even management could not come up with an answer. At that moment, I recalled one manager's remarks during the intake: "We don't talk about mistakes here! Our people are all professionals with years of experience". During the whole project we kept an eye on why people could not learn from experiences. *Many reasons* surfaced, amongst one the collusion around the need to conceal incompetence and an excessive concern not to disappoint or hurt anyone, directly. Some managers even needed to be protected. Furthermore, the avoidance of paying due attention to deviations from the expected was also neatly covered up by a persistent, generalised emphasis on creativity and enjoyment of work. However, satisfaction at work could equally be derived from doing one's job right the first time. Without removing all these reasons for not learning from mistakes (experience) the improvements in efficiency and effectiveness of the firm would only have yielded temporary results.

In psychodynamic inquiry one does not take answers to a direct question *readily for granted*. One keeps an open mind to allow oneself to become aware of possible answers revealed: (a) in elaborations by the person(s) concerned, (b) in recognisable patterns of interactions or behaviour; (c) in slips of the tongue, unattended revelations in informal conversations, gossips, jokes or graffiti; (d) in observable sources of tensions, discomfort, fears and negative anticipations that either need to be controlled or avoided; (e) in secondary benefits that are more rewarding than the obvious discomfort (like the famous headache during exams to alleviate being fully responsible for unsatisfactory results); and (f) in observations of how problems and suffering become displaced, dislocated from their causal context, or fragmented in the organisation for valid reasons or through defensive processes (we'll come back to this issue of locating the problem in Chapter 8). In other words, the psychodynamic perspective driving inquiry is always present. Even when exploring an issue with frames from other disciplines, it stays there in the background of our minds triggering questions.

Psychodynamics as a Way of Creating Conditions

A reciprocal interaction exists between understanding a situation and taking action. They enrich one another: "Understanding to transform, transform to understand"(Clot, 2001). Actions may take the form of a direct intervention, for example, a question to explore what is happening beneath the surface, or of sharing one's understanding with the client system. Taking action may also be creating conditions that (a) facilitate task accomplishment, and/or (b) enable psychic processes to do their work, and/or (c) change the conditions of the system and its dynamics in a more enduring way. Although these conditions or interventions may and often do overlap, we like to distinguish them for practical purposes and theoretical interests. The first kind of conditions we call *'facilitating structures'*. They include a rich variety of alternating group compositions (homogeneous and mixed groups) to tap group, identity, and/or role experiences; various ways of expressing and sharing data (verbal or written reports, drawings etc.); and research methods and techniques that encourage shared data collection and processes that facilitate task accomplishment without determining its outcome. From the very start, Organisation Development and Action-Research have highlighted the importance of making the social sciences and their investigation techniques accessible to the common people, so that they can fully own and participate in improving their work system, their organisation or their community. They produce a repertoire of ideas that can be used in creative ways to fit the particularities of a given situation. Most of these 'facilitating structures' – sometimes called 'minimal structures – reduce the degree of complexity and chaos to a level that is bearable for the people to work with effectively. We think of the structures in 'search conferences' (Emery, 1997), in 'future search' (Weisbord & Janoff, 1995) and the establishment of 'the rules of logic' (Gray, 1989) for dealing with issues of collaboration between different interest groups, and the minimal structures advanced by Barrett (1998) for organising work. Other facilitating structures intend to ease the tensions and fears in the setting. Krantz, (2001) cites, for example, 'transition planning' and 'outplacement' as a means of supporting people in organisational change processes.[8]

---

[8] Facilitating structures like some research methods, in particular when they expose and confront people with new realities, may evoke transitional processes as indicated by Raminez & Drevon (2005) and reflected in our own work described in Part Three.

The second category we have called '*supportive process structures*'. These are intended to enable healthy mental processes to emerge and take their own course. In Part One, we have already discussed two of them: 'containment and holding', and 'transitional processes'. There are, however, others designed to enable the 'working through' of experienced loss of a real 'object', of confidence or trust, and to allow for 'reparation'.

Containment or that capacity to absorb and hold on to tensions generated by others does provide a favourable condition to allow human beings to function until they are able to face up to the tensions. Containment can be present in a person or in a group, but can it be purposefully created? The capacity to contain appears to be rather specific. A manager or consultant, for example, may be able to contain the tensions generated at work, but may get hopelessly lost in the family situation or vice versa. On the other hand, it looks like we can learn to withhold spontaneous, tension-increasing responses in particular situations and that many people can learn to sort out their own experiences of tensions from those put into them. Furthermore, one comes to feel more self-confident, less anxious with the accumulation of positive experiences in handling tensions proper to consulting or managing.

Holding becomes expressed in facilitating structures that either prevent overexposure to all sorts of tensions or regulate through step-wise approaches the amount of complexity and uncertainty in working on the task. For example, keeping the media at bay during the first try-out of large organisational change, or during negotiations between different interest groups.

Supportive process structures that enable *transitional processes* to emerge or that facilitate *working through* or *reparation* of painful experiences will be discussed in the subsequent sections of this chapter. They deserve more elaboration because of their particular importance in organisational and community life.

In a third category of interventions, named *system's conditions*, we group together all efforts and activities to *create or change existing conditions of the system to improve its dynamics in a more lasting way*. The intent of these interventions is to establish conditions that further organisational effectiveness while enabling psychic and social development. These interventions include work systems and organisational design, and community building.

Already in the 1950s, Eric Trist and Ken Bamforth (1951) discovered through reflection on their work in an action-research project in the coalmines, the great impact of technological conditions on the social behaviour of the people in the system. Their new concept of a social-technical system posits that the performance of a work system is a function of the optimisation between the technological demands of the work (e.g. technology, lay-out) and the psychological requirements of its members. The concept was further developed by a number of social scientists, in particular by Fred Emery (1972) and Albert Cherns (1976) who specified the minimal psychological requirements. Subsequently a great number of social scientists from all over the world took this notion as a cornerstone in work systems design and redesign. Even today, the concept continues to inspire consultants and managers in their organisational praxis.

From this basic notion, Trist (Trist, Higgin, Murray & Pollock, 1963), Herbst (1976) and later Jaques (1989) opened up organisational design alternatives that promise more effective and satisfying conditions. Perlmutter (1965a, 1965b) advanced the notion of 'the social architecture of organisations' in which he included ethnic variables and nationality in the manning of multinational organisations. Many more recent authors could be named, but with the exception of a few the emphasis in recent organisational design is more readily put on generating financial benefits alone.

The tendency to design work systems and organisations to maximise performance and/or financial benefits not only increases stress and temporality in work systems, but erodes the *social* gratifications of work itself. In the Western industrialised world with its well-developed social security systems, people don't just work to earn a living, or to be the best, or to make a career. If the workplace offers only those minimal opportunities, one must not be surprised that a majority of employees want to quit before the age of retirement. The workplace is not just for self-engagement in the 'primary task' per se, or in task accomplishment per se. It is a place where people can engage with other human beings, develop meaningful relations, test reality while contributing something valuable to society. Yet, when all slack (e.g. tea/coffee breaks, lunches, informal conversations) is cut to the limit of what is physically bearable; when all appreciation becomes based on individual performance, when persons become tied to individual workstations; when the emphasis is on 'employability' (the individual's responsibility to enhance one's attractiveness in the labour market), voluntary help, friendship and social life at work are eaten away. This undermines the sustainability of the workplace and indeed of the social system as a whole.

Marie-Jeanne Vansina-Cobbaert (2005) distilled from her years of work in a *therapeutic community* six critical conditions that facilitate psychological growth and well-being. These conditions could equally well be created and developed in work systems and in work and neighbourhood communities whereby the erosion of social relations is to be countered (see: Part One, Chapter 2). At this time, it is too early to report some life experiments on these six conditions. However, earlier studies (e.g. Emery, 1972) and the empirical findings about the attractiveness of the workplace (Buckingham & Coffman, 1999) have already pointed to the importance of having at least one friend in the work community with whom one can share personal concerns and issues, as well as enjoy his/her company. They give some support to our attempts to build social sustainability in (work) communities. These six conditions, however, are things to be developed over time; they can't just be installed by decree or by sheer work systems design. They require continuous attention, even at times some facilitation.

This brings us to a very important point: the system's conditions are never imposed on the people but are developed in active participation with all or a large section of them. Conditions are proposed, discussed and explored in their likely consequences, but they are rarely the clean product of the consultant or managers. The way they are created appeals to the creativity of the people involved, allows them to grow into them and acquire ownership.

The psychodynamic approach as we have tried to define it for managers and consultants is much more than applied group relations within organisations. It is at the same time an evolving body of knowledge that shapes a perspective, but most of all inspires inquiry to gain a more profound understanding and share it with the system under investigation in order to take jointly more appropriate action, either directly or by creating new conditions. The value base and the intent are to create more sustainable improvement of the system's effectiveness, while enabling psychic and social development for the people involved.

CREATING SUPPORTIVE PROCESS STRUCTURES

The primary purpose of consulting or managing may not be to facilitate personal development, but to improve in a sustainable way the performance of a work system. Yet, organisational and personal development cannot be taken as independent processes. Several empirical studies show that long-term organisational performance is positively related to investment in personal development and attentive personnel management (e.g. Collins & Porras, 1994; Pfeffer, 1994; De Geus, 2002; Pfeffer & Sutton, 2006). Furthermore, when the purpose of organisations in society is rightly considered to be more than just yielding sustainable benefits to the shareholders, but to include generating benefits for the other stakeholders as well (e.g. employees, clients and communities), the importance of personal/social development in organisational development becomes even more obvious. Consultants and managers can contribute to these endeavours. Yet, it would be naïve to think that their impact is lasting, even when special attention has been given to embed the project in the organisation by preparing the system to take over the developmental conditions and processes. Managers familiar with the psychodynamic approach are in a better position to produce more lasting results. Because of their authority and power they are often more able to modify conditions of the system they are accountable for and find ways to engage the adjacent systems in developing less disturbing and more collaborative relations to benefit the whole. Consultants are often restricted in their efforts to move into connecting systems for several reasons. Consultants' probes may be seen as attempts to turn the project into something much bigger, and/or the sponsor may fear losing control over the project and becoming involved in political arguments with other managers. However, even managers do not have the omnipotence to produce enduring results because of changes within their work system, or within the decision-making structure of the organisation and/or in its wider environment. For example, it is rather omnipotent thinking to expect that a successful, strategic restructuring project of the production plant of one business unit will become a most influential factor in the decision-making process at headquarters. Nevertheless it is always worth the effort to create favourable conditions, because one does not know in advance whether they will have a more lasting effect. Even when they don't, they do provide some temporary work experiences to hold on to as a good memory.

In this section, we will focus on the creation of *supportive process structures* within the psychodynamic approach to enable healthy psychic processes to develop along the way of attaining the project objectives. We are not talking here about creating conditions that will eventually change the system's dynamics for the better, but about some specific supportive conditions that enable people to get there without yielding to coercion, collective denial, and persecutory anxieties. The focus here is on the psychic processes along the way of getting there.

We have already drawn attention to the fact that one can create appropriate supportive process structures to enable psychic development, but it is simply impossible to take it over from someone else. The persons involved can use or fail to use the offered opportunities.

Enabling Transitional Change

Even before Gilles Amado and Tony Ambrose published the book: *The Transitional Approach to Change* (2001), several members of the discussion forum who met over several years, started working with the new notion of transitional change. Winnicott's (1951) original concepts of 'transitional object' and 'transitional space' were seen as relevant in the world of adults confronted with organisational and personal changes in their lives. In this adaptive process some concepts acquired a different meaning. As usual during a period of conceptual rethinking, it also brought along some confusion, conceptual un-clarity and some people jumping on the bandwagon providing cases of their work that could look like transitional change. Time has come to clarify the concepts, thereby distinguishing them from other notions and change processes. In Part One, we already discussed transitional processes at length. Here we will discuss these processes in relation to the recent notion of *transitional change*.

Winnicott, a British psychoanalyst and paediatrician, studied mostly young children. From his observations he concluded that infants make use of transitional objects to separate the 'me' from the 'not-me', and move from absolute dependency into a stage of relative dependency. When born, the infant is completely dependent on others for nourishment, cleaning and feeding. Without helpful people around him, the infant would not survive. Furthermore, in the very early stages the infant does not seem to make a distinction between his need to be fed, cleaned and nourished, and the other need-providing persons around him. He is hungry, he cries and he becomes nourished. It is the time that the infant is assumed to feel omnipotent. He only needs to cry and he becomes satisfied. Gradually, the infant comes to see that the mother or mother figure is not always around, providing for his needs, but leaves the baby to engage in other activities. The gradual breakdown of the illusion of omnipotence brings with it a growing distinction between 'me' and 'not-me'. We assume that this can't be easy 'work' for the very young child. The mother figure is no longer an adaptive and providing part of oneself, but a separate and independent person: one has to learn to stand on one's own feet, so to speak.

Winnicott's thinking about child development differs from that by Freud and M. Klein. While Freud assumed a movement from the 'pleasure' towards the 'reality principle', Klein focussed on the inner world and the child's phantasies. Winnicott posited *a third space* of *experiencing* (sometimes referred to as a neutral, or a transitional space) between the inner and the outer world of the human being that allowed for transition from his own subjective state to a more objective state of experiencing the world. In this third space, the human being *perceives and creates* at the same time, and allows for using symbols when he has become able to distinguish between fantasy and facts, between inner reality and external objects.

> ...there is the third part of the life of a human being, a part that we cannot ignore, an intermediate area of *experiencing*, to which inner reality and external life both contribute. It is an area which is not challenged, because no claim is made on itself except that it shall exist as a resting place for the individual engaged in the perpetual human task of keeping inner and outer reality separate yet inter-related (Winnicott, 1951, p. 230).

Somewhat further, Winnicott writes in cursive characters:

> *The intermediate area to which I am referring is the area that is allowed to the infant between primary creativity and objective perception based on reality-testing* (p. 239).

The third space is the space in which human beings are living in health, pursuing cultural activities and enjoying themselves:

> ...playing and cultural experience are things that we do value in a special way; they link the past, the present and future; *they take up time and space.* They demand and get our concentrated deliberate attention, deliberate but without too much of the deliberateness of trying (Winnicott, 1971, p. 109).

Winnicott came to posit this third space from observing the newborn baby's use of his fingers and fist and the ways the older infant (3 to 12 months) played with a teddy bear, or a soft toy. This favourite doll or soft toy he called a *transitional object*. This object does not need to be a real object, it can be a tune, a word, but in general we are inclined to picture it as teddies, or dolls. Yet, it is something that the infant *creates from what the world supplied*. In this sense it is his first, real possession. It is at the same time 'me' and 'not-me'. In essence, it is the object that bridges and makes "...contact possible between the individual psyche and external reality" (Winnicott, 1955,

p. 149), and "... gives room for the process of becoming able to accept differences and similarities" (Winnicott, 1951, p. 234). Whatever the transitional object, a teddy bear or a tune, it figures in that third space: the transitional space.

The function of a transitional object was originally defined to further the infant's psychic development. But its function can also be conceived as to allow the human being to become familiar and to adapt to an external reality (not always in the future). In this process one relinquishes the illusion of omnipotence. This latter way of wording – in more general terms – points to the relevance of 'transitional objects' also for adults. Once this function is fulfilled the transitional object loses its relevance. Yet, people may remember it much later with pleasure(Vansina-Cobbaert, 2005).

When, some 15 years ago, a small group of social scientists took the ideas of Winnicott into the world of adults and organisational change, the notion of *transitional space* became significantly changed (Amado & Ambrose, 2001). In my understanding of the original thinking of Winnicott, the third part, the intermediate area, the neutral or transitional space referred to the *internal space of experience* between the inner and outer world of the human being. Now, transitional space comes to refer to *external conditions* of time, space and sanction to be provided for the adult to enable those healthy, creative psychic processes in the inner third space to do their work. Another difference can be observed. The young child and his transitional object become involved in developmental and adjusting processes to adapt himself to a subjectively perceived – even imagined – external reality that is presented in some form or another, for example, the coming and going of the mother figure, the caring and punishing adult. In the life of adults, transitional processes evolve *not only* around presented new external realities, but also around new realities to be *imagined and created*. In other words, the developmental and adaptive transitional processes of the young child point predominantly to the adjustment of his inner world to the outer world, while in adults they deal with both: the adjustments of the inner *and* the outer world. Both adjustment processes are included in '*transitional change*'. Transitional processes may occur in various settings, but for managers and consultants it is most appropriate to focus on creating supportive process structures enabling transitional change. The transitional approach to change can then be defined as the provision of *enabling conditions* to help human beings to work through the tensions of moving from the past to a future that is only partly known, partly created and largely imagined.

Harold Bridger, according to Ambrose (2001, p. 27), identified four conditions for enabling transitional change in organisational settings: *time* (allowing time for thoughts and reflections), *space* (a place to engage in thinking and reflective activities), *sanction* (a tolerance of the system to engage in these mental activities), and the group's *capacity to contain* creative thinking, and self-reflection. In the second book on transitional change (Amado & Vansina, 2005, p. 4), we compared the conditions created by consultants in their projects with a transitional approach to change in which transitional processes are claimed to have taken place. We identified the following *conditions*: (1) the provision of *time and space that is psychologically safe enough* to (a) enable the persons concerned to reconcile their inner and outer worlds through reflection and checking reality (partly known, partly created and imagined) as it becomes revealed in the intersubjective exchanges and pieces of data; (b) work through the tensions present in the 'here-and-now' between the past (e.g. partial or whole experiences, learned practices and mental frames) and the future (partially known, imagined, created, anticipated and wished for) through interactive mental processes of 'working and worrying through' of identified or anticipated benefits and costs; (2) the provision of *reality objects* that can serve as a 'good enough cover' (a transitional object in Winnicott's thinking) or a vehicle with an external '*raison d'être*' (Bridger, 2001); and (3) the appropriate role of the consultant/manager to facilitate transitional change processes (e.g. containment, patience), including an absence of interpretations of what goes on in that third space that might stop the unconscious doing its work. And we should include a final condition: the change should be more or less open-ended (Amado & Amato (2001)). If not, creative work of the persons concerned is largely excluded.

Some of these conditions are similar to what Harold Bridger, according to Ambrose (2001), describes as three different though related *experiences* in a transitional space:

- Relinquishing earlier dysfunctional, but still valued, roles, ideas, and practices.

- Creating, finding, or discovering new, more adaptive and viable, ideas and ways of thinking and acting.

- Coping with the instability of the changing conditions, both outside and within the organisational system, and with the sense of insecurity arising from it (p. 14).

These experiences go together with tensions that Bridger noted in observing managers and executives, as they struggle with illusions of omnipotence in thinking, in one's relation with the organisation, and in one's power position; struggles with distinguishing the 'me' and the 'not-me' as one has identified oneself with the organisation; and with the loss of personal identities as long-standing practices (that have often outlived their usefulness) are to be given up.[9]

The concepts that we use to talk about transitional change are not yet crystallised. The same realities are sometimes talked about in terms of the *minimal starting conditions* or as *supportive process structures*; others prefer to describe them as *experiences* within the transitional space. These different dimensions are relevant, and complementary. The description in terms of conditions is valuable for practice by managers and consultants to enable transitional processes to occur. The description in terms of experiences allows us to understand whether or not these transitional processes are operative. More regretful is the introduction of new, undefined notions that blur the distinction between transitional, organisational change and organisational change in general. The 'transitional situation' is such a confusing concept (Ambrose, 2001, p. 25).

As Winnicott already observed (some examples were given in Part One), not only objects can serve as a transitional object, it can also be a word or a ritual. However, to replace the transitional object by anything that facilitates or acts as a *catalyst* in the development or change process opens up a whole range of possible misconceptions about transitional change. Not all catalysts function as transitional objects. A transitional object is much more than a catalyst; it involves emotional processes of reconciling the inner and the outer world. In order to function as a transitional object it needs to play a part in the 'here-and-now' in dealing with experiences of tensions of moving from the past to the future. Otherwise, the means (external reality) provided may only serve as a 'facilitating structure', or in other words, a structure introduced to facilitate a task, for example, 'role playing the product' in a work-flow analysis (e.g. the consultant uses himself to represent the body of a car to be painted). Installing a coffee machine in between two departments in order to facilitate contact between them does not necessarily turn the coffee machine into a

---

[9] Consequently, human beings become confronted with some experiences of 'letting go', of loss. But, we see it as an impoverishment to equate transitional processes with 'working through' losses of one kind or another.

transitional object. Facilitating the working through of the consequences of an already *implemented* organisational change may be valuable work, but we can't consider it as standing for transitional change. It deals primarily with the working through of changes already implemented.

The most clear-cut example of transitional change I have come across in my consulting practice was during the redesign of the paint factory of General Motors in Antwerp, Belgium (1987–1988) from a highly hierarchical and functional organisation into a plant designed to foster teamwork. During the intensive preparation of the project with top management, the unions and the employees we had shown the movie on Nummi, a project of a team-designed plant, jointly operated by GM and Toyota in California. Yet, from the outset it was clear that we didn't intend to duplicate that model factory in Antwerp. 'Study groups' of various kinds were set up to rethink the work organisation and to study particular issues with the employees concerned and some union representatives. The generated proposals were laid down in brief reports and presented to the 'workgroup' composed of a diagonal slice of the factory and the union representatives, together around 40 people. The task of the 'workgroup' was to study the proposals and to either approve them or to send them back to the 'study group' for further study. Eventually, the approved reports were sent to the Board for final decision making. The external consultant took part in most of the 'study groups', chaired all of the 'workgroup' discussions, and attended all Board meetings relating to the change project. Most of the change proposals of the 'study group' did not generate too much debate in the 'workgroup', except two. The first one suggested the reduction of the existing three restaurants/cafeteria to one with the same portions and the same quality for everyone irrespective of rank (like they did in the Nummi film). The second was the introduction of one standard work dress for everyone in contrast to the different colours and cuts proper to the various functions and hierarchical levels currently in use. This proposal took up several meetings of the 'workgroup'. The discussions became emotional; objections ranged from the need for privacy for managers and guests to convenience in recognising one's own employees just by looking at their work outfit; while others advanced an expected increased ease in communication and informal contacts. They could not reach a conclusion. After some strenuous meetings, the most senior manager of the 'workgroup' became concerned and told me: "Lee, we should change the name of this group because the 'workgroup' is not working!" I said something like I thought that they were working, and that we were lucky not to have implemented the already agreed changes if in the virtual world they still could not agree to work differently. Finally, the 'workgroup' came to a decision to have only two cafeterias and one uniform or work dress. If we reflect on this episode the restaurants and the work dresses were a 'cover' that allowed the members to discuss – often in covered ways – their anticipated concerns of working with less hierarchical and functional differentiation; with less status differences and less clearly delineated role-identities. Those little things that matter so much could not be discussed in a direct rational way; they needed to be 'worked through' and 'worried through' in an indirect way until a sufficient number of people revealed – in one way or another – their willingness to commit themselves to the new largely imagined work practices in the future. The Nummi movie had provided them with a medium to which they could link their own aspirations, longings and fears. I don't believe many people realised after the decision what had really happened. They approved the 'modified' proposals and passed them on to the Board. They were implemented. Some years later one of the two restaurants was closed too. The need for that extra distinction had vanished.

According to the plan, the paint shop project was spread over the remaining shops making up the total factory. Management now knew how to bring these transformations about. The major difference was that they left out the 'work-group'. I was told, much later, that they never reached the same enthusiasm and successful implementations as in the paint shop.

Specific supportive process structures enabling 'working through'

We used the concepts of 'working through' and 'worrying through' earlier. It may, however, be important to describe these mental processes more precisely, so that one is enabled to make more refined distinctions in the conditions to be created to facilitate these healthy mental processes. This is all the more important because 'working through' is often referred to under the more general label of 'mourning' or in French 'faire le deuil'.

The notion 'working through' refers to the healthy process of integrating painful experiences *after* they have taken place: for example, troubling insights in oneself, the loss of someone, something dear (an object in 'object relation theory'), or a failure. In general it requires some time and space to 'lick one's wounds' or to mourn the loss before one is able to find new meaning in life. On the other hand, 'worrying through' is a concept introduced by Irving Janis (1959, 1969) to point to the healthy process of processing *anticipated* gains and losses for oneself and significant others, which are part and parcel of taking irreversible decisions. Such processes are not restricted to rational and conscious mental activities; unconscious mental processes are likely to become activated. From empirical evidence, we find that 'worrying through' results in both the development of mental strategies to control anticipated negative consequences when they do occur, and the creation of some psychic immunity that enables human beings to face them eventually. Although both 'working through' and 'worrying through' processes take place in transitional change, one may not reduce the latter to one of them. 'Worrying through' processes are facilitated when the person concerned is provided with realistic and accurate data – without stirring up too much anxiety – *before* committing oneself. Although both mental processes – in interaction – can be observed in transitional change, one may not conclude from the occurrence of one of them – often 'working through' – that the latter is sufficient to name it transitional *change*. Although some rituals may ease the transition from one state of being to another (e.g. the funeral ceremonies in the transition from husband to widower), working through real loss is a quite distinct psychic process.

Psychodynamics is about inquiry. In a following part, we will illustrate by three different consulting projects how a manager or consultant can create more specific, supportive process structures to enable healthy mental processes to deal with three specific kinds of loss in organisational life; three different kinds of loss, which at first sight find their expression in the same lack of energy amongst the people, a low mood even touching on a depressed state of being and controlled aggression against management. It is only through exploration of the organisational context and history that we come to distinguish the real loss of work relations, jobs and friends, from the loss of an illusion and the loss of trust. Each of these kinds of loss demanded distinctive conditions to work through the hurt and pain, before the people were able to invest and engage themselves again in the organisation.

Supportive process structures for dealing with real loss of work relations

Organisational restructuring, downsizing and/or strategic repositioning almost always lead to redundancies, changes in jobs, career perspectives, social identity, work relations and the meaning given to one's old role. The latter losses may appear to be easier to overcome than the loss of one's job. That is not necessarily the case. Most restructuring projects result in a mixture of different kinds of losses.

Not only the employees who are made redundant but also those who survive the re-organisation, including managers, suffer from such losses. When the first wave of restructuring and downsizing came over Europe in the early eighties, Harold Bridger from the Tavistock Institute commented: "How one deals with all those people who have to leave the company will determine how the survivors feel!" Indeed, the most loyal and dedicated employees suffered most severely from the downsizing (e.g. Brockner, Tyler & Cooper-Schneider, 1992). Only those employees who had an instrumental relationship with the organisation more or less escaped from this collective response to the experienced losses: depressive mood with some controlled aggression towards management. To make things worse, a depressive mood is not well tolerated by management. It is definitely not part of an American management culture in which everyone is supposed to be positive and assertive. Unfortunately, that management culture is also penetrating the European management circles. Consequently, people who do feel depressed come to feel also *ashamed of it,* as if being down is something abnormal and definitely not considered manly. The emotional responses to experienced losses become thereby *undiscussable.*

Indeed, 'working through' as Enriquez (1997) remarked, is a process that runs counter to the general psychodynamics of organisations. It appears impossible to question the loss of something important, to even recognise insurmountable shortcomings. Such explorations and discussions may lead into unpredictable domains and conclusions. Therefore they must be avoided. Nevertheless, over the years, and in several businesses we have *negotiated* conditions with management to create time and space to make the *undiscussable* discussable, and to help people in the process of re-engagement in their organisation (Vansina & Taillieu, 1996). In other words, the specific supportive process structures contain two elements enabling the people concerned to work consecutively on the task of 'mourning' the real loss of an object and on the task of re-investing oneself in the 'new' organisation. Let us take a closer look at these two basic elements.

Condition one: an exploring space

Taking time out of the regular working hours to create – what we called – an exploring space where employees and managers with assumed similar experience of drastic change in roles or jobs could come to share freely their experiences. The half-day meetings started with a full recognition by management of the pending changes, the reasoning behind them, their eventual irreversibility and the possible hurt that it may and will cause people. Then, the consultant gave a talk on the *normal affective* responses of human beings when confronted with loss of something important and dear to them. The study of Kübler-Ross (1969) and a later publication by Bridges (1986) are often used to describe the normal sequence of emotional responses to real loss: denial, anger, depression and search for new meaning. It is a simple set of affective stages, although people can and do often regress from one into another, before moving on. Some remain stuck and don't seem to find new meaning. It is important to communicate that such feelings and regressions are normal human responses to loss and that they can be shared. After a brief discussion of Kübler-Ross's findings, we organised a coffee break. After the break we checked whether new ideas or questions had come up during the break that anyone would like to share. At the same time, it provided us with another opportunity to check whether we were in or out of tune with the employees. When this was done, the consultant told an allegoric story of a young man in transition from adolescent life to adulthood (see: Bridges, 1986). The story stems from another culture, but was told in such a way that some similarities with the current situation could be recognised, so that some identification with it was facilitated. While telling the story, we paid attention to the non-verbal and verbal responses, which could have indicated persons needing further professional attention. After the discussion, we prepared a 'walking' cold buffet to allow people to mingle freely and talk informally with friends or colleagues, move to another small group, or change the subject completely. Indeed, human beings differ in the way they wish to work through their experiences of loss, either by sharing and talking, or by forgetting, or at least: 'let's not talk about it'. Yet, we always came back together in plenary to share on a voluntary base whatever they wished to bring into the group.

It must be said, that for most people such a session was enough to continue the process of mourning without further guidance. For a few it was not at all sufficient. We faced many painful moments. I will never be able to forget some of them. While re-structuring the earlier mentioned paint shop at General Motors, the supervisors were given a new role by which they became the leading member in the team on the line for 80% of their time. The other 20% was reserved for other activities off the line. After the 'walking' buffet lunch a supervisor came up to me and told me: "You just wiped out twenty years of my life. For twenty years I have worked to get away from that assembly line, and now I am back on it!"

Condition two: a space and tasks, facilitating reinvestment

After a couple of weeks when we felt that people were ready to think again about the future, we brought them together for a couple of half-day meetings. Each with a roughly defined set of tasks inspired by Ackoff (1981): (a) to become familiar with the new strategic objectives and tasks formulated in operational terms, appropriate for that particular hierarchical level; (b) to explore one's influence through co-ordinated effort towards future success; (c) to re-establish vital internal and external work relations; and (d) to formulate progress indicators to be used in regular review sessions.

The specific conditions and tasks vary with the concreteness of the organisational context. The reader may get a feel for what is possible in the following brief review of a project with an engineering division, which was downsized and merged with another independent engineering firm from the same industrial group. Besides the re-structuring the work was drastically changed from being a research centre for projects financed by a central budget into a knowledge centre that had to sell promising projects to the business units.

About six weeks after some sessions, organised to explore and work through the losses brought about by the reorganisation, the 70 engineers came together again to hear and discuss the new strategy for the division. Subsequently, they moved into the newly formed 'knowledge cells' to formalise their objectives and contributions to the new strategy (including what they needed to get right in the short term so as to become effective in relation to the new strategy). That work was started in the working conference but was later completed during normal working time. In a subsequent meeting, every 'knowledge cell' presented their objectives and contribution so that every other cell knew and could relate to them. Then the knowledge cells visited one another to meet each other's members and begin to establish new work relations. In each knowledge cell the members discussed two questions: 'What do we want to do to make you successful in your work?' and 'What do we ask you to do for us to make us successful in our work?' (Note that the emphasis here is on voluntary behaviour and on 'asking'.) Again this work was started during the meeting but completed during normal working time. In the last meeting these discussions were reviewed and completed and a method was presented to formulate progress indicators, needed for reviewing their progress and identifying possible work domains needing adaptation. During this period the consultants and the director remained available for further assistance or personal talks.

Supportive process structures for working through dis-illusionment

At first sight, the emotional response to the loss of 'an illusion' or to the loss of a real object is not much different. People are down, depressed, often looking for a scapegoat and show a general inability to rethink their current position, even less to plan in a creative way for the future. Major indicators for disillusionment can be deduced from the history of the organisation. Yet, they need to be explored with the persons concerned.

Strategic repositioning, restructuring, de-layering and reorganisations follow one another in waves. The more people have invested in the success of a reorganisation (e.g. joined in the formulation of shared mission definitions, taking new roles, working with new technologies, having believed management's rhetoric that everyone can become successful) the more likely they have developed a belief that through joint efforts one can make one's work unit, or one's organisation successful. That belief may gradually turn into an illusion of omnipotence. Disillusionment comes about when awareness emerges about our illusions. In organisations the awareness of failure, the shattering of illusions can come abruptly with the realisation that despite all efforts one has not been able to keep the work unit as an independent unit in the market. The awareness may kick in by the announcement of a new reorganisation or a management decision to sell off the business unit or to simply close the work unit because it no longer fits in its core strategy, and the owners can more profitably invest in another business. The meaning and the inexplicability of failure determine the emergence of what we call a *basic depressive response*. Not depression in the psychopathological sense of the term as it also contains a positive element to the extent that it makes room for adaptive processes to reality, mobilising efforts and processing information to repair the situation. Yet, one has lost self-confidence, feels down and often suffers from sleeplessness (Gut, 1989, p. 31–32).[10] In the face of such situations, the organisational culture seldom allows for space to work through the disillusion, neither does it provide favourable conditions for vigilant analysis of the situation, or innovative, proactive thinking about strategic alternatives (Whetten, 1980; Krantz, 1985; Hirschhorn, 1988). The focus is more on finding external factors accountable for the problems than on the analysis of how

---

[10] Dis-illusionment, or even better working through illusions brings people back into contact with reality. As such it is a healthy mental process (Gutmann et al., 2005). Yet, whenever the illusion served a defensive purpose, its removal brings forward the original fears or anxieties.

we got ourselves in that problematic situation in the first place. Janis (1992) rightly warned policy makers in his 'theory of constraints' of the tendency of human beings to abandon rigorous problem solving when they consciously or unconsciously feel incapable of dealing with the actual and potential difficulties and constraints. When we feel that we can't control the problem situation we fall back on politics (pleasing senior management or the shareholders), and/or a search for satisfying self-serving solutions.

The conditions and the tasks for working through disillusionment are however different from those for mourning real loss. We need to create space, but space for reflection to explore why we got caught in the illusion of omnipotence in the first place. It leads us to understand the processes, context and factors that led us to believe in our capacity, through joint efforts, to overcome all difficulties, even macro-economical factors, and also led us to forget that we only have a limited influence on our future; a limited influence but an influence worth using. We also need a space for reflection to explore what factors we overlooked or even denied in our strategic efforts. Finally we need a space to study how and why we overlooked early signs and warnings that the followed course and efforts were not sufficient in real terms or in the evaluation of headquarters. This critical and rigorous organised retrospective analysis facilitates working through as well as learning for the future, which includes insights in all kinds of defensive behaviour that got us into a state of illusion and prevented us from understanding the full reality of working in an organisation (Vansina, 2004).

Supportive process structures for working through "failed dependency"

"Failed dependency" as Miller (1998) coined it, or loss of trust in management can be found in organisations where a radical change took place in the relation between senior management and the rest of the organisation, namely from a leadership that is experienced as *protective* towards leaders who are *threatening* the (job) security of the employees, even more so than the competition. In fact the new managers become seen as the enemy within the organisation. The behavioural signs are somewhat similar to the other forms of loss discussed above: a refusal or inability to engage in creative and serious, strategic thinking, a depressed mood, controlled aggression, lack of involvement and in addition: (a) distrust in management and (b) 'calculated sincerity': carefully checking what to tell management, 'willing' obedience bordering on compliance, not as a learned attitude but as an intentional response. The latter two emotional responses and the history of the organisation form the distinctive diagnostic features. Rather than starting a mourning process about the loss of trust, the task here is to create conditions for trust to become *restored* by providing *transparency*, *sharing business data* and *joint information process-ing* with a broad segment of management to enable them to gain confidence in taking power, before the managers can subsequently become involved in joint strategic thinking. Senior management must – in the first place – re-gain the trust of a broad layer of managers, before trust can be re-established within the organisation (Vansina, 1999). Let us illustrate this with a concrete project.

During the previous management a rather brutal re-structuring process took place, putting a business unit up for sale. McKinsey had made their calcu-lations, designed a slimmed-down organisation that would be attractive on the acquisition market. The business unit was conceived as not fitting any longer in the strategic core of the international chemical parent corporation. The implementation was executed by management resulting in a radical break with the culture of the organisation in which reliable employment was a ma-jor feature. Four years later, not one organisation had shown an interest in buying the business unit. A new manager was appointed, and after some rig-orous calculations of data collected over a longer time period to overcome the typical seasonal results, he came to the conclusion that the unit was not only viable, but also yielded over time a significant profit for the corporation. His management team, shocked by the brutal downsizing and the absence of any prospective buyer, was still pretty much depressed and rather distrustful of the new manager. Notwithstanding all this, the new business unit manager had obtained permission from headquarters to start a new strategic round ac-cording to the strategic orientation procedures established by McKinsey. The new manager called me in to organize a *qualitative* strategic round with his management preceding the start of the formal standard procedures that were estimated to take at least two months' work from some senior managers. On the basis of a discussion and some explorative interviews with his management team, management agreed to adopt an action-research approach. All relevant information about the business and our joint work would be brought in and processed by a broad segment of managers. For this purpose, a two-day resi-dential, strategic working conference was set up with the top three layers of his organisation, in advance of the strategic 'planning' round formally requested by headquarters. Top priority was re-gaining the trust of the managers. After the usual opening, the group of around 14 managers were divided in three small parties: the management team of the business unit, the managers of the primary process, and the managers of staff and support personnel. We asked for their responses about respectively 'What is it like to manage here?' and 'What is it like to be working here?' The answers processed in plenary revealed the differences in work experiences. The management team saw the situation as a set of obligations, not opportunities. The support services took pride in the safety regulations and records of the chemical plant. The primary process managers struggled with the employees' feelings of being the underdogs of the corporation. From the ensuing discussions a shared general understanding emerged as well as an appreciation of the different perspectives. From then on we could continue our explorations of the strategic round, alternating small mixed groups and plenary sessions. Managers started to come forward with their understanding, using the influence of their conviction, while regaining trust in their new business unit manager.

In these three projects similar features can be observed: depressive mood, anger, somewhat covered aggression, distrust as well as the inability to become engaged in creative thinking or in the life of the organisation. Yet the consultant/manager creates different supportive process structures enabling healthy psychic processes to deal with respectively real loss, loss of self-confidence (disillusionment) and loss of trust in management. The differences between these organisational situations and psychological states can only, or at least more readily, be detected through an exploration of the whys of the behaviour and by knowing something of the recent past of the unit under study.

Supportive process structures to facilitate reparation

The reparation we talk about here is a healthy mental process by which human beings try to make good whatever damage they may intentionally or unintentionally, imagined or for real, consciously or unconsciously have done to other people, or to things that are dear to them. Reparation is grounded in respect and care for the other and often contains an element of creativity.[11] In Kleinian thinking it is the repair – in phantasy or in reality – of the inner world that is intended through repairing the external one. We deviate somewhat from this thinking. We see reparation in the inner world as the *consequence* of

---

[11] Other forms of reparation exist that in a defensive way try to reduce guilt, or reparation that carries some triumph over the 'victim' that is always seen as ungrateful for the restoration (Klein, 1940).

purposeful efforts to make good in the external world what one did wrong. We see more other-directedness than self-directedness in the process. Reparation furthers maturation processes by helping to control destructiveness by love and care and to increase trust in one's own love. Furthermore, it is said to increase one's capability of experiencing deprivation without being overwhelmed by hatred (Segal, 1973). Neither an apologetic 'sorry' nor a begging for forgiveness may be sufficient to repair the 'damaged' relationship. Something must be done to express concern and respect for the 'damaged other' to *start* a reparation process. One can't expect some magic from one's honest attempts to repair, like expecting the 'damaged other' to immediately forgive and forget what has happened. Furthermore *both parties*, the 'damaging' and the 'damaged' must be ready to engage in a time-consuming healing process. It is obvious that supportive process structures can't create remorse and concern, but only make it easier for human beings to mobilise what there is deep down and to facilitate its expression in one's own creative ways.

Reparation may come about spontaneously in or after intense argumentations and debates over organisational issues, in interpersonal or interdepartmental conflict, or accompany processes of working through loss of trust and loss of something dear. But, when we talk about supportive process structures to enable reparation we refer to something more elaborate. In our consulting practice, we have only had experiences with reparation during intensive re-structuring projects. The supportive process structure took the form of preparing the most senior manager for a meeting (or meetings) with his employees in which he would give first, an honest report about the necessities and objectives of the re-structuring. Furthermore he talked about his best estimations, at that point in time, of the implications for the employees, for example, redundancies, changes in jobs and work relations, and he explained the way the re-structuring would be organised (e.g. ways of providing for a modicum of control through participation), and the envisaged social support like outplacement, training and extra legal compensations. He was mentally prepared to listen and respond to the questions, negative fantasies about the worst that was going to happen and to comments with honesty and respect, even when addressed in an aggressive way. In this way management expresses openly an acceptance to 'bite the bullet'.[12] Here it is the manager who takes

---

[12] According to Jerry Harvey, the original meaning of 'biting the bullet' goes back to early war time in which a wounded soldier was given a bullet to bite on while a limb was sawed off, without anaesthesia.

and bites the bullet while restructuring the organisation. S/he suffers too while doing the job.

Such a supportive process structure is not devoid of any risks, most importantly the danger is that it turns into a selling of ideas, or into making unrealistic promises rather than an empathic listening to and registering of the experiences and concerns of the employees, which invokes pain and concerns in the listener. It may be beneficial to set up similar meetings and exchanges in situations where management or the leader is experienced as 'betraying' the confidence of his people for the best of intentions (Krantz, 2006): for example, when the French president Charles de Gaulle, on a presidential election ticket to maintain Algeria as a French colony, betrayed his electorate by granting independence to its colony. Unfortunately such meetings and exchanges were not organised then.

The most illustrative supportive process structure enabling reparation was set up and organised in South Africa, after the collapse of the Apartheid regime under the name of the 'Truth and Reconciliation Commission'. More than 20 truth commissions in several parts of the world have been set up and studied (Hayner, 2001). They all move beyond the Law of Talion: "An eye for an eye and a tooth for a tooth" or "Let the punishment fit the crime" for the cause of reparation and restoration of human dignity.

Archbishop Desmond Tutu, Chairman of the Truth and Reconciliation Commission, underlines in his introduction of the report (2003) the deeper purpose of all the efforts: to set in motion "...a process of healing a traumatised and wounded people". He further recognises that "...ourselves have been wounded healers" yet, wounded healers are fully aware that "There is not much future for them without forgiveness, without reconciliation". The Truth and Reconciliation Commission oversaw three other committees, one for 'Human Rights Violation', one for 'Reparation' and one for 'Amnesty'. This basic structure secured that amnesty would be granted to those persons who (a) had violated human rights in an act associated with a political objective, (b) had made full disclosure of all the relevant facts without threat of prosecution, and (c) had accepted guilt for these incident(s). The victims of gross human rights violation were invited to testify and give openly and fully an account of the endured suffering in a setting in which perpetrators and victims could listen and empathise. The victims would receive some reparation by the State in the form of either financial or symbolic means or some administrative measures and community rehabilitation. From a psychological point of view the

Truth and Reconciliation Commission provided a structure that enabled the perpetrators to reveal the truth and to express feelings of guilt normally associated with the violation of human dignity. Furthermore, hearing the suffering and pain of the victims may invoke genuine feelings of pain, concerns and regret that in legal settings are more easily repressed or fabricated to evoke a milder sentence. The victims on the other hand, are allowed and encouraged to talk in detail and openly about the human right violations and the suffering they have been subjected to. However painful and shameful telling the stories may be, the victims no longer feel alone with what was done wrong to them. In this respect both perpetrators and victims mourn in the reparation process. Genuine begging for forgiveness and forgiving does not come easily, it implies respectively the realisation that one has caused hurt and a wish to repair, while the victim accepts both the human frailty and the wish to repair as a minimal support to work through the inflicted pain and suffering. Both parties have their own internal struggle: one against a rejection of guilt and the other against the Law of Talion.

SMALL THINGS THAT MATTER: A LOOK AT SOME NEGLECTED POTENTIAL BENEFITS OF A PSYCHODYNAMIC APPROACH TO ORGANISATIONAL ISSUES

From the previous discussion, it is clear that in our view psychodynamics can seldom be the only perspective for dealing with organisational or management issues. Other perspectives from other bodies of knowledge and practices need to complement it. Organisational and management issues are multi-faceted and cannot seriously be dealt with by one discipline or by one perspective. In particular psychodynamics should be combined with organisational theory. Organisations should not be conceived as a collection of people but as an interconnected system of roles (positions) taken by requisite persons (with appropriate mental capabilities) and with explicit or implicit mutual accountabilities and authorities (Jaques, 1989). A psychodynamic approach is interested in understanding the whys of organisational behaviour, it attempts to remove causal factors of dysfunctional behaviour that are not always obvious, thereby contributing to *more lasting* improvements and *developments*.

Its value and relevance is most often appreciated by the *effectiveness of the actions* undertaken and the *conditions* created to deal with an organisational issue. We pay much less attention to the potential of a psychodynamic approach for the psychic developments of the people involved. We are careful in using the word 'potential' because the impact of a psychodynamic approach varies in intensity and length. It is evident that such potential is less likely to become realised by a few work sessions, while projects that last over six months form a more solid ground for psychic development to take place. The psychic developments we have come across in our work as consultants are of two kinds: an *increased human capacity* to relate to and handle the changing realities, and *psychic developments in one's affective life.*

The Capacity to Deal with Changing Realities

The human capacity to relate and handle changing realities can further be operationalised as an increased potential for *reality exploration, reality testing* and *reality acceptance.*

Reality exploration implies a capacity to be fully present as a person and to listen and compare observable behaviour with what is being said, with an interest in finding out what is happening in, or with the system in its context of which one is part. Understanding why things are or are not becoming, is coupled through reflection with reality testing. The latter refers to the capacity to withhold acting upon one's impressions, assumptions or understanding of people and systems, until they have been sufficiently explored as to their validity. In other words, there is nothing wrong with having assumptions about people and systems as long as one doesn't take them as truths, until they have been further explored and verified. This does not mean that one readily accepts the interpretations or views of others as more valid than one's own experiences, they are, however, taken into consideration like any other data, before making up one's mind. Reality testing is closely related to one's capacity to distinguish one's expectations from what is really out there, whether it is pleasant or not.

Reality acceptance refers to willingness and a capacity to make *conscious choices* either to accept and adapt to the changing realities, or to take action to change, to counter or to control the new evolving realities or to protest against a faked reality. Reality acceptance is therefore not an automatic adaptive response, but the outcome of a *process of questioning the reality* and subsequently, a willingness to accept the risks inherent in choosing.

Psychic Developments

Members of the client system may benefit from the experience of a psychodynamic approach to organisational issues and develop their psychic functioning further. From our own observations we identified two important dimensions of development. First, members' capacity to more readily make distinctions between their own psychic inner worlds and those of others, seems to be increased. Although empathising with others, they more readily comment on the differences between their own particular experiences and those of others. 'Not quite like that, but somewhat similar . . . ' is often an opening statement to an elaboration of what went on *in themselves*. It leads us to speculate that persons have learned somehow to recognise important differences in the inner world of their colleagues and themselves. Second, members more frequently communicate their feelings and the affects triggered by interactions with other persons or objects, rather than to act on them. We observe an increased use of words expressing feelings in general, whether they are feelings of anger, of being neglected, of being insecure, or of gratefulness, or joy.

This brings us to the rather recent notion of *affect regulation*. It refers to the capacity to monitor, evaluate and modify the intensity and form of expression of affect in the pursuit of goals. Fonagy et al. (2004, p. 92–96) have developed this notion by pointing to specific aspects. As reflected in the earlier definition, affect regulation can serve to regulate the self that experiences the affects. It also implies choice to maintain a certain equilibrium; subsequent actions may be considered but they can also be spontaneous and without reflection. Another aspect in affect regulation is the meaning that affects have for particular individuals. Rather than to 'expunge' the affect by cognition, one allows the affect to be felt for the sake of *self-understanding*. Fonagy et al. (2004) places affect regulation within the process of 'mentalization' whereby the notion receives another quality. "Mentalized affectivity" is consequently defined as "An adult's capacity for affect regulation in which one is conscious of one's affects, while remaining within the affective state. Such affectivity denotes the capacity to fathom the meaning(s) of one's affect states" (p. 96). In other words, one comes to 'understand one's feelings experientially in a way that is emotionally meaningful (vs. intellectually)'.

We do not want to say that these potentials in a psychodynamic approach are realised in all organisational consulting projects. We have not conducted any rigorous research to test our assumptions. Yet, we have observed meaningful psychic developments in some of the members of our consulting projects, discussed in subsequent chapters of this book. Certainly, we do not claim that all psychodynamic approaches will equally enable these potentials to become realised. Indeed, we have some doubts that an approach focussing more on psychic defensive processes, while neglecting the importance of creating conditions that enable psychic and social development, will generate similar outcomes.

FINALISING COMMENTS

In this chapter, you may have noticed some assumptions in our attempts to define psychodynamics. These so called 'premises' are in fact statements that are supported by empirical evidence from the social sciences. Here, we only list them under premises, because we don't think it is appropriate to review all the compiled evidence.

- Meaning attribution is an intermediate process between a reality (a stimulus) and human response or behaviour. Meaning attribution is, however, not just an individual, but also a social process. The meaning, for example, of being unemployed has changed over the last decennia from a problem with one's personal identity (something that dismissed employees and managers tried to hide) towards a diminutive label: 'I'm in transition, or I'm looking for an interesting job'. And the meaning is still changing.

- Human behaviour is most often the product of conscious and unconscious mental processes leading to partial contact with reality, partial experiences, and selective attention and self-censoring. Consequently, what we grasp and call 'reality' is only part of what is out there. Other elements are unconsciously constructed by the human being or projected onto reality.

- Human beings in general tend to avoid pain, anxiety, tensions and uncertainty, while they try to protect and enhance self-esteem. This is what we consider 'normal' behaviour. Tensions, anxieties, internal or external conflicts are inherent to life and human beings do attempt to avoid them.

Consequently, one may expect defensive processes of all sorts to diminish, to resolve or to avoid uncomfortable or embarrassing situations.

- Human beings are basically oriented towards social interaction and contact with reality. Not just in order to survive, to control what is out there, but also to explore and to understand the world and one's existence and to enjoy being alive. Human beings have the capacity to unveil or uncover the reality ('devoiler la réalité') behind the realities directly accessible to our senses, or indirectly through the accounts of others. The realities one finds may be unpleasant, disappointing or even scary, and people may run away from them, but without social interaction and exchanges with reality, the human being develops hallucinations and becomes, psychologically speaking, ill.

- The human being is a whole (psyche and soma) trying to maintain a congruent wholeness of the self: values, beliefs, knowledge, feelings and behaviour. Internal contradictions are avoided, made more congruent or they become disconnected.

We would like to round off the chapter with some brief reflections on the critical competences of persons engaged in psychodynamic work.

- A capacity to maintain a dual attention to the manifest (e.g. content) and the latent, revealed in the languages of images, action and relations. The psychodynamic perspective remains always in the background of the mind. It is the basis for raising questions or for revealing additional meaning to what is happening.

- A capacity to reflect on oneself in action (what one is doing to a system and how the latter 'talks back') and on the soundness of one's involvement. The practitioner allows him/her self to be guided by an ethic of responsibility or a willingness to be accountable for the consequences of one's actions to the extent that they can be foreseen.

- Enough creativity to introduce facilitating and supportive process structures, and system's conditions facilitating goal attainment while enabling healthy mental processes to take their course.

- In view of theoretical curiosity and scientific progress, and for purposes of professional development it may be important to make clear distinctions between concepts, but in practice one avoids using theoretical labels in favour of working with one's understanding of what seems to be required to further development.

- Exercising sound judgement on the appropriateness of the expected results and their consequences in the short and the long term for the system itself, its members and the wider environment. This implies the capacity of 'critical thinking' about one's own work and its implications for the life of future generations. Critical thinking about society holds a central place in psychodynamic work. It serves as an antidote against the trend to educate consultants and managers more as leaders in following the market, than in becoming 'leading parts' in serving mankind.

REFERENCES

Ackoff, R. (1981). *Creating the Corporate Future*. New York: John Wiley & Sons, Inc.

Amado, G. (1980). Psychoanalysis and organization: A cross-cultural approach. *Sigmund Freud House Bulletin*, Vol. IV, 2 (Winter). Also published in: M. Hofman & M. List (Eds) (1994). *Psychoanalysis and Management*. Heidelberg: Psysica-Verlag, 13–22.

Amado, G. (2007). Vida psíquica e organizacao: entre Thanatos e Eros. In: R. Facchin & T. Fisher (Eds) (2007). *Analisis das organizaçoes, perspectivas latinas*. Press Universidade Rio Grande do Sul.

Amado, G. & Amato, R. (2001). Some distinctive characteristics of transitional change. In: G. Amado & A. Ambrose (Eds), *The Transitional Approach to Change*. London: Karnac, 87–117.

Amado, G. & Ambrose, T. (Eds) (2001). *The Transitional Approach to Change*. London: Karnac.

Amado, G. & Vansina, L. (Eds) (2005). *The Transitional Approach in Action*. London: Karnac.

Ambrose, A. (2001). An introduction to transitional thinking. In: G. Amado & A. Ambrose (Eds), *The Transitional Approach to Change*. London: Karnac, 1–29.

Balint, M. (1968). *The Basic Fault: Therapeutic Aspects of Regression*. London: Tavistock Publications.

Barrett, F. (1998). Creativity and improvisation in jazz and organisations. *Organization Science*, **9**, 5, 605–622.

Bennis, W.G., Benne, K.D. & Chin, R. (Eds) (1961). *The Planning of Change: Readings in the Applied Behavioral Sciences*. New York: Holt, Rinehart and Winston.

Bion, W.R. (1961). *Experiences in Groups, and other papers.* London: Tavistock Publications.

Bollas, C. (1987). *The shadow of the object: Psychoanalysis of the unthought known.* London: Free Association Books.

Bradford, L.P., Gibb, J.R. & Benne, K.D. (Eds) (1964). *T-group Theory and Laboratory Method: Innovation in Re-education.* New York: John Wiley & Sons, Inc.

Bridger, H. (2001). The working conference design. In: G. Amado & A. Ambrose (Eds), *The Transitional Approach to Change.* London: Karnac, 137–160.

Bridges, W. (1986). Managing organizational transitions. *Organizational Dynamics,* 24–33.

Brockner, J., Tyler, T.R. & Cooper-Schneider, R. (1992).The influence of prior commitment to an institution on reactions to perceived unfairness: The higher they are, the harder they fall. *Administrative Science Quarterly,* **37**, 241–261.

Buckingham, M. & Coffman, C. (1999). *First, Breaking all the Rules: What the world's greatest Managers do differently.* New York: Simon & Schuster.

Cherns, A. (1976). Principles of socio-technical design. *Human Relations,* **29**, 783–792.

Collins, J.C. & Porras, J.I. (1994). *Built to Last: Successful Habits of Visionary Companies.* New York: HarperCollins.

Clot, Y. (2001). Clinique du travail, clinique du réel. *Journal des psychologues,* **185**, 48–51.

De Geus, A. (2000). *The Living Company.* Boston, Mass.: Harvard Business School Press.

Emery, F. (1972). Characteristics of socio-technical systems. In : L.E. Davis & J.C. Taylor (Eds), *Design of Jobs.* Harmondsworth: Penguin, 177–198.

Emery, M. (1997). The search conference. In: E. Trist, F. Emery & H. Murray (Eds), *The Social Engagement of Social Science: A Tavistock Anthology. Vol. III: The Socio-Ecological Perspective.* Philadelphia: University of Philadelphia Press, 389–411.

Enriquez, E. (1997). *Les jeux du pouvoir et du désir dans l'entreprise.* Paris: Desclée de Brouwer.

Fromm, E. (1941). *Escape from Freedom.* New York: Henry Holt and Co.

Fonagy, P., Gergely, G., Jurist, E. & Target, M. (2004). *Affect Regulation, Mentalization, and the Development of the Self.* New York: Other Press.

Gray, B. (1989). *Collaborating: Finding Common Ground for Multiparty Problems.* San Francisco: Jossey-Bass.

Greenwood, D.J. & Levin, M. (1998). *Introduction to action research: Social research for social change.* London: Sage.

Gut, E. (1989). *Productive and Unproductive Depression: Success or Failure of a Vital Process.* London: Tavistock-Routledge.

Gutmann, D. et al. (2005). *Disillusionment, Dialoque of Lacks.* London: Karnac.

Hayner, P. (2001). *Unspeakable Truths: Facing the Challenge of Truth Commissions.* London: Routledge.

Herbst, Ph. G. (1976). *Alternatives to hierarchies*. Leiden: Martinus Nijhoff.

Hirschhorn, L. (1988). *The Workplace Within: Psychodynamics of Organizational Life*. Cambridge, Mass.: MIT Press.

Hjelholt, G. (1973). Group training in understanding society: the mini-society. In: B. Madsen & S. Willert (Eds) (2006). *Working on Boundaries*. Aarhus: Aarhus University Press, 259–271.

Janis, I.L. (1958). *Psychological Stress*. New York: John Wiley & Sons, Inc.

Janis, I.L. (1959). Decisional conflicts: A theoretical analysis. *J. Conflict Resolution*, **3**, 1, 6–27.

Janis, I.L. (1969). *Stress and Frustration*. New York: Harcourt Brace Jovanovich, Inc.

Janis, I.L. (1982). *Groupthink*. Boston: Houghton Mifflin Co.

Janis, I.L. (1992). Causes and consequences of defective policy making: A new theoretical analysis. In: F. Heller (Ed.), *Decision-making and Leadership*. Cambridge: Cambridge University Press, 11–45.

Janis, I.L. & Mann, L. (1977). *Decision making: A psychological analysis of conflict, choice, and commitment*. New York: Free Press.

Jaques, E. (1955). Social systems as a defence against persecutory and depressive anxiety. In: M. Klein, P. Heimann, & R.E. Money-Kyrle (Eds), *New directions in psychoanalysis*. New York: Basic Books, 478–498.

Jaques, E. (1989). *Requisite Organization*. Arlington, VA.: Cason Hall.

Johnson, Ph. (2004). Shared thinking and interaction in the family business boardroom. *Corporate Governance*, **4**, 33–51.

Kelman, H.C. (1958). Compliance, identification, and internalisation: three processes of attitude change. *J. Conflict Resolution*, **2**, 1, 51–60.

Klein, M. (1940). Mourning and its relation to manic-depressive states. *Int. J. Psycho-Anal.*, **21**, 125–153.

Krantz, J. (1985). Group process under conditions of organizational decline. *J. Applied Behavioral Science*, **11** (1), 1–17.

Krantz, J. (2001). Anxiety and the new order. In: E.B. Klein, F. Gabelnick & P. Herr (Eds), *The Psychodynamics of Leadership. Madison*, CT.: Psychosocial Press, 77–107.

Krantz, J. (2006). Leadership, betrayal and adaptation. *Human Relations*, **59**, 2, 221–240.

Kubler-Ross, E. (1969). *On death and dying*. New York: Macmillan Press.

Lapassade, G. (1971). *L'Analyseur et l'analyste, recherches institutionelles*. Paris: Gauthier-Vilars.

Lévy, A. (1997). *Sciences cliniques et organisations sociales*. Paris: Press Universitaire de France.

Levinson, H. (2002). *Organizational Assessment: A Step-by-Step Guide to Effective Consulting*. Washington, DC.: American Psychological Association.

Lewin, K. (1951). *Field Theory in Social Science*. New York: Harper & Brothers.

Lhuillier, D. (2006). *Cliniques du travail*. Ramonville Saint-Ange: Eres.

McClure, B.A. (1990). The group mind: generative and regressive groups. *J. for Specialists in Group Work,* **15**, 159–170.

Mendel, G. (1992). *La société n'est pas une famille. De la psychoanalyse à la sociopsychanalyse.* Paris: La Découverte.

Menzies I. (1959). The functioning of social systems as a defence against anxiety. In: I. Menzies-Lyth (1988). *Containing Anxiety in Institutions.* London: Free Association Books.

Menzies-Lyth, I. (1988). *Containing Anxiety in Institutions. Selected Essays, Vol. 1.* London: Free Association Books.

Menzies-Lyth, I. (1989). *The Dynamics of the Social.* London: Free Association Books.

Miller, E.J. (1998). The leader with a vision: Is time running out? In: E.B. Klein, F. Gabelnick & P. Herr (Eds), *The Psychodynamics of Leadership.* Madison, CT.: Psychological Press, 3–26.

Moscovici, S. & Doise, W. (1994). *Conflict and Consensus: A General Theory of Collective Decisions.* London: Sage.

Pagès, M. (1968). *La vie affective des groupes.* Paris: Dunod.

Pagès, M., Bonetti, M., de Gaulejac, V. & Descendre, D. (1979). *L'Emprise de l'organisation.* Paris: Presse de France.

Pateman, C. (1970). *Participation and Democratic Theory.* Cambridge, UK: Cambridge University Press.

Perlmutter, H.V. (1965a). Towards a Theory and Practice of Social Architecture. *Tavistock Pamphlet No. 12.*

Perlmutter, H.V. (1965b). L'Entreprise internationale: trios conceptions. *Revue Economique et Sociale.* Université de Lausanne, May.

Pfeffer, J. (1994). *Competitive Advantage Through People: Unleashing the Power of the Work Force.* Boston, Mass.: Harvard Business School Press.

Pfeffer, J. & Sutton, R.I. (2006). *Hard Facts, Dangerous Half-Truths and Total Nonsense: Profiting from Evidence Based Management.* Boston, Mass.: Harvard Business School Press.

Raminez, R. & Drevon, C. (2005). The role and limits of methods in transitional change process. In: G. Amado & L. Vansina (Eds), *The Transitional Approach in Action.* London: Karnac, 195–226.

Redl, F. (1942). Group emotions and leadership. *Psychiatry,* **5**, 573–596.

Resnick, L.B. (1993). Shared cognition: thinking as a social practice. In: L.B. Resnick, J. M. Levine & S.D. Teasley (Eds), *Perspectives on Socially Shared Cognition.* Washington, DC.: American Psychological Association, 1–22.

Schein, E. (1985). *Organizational Culture and Leadership.* San Francisco: Jossey-Bass.

Segal, H. (1973). *Introduction to the Work of Melanie Klein.* London: Hogarth Press.

Sutherland, J.D. (1985/1990). Bion revisited: Group dynamics and group psychotherapy. In: E. Trist & H. Murray (Eds), *The Social Engagement of Social Science.*

Vol. I: The Socio-Psychological Perspective. London: Free Association Books, 119–140.

Sherif, M. & Sherif, C.W. (1953). *Groups in Harmony and Tension.* New York: Harper & Brothers.

Stolorow, R., Atwood, G.E. & Brandchaft, B. (Eds) (1994). *The Intersubjective Perspective.* London: Jason Aronson Inc.

Tjaifel, H. (1982). *Social Identity and Intergroup Behaviour.* Cambridge: Cambridge University Press.

Trist, E.L. & Bamforth, K.W. (1951). Some social and psychological consequences of the longwall method of coal getting. *Human Relations,* **4**, 3–38.

Trist, E. & Murray, H. (Eds) (1990). *The Social Engagement of Social Science. Vol. I: The Socio-Psychological Perspective.* London: Free Association Press.

Trist, E. & Murray, H. (Eds) (1993). *The Social Engagement of Social Science. Vol. II: The Socio-Technical Perspective.* Philadelphia: University of Philadelphia Press.

Trist, E., Emery, F. & Murray, H. (Eds) (1997). *The Social Engagement of Social Science. Vol. III: The Socio-Ecological Perspective.* Philadelphia: University of Philadelphia Press.

Trist, E., Higgin, G.W., Murray, H. & Pollock, A.B. (1963). *Organizational Choice.* London: Tavistock Publications.

Truth and Reconciliation Commission Report, (2003). Date of issue: 23 March 2003. Internet.

Turquet, P.M. (1974). Leadership: the individual and the group. In: A.D. Colman & M.H. Geller (Eds) (1985). *Group Relations Reader 2.* Washington DC.: A.K. Rice Institute, 71–88.

Vansina, L. (1998). The individual in organisations: Rediscovered or lost forever. *European Journal of Work and Organizational Psychology,* **7**, 3, 265–282.

Vansina, L. (1999). Leadership in strategic business unit management. *European Journal of Work and Organisational Psychology,* **8**, 1, 87–108.

Vansina, L. (2000). The relevance and perversity of psychodynamic interventions in consulting and action-research. *Concepts and Transformation,* **5**, 221–248.

Vansina, L. (2004). Over zin en onzin van psychodynamiek voor organisatieadviseurs. In: W. Varwijk & R. van Zijl (Eds), *Strategie moet je samen doen.* Tandem Felix Uitgevers, 159–177.

Vansina-Cobbaert, M.J. (2005). A therapeutic community: A space for multiple transitional change. In: G. Amado & L.Vansina (Eds), *The Transitional Approach in Action.* London: Karnac, 41–70.

Vansina, L. & Taillieu, T. (1996). Revitalisering: een essentieel psychisch proces by strategische herpositionering. In: R. Bouwen, K. De Witte & J. Verboven (Eds), *Organiseren en veranderen.* Leuven: Garant, 211–234.

Weisbord, M.R. & Janoff, S. (1995). *Future Search: An action guide to finding common ground in organizations & communities.* San Francisco: Berrett-Koehler Publ.

Winnicott, D.W. (1951). Transitional objects and transitional phenomena. In: *Collected Papers: Through Paediatrics to Psychoanalysis* (1958). London: Tavistock Publications.

Winnicott, D.W. (1955). Group influences and the maladjusted child. In: *The Family and Individual Development* (1965). London: Tavistock Publications.

Winnicott, D.W. (1971). The place where we live. In: *Playing and Reality*. London: Tavistock.

Whetten, D. (1980). Sources, responses and effects of organizational decline. In:

J. Kimberley, R. Miles & Associates (Eds), *The Organizational Life Cycle*. San Francisco: Jossey Bass.

CHAPTER 7

'Me' in the Problem Situation

Leopold Vansina

Werner Heisenberg, a quantum physicist, made a remarkable observation, which he condensed into just one short sentence: "The observer is part of the field". In the social sciences this observation has a double meaning. The observer not only affects what is observed, but s/he is also affected by what is observed. Practically it means that whenever we enter a social situation we become part of it.[1] Furthermore, when we are part of the situation and a problem arises we are very often not only part of the situation, we are also part of its problem. The idea of taking a neutral observer stance is an illusion. It is cherished by many and broken at one time or another. I would say the sooner, the better. I still vividly remembered when it happened to me.

One Friday evening, coming home from a week-long assignment abroad and looking forward to a relaxing, cosy weekend, I was greeted at the door by my wife. Her face told me something was wrong. On our way to the living room, I asked her with my last reserve of energy: "What has happened?" Without hesitation, she poured out to me a complicated, long and confusing story about the children ... I was all understanding, although overwhelmed,

[1] These findings are currently seen as essential components in psychoanalytic practice (Ferro, 2006; Baranger, Baranger & Mom, 1983).

and sat down beside her. As a good consultant should, I listened carefully to grasp the essence of the problem. When she paused, I was ready and shared reassuringly my understanding of children growing up. I started to feel pleased with myself, with my ability to put the issue in proper perspective, especially after such a tiring week. Suddenly she rose and said in a tone that left no doubt that she was earnest: "Leopold, you are part of the problem. You are too often away from the family!"

Some consultants may think that this incident is more telling for managers. Consultants, at least external ones, come in from the outside. This is true, but it may unjustifiably reduce the relevance of my painful, but enlightening experience. How often do we secretly blame people for resisting our efforts, even when they are trying hard to make us see that our definition of the problem does not match their understanding and/or their expectations about a more satisfactory situation?

In this chapter, I will discuss first some of the major factors that may influence me as well as the other stakeholders in the problem setting. Second, I will suggest some ways of building continuity in the development of the client system after one has left the work on a project. Third, I'll review some of the issues one may face in terminating the work. And I'll end this chapter with a review of the transference and counter-transference an individual actor may experience during the project.

THE PROBLEM WITH PROBLEM DEFINITION

Managers most often grow into a work situation, getting used to the routines of work and the often hectic life of dealing with the daily issues. They are easily drawn in the system, whereby they lose sight of what can and does need improving. In fact many managers no longer work *on* the system, but they are *in* the system, as Tribus (1983) observed years ago. Managers become accustomed and adapted to the daily life of the system. Self-reflection and reviewing may help to take some distance from the work situation, thereby enabling them to get a clearer picture of themselves in the work setting and *see the system at work*. If not, they risk being woken up too late, so to speak, by alarming events or a major incident. Managers entering the situation from the outside (through hiring) may find it easier to sense that something needs to be done. They are in a similar situation to external consultants who have neither been part of the history of the situation, nor part of the organisational dynamic context. They don't carry with them the blind spots of the work routines and the organisational culture. Yet, it would be wrong to think that consultants or newly appointed managers from the outside are privileged to look at the situation with an unspoiled, open mind. They too carry with them their history of experiences, successes and failures that will affect their perceptions and interpretations of a problem, emerging or established, and of their relation with its stakeholders. Only exceptional managers or consultants have sufficient self-confidence, self-understanding and an interest in *finding out* to understand the specificities of the new situation (Vansina, 1988). However, entering an organisation or a particular problem setting with its physical and social qualities, provides unique opportunities to *experience* what is going on and what the system is doing to the newcomer, what the range of expectations of its members is and how the system 'talks back' to early comments or even one's presence. These early experiences are not just cognitive or affective, but the encounters touch our senses and penetrate our bodies. Or, as Lhuilier (2006, p. 75) puts it so properly, one's "listening is incarnated" ("L'écoute est incarnée"). At first, many of these experiences may not be fully understandable, but we hold them till they may become comprehensible in later interactions. Furthermore, these early impressions and sense-making endeavours are likely to differ from people living in the system: the actors, the sponsors or the hierarchy. And so we have entered the domain of 'me' in the problem setting.

Up till now, the scientific disciplines have not come up with a generally acceptable scientific method to define organisational problems from the problem setting. We minimally define a 'problem setting' as an existing situation with all its aspects (e.g. social, technical, physical, economic) in which *dissatisfaction is felt*. The dissatisfaction may vary from discontent with the state of affairs or events to displeasure stemming from the realisation that the full potential of a system, or an inspiring vision is not being materialised.

Problems in organisations and communities never present themselves in a neatly defined form. They emerge in diverse symptoms, for example, complaints, delays, breakdowns, poor quality, incompetence, lack of creativity, sickness leave, accidents. Even when the hierarchy, the sponsor or client presents us with a well-defined organisational problem we can't take that definition for granted. We need to explore how one arrived at that definition.

In the real world, problems are generally messy, fuzzy with a degree of complexity and a need to be *constructed*. Indeed, science-based methods like the *Impact Diagram* derived from operations research and cybernetics (Maruyama, 1963); methodologies like the *Soft System Methodology* (Checkland, 1981) and *System Analysis* (Senge, 1990) originating from systems theory are insightful and useful methods for understanding the complexity of the situation. However, they cannot eliminate the human processes of giving meaning. A problem definition is and remains a *social construction* formed from *the givens* in the problem setting and the *persons involved*. The requisite base is a rich picture of the problem setting: likes and dislikes, all sorts of deficiencies, shortcomings, delays, disappointed expectations and waste of time, space and resources – you name it – from which the stakeholders make sense and relate to. The minimal stakeholders that need to become involved in a problem definition are: (a) the client-system defined as the actors in the system that will endure the change and all those that will benefit or suffer from it; (b) the sponsor of the consultant, or the hierarchy of the manager; and (c) the consultant or manager concerned. Their participation in the construction of a 'good enough' problem definition can either take the form of a joint exploration or of a sequential discussion of the different definitions to arrive at a common ground. However, achieving agreement on a problem construction is not just the outcome of a negotiation process amongst the stakeholders, but of a search process, with all our senses, about assumed causal factors, positive dispositions for improvement and opportunities for anchoring change. Starting with separate provisional definitions is therefore preferable. Furthermore the boundaries of the client-system may change with each problem construction bringing in different persons with different ideas and knowledge. Consequently, we have to accept that problem construction is an *ongoing process* resulting in a 'good enough' definition to start with and that continuing attention should be given during the course of the work to major new insights and developments that call for another meeting with the stakeholders; a meeting to review and eventually re-think or better re-construct the problem from the new data.

The process of problem construction is riddled with partial and ambiguous data. We face all the uncertainties proper to an inquiring dialogue with the problem setting in which we alternate figure and background, symptoms and assumed causes, business and social interests; attempts to reconcile removing dissatisfactions and achieving short and long term objectives; and in which we extend and shrink the boundaries of the organisational setting to locate the primary causes of the problem. Indeed, simply working with that part of the organisation where the problem is experienced may leave the real causes aside, as we will see in chapter 8.

It is evident that such processes engage the stakeholders *personally*. We should not be surprised that in such processes differences in perceptions, judgements, and sense making surface as well as differences in one's relations to the problem setting. The situation itself is conducive for all kinds of defensive reasoning and power plays. Nevertheless, the exchanges of views and relations amongst the major stakeholders are essential to compensate for the inevitable limitations of our human views on issues of importance and to gain commitment.

Some Variables Affecting Knowingly or Not Problem Construction

Values, expectations and objectives. Until we achieve agreement on the desired outcomes, or the objectives of the implied efforts we don't have a project. Yet, implicit goals and visions of the future influence the ways in which we formulate the problem from the problem setting. In some instances, problem settings are manipulated or even created to achieve political ends.[2] Objectives and expectations, however, are easier to debate than values. Differences in values are not readily discussed. Most often this kind of disagreement is brushed aside as a sign that one has 'not fully understood the situation' or one is 'not sufficiently familiar with the way things are done over here!' If not listed in the official value statement of the organisation, values are likely to be considered as private. Yet, values become revealed in how we define organisational issues, and in the anticipated actions to achieve desirable ends. Consequently, values are influencing the way we appreciate the givens and data from the problem setting. For example, engineers tend to see problems in a way that demand technological solutions; financial specialists readily find ways to reduce costs, while H.R. managers often expect solutions from training programmes. Likewise, consultants almost always frame the problem in such a way that they can be helpful. Not necessarily because of commercial interests (or a need to show off), but they may see the problem from the

---

[2] Noam Chomsky, professor at M.I.T. has described several instances in the USA where public "consent was manufactured" to carry out "planned" wars, for example, Vietnam and Iraq. They are very illustrative for what also, may be it less extreme, takes place in our democratic states and in organisations (Mitchell & Schoeffel, 2003; Chomsky, 1987).

same value-system that encouraged them to study a particular discipline or chose a vocation. Most people therefore, spontaneously frame the problem in line with their domain of expertise, and/or in congruence with their preference for a solution. Furthermore, one's position in the organisation makes people see the problem from that perspective. The general manager, for example, may see what emerges as a production scheduling issue in the production department as deficiencies in the management of the flow from customers' demands over production, delivery and invoicing. The problem owner on the other hand, may define it in terms of the difficulties s/he encounters daily, or in other words from where the energy is to do something about it. In order to counter the difficulties with diverse organisational perspectives and values, affecting problem definition without being fully aware, it is recommended that we bring together a multidisciplinary and multilayered team to explore further the experienced problem in view of arriving at a good enough definition that seems to hold desirable and achievable solutions, and is capable of mobilising sufficient energy to take proper action.

Expectations become expressed in the language people use to talk about the issues at hand. We pay particular attention to the verbs one uses: repair, mend, improve, expand or rethink the problem situation. These verbs reveal expectations about the manager or consultant to simply remove the symptoms, improve the functioning of a system, develop, expand or transform it.

Once the problem becomes formulated, it further influences the selection of the kind of consulting or management skills and expertise. The consultant or manager has either been part of the problem construction, or that problem definition was already in the sponsor's mind. In any case, the formal selection of the consultant or project manager increases the chances that the original, implicit or explicit, problem definition, right or wrong, becomes confirmed.

Boundaries of time and space. The boundaries that fall within the authority of the sponsor are often spontaneously taken as the boundaries of the problem situation. If one does venture outside those confines one often meets reservations even clear embargo for a variety of reasons. One may wish to avoid expanding the problem situation, to maintain ownership of the problem, or opening up an issue that will trigger difficult responses from one's peers and boss. Yet, extending and retracting the boundaries of the problem setting may be a legitimate requirement to come to a good understanding of the interdependencies with adjacent or connecting systems before we can soundly define the problem. Furthermore, boundaries may serve as a defensive purpose to the extent that the manager or sponsor can either include or exclude him/herself from the problem setting. This is to avoid facing one's part in the problem and/or one's active involvement in its solution. Likewise boundaries of time may become established whereby the history of the problem situation becomes either included or excluded. Yet, as we have seen, the history of the problem situation is an important factor in how we define the problem and the actions.

Mental capabilities. The fuzziness of data and the complexity of the problem setting, the values, expectations and objectives, the boundaries of time and space all interact in the process of problem construction. They challenge our mental capabilities as well as our personal integrity, while struggling with uncertainties and tensions. Mental capabilities refer to the person's ability to work (the exercise of judgement and discretion in making decisions in carrying out goal directed activities), which is function of his/her complexity of mental processing of information (Jaques, 1989). Mental capabilities or work capacity correlate only mildly with intelligence. Yet, they can be reliably measured and predict future developments in work capacity (Jaques & Cason, 1994). In order to build requisite organisations the mental capabilities of a person must match the mental requirements of a position at any level in the organisational hierarchy. A mismatch leads to underperformance and stress on one hand, or boredom on the other hand. A useful indicator of a person's mental capabilities is time-span or the longest task a person can envisage and undertake independently, before it can reach completion. The required time-span and scope increase the higher one moves up in the organisational hierarchy. Some managers may become promoted as recognition for their past performances, or because they were the best available candidate, but may reach a level beyond their mental capabilities. The consequence is that they organise the work and construct organisational issues in line with the limits of their capabilities. The same applies for consultants. Not all consultants have the mental capabilities, plus the necessary skills and knowledge, to deal with the range of issues that one faces at various levels in an organisational hierarchy. Yet, as all human beings, we non-consciously construct the problem according to our limited mental or work capacity. In practice it means that a consultant having the mental capabilities to work effectively on issues at the level of business unit manager may be unsuited to solve issues proper to the corporate level. Issues of teambuilding or negotiations skills may well be dealt with effectively at that higher level since they don't require the mental capabilities to engage in collegial disputes about the content of the tasks proper to the corporate level. If the latter is the deeper cause of disagreement within the corporate board, only the psychodynamic aspects of the issues will be dealt with. It is therefore important for a consultant to know one's mental capabilities as a precondition to accept work within one's mental limitations. Without such awareness one may conceive and construct the project according to one's available work capacities.

All these factors are grouped together under the notion of a frame. A *frame* is any kind of structure that organises a person's experiences of occurrences perceived as outside (e.g. an accident, a problem setting) or inside oneself (e.g. a headache, an increased heartbeat) and render them meaningful. Goffman (1974) conceives frames as that which governs our perception and representation of the situation in which we are acting. They facilitate people to locate, perceive, identify and label phenomena. He distinguishes two kinds of frames: natural frameworks identify occurrences as purely physical, without any human interferences; and social frameworks that "provide background understanding for events that incorporate the will, aim, and controlling efforts of an intelligence, a living agency, the chief one being the human being" (p. 22). Frames are implied in human responses to a situation. Entman (1993) in his definition focuses on the *active* function of frames: "to frame is to select some aspects of perceived reality and make them more salient in a communicating text, in such a way as to promote a particular problem definition, causal interpretation, moral evaluation, and/or treatment recommendation" (p. 52).

Frames can be taken as the object of study. This may however take the researcher to see frames as divorced from the individual characteristics of the person selecting, consciously or unconsciously, a particular frame. Frames can be learned, consciously by attending teaching classes, or unconsciously through social interaction. Frameworks are largely, socially embedded (Schruijer & Vansina, 2006). It has been found, for example, that political parties, churches and other institutions provide their members with schemes of attributions for common and problematic occurrences (Semin, 1980).

The Importance of Problem Definition

Problem construction is an important process in consulting and project work. First, it defines knowingly or not the boundaries of the client-system; thereby including or excluding the parts of the organisation that need to be *involved* in the improvement efforts. Second, without a good enough agreement amongst the stakeholders on problem definition, values, approach and desired outcomes one does not have a genuine project. Such an agreement is, however, not static, it may fall apart in the light of new information or changes within or outside the organisation. Third, a problem definition leaves an imprint in the mind that can only become modified by an extra effort of reframing, or a confrontation with a differently framed definition.

Let me try to illustrate how a problem definition (a) shapes our conception of the client-system, and (b) channels our thinking about action alternatives. Since the drug issue leaves not one of us untouched, I use the drug problem, rather than an example from organisational life.

The late president Ronald Reagan in his first term of office summed up the problem as: "the uncontrolled production of cocaine by Columbian farmers". Let us reflect a moment on what such a definition leaves as an imprint in our minds. Implicitly, the action to be taken is mobilised towards controlling the production of cocaine abroad and controlling its influx in the country. In this way, the client-system becomes divided into those who have to suffer from the action: the Columbian farmers and those who will benefit from it: the American society. Society as such does not have a problem, although its citizens are buying the drugs with all its terrible consequences. Yet, the American society as a whole is seen as benefitting from the change! After years of experienced failure and conflicts in Columbia, President George Bush senior, framed the drug issue in his inaugural speech in the following words: "There are few clear areas in which we as a society must rise up united and express our intolerance. The most obvious now is drugs. And when that first cocaine was smuggled in on a ship, it may as well have been deadly bacteria, so much has it hurt the body, the soul of our country. And there is much to be done and to be said, but take my word for it: This scourge will stop" (Bush, 1989). Again we are made to think that the cause of the problem lies abroad. Society has to rise and eradicate the importation of drugs. American society does not have a problem. The problem boundaries are drawn in such a way that the citizens are seen as playing no active part in the problem. And again the American society is the beneficiary of whatever efforts are organised against illegal imports. In both examples, the boundaries are drawn in congruence with the dominant political and cultural value frame: America can't have any problems except those created by an outsider. At least, that is how these American presidents frame problems for their citizens.

Imagine that we frame the problem differently: In our modern societies, we find a number of human beings, willing to do anything to escape from the painful, existential realities of daily life, by either taking drugs, in whatever form, or by making money in a fast and easy way. In line with this problem construction, we might legalize drugs, as eventually was done with alcohol; thereby, reducing the killings amongst drug-dealers, and the huge financial profits from the drug business, which often result in political and military corruption. It would enable the respective administrations to relocate the huge budgets of the anti-drug brigades, the criminal courts, and the prisons to study and remedy the causal texture in society that encourages 'escaping from the existential realities of daily life'. A different client-system emerges in our minds, in which those who have to endure the action are also the likely beneficiaries; we as citizens are all part of the client-system. In the construction process different values and responsibilities are activated; and a new range of actions and approaches – short and long term – can be considered as relevant.

From this example, we may have noticed that a problem construction leaves an imprint in our minds that modifies our way of looking at the problem setting, and the stakeholders involved. It even shapes the meanings of the givens in the setting. Consequently, through the act of trying to make sense of the givens, we become responsible and accountable to the problem setting. We set a frame for action to deal either with the supply side leaving the customers in peace, or we include dealers and drug addicts as symptoms of our modern societies. Reframing the problem, although of utmost importance, demands an extra effort to overcome the imprints of earlier problem definitions.

Often and beyond our awareness, problem construction draws our whole selves into the process, our experiences, our values, our imagination, our expectations and expertise in what could be the causes of the difficulties, our ways of coping with tensions, and in what could be done to achieve a more desirable future. All these factors become more active and complex in the course of the discussions to achieve a 'good enough' shared definition. Power and politics enter the scene and we may be tempted to formulate a problem definition that is more acceptable than effective, easier to mobilise energy for action than to solve or dissolve the problem, more designed to appear as 'doing something' than to take appropriate action. Or we accept a definition in the hope that during the project we may be able to achieve acceptance of a more proper problem definition, based on data collected in the meantime. Not so seldom, the exchanges amongst stakeholders slip into a debate about what definition is right, and away from appreciating the added value of different views for understanding the problem setting, our relations to that setting and the persons involved.

Underneath this complex interplay of factors, the sponsor or client-system may be responding to the views of the new manager or consultant which may draw light on blind spots, touch upon what may not be recognised, or stir up fears and anxieties about what might happen if one accepts their problem definition, its implied values, actions and desired outcomes. These aroused fields of tensions, concerns, hopes and expectations need to be checked on their reality base, relevance and subsequently be worked through. Therefore it is important to realise that the *'consulting work'* or *'consultative management task'* begins with the problem construction and achieving agreement on the necessary conditions for good project work. In my experience, it is not exceptional that these discussions take several meetings, spread over several months before a workable agreement and realistic work relations can be achieved. Too often this is simply conceived as the *contractual* phase. In fact the underlying process is about gaining *insights, confidence, developing workable relations* and finding enough *security* to face and accept the inevitable uncertainties and fears about what might come up *during* the project and *afterwards*.

Two important remarks: first, the so-called diagnostic and contractual phase *are not phases* in the proper sense of the word, but exchanges between the stakeholders about the changing problem setting and/or new insights, relations, concerns, fears and anxieties. The interplay between diagnosing and contracting requires continual attention and time of managers or consultants resulting in periodical exchanges and reflective discussions with the stakeholders. Whenever the sponsor or hierarchy is part of the client-system these exchanges become natural and are easy to organise. More energy is required when the sponsor or hierarchy is located outside the client-system. In both cases it is important to keep the history alive: where we found ourselves at the start, where we currently are, and our views on further developments. Second, diagnosing and contracting are processes that affect the 'me' in the situation as well as the other stakeholders. Uncertainties about the correctness of one's views and one's relationship with the other stakeholders are aroused. One's professionalism and integrity are questioned in self-reflections about ones interventions. In other words, managers and consultants are working on *two tasks*: the task of achieving and maintaining agreement on the problem construction, and the other task of recognising and managing the 'me' part.

BUILDING CONTINUATION

In the context of problem construction and building continuation, it is worthwhile remembering the wise advice of the late Harold Bridger: "One always starts from where the client is". The 'client' here may either refer to the sponsor, one's boss or the client-system. Harold's statement is often misunderstood as meaning *going along* with the client's views and thoughts! Or, *staying* with the issues that hold the client's energy! In fact, he meant something quite different, namely that we always keep in mind where the 'client' is in *the level* of sophistication of our discussions with him or her; in building on *how s/he sees the problem* and the *expected outcomes* and what *action taking* s/he has in mind. It means *working from* where the client is *towards* where the client could or should be in order to deal effectively with the problem setting. Working towards means helping the 'client' to see other aspects in the problem setting and/or in him/herself – which may be disquieting – and may eventually lead to another problem definition, other objectives and other ways of solving it. Harold Bridger was quite aware of the fact that the client's first conception of the issue may be partially correct, but also partially riddled with personal and contextual preoccupations, which need to be clarified, understood, and worked through. This working towards, starting from where the 'client' is, is genuine *consulting* or *consultative work*. Whenever the client has moved forward through new insights, and a joint agreement on a new problem definition is achieved, we keep in mind where we started. In later discussions, or progress reviews, we may recount the original request of the 'client' and how we jointly arrived at new insight into the issue or at a new approach so that progress can be seen rather than forgetting the original request.

Psychodynamic consultants – managers very seldom – may forget that they are a source of knowledge and experience, besides simply being a process consultant with the additional functions of holding and containing. The *dissemination* of knowledge and skills remains an important function. We not only share our frameworks, our ways of mental processing of data and our ways of solving problems, but we are also actively involved in creating 'facilitating structures', 'supportive process structures' and let's not forget, conditions to improve the dynamics of work-systems in more sustainable ways. First, there is dissemination of knowledge as part of building continuity of development and dealing with corrective actions in turbulent times. Consultants, more so than managers, are concerned about what must be left behind so that the organisational and personal processes of development can continue their course when one has left the organisation. Creating conditions for continuation and anchoring the project in the organisation are critical tasks that should be on one's mind from the beginning, and not just picked up when the project is reaching its final stage. In a way, the consultant/change manager is like a surgeon performing a heart transplant. The sheer transplantation of a heart does not appear to be the most critical part in the surgical intervention. Taking care that the new heart is not rejected as a foreign body is. The better the 'new' system becomes linked to the wider organisation (clarifying and working through the new interdependencies with connecting systems), and related to the history of the organisation, the more that 'foreign body' becomes integrated. Moss-Kanter (1985) used the notion of 're-writing history' not to encourage falsification of the company's history, but to highlight values, periods or events in the past to expose continuity over changes and over time. Integrating and implementing improvement ideas of the actors in the system, the so-called 'local theories', and building on existing 'good practices' and/or informal, innovations can also strengthen the anchoring of introduced changes. Second, dissemination plays an important role in learning. The consultant/manager is also concerned that all the endeavours will enable the client or work system to solve similar problems in the future, independently from an outside intervention; in other words that they have learned from the experience and gained sufficient confidence to work with it. In this domain of dissemination, managers have a great advantage over consultants. They are more familiar with the contextual variables and they are with their presence and position an important continuing actor.

'ME' IN TERMINATING A PROJECT

When I drive or fly home after rounding off a consulting project, my mind wanders over the work we did and I come to feel that now, at the end, I finally understand what the issues really were. Yet, I am quite sure, that if I started where we left off with this new understanding, that after some work and at that new ending, I again would come to a different view on the organisational issue. I often wondered why? Is it that when ending intensive joint work, we have gathered so much information and experience that in retrospect we see a different picture, which we believe to be more accurate? But, also during the course of our work we develop new insights and adjust/change the original problem definition and courses of action. What is than so special about ending? Is it the end itself that makes our reflections more profound and leading to a rounded-off whole which is unchangeable because new experiences with the client are unlikely to come about and perturb that 'Gestalt'? Or, is it that issues in an organisation are always moving along with changes in the organisation and/or in its environment? I believe there is another important reason as well. We start a project with information that we are told and with some hunches about what might be going on in the organisation. While we are working, however, more information surfaces that could not be revealed earlier because it was unconscious or it had to remain concealed. Furthermore, working with this additional information and in our attempts to set a developmental process in motion, we often touch upon other issues, old and new ones. So for various reasons we arrive with a 'Gestalt' at the end of an assignment. Yet, it is against that final 'Gestalt of understanding' that we largely come to appreciate how well we worked as managers or consultants.

Terminating a project of some importance confronts the 'me' in the situation with at least two issues. An appreciation of how successfully we worked as professionals and a meeting with ourselves in 'letting things go'.

Success is a very general notion, often felt as the final note in a concert. Yet, it should always be clarified by the criteria in use. As consultant, I use three criteria. The first one deals with the *quality of my work* appreciated in three aspects: the quality of *professional standards* adhered to; the extent to which *processes of development* were set into motion while achieving the project objectives; and the degree to which the work was congruent with my *social responsibility* as a professional and as a citizen of the world. The second deals with the degree of *satisfaction of the stakeholders*, not only the sponsor and the client-system, but also the people in the organisation and those with whom they work (e.g. suppliers, contractors and customers). The third criterion tries to estimate the extent to which the project was completed without unnecessary *depletion of the client's resources* (waste of time, money and materials). The three combined produce a global, subjective self-appreciation, with all its limitations. The satisfaction of the sponsor and the client-system can readily be assessed in a more objective way, but this is seldom done. More frequently, follow-up studies are organised either by myself or by a third person to evaluate the outcomes of the consulting work. From these reports one can learn. They may change the original self-appraisal, one way or another. However, it is the global, subjective self-appraisal at the end of the project that largely affects our experiences of 'letting go' and letting the client carry on with the work.

The 'me' seems to respond differently when we terminate good or dubious work. Leaving a client-system with whom we worked hard and well, may stir up some ambivalent feelings of being pleased with the progress made, some gratitude for the learning and at the same time some sadness at breaking off important relations and sometimes ... of being no longer needed. The ending on the other hand of a dubious project may generate quite different mixed feelings of anger and frustration with oneself and/or with one or more stakeholders, and some kind of relief that it is all over. These feelings are likely to impact how we terminate a project and what we can learn from exploring the work in some depth.

Self-appraisals don't come up just at the end of the project; they are part of an ongoing process. However, at the end they obtain that special quality we referred to earlier. During the work, if we don't progress as expected, there is still hope and energy to redress the situation; yet, hope and energy that gradually diminish as the end comes in sight. It is the impact of this emotional state that I like to explore a little further. Ideally, the ending should be planned so that it does not come like a sudden departure, an abandoning of the client, but takes the form of a gradual fading out of the project: less frequent meetings, a more coaching role towards the client who is picking up the slack or just taking over. Then the last meeting may be organised as a joint overall review with a serious promise of a follow-up, to be planned at a much later stage. A follow-up is then an opportunity to appreciate the continuity in the initiated improvements, which may end with some suggestions or encouragements to deal with unforeseen changes or consequences, and an honest recognition of the joint work achieved.

When not much progress is realised in the project and the time has come to terminate, hope and energy may have been drained to such an extent that one – consciously or not – lets the project end like a burning candle. Such projects are however most interesting to learn from, if the client too is willing to join in a review. More often than not the stakeholders don't wish to invest in such an event. In one instance, I did succeed in bringing them together for a half day. It was amazing how often we misunderstood one another. Eventually, we became so interested in why it all went sour that we decided to pick up where we left off and continued our work with a newly formulated project.

It does happen that a project is stopped *before* completion. For example, because of decisions taken higher up in the organisation (e.g. merger and acquisitions, mutations of sponsor, introduction of a new manager or radical changes in strategy and/or new developments in the environment). The project can also be stopped because of a breakdown of confidence. Each of these unplanned terminations calls for a special response. In the first instance, when changes higher up in the organisation disrupt the project, we can try to arrange a meeting with the (new) management to review the situation and explore whether a continuation or a reframing of the project is meaningful. If not, I suggest that the sponsors inform the client-system of the changes in the business situation and the reasons why the project needs to be terminated or postponed. If at all possible, I like to be present out of respect for the work that we did together in the client-system and to indicate my consent with the decision. To my recollection, I have never had a termination of the project due to a breakdown in confidence. As a standard practice, I include in the contractual agreement the provision that the contract can be terminated after a joint review of our experiences. Insurmountable differences in views on the problem-setting, however, have led to a decision on my part not to continue the relationship; either because the necessary conditions for effective work could not be provided, or because of differences in values. For example, when after a first discussion of the data on the organisational diagnosis, the sponsor did not wish to invest in taking further actions, I tried to and obtained his permission to talk to the board in his presence. However, at the board meeting only he and his wife showed up and they could not choose between either continuing with the current centrally controlled management practice or securing the survival of the company by setting up business units managed by competent persons. Five years later the company went bankrupt. On other occasions, it was me who couldn't agree with the sponsor's way of dealing with the issue. The discussion then ended with my resignation, but I did inform the client-system about my inability to deal properly with the issue without further elaboration of the reasons of my decision.

Leaving a client when you have been working together intensively is not easy, even when one prepared the transition well. A relationship has been formed and has come to an end, at least materially. There is usually a longing to hear something about how 'what is left behind' is developing. Some consultants may struggle with the absence of being needed. This is not much of an issue if one has a fully booked agenda. One moves on to other projects, which carry some promises of new things to discover.

Departing from a disappointing experience is even more difficult, in particular when one didn't have any review with the client. Whenever that happens to me, retrospective reflections keep popping up in my mind and I have to process my project experiences with my colleagues. I need to understand why things happened the way they did. Without some working through, this experienced failure becomes a burden and an interference with effective work in the future.

WHAT ABOUT TRANSFERENCE AND COUNTER-TRANSFERENCE IN OUR PRACTICE?

At a symposium of psychoanalytic-informed consultants, I was asked to talk about my way of teaching a class of more than 350 engineers at our University. During my presentation, one consultant rose and asked me what kind of transferential relationship I experienced with these students. The question came as a surprise. I told them – as best I could – about the kind of cartoons some of the students had drawn and that I was sometimes portrayed in their annual 'burlesque'. I went on to how the relation with the class varied with the topics discussed and my successful or unsuccessful attempts to keep their minds on the subject. But the consultant insisted and wanted to know whether the students took me as a father figure or an older sibling. I told her that I had never taken that perspective, and then went on with what I had felt in my interactions with the class.

I recount this event, because many psychoanalysts who are interested in consulting put a heavy emphasis on the importance of transferential relations in their practices as if they are very special relationships. Quite a few practitioners still take those relations back to early experiences in the family. Thereby they make them not only reductionistic, but also unsuitable to work with as a consultant or manager in an organisation. I hold a different and more 'nuanced' view.

Czander and Eisold (2003) emphasise the ubiquitous presence of transference and counter-transference in all relationships. This is very true; our experiences affect our current relations. But what is their relative impact on the work? And, if they do, to what extent should these transferred experiences be traced back to their origin in the context of consulting work? Work experiences of the recent past could be accessible and relevant, but I won't touch experiences that may go back to early childhood or family life. In my view, the focus on transference and counter-transference is somewhat one-sided in the client-consultant relation and at the expense of the relation with the problem situation both the client and the consultant/manager are confronted with. I like to distinguish three different relations: (a) relations of stakeholders (including the consultant or manager) with the problem setting; (b) the relations with the organisation or the broader system in its context in which the problem setting is located; and (c) the relations between and amongst the various stakeholders and the consultant/manager. All three, as we have seen in discussing the problem construction, have an impact on the way we conceive a problem, achieve a contractual agreement and on the effectiveness of the work. Here, I want to share my experiences of the 'me' in my relations with the stakeholders.

As a general working principle, I always try to stay in touch with what I feel is going on in my *interactions* with other persons during my work and be attentive to what may come up from 'Atlantis' within that space. After sorting out what is 'me' and 'not-me', I'll work with these feelings and their possible meaning if and when deemed relevant to the task in front of me. Working with them may take the form of modifying my interactions or using these feelings for inquiry, or I may bring them in for further exploration. The quality of these feeling may range from 'having to be the best consultant', 'not being good enough', 'distrust', 'willingness to accept any of my proposals', 'never getting enough out of my contributions', 'presenting the issues in human or social terms only', 'making me feel that I can help them', 'giving me time and space, but not continuing the work while I am absent', 'feeling that we are making progress, or of not being helpful', 'doubts about my interest in their problem', 'having to be careful not to come across as judgemental', to 'feeling that I can speak my mind'. There are many more experiences, too many and often too complex to list them in a few words. However, I'll never in my consulting work categorise or bring those in relation to early family experiences. I may inquire into them in words or feelings used by the client to communicate openly or in more covered ways his expectations, fears and concerns about talking and/or working with me, and how s/he (or they) want to use me. An often-sensitive domain is when I come forward with suggestions or interventions that are felt to pertain to managing the organisation. It is as if one does not expect from a psychodynamic consultant that s/he will intervene on the content itself; as if this remains the prerogative of the manager in charge. Combining content and process, and advancing possible linkages often seems unsettling the client. It is often that part of my role that is stirring up more 'unhappy learning', than working on the group or intergroup dynamics.

A helpful way in sorting out the 'me' from the 'not-me' is to work on more than one consulting project at the same time. We can then compare and differentiate our experiences. Important is that we don't take them readily as 'transferential' in the psychoanalytic sense of the word, but work with them as *my experiences* in the evolving relationship/interactions. Often earlier experiences with consultants or managers may indeed be carried over, but whether they stem from early childhood or not is not so important as long as we work with them to clear out relations that affect the task.

Consulting is not coaching, although personal talks (either with sponsor, the client or some actors within the client-system) are part of most consulting projects or managing. Most of the consulting work takes place in teams, in large groups or loose groups of people (task forces, project teams or larger work units) relevant to the subject. The social context of these work settings often obscures transferential phenomena because they are spread out over different persons, not just the consultant. In such settings, we may get a feeling about something that is part of the culture of that organisation or work system. Differentiating organisational culture from transferential relations with me as a person, and not with my role is facilitated when working with more than one consultant on the same project, for example, with an internal consultant. However, when working alone, we can observe whether the same attitude is displayed with other persons in the organisation or with other suppliers, currently or in the recent past. But this distinction may be less important that one's willingness and skills for working through the experiences of the relation.

A more difficult issue in my experience is counter-transference in its various, multi-coloured forms: liking or disliking to work on particular organisational problems (e.g. lay-offs, intercultural issues) or for particular clients (e.g. banks, public authorities, or persons e.g. older, younger, men, women). Counter-transference may reveal itself, first during the discussions on problem construction, and later during the work on the project. In the problem construction it may be blended with the first experiences, and differences in values and objectives. It tells me something about myself or about something in relation to the client that may be important to explore. The problem construction 'phase' is a suitable testing ground where one can do this exploration: find common ground, a match of our 'chemistries' and a possibility of working with or through 'troubling' relations. Self-reflection and integrity are critical here. If in one's subjective appreciation, it does not feel that one can work together, one had better turn down the assignment, and refer the client to another person. Counter-transference experiences, however, may come up during the project itself, like feelings that one is not being told the whole truth, suspicion that confidentiality is misused or impressions about other intangible things. Here, the value of having the agreement that the project can be reviewed comes in handy. There is time to explore and to work on it and if this is impossible, one may even terminate the relation by mutual consent. Also clients don't want to work with consultants who don't feel good in their relations with the problem, the sponsor or the client-system. These are extreme cases and rather exceptional. But what about those incidents less tangible in which one feels awkward and one doesn't know why? Something is happening *between* 'me' and the stakeholders or the problem setting. Self-reflection does not make me any wiser. It may be something out there that triggers in me an oversensitive spot or something that I have not properly worked through. Or it may be something that is induced in me, *projected into me* so to speak, like a feeling of guilt that I can't place or justify, or a feeling of being incompetent, while I know that I have solved similar problems quite successfully in the past. In both cases, it is best to talk about it with a trusted colleague to clarify its nature, before taking it back to either the relationship (counter-transference), or to the work situation in which it was induced (projective identification). In this last instance one should be careful, sensing whether the people in the work situation are able to bear these feelings of guilt or incompetence so that their basis can be explored. These explorations are ways of enabling 'working through'.

The psychodynamic perspective is not another role the consultant or manager takes when deemed relevant; a role or a hat taken when one gets stuck in the work, or when a social or personal issue can no longer be avoided or denied. The psychodynamic perspective is part of 'me' and the 'me' becomes interwoven in the perspective on what is going on in our world. In the beginning, we may be rather clumsy in inquiring, in working with a psychodynamic approach, but with time and effort we can grow into it, like in a profession (Skovholt & Rönnestad, 1995).

In this chapter, we discussed primarily the field of tensions consultants may face in their practices. However, managers may meet similar issues in working on their projects or assignments. There are, however, major differences between both professions. While consultants are called in to solve issues, managers are often problem creators. Part of their responsibilities is to identify trends in technological developments, detect strategic changes in the moves of competitors, in customers' expectations and in the wider environment that will affect their business or work unit; developments that call for a break with the status quo. By talking about these developments, as a way of announcing forthcoming changes, they create problems for their people. In other words, managers themselves create projects they will have to carry out. They are responsible for initiated projects and largely for their effective implementation. Consultants are responsible for their advice and interventions, and only accountable for the proper implementation. Furthermore, managers may not enjoy the same degrees of freedom to turn down projects; their stakes are much higher since their careers in the organisations are put (or at least felt) at risk. For managers in particular, the question stands: 'What are the alternatives?'

REFERENCES

Baranger, M., Baranger, W. & Mom, J. (1983). Process and non-process in analytic work. *International Journal of Psychoanalysis*, **64**, 113–28.

Bush, G. (1989). Administration of George Bush, January 20. *Weekly Compilation of Presidential Documents, January 27*.

Checkland, P. (1981). *Systems Thinking, Systems Practice*. New York: John Wiley & Sons, Inc.

Chomsky, N. (1987). The manufacture of consent. In: J. Peck (Ed.), *The Chomsky Reader*. New York: Pantheon.

Czander, W. & Eisold, K. (2003). Psychoanalytic perspectives on organizational consulting: Transference and counter-transference. *Human Relations*, **56**, 4, 475–490.

Entman, R. (1993). Framing: Towards clarification of a fragmented paradigm. *Journal of Communication*, **43**, 4, 51–58.

Ferro, A. (2006). *Psychoanalysis as Therapy and Storytelling*. London, Routledge.

Goffman, E. (1974). *Frame Analysis: An Essay on the Organization of Experience*. Boston: Northeastern University Press.

Jaques, E. & Cason, K. (1994). *Human Capability*. Arlington, VA.: Cason Hall & Co.

Jaques, E. (1989). *Requisite Organization*. Arlington, VA. : Cason Hall & Co.

Lhuilier, D. (2006). *Cliniques du travail*. Paris: Erès.

Maruyama, M. (1963). The second cybernetics: Deviation-amplifying causal processes. *American Scientist*, 51, 164–179.

Mitchell, P.R. & Schoeffel, J. (Eds) (2003). *Understanding Power: The Indispensable Chomsky*. London: Vintage.

Moss-Kanter, R. (1985). *Change Masters: Corporate Entrepreneurs at Work*. London: Unwin Paperbacks.

Schruijer, S. & Vansina, L. (2006). The meaning of 'social' in interpersonal conflict and its resolution. In: M.S. Herrman (Ed.), *Handbook of mediation: Bridging theory, research and practice*. Oxford: Blackwell Publishing, 326–343.

Semin, G. (1980). A gloss on attribution theory. *British Journal of Social and Clinical Psychol.*, **19**, 291–300.

Senge, P. (1990). *The Fifth Discipline.* New York: Doubleday.

Skovholt, T.M & Rönnestad, M.H. (1995). *The Evolving Professional Self: Stages and Themes in Therapist and Counselor Development.* New York: John Wiley & Sons, Inc.

Tribus, M. (1983). *Managing to Survive in a Competitive World.* Center for Advanced Engineering Study. M.I.T.

Vansina, L. (1988). The general manager and organisational leadership. In: M. Lambrecht (Ed.), *Corporate Survival: Managing into the Nineties.* Leuven: Leuven University Press, 127–151.

CHAPTER 8

Groups as the Tip of an Iceberg: Locating Issues in Their Context

Leopold Vansina

INTRODUCTION

Too easily organisational problems become localised in groups like boards, management teams, project teams or work units while the causes of the difficulties may reside elsewhere in the organisation or even in the community. Groups form a social entity, which is readily recognised and often serve as a platform on which difficulties emerge or become acted out. Consequently, its members are the first to experience the discomfort within their own territory and energy can more readily be mobilised to do something about it. Furthermore, groups have been and are in focus in the literature and in a variety of management programmes, for example, Group Relations, team building and as semi-autonomous building blocks for organising work. Groups, however, are embedded in organisations and communities, a real context from which difficulties become exported, consciously or not. In analogy with an organic system, I say that it may not be wise to look too closely for the problem causes there where the pain and difficulties are experienced.

In this chapter, I will present some ideas and findings that will help managers and consultants in locating the problem within its wider social embeddedness.

First, I'll briefly discuss some of the common factors that may prevent us from looking beyond the group: context and history, boundaries, and human efforts to maintain a relative autonomy. Secondly, I'll put the focus on management teams as the tip of the iceberg and provide a project to illustrate a useful model to work with this phenomenon. In a third paragraph, I look at project teams, which may also be just the tip of an iceberg, namely a platform for acting out inter-group conflicts. Finally, I'll review and discuss the import and export mechanisms of problems from one part to another in organisations.

Common Factors that Obscure the Embeddedness of Groups

Inaccessibility of context and history

Managers in particular are sensitive to interpersonal frictions that interfere with their real work to achieve task accomplishment. They wish these would go away and if this does not happen they call in consultants to provide some training in interpersonal relations or to work on the team. Little attention is paid to the physical and system realities: context, goals, roles, resources, procedures and technologies the group is exposed to and to its history. Yet, they pertain to the responsibilities of management in general.

In psychology, we don't have many formulas. Kurt Lewin produced one, which is extremely simple as well as practical. *Behaviour* (performance) is a function of the *individual* (dispositional) and the *situation* (situational factors). Situation stands here for the social and physical conditions, as well as for strategies, systems, structures and technologies to which that person happens to be exposed. Whenever one assumes that the causes of the difficulties reside *only* in personal dispositions and psychic processes (intra-, interpersonal and/or psychodynamics), one risks *'psychologising'* the issues. On the other hand, reducing the complexity by neglecting the possible psychological components is likely to result in temporary solutions. Working on these two aspects of human behaviour in sequence may make it look simpler, but one loses the richness of the interactions and interdependencies between persons and the given structural situation, in other words, an understanding of the realities of work as a whole. The two aspects must be taken into account simultaneously by studying the interactions between human beings and the given situation like made explicit in socio-technical system thinking.

Consultants from outside the system work with the knowledge they have about a system and with the information they can derive from inquiry, from listening and sensing what that system is doing in the here-and-now. The problem with contextual variables is that they are difficult to get access to when consulting is restricted to a management board, a team or a project group in *a retreat*, in 'isolation' from the organisational setting and history. Either because the sponsor has localised (confined) the issue in a particular group or because further access to contextual and structural conditions is denied or seen as irrelevant for the work of a good subcontractor, be it a coach, a consultant or a team facilitator. The organisational context then may disappear into the background. It becomes hidden but also revealed in the members' interactions and in the behaviour of the group. Or the context is talked about in more or less distorted ways, and/or may become projected on the staff and into the conference design.[1] For example, the organisational context may become expressed in: (a) sporadic references to strategic decisions, financial and other empirical data, and/or imposed conditions and constraints; and (b) through blurring phenomena, for example, basic assumptions (Bion, 1961). Members of the organisational unit take their assignment or task as sacred, as if an omnipotent, unquestionable sponsor or boss is mentally present in the group (which might reveal dependence). The group is stuck in criticising shortcomings in information, resources or time, as if task completion would otherwise be easy to achieve (maybe related to fight-flight). Or the group invests all its hope for success in the additional study groups they create in dealing with a difficult assignment (which may be a constructive proposal or it might refer to the underlying basic assumption of pairing).

While working on the assignment, the restrictive view on the group can be widened by taking an appropriate *mental frame*. The frame consists of three dimensions. Each of them can be defined by its extremes, which can be separated by a boundary that is not a line but an area of interplay. The first dimension is well known and can be labelled as the 'manifest' and the 'latent'. The second one can be described by 'personal' and 'situational'. And the third dimension stretches from the 'here-and-now' (the group in operation while being studied) and the 'there-and-then' (the group in its operational

---

[1] From this perspective, one may gain a different understanding of the dynamics described by group relations consultants when they work with organisational issues, for example, Rina Bar-Lev Elieli (2005), A journey towards integration: a transitional phase in the organizational life of a clinic. In: G. Amado & L. Vansina (Eds), *The Transitional Approach in Action*. London: Karnac, 83–106.

context, its history and its future). This frame is commonly known as an open system's perspective.

Prior to embarking on a group intervention one can avoid the lack of contextual understanding in several ways. First, by taking an active part in the problem definition. Second, through individual or group interviews exploring the organisational context and history of the designated client-system, in particular the connecting or related parts of the system, or by an overall organisational diagnosis.

Organisational boundaries

In general, boundaries can be understood as mental frames that *separate* and *relate* what is *within* from what is *outside*. At the level of individuals it leads to distinctions between the 'inner' and 'outer world', between 'me' and 'not-me'. At the social level one finds demarcations between 'one of us' and 'one of them' and/or 'within' and 'outside our group'. Boundaries are most often inferred from the interactions and are seldom clear-cut like a line. Furthermore, they can be appropriate or inappropriate in relation to the object of study, the work to be done, and/or psychic development of its members.

In organisational psychology one distinguishes between *mental boundaries* that organise our perceptions and action from *social boundaries* that relate to identity and social bonding, and *physical boundaries* that relate to formal rules and physical structures. Most of our mental boundaries are invisible, or at least blurred, while social and physical boundaries can be and often are more tangible. Hernes (2004) sums up some major features of boundaries in organisations: (a) boundaries are intrinsic to organising and central to understanding organisations; (b) they are composite in the sense that organisations operate within multiple sets of co-existing boundaries; (c) they are continuously constructed and reconstructed through interaction; some may be rather stable, others are changing. Being on the boundary – or more correctly within the boundary area – generates tensions, since boundaries are tested both from within and from the outside, but it also provides opportunities for transitions.

Boundaries fulfil different functions in an organisation: *ordering* or regulating internal interaction; *distinguishing* or demarcating inside from outside; and *thresholding* or regulating the flow or movement from inside to outside, for example persons, material, information. In many of our modern organisations, characterised by strategic alliances, networking and outsourcing, boundaries have become more difficult to identify, not only because they are composite, but also because they have become fluid.

In sociology one distinguishes symbolic from social boundaries. *Symbolic boundaries* refer to conceptual distinctions made by social actors to categorise objects, people, practices and even time and space. *Social boundaries* are objectified forms of social differences manifested in unequal access to and unequal distribution of resources (Lamont & Molnar, 2002). Symbolic boundaries can turn into social ones when they achieve wide agreement.

Although we can see an overlap in the conceptions of boundaries in psychology and sociology, the latter definition of social boundaries is of particular relevance for locating issues in organisations. Groups or work systems often have, within their context and history, unequal access to resources, like information and power, from which they derive unequal influence. Furthermore, the differences in influence and power create dependency relations that may hamper effective work or may stir up frictions between units and strife for power.

Physical and geographic boundaries surely, but also hierarchical boundaries often do exclude relevant elements that are part of the problem, or have a direct impact on solving them.

In community work we regularly see that the socio-economical developments become confined to an island while in fact it can only be dealt with effectively when conceived as a regional development project. When we overcame our perception of an oil tanker as a socio-technical unit without taking the shore services into account, the management on the ship could take a lot more responsibilities at sea. Technology helped us to cross the artificially conceived boundary of the ship by water.

The need to maintain a relative autonomy

Boundaries may obscure the proper location of problems, but they also are useful to maintain a relative autonomy. However, the healthy drive to maintain a *relative* autonomy may foster the illusion of *full* autonomy, which in turn may hamper the location of the problem. What constitutes too little or too much autonomy is critical in effective *boundary management.*

Human beings enjoy a *relative autonomy* from other persons, groups, organisations and even society. They are influenced, but not determined by their context and history. Evidence has been given that some individuals and groups can resist extreme or subtle pressures in religious, ideological or political prosecutions, torture rooms, and concentration camps. Individual resistance to influences from the presence of others (a group setting) has been confirmed in social experiments of Asch (1955), Milgram (1963), Haney, Banks & Zimbardo (1973) and of many others in different cultures. On the other hand, the same experiments and other studies on social identity theory (Hogg & Reid, 2001) point to the omnipresence of groups in the individual's mind. Other studies demonstrate the effect of the sheer presence or absence of another person on cognitive performance and ethical behaviour. In other words, the social environment has an influence on individuals and groups, an influence one may not always be aware of. The social operates also on an unconscious level, and it is not always easy to distinguish them from personal dispositions. From the individual perspective these social 'pressures' are understood in terms of unconscious needs to belong, to identify with, to be dependent on etc. While from the social psychological perspective, the same and a whole variety of social conditions (pressures) are studied in terms of their impact on human behaviour: for example, conformity.

In experimental studies on conformity and obedience one generally finds that about two-thirds of the persons yield to social 'pressure', while only one-third are more able to control its impact. In situations of ambiguity, they hold on – for various reasons – to their own observations, opinions and views, although feeling the pressure to conform. However, many forms of influence on individual judgement, and behaviour operate at the unconscious or non-conscious level. Being in a position of power is by some persons 'experienced' as an *entitlement* to seek gratification for selfish needs, objectives, and views, and not *as taking advantage* of their power position. Politics too are often experienced as right or legitimate guidelines, not as rules imposed from outside oneself by persons/groups with questionable objectives (Vansina, 2001; Vansina, 2007; Lee-Chai & Bargh, 2001). Some persons in power become, however, concerned and feel more responsible for what they do and its consequences for others. These persons are conscious of the interdependencies amongst people and subordinate their own interests to service and social responsibility (Chen, Lee-Chai & Bargh, 1999).

This relative autonomy is at the same time an outcome and a critical capacity essential for *boundary-management*, by which human beings become not only able to distinguish what is my personal understanding, experience from those of others, but also to listen to the others' views, process the data on their relevance and value without yielding to social pressure. In other words, boundary management means that one separates and relates, but also regulates what views should be considered and what conditions should be accepted as genuine, legitimate and appropriate in order to continue with the work. The 'keeping out' here should not be confused with *denial* or dissociation from outside realities due to concentration of attention. We only speak about boundary management when the separating, the relating and the regulating of what is allowed in are based on *conscious choice and efforts*.

Individuals (and groups) differ in their ability to exercise their relative autonomy and manage their boundaries. Some persons may yield easily to the pressures (conscious or unconscious) of the group; allowing the pressures from outside their work system to come in and upset their lives and work. Different situations may exert a different impact on the same individual or group. Furthermore, boundary management, although helpful, does not provide a foolproof guarantee for the exclusion of all undesirable influences from the outside.

Too little boundary management may facilitate the import of disturbances into a social unit that erode its identity, while too rigid boundary control may lead to a denial of interdependencies with environment and a strong social identity. Both extremes create additional difficulties in locating the problem.

MANAGEMENT TEAMS AS THE TIP OF AN ICEBERG

Fry, Rubin & Plovnick (1981) have described how upper and lower management levels often influence middle managers. What appears as interpersonal or team problems of middle management are often forms of acting out/responding to the dynamics and conditions imported or created by top management. Fry et al. label it a "mirror image". "This is a phenomenon whereby a middle group experiences the effects of a problem reflected upon it by a group, higher up in the organizational hierarchy, usually an executive level, or policy *setting* group" (p. 41). They continue to say that the middle managers' group style of decision making, ways of running meetings, ways of dealing with conflict, etc. often mirror the way things are done in the top group(s) in which the leaders of the middle management group take part. In other words, work systems – in particular at the middle management level – may fail to create the systems' characteristics requisite for their own specific tasks by taking over those that dominate the top. This phenomenon may well explain why psychoanalytically-informed consultants claim to work with the overall organisation while in fact they are only consulting a management team in which the organisational context is *reflected*. The behaviour in the team studied is in other words either related to, or influenced by organisational factors, outside the immediate control of its members. One can hardly expect to understand the dynamics of top management by looking at reflections, let alone improve the organisation by leaving middle management with the task of changing their bosses.[2]

Groups at lower hierarchical levels are less affected by the beliefs and values of top management. Shop floor levels are more distant from the executive suites and have norms and standards that reflect more their function, task or physical environment (Fry et al., 1981, p. 43). The concreteness of the tasks and environments, as well as the distance from the top, facilitate the exercise of relative autonomy.

'Mirror effects' must first be recognised as the reflection of organisational issues, and not simply dealt with as intra-, interpersonal or group problems by designing team building, or outdoor exercises/adventures. In order to avoid this trap, Fry et al. suggested a model. This model is a copy of what Rubin and Beckhard (1972), derived from their field study, but completed by pointing to the causal linkages between the *system* (organisational context) and *goals, roles, procedures and interpersonal relations*. If these elements – in this logical sequence – are not sufficiently understood and dealt with, the experienced problems and conflicts will not be resolved. On the contrary, it may lead to more frustration, stress and defensive behaviour.

---

[2] Andre Schonberg (1998) calls this pseudo-systemic monism. "It is the tacit belief and assumption that all the dynamics of the organisation are in fact represented in one of its parts, either a particular element in the organisation, for example, top management, or any part whatsoever of the organisation" (p. 9).

System or Contextual Elements

- The task of middle management is most often ambiguously defined: to *execute* and to *manage* policy! Indeed, to execute means to carry out well-defined operational objectives yourself, while to manage is to "infer objectives and to see to it that others own them clearly, and carry them out" (Fry et al., 1981, p. 45). The first implies an active doer role, while managing implies a more supportive role: creating conditions for the work systems at a lower level to carry out their work. These two tasks are quite different from top management who are responsible for defining/setting policy. Yet, there is pressure from top management to function in line with the top with respect to problem definition, role allocation, procedures, conflict management etc.

- Headquarters regularly visit the divisions or strategic business units to "keep in touch" or to "avoid surprises" as Mintzberg (1979) puts it. There are real pressures from the top. The efforts – in the last decennia – to establish a 'strong corporate culture' and to make everyone in the organisation identify with the objectives and core values often aim at the development of a monolithic social entity. Thereby organisations are less likely to be conceived as inter-related work systems with different tasks, time-span, scope and technologies. The real risk is then that managers at different hierarchical levels start subsequently doing the same work, but from different positions. It leads to an expensive duplication and overlap in roles, with blurred accountabilities.

- Middle managers also scrutinise top managers to detect their expectations and to mould "them into acceptable statements of their group's core mission, goals, and priorities for others to use" (Fry et al., 1981, p. 45).

- Many middle managers aspire to advance in their careers. These aspirations can influence them to please their boss rather than doing the things from their organisational position and role that are required to make the organisation successful.

Boundary management and maintaining a relative autonomy may be very difficult for some middle managers facing these social pressures. But there are also *technological* factors that may impede boundary management efforts.

When Apple Computers was enjoying its early hey-days, I happened to be a consultant to them to help them cope with turbulence outside and within the company. American headquarters were regularly modifying or changing the emphasis in their strategic objectives. In some European countries while not in others, the computer linkages to headquarters were direct. Everyone in that country organisation had direct and instant information about American headquarters' decisions or thinking. In other country organisations, senior management *controlled* that flow of information by technical means. Managers of the latter countries appeared to have a clearer view of the company's strategic objectives, had more stable and consistent strategic action plans; there was less internal turbulence (stress) than those that had direct, unfiltered information from American headquarters. The latter were having more formal and informal meetings to adjust, clarify, and co-ordinate their activities.

Mission and goals

From the discussions above, it is clear that playing it safe by accepting the expectations of top management without interpretation in terms of one's own systemic hierarchical level (Jaques, 1998) maintains the confusion of objectives by keeping them too general and not specific enough to initiate goal-directed action. Roles, procedures and interpersonal relations must consequently remain unclear and conflicting. Fry et al. (1981) illustrate how the opposite happened with a case in which the Construction Division of a large high technology electronic company tried to define its mission.

The Divisional Manager wrote: "To construct all site and building facilities and chemical installation from information supplied by the engineering departments and/or customers".

The Personnel Representative wrote: "To construct facilities in the most efficient manner possible, utilizing the talents of the organization".

The Engineering Service Representative wrote: "To manage all space and facilities construction as defined by engineering services to insure least cost, highest quality, and minimum interruption of corporate functions".

Schedule and Cost Control Liaison wrote: "To efficiently provide a construction service to the Corporation by the management of and/ or participation in all construction projects. Completely controlling costs, quality, manpower, and schedules".

In this case, the confusion that had led to the consulting assignment became evident in trying to define the mission of that division. Until then, it had been the basis for misunderstanding and interpersonal problems in the management team.

Simply writing a mission, or having some consultants write it for you does not help. If a mission statement is not *authentic*, the organisation is less able to find and develop a systemic capacity for reflection and effective action (Krantz, 2005). It is only a nice flag to impress the outside world, not a guiding document for work.

Roles

Organisational roles can only become defined when the system's tasks – in relation to the whole – have been specified, the mission statement is owned, and the strategic objectives are clear. Roles are to be defined in relation to other roles or pattern of roles so that role interdependencies and tensions become visible and discussable. In current organisations, roles cannot appropriately be defined in functional or discipline responsibilities, nor in a set of activities to be carried out, yet should be defined in terms of *core tasks*, or agreed *contributions* to the system's tasks and objectives. In this way, enough space is provided for initiative taking, while the accountabilities can become clarified. Consequently, there are several reasons, besides personal and interpersonal factors, why role clarification can go wrong.

- The ambiguity in the role of managers 'doing things oneself' or 'co-ordinating and creating conditions so that these things get done' is often one of the major stumbling stones. Take a product manager for instance. Is s/he personally responsible for making and overseeing the implementation of all decisions regarding the product, or is his/her core task to create conditions so that others, responsible for the product (i.e. marketing, manufacturing, engineering, R&D) together can take and implement all product-related decisions; or is s/he responsible for the co-ordination of the activities in the team?

- Role conflicts may be the outcome of career concerns: what is good for my career versus what is good for the business. The increase and social acceptance of mobility has tilted the balance even more towards what may enhance my career prospects in the labour market. Doing the things yourself is likely to give you more exposure, as well as control, that the activities are carried out in your preferred way. Furthermore, one may feel more confident in doing so, because these are the domains in which one has a recognised competence. Professionals are inclined to subscribe to the belief: 'If you want it done right, do it yourself!' Here we get a glimpse on how over-determined a particular role preference can be.

- Fry et al. (1981) give yet another reason. Middle managers come from various backgrounds and disciplines; their perceptions about what is an appropriate role are likely to differ.

Even when roles are properly defined but the person in role does not have the requisite knowledge and skills to carry them out, process consultation (Kaplan, 1979) or team-building training will not enhance task performance. The elimination of 'process loss' due to deficient workgroup processes is not likely to compensate for members' lack of task-related competences.

Procedures

Many procedures and conflicts over resources find their origin in unclear goals and inappropriate role definitions and/or allocations. Furthermore, agreement on how we should work together becomes more difficult to achieve because of:

- the felt pressure to mirror the procedures of the group higher up in the hierarchy;

- limited career opportunities may increase the competitive pressure to 'look good' to top management.

Interpersonal issues

The ambiguities of tasks, goals, roles and procedures increase the levels of stress thereby stirring up anxieties, which can lead to interpersonal friction and defensive behaviour. Without following the *sequential* steps in the model it is most often impossible to distinguish and appreciate the overlap between *real* interpersonal, *genuine* intergroup conflict and *justifiable* defensive behaviour originating from *organisational conditions* on the one hand from conflicts and frictions grounded in more pure *psychological factors* like personal incompatibilities, in social identity conflicts between groups, or psychodynamics. The reduction of the former to the latter, however, would be *'psychologising'* organisational issues.

An Example to Illustrate the Value of the Model

I was called in to consult the management team of a business unit, the largest and most profitable of the corporation. The General Manager was the first of the new generation of management. He told me that he had waited a few years to organise an OD workshop with his management team. He still felt a little unsure about his position in the team. In his career within the corporation, he had held posts in different functional areas and hierarchical levels. On important issues, he did consult his team, subsequently he would take their ideas and emotional reactions with him, worry them through personally before taken the final decision. The team, he thought, seemed to have some difficulties with this way of taking decisions and managing. During this first meeting, I got the impression that there was not enough space between some of the key managerial roles. There appeared too much overlap. His team consisted of 10 directors, 2 managers and a secretary. He told me that he wanted to keep the team that large until he felt sufficiently familiar with the whole business unit. Yet, there was a general feeling amongst all members that the team was not working as well as it could. This feeling was strengthened by the success of a designated team of colleagues that handled a nationwide business problem. These members had worked overtime, almost till exhaustion, but they had done the work for the sake of the corporation, not on behalf of the management team.

During this first meeting, I discussed my first impressions with the General Manager and suggested that we might work first on the definition of the tasks and responsibilities of the business unit's management team. However, before starting on any course of action, I asked him to have individual interviews with each of the members to hear their views on the way the team was working in the organisation, and to establish a working relation with each of them. Thereafter, we could discuss the design of the project.

At a subsequent meeting with the General Manager we discussed some major findings and decided to start a two-day, off-site, workshop. After a brief review of the aims and of some standard procedures in a workshop, we discussed the interview data. Then, we commenced the work on the tasks, responsibilities, and accountabilities of the management team of a 'business unit' in the corporation. When that was clarified, we would define the requisite roles in the management team.

Situating the business unit as a system within the corporation

A lot of insight was generated about the organisational context and the system's dynamics:

- Internal training programmes and management development devices had kept the organisational boundaries (too) highly permeable.

- The founder and late president had established a council for "Exploring Futures" to which all senior managers of all business units were invited together with the complete Corporate Board. This council was kept alive and met three to four times a year.

- The Corporate Personnel and the Corporate Finance Directors were also members of the management team of the business unit under study.

- The Chairman of the Board had regular personal reviews with each of the senior managers of all business units. The content went beyond the appreciation of career expectations, opportunities and competence development, into their personal views about the business.

- The open communication policy created by the founder was maintained. Each senior manager had direct access to the Chairman.

- There were wide divergences in their conception of the task of the management team.

The Management Team of the Business Unit

- Interesting ideas from the special council for "Exploring Futures" were further developed in more than 40 project teams with members from deeper down in the business unit, called "Breeding Centres for Continuous Change". Most of them were chaired by the General Manager providing him with information about what was alive deeper down in the organisation.

- The two managers of one of the directors had been made members of the management team, thereby eroding hierarchical differences.

- The General Manager held regular personal meetings with the members of the management team.

- The 'house style' required directors, managers and to a lesser degree the employees to learn to live with ambiguity, uncertainty, boundary crossing and open confrontation, and to attach little importance to social status, but instead care for others.

My observations from the interviews and the discussions within the management team show clearly the *mirror image* of the organisational context. The members of the team had to invest a lot of energy in the maintenance of individual role boundaries to ensure their relative autonomy. The lack of boundary management around the business unit was not consciously experienced as a problem, although one could not define the task of the business unit within the corporation. Consequently, the management team – as an organisational unit – lacked a firm identity in the organisation. The directors and managers were only recognised in their respective *functional* roles, not as members of the deciding management team ('la Direction'). The absence of boundaries around the management team was accepted as part of the 'house style'. The members were not aware of the reasons why they had to invest so much energy in maintaining their relative autonomy in role, and as a person. In the team they had to be attentive and claim the right to openly protest whenever their colleagues did not respect their minimal *functional, role boundary*. The *personal boundary* issue became expressed in their complaints about "the lack of control over their diaries" (through the computer system), and about the company's "claims" on their private time.

Some outcomes of the workshop were:

- The definition of the task, responsibilities, and accountabilities of the Management Team allowing them to draw responsibility and accountability boundaries, while accepting informational boundary crossings.

- The 'house style' was carefully kept as a critical success factor.

- The team underlined the fact that the corporate Personnel Director and the Director of Finance had to report first to their business unit for issues that were proper to the business unit, before using that information in the board.

- The "Breeding Centres for Continuous Change" were maintained as a valuable work method to create and support 'transitional change'.

- The Management Team was restructured into a smaller Management Team and an 'extended' management team, which met at times to work on issues that required broad involvement and commitment.

- The computer diary system was changed to allow the manager to block time for him/herself.

- Steps were taken to reduce overtime work and to facilitate doing some office work at home, thereby eliminating travel time.

Some months later, management organised another two-day meeting with the extended management team to formulate a strategy and strategic objectives for their business unit. Its outcomes were presented to the Chairman of the Corporate Board, where they were subsequently approved. During the strategy meeting, I commented casually about the lack of warmth in the team. Some months later, the management team took a week off for a team-building project with a facilitator.

From this example we can note a few things. First, if we had taken the original request at face value, 'interpersonal and team issues' would most likely have passed over fundamental, *organisational* questions: the situating of the business unit in the corporation, the joint definition of management's core task as a team and the formulation of a strategy. Second, the strategy proposal allowed them to differentiate them from other business units and affirm their identity in relation to the chairman. Strengthening its boundaries allows for the development of the system characteristics that are appropriate for carrying out its strategy. It will thereby generate distinctiveness amongst the different business units and their respective product-technology markets. Cross fertilisation and collaboration amongst the business units may subsequently become more difficult to manage, but there is more to gain for this growing corporation. Third, the 'house style' or the culture, which was seen as a critical success factor in a flexible organisation, had penetrated the whole organisation. The question remains then what in that culture is beneficial to the further development of each of the business units within that corporation? And finally, the organisational work done in the two workshops did not prevent the continuation of work at the level of the team.

THE ICEBERG IN PROJECT TEAMS

Not only management teams have to be understood in their context. The now common multi-functional or multi-disciplinary, even multi-organisational teams for, for example, product development, complex consulting projects, or for multi-specialists interventions in health care systems are all operating in an organisational context that often provides a breeding ground for what mistakenly may be seen simply as 'difficult person(s), interpersonal conflicts, or group problems'. While in fact the project group *may* just be the platform upon which the organisational dynamics are played out.

Hirschhorn and Gilmore (1992) called organisations that rely heavily on flexible work and project teams "boundaryless corporations". Here, members rapidly move from one project into another with different roles: at one time they are a regular member and their boss is the project manager, while in the afternoon in another project one is the project manager of a team in which one's boss is a regular member. These authors argue that without a minimum of psychic boundaries the individual would be at a loss. Four psychic boundaries are advanced: authority (Who is in charge of what?), identity (Who is and isn't us?), task (Who does what?) and political boundaries (What is in it for us?). Those boundaries could be grounded in not further specified organisational and/or personal factors.

The four boundaries are posited as conditions that allow for effective project work.[3]

Human beings are likely to belong to different groups within and outside an organisation. They 'enjoy' multiple memberships, social identities and loyalties that become salient when the situation evokes a particular group-belongingness. The members of cross-functional or multi-organisational project teams or task forces are likely to belong to at least two groups. The *sentient* group is the one on which the member depends for emotional gratifications (recognition, rewards, career advancement, etc.), while the *task* group generates only meaning derived from doing the task (Miller & Rice, 1967). Project groups for product development, for example, are a special kind of multi-party group. They are commonly composed of members from different functional departments or disciplines. They need to collaborate to get the work done in the project team (task group). Each member brings to the task the distinctive knowledge, skills and perspectives needed to create a successful product. At the same time, the members represent their respective departments and group interests (sentient groups). This dual membership contains a potential role conflict between meeting the requirements for task accomplishment and representing the interests and perspectives of one's organisational unit. One frequently observed defence is to lower the diversity in language and thinking by falling back on a common denominator. Thereby members diminish the very reason for being part of the team, namely to bring different perspectives, knowledge and skills to bear on the project. In so doing, the members reduce the uncertainty to be understood and accepted; avoid interpersonal conflict and the stress proper to their individual boundary roles.[4] The more the different departments, and eventually the representatives,

---

[3] Isabelle Vincent (1997) made a first effort to verify these boundary claims in a petro-chemical research centre of an international oil company. In the absence of valid productivity measures per project, she relied on work satisfaction rankings across the many projects an individual employee was taking part in. Three out of the four of Hirschhorn and Gilmore's mental boundaries were not significantly related to work satisfaction. The only mental boundary that did significantly relate to satisfaction was the individual's capacity to feel comfortable with changing authority relations: the so-called 'authority boundary'. Whether this mental boundary is grounded more in a personal disposition than in the organisational context, still needs to be sorted out.

[4] A boundary role refers to a psychological and structural location an individual occupies in which s/ he has a dual membership, both with his/her 'parent' or 'sentient group' of constituents and with 'outsiders' or the 'task group'; s/he spans the two groups.

see the project group as working in a hostile (competitive) environment, the more the representatives find themselves operating from a rigid and highly controlled mandate. While exactly flexibility and creativity in thinking is demanded to get the task done. Whenever the project manager is perceived by the members as favouring a particular perspective (of one or other department) s/he loses his/her neutrality and becomes seriously handicapped in creating conditions that will facilitate trust building, respect for diversity, and collaboration.

Diverse project teams and task forces face still another source of stress, ambiguity and uncertainty, which is the direct result of its heterogeneous composition, namely members with different, distinctive knowledge and perspectives. Diverse teams are found to be more creative, innovative and are likely to produce higher quality decisions. They also demand more time to reach agreement. Because of the high level of stress, the ambiguity and uncertainty, and the potential boundary role conflict, one may expect more interpersonal conflict and defensive behaviour. Only dealing with these intra-group problems, without consideration for the organisational context, however, easily leads to '*psychologising*' the issues.

What needs to be achieved in the *organisational context*, and what needs to be worked through in the *project group* in order to create favourable conditions for productive work?

In the organisational context one needs to develop and maintain:

• Saliency of a jointly conceived mission of the organisation or project.

• The relevance and importance of the project team for the organisation(s).

• Non-competitive relations between the different functional departments, disciplines, professional specialties, or different organisations by reducing competition for resources, advancement, social status and power.

• Sufficient social support, time and resources for professional development within one's function, discipline, specialties or organisation.

• A system that secures the appointment of project managers, who are able to create conditions that enable trust and respect to develop and facilitate collaborative processes, without relying on positional power.

Within the project group one can:

• Socially ratify the importance of diversity for the work to be done.

• Help the group to understand the inevitable stress proper to working from boundary roles.

• Assist in containing the tensions proper to innovative and creative work in groups, so that they are enabled to hold on to ambiguity until various good ideas have been generated, not just one.

• Support initiatives in trust building, respect for and exploration of differences; encourage collaborative processes (e.g. interest versus positional bargaining) and recognition.

• Establish regular review sessions of how the project group has been working.

Note, that none of these conditions are bureaucratic. They can't be established by decree, but need to be worked on. They are to be achieved.

IMPORT AND EXPORT MECHANISM OF PROBLEMS

So far we have demonstrated that groups or teams cannot be genuinely understood without paying attention to the organisational context and history in which they are embedded and the critical function of boundaries in organising processes. The 'mirroring behaviour' is nothing mysterious. It is the product of the human response to the real or assumed – sometimes-fantasised – context and the absence or erosion of boundaries. The human response, however, may subsequently lead to problems in a given management or project team. Some psychoanalytically-informed authors have wrongly labelled this phenomenon as displacement. Long (2000) even goes so far as to state that all conflicts in the workplace are inevitably the product of displacement through unconscious, defensive processes like splitting and projective identification. Although unconscious processes may and do take place, such categorical statements don't do justice to the human efforts to search, explore, test and deal with reality. It forecloses making a distinction between unconscious processes, the pervasiveness of the organisational context, the absence of the work system's differentiation and boundary management, and the conscious location of conflict in parts of the organisation where they can most appropriately or more conveniently be dealt with. These distinctions are important to make since different processes call for different interventions. In the case of our business unit management team, there were no indications that the problems within that team had been 'displaced' by corporate management. The lack of differentiation and boundary management resulted in adopting conditions appropriate or favourable for the work in one part of the organisation while they were not (or no longer) appropriate and effective at another hierarchical level. The reasons behind that lack of differentiation of work systems and boundary management needed to be explored and dealt with. In line with this view, I will first say something more about the pervasiveness of context in which conscious and unconscious processes may be active. Second, I'll discuss some examples of transfer of problems by conscious choice. Third and finally, I'll review and illustrate some of the more frequently observed unconscious 'displacement' processes.

The Pervasiveness of Context

DNA-analyses inform us that most of us are descendants of the human beings that managed to survive in the ice-age thousands and thousands of years ago. Recognising and dealing with the environment is a natural, healthy capacity, essential for survival. We are outwardly directed. We want to explore, to understand and make use of the wider context in which we live.[5] We may even resonate with events happening in that outside world (Amado, 1990). The environment and organisational context are therefore likely to be within us, although we may not be aware of these. We may be so used to relating to particular, standard parts of that environment that we engage in activities as if we are driving a car using our human 'automatic pilot'. The pervasiveness of context is likely to increase with the now frequently noticed erosion of boundaries (e.g. hierarchical and functional), the emphasis on flexibility, on temporary assignments, the exposure to world media and the easy access to data. In the examples given so far one detects a combination of learning or internalisation, compliance and identification processes of which we are not always aware. People learn from direct and indirect dealings and encounters with the organisational context and management's actions. Not only through

---

[5] Yet, we may become scared and run away from what we discover out there and within ourselves.

what is relevant and valuable for work and organisational goal attainment, but also what particular behaviour is rewarded or keeps a person out of trouble. Those in power impose their frames, ideas, values and views about management and the organisation (views which may have been linked to success in the past) onto the less powerful. Advancement in the organisation often does dependent on adherence to these views. In other words, compliance is at least perceived as being rewarded. Finally, identification processes with leading figures or groups – expressing our desire to be like them, to be included – may result in imitative behaviour: language; mannerism, priorities and actions; attitudes towards, and views about, for example, work, conflicts, values and goals, how to manage and to organise without being fully aware of it.

Transfer of Organisational Issues as a Deliberative Choice

In the early sixties, Marie Jahoda once said: "You always have to look for those parts in the organisation that must be kept happy". As I remember she did not make a distinction between considered choices or unconscious processes. Yet, her insight is extremely useful.

Decisions to *locate* an organisational problem, either of a sporadic or a repetitive nature, can be based on the rationale that problems should be 'placed' there where they can be solved most effectively and most efficiently. Different criteria may then be used like: where they can be noticed first; where people have the proper resources and competences to deal with them; where one has ready access to feedback on attempts to deal with the problem, etc. The location can also be based on weighing the pros and cons of dealing with them directly versus moving them to other places. Transfers of problems, however, can also emerge from the shared feeling of not wanting to be bothered by those issues! Rational reasons may then be found to cover this up, because 'keeping oneself happy at the expense of others' does not sound right. Whatever, the latter leads to situations where parts of the organisation experience a problem that originated elsewhere.

> An international chemical corporation contracted me to introduce and develop a total quality management system. The approach (Vansina, 1989/90) had been discussed and approved of by top management. During our work at the operational level the multi-functional team experienced serious difficulties dealing with the quality problems of an innovative, promising product.

Eliminating defects in the product took too much time, threatened market penetration, and even risked possible legal suits. A closer study revealed the following structural problem:

- Purchasing worked on buying at the lowest costs, so they bought large quantities of basic materials – that deteriorated over time – from a wide range of suppliers. The impact of this practice on quality and reliability of the basic materials escaped their attention. The problems surfaced only in the production department. Purchasing, however, could show management a favourable picture.
- Production had invested in automated technologies to make long production runs. They worked with the principle of maximum utilisation of machine capacity, and kept an inventory of products in anticipation of difficult product mixes. Consequently R&D had difficulty in squeezing in some test runs of improvements of the product concerned. Awaiting the results of the test runs, the scientist in the laboratory came up with alternative solutions and product improvements, increasing the number of requests for test runs on that product and thereby further upsetting the production schedule.
- Planning and Warehousing operated on serving the customer upon request, at all times. Consequently they planned for and kept large stocks of finished products that lost their qualities over time.

When I discussed with the top management team the negative consequences of their departments working only on their own objectives, which lacked integration, they decided not to do anything about it. They preferred to keep their team conflict-free and to put all quality issues on the plate of the quality circles to be instituted. *At times, people prefer to live with the problem, rather than bear the anticipated consequences of a solution, in particular the fear of having to handle conflicts.*

Unconscious Import–Export Mechanisms

Tension producing issues may unconsciously be displaced to another part of the organisation to the relief of the original owners. Consequently, they no longer bother them.

Mergers and acquisitions are almost always decided at corporate level. The formal agreement to a merger or a friendly take-over often results in the formation of a new board. It is a delicate process in which power-, social status-, and competence issues are to be balanced between the merging partners. The outcome can often be qualified as 'suspended tensions' between the parties. The further integration of the business is subsequently delegated to a steering group and project teams, assisted or not by consultants. There may be good reasons for the board members to claim time for themselves to become established. Unfortunately it may also be an unconscious displacement.

> A large bank merged with a highly profitable, and successfully managed smaller bank in the same market. Their management systems, for example, promotion and reward systems, the relations between hierarchical levels, differed widely. Soon after the merger was formally concluded, the chairman of the new board – which had been constituted with great pain – went to visit the managers of the two parties separately. In his talk he reassured the largest partner (where he had been the chairman) that they did not have to worry since their management systems were going to be kept in place. Subsequently, he informed the smaller, more profitable partner (meeting in another hotel) that the best management practices would be introduced into the total, new organisational entity. The integration project team was subsequently confronted with the conflicting expectations as well as the differences in management systems. We didn't have any indication that the chairman made a deliberate choice to saddle the project team with this extra problem.

Projection may follow an unconscious process of splitting by which the 'good' or desirable parts become separated from the 'bad' or undesirable part of the same object or issue. The recipients of the 'good parts' become subsequently idealised, while those of the 'bad parts' become blamed, victimised, even eradicated as centres of evil.

> Senior management and workers blamed the maintenance team in a motor manufacturing company for the frequent breakdowns in quality in the production department. The product was a jewel of engineering sophistication and as such that department was glorified for its innovative capacity. The blamed maintenance team put in extra efforts to keep the available technology in operational conditions, but in vain. They came to the conclusion that the production requirements of that product exceeded largely the 'process capabilities' of the existing technology. They talked to the chief engineer wondering whether a more 'robust quality' could not be designed into that product. It only aggravated the situation. Maintenance was now seen as blaming 'engineering' for their ascribed negligence.

It is not easy for the victims of projected 'bad parts' to correct the unjustified negative image. Efforts to improve their image by pointing to the mistakes or unfair dealings of the glorified party, – although correct – are readily turned back to confirm the original negative image. A minimal condition for bringing together the 'good' and the 'bad' parts is the mutual recognition by the parties of their own contribution – how limited it may be – to the blaming and the idealisation.

The basic human ambivalence towards change often leads to the emergence of proponents (advocates) and opponents to change. Efforts to convince the other group of the anticipated negative or positive consequences are likely to fail without any recognition of the basic ambivalence. The splitting and projection onto opponents and proponents of a certain course of action may become expressed in an interpersonal or intergroup conflict.

A consultant was called in to mediate in a year-long conflict between two doctors in a general hospital. The intake interviews revealed that there were many layers on which the two persons as well as the staff were divided, for example, for or against organisational change. This led the consultant to conclude that: "Their departments as a whole were acting out the conflict on behalf of the whole system" (Hambleton, 2002). Unfortunately, the issue was dealt with as if mediation between the two doctors was sufficient to solve this particular conflict, defined as 'interpersonal' by the sponsor!

An outsider may understand the underlying processes in the presented case in different ways from either the sponsor or the consultant. Of crucial importance is that these different hunches become explored and validated in direct interaction with the client system, how difficult that may be. Without inquiry in the real setting, one can only make guesses, or worse, 'wild interpretations'. Consequently, I can only *venture* some plausible, alternative hypotheses. One such hypothesis is that two social categories are formed around proponents and opponents to organisational changes, either based on *splitting*, or on a different but careful deliberation of the anticipated advantages and disadvantages of change. It is not uncommon that the consequences of an organisational change (or a merger) have a marked different impact on different parts in the organisation. This may provide ground for proponents and opponents of the very same project. In this instance, the interpersonal conflict between the two doctors could be the expression of a *real intergroup conflict*. In other words, the two doctors have become representatives of their respective groups/departments or even social categories, while the groups can stay off stage. Under this hypothesis, the members may or may not be aware of the existing conflict. Resolving the dispute could then only be achieved in an intergroup setting in which everyone is encouraged to own up to his/her ideas so that the pros and cons of a possible change can be brought together and evaluated against agreed shared desirable outcomes for the overall hospital, and appreciated against the available means either to control the undesirable consequences or to spread them in fair way. Another hypothesis is that each of the two doctors (who may or may not like one another) may have advanced outspokenly a position, which the other members of staff have come to *identify* with. In this instance an intergroup approach should best precede an *interpersonal* mediation effort. Still another possibility, advanced by the consultant of the project, is that the two doctors are the objects of *projective identification* by the whole organisation of its split ambivalence towards change. Whatever, each hypothesis should be backed up by *indicators* and subsequently verified before a label can be put on it or a particular intervention strategy can be executed.

Projective Identification

This psychic mechanism has extensively been discussed in Part One. In short, it stands for a defensive process in which also the manager or consultant becomes the recipient, requiring him/her to engage in the hard work of 'sorting out' the 'me' from the 'not-me'. The following vignette may provide you with an illustration of its existence as well as the difficulties in working with projective identification.

> The staff group of a Harold Bridger-type working conference (non-residential) was composed of three senior (of which two were males) and two junior female consultants. Each junior worked with a senior consultant, while the third female senior consultant took a group on her own. The participants consisted of a majority of last year's students without any previous experience in group-relation conferences of any kind, and about six participants who had had some experience in at least one Tavistock/Leichester-like programme. The latter, by and large, considered themselves as one step ahead of the others, which was true in the sense that they were no longer

novices in the field. They were spread over the three learning groups. In all groups they experienced difficulties in participating as regular members. While the junior consultants behaved like regular staff. The emerging power relations between the 'non-novices' and the 'students' became expressed in attempts to impose their views onto the others and in their attempts to take a special role, somewhat similar to that of a consultant. These issues had been discussed and worked on in the learning groups as well as in the large group meetings. Due to the non-residential character of the working conference the staff meetings had not continued late into the evening because of family commitments and traffic problems. The distinction between senior and junior consultants had emerged early in the conference, for example, in the allocation of roles and by an incident. Namely, one senior consultant had clarified and completed an instruction that a junior consultant was giving to the conference group. The junior consultant felt let down, and not helped by the staff. Yet, another quality began to colour the staff meetings. It happened regularly that sweeping interpretations were made about the dynamics in the conference. One of the senior consultants repeatedly asked for data in support of these interpretations, before accepting them as possibly relevant. By and large the differences between members of staff and some more stable, similar minded alliances had emerged: the two senior male consultants stayed together in the evening; the junior and the senior female consultant often found common ground in their interpretations in the staff meetings. Furthermore, that junior consultant and the senior female consultant working on her own deplored in particular the lack of time for staff discussions. At the final staff meeting, after ending the conference, when this neglect was raised again by the same junior staff member and being discussed, she broke in with the interpretation that "the staff are acting out the problems for the participants" (the staff were the subject of a projective identification of the participants). The focus switched to speculations about the ex-participants (inquiry was impossible since they had in the meantime left the premises) and away from exploring the felt neglect with the consequence that no time was left either to reflect upon the internal dynamics of the staff group, or to round off the work.

The vignette illustrates a couple of points. First, the statement: "The staff are doing the work for the participants!" is a popular interpretation by 'group-relation' consultants in various contexts, even in the absence of any unusual feeling like being overburdened by the work. Second, nothing more is done by that person and the rest of the group to further inquiry into the underlying dynamics in order to help the conference group move beyond *hearing* the interpretation to a more *effective state of functioning*. Simple awareness is taken as sufficient. Third, similarities between issues in the group of participants and the staff are seen – without further inquiry – as the outcome of projective identification. Other alternatives, for example, that both groups under similar conditions may really have *similar* problems are not considered. Fourth, "The staff are doing the work *for* the participants" implies that neither the participants, nor the group of staff is doing their proper work. The staff group may well feel that there is a real issue between the more experienced and the less experienced members of staff, and consequently work on that issue as if it was only their own. Not as a deliberate choice to learn from in order to be in a better position to help the delegates to work through their 'non-novice' and 'student' statuses. Fifth, projective identification is an unconscious process by which emotional experiences are induced in the other person (or party). The experience of discomfort here would be essential. It is this actual, emotional experience – accompanied by reflections on the context – that leads to a painful process of sorting out what is really 'me' from 'not-me' (an internal staff issue or something induced from outside) that is "out of character", as Krantz and Gilmore (1991) phrased it. The hard, reflective work of 'sorting out' seemed to be reduced to remembering a popular interpretation. Insights don't come that lightly as ideas about similarities come to mind. When one is really the object of a projective identification, the insight leads to a modification of behaviour of the recipient. In the absence of the other party, a validation is, however, impossible. Consequently, one cannot learn, nor develop from an eventual exploration.[6] Sixth, interventions like these turn the attention to the other(s) (often absent), who become responsible for the implied problems, thereby deflecting from taking a good look at oneself first. However, such statements may provide a false, temporary relief, much like other offered escapes. It is therefore crucial to understand the function of such an intervention and what the group does with it. Here, the experienced neglect within the staff group was removed from the agenda, since the neglect was allegedly induced by the participants and the experienced differences in gender, for example, became deflected.

---

[6] An individual or a group can gain some notion that projective identification might be present, but it can only be fruitfully explored and learned from in the presence of the parties concerned. More concretely, in group relations conferences such assumptions should be explored in the 'learning community' in which participants and consultants meet to review their work together.

Identification with Different Parts of an Organisation

I would like to draw attention to another phenomenon, facilitated by the division of work in project or study teams that coincide with existing different social identities in these teams. For example, the management of merging companies may form project teams to study and design further integration, but allocate the work along the lines of the two merging entities. Members of company X study parts of company Y and vice versa. Worse, each may study parts of their respective organisation. Or two consulting firms may study different parts of one organisation. Consequently, we may expect that existing conflicts in the client system become subsequently enacted in the management or consulting teams.

The psychology department of the University of Leuven (Belgium), at that time consisting of French and Flemish faculty members and students, was asked to study a particular prison. The work was divided so that the French team members would study management and the wardens, while the Flemish members would research the prisoners. When the data was brought together the trouble began. Each party within the research team started to defend the concerns and interests of that part of the organisation they had studied. In this process group membership became salient and activated the wider community conflict between the French- and Flemish-speaking groups. When they realised what was going on, they still could not resolve the issue. Consequently, they did not succeed in producing an integrated report on the prison.

The point here is that the composition of research or consulting teams and the division of work can create conditions that activate existing intergroup conflicts and provide fertile ground for various kinds of defensive mechanisms. The different parties may, for example, come to identify with the organisational unit they study or work in. Subsequently, the parties land in a situation where it is difficult to distinguish the client's or company's concerns and interests from those that are associated with their own group membership.

SUMMARY

Groups never exist in a vacuum, but within a context and a history. The latter are far from being univocal and often not directly accessible, although they do influence the dynamic processes in a non-conscious or unconscious way. Consultants with a too narrow specialisation, or lack of interest in the organisational context and history may locate too easily the problem where the difficulties are experienced and where the energy exists to do something about it.

Boundaries, mental, social or physical are essential for organising and for understanding organisations issues. The more these boundaries become blurred, composite and rapidly changing, the more difficult it is to locate the problem or its real causes in the organisation.

Mental boundaries, like role boundaries, may help to maintain a relative autonomy required to withstand undue social pressures and to regulate what information, views and preferences should be considered. Organisational boundaries and problem definitions also create mental boundaries, thereby rendering difficulties in reframing problems and/or exploring the wider organisational context. Furthermore, various import and export mechanisms may move discomfort and problems across boundaries, thereby giving credit to the commonsense saying: in systems do not look too closely where the troubles are experienced to find the real causes of the problem.

Whatever, if one wants to avoid '*psychologising*' social issues, and at the same time one wishes to increase the effectiveness of one's consulting or management efforts, one needs to gain an understanding of the contextual dynamics.

REFERENCES

Amado, G. (1990). Identité psychique, crise et organisation: Pour une théorie de la resonance. *Psychologie clinique*, **3**, 115–28.

Asch, S.E. (1955). Opinions and social pressures. *Scientific America*, **193**, 5, 31–5.

Bar-Lev Eleili, R. (2005). A journey towards integration: A transitional phase in the organisational life of a clinic. In: G. Amado & L. Vansina (Eds), *The Transitional Approach in Action*. London: Karnac, 83–106.

Bion, W. (1961). *Experiences in groups*. New York: Basic Books.

Chen, S., Lee-Chai, A.Y. & Bargh, J.A. (1999). Does power corrupt? Relationship orientation as a moderator of the effects of social power. Manuscript submitted for publication (cited in: A.Y. Lee-Chai & J.A. Bargh (Eds) (2001). *The Use and Abuse of Power: Multiple Perspectives on the Causes of Corruption*. Hove: Psychology Press.

Fry, R., Rubin, I. & Plovnick, M. (1981). Dynamics of groups that execute or manage policy. In: R. Payne & C. Cooper (Ed.), *Groups at work*. New York: John Wiley & Sons, Inc., 41–55

Hambleton, L. (2002). *Clash of the titans: Powerful individuals in conflict and the role of the process consultant*. Paper presented at the annual symposium of the International Society for the Psychoanalytic Study of Organisations, Melbourne, June 20–22.

Haney, S., Banks, C. & Zimbardo, Ph. (1973). Interpersonal dynamics in a simulated prison. *International Journal of Criminology and Penology*, 1, 69–97.

Hernes, T. (2004). Studying composite boundaries: A framework of analysis. *Human Relations*, 57, 1, 9–30.

Hirschhorn, L. & Gilmore, T. (1992). The new boundaries of the 'boundaryless' company. *Harvard Business Review*, May–June, 104–115.

Hogg, M.A. & Reid, S.A. (2001). Social identity, leadership and power. In: A.Y. Lee-Chai & J.A. Bargh (Eds), *The use and abuse of power: Multiple perspectives on the causes of corruption*. Ann Arbor: Psychology Press, 159–180.

Jaques, E. (1998). *Requisite organization*. Arlington, VA.: Cason Hall & Co.

Kaplan, R.E. (1979). The conspicuous absence of evidence that process consultation enhances task performance. *Journal Applied Behavioral Science*, 346–360.

Krantz, J. (2005). Einige Gedanken über Reflexion in Organisation. *Freie Assoziation: Zeitschrift für das Unbewusste in Organisation und Kultur*, 8, 2.

Krantz, J. & Gilmore, T.N. (1991). Understanding the dynamics between consulting teams and client systems. In: M.F.R. Kets de Vries et al. (Eds), *Organizations on the couch: Clinical perspectives on organizational behavior and change*. Oxford: Jossey-Bass, 307–330.

Lee-Chai, A.Y. & Bargh, J.A. (Eds) (2001). *The use and abuse of Power*. Ann Arbor: Psychology Press.

Lamont M. & Molnar, V. (2002). The study of boundaries in the social sciences. *Annual Review of Sociology*. Vol. XXVIII, 167–508.

Long, S. (2000). Cooperation and conflict: Two sides of the same coin. In: R. Wiesner & B. Millet (Eds), *Current issues in organisational behaviour*. Brisbane: John Wiley & Sons Australia, Ltd, 1–13.

Milgram, S. (1963). Behavioral study of obedience. *Journal of Abnormal and Social Psychology*, 67, 4, 371–378.

Miller, E.J. & Rice, A.K. (1967). *Systems of organisations: The control of task and sentient boundaries*. London: Tavistock Publications.

Mintzberg, H. (1979). *The structuring of organisations*. Engelwood Cliffs, NJ.: Prentice-Hall.

Rubin, J. & Beckhard, R. (1972). Factors influencing the effectiveness of health teams. *Milbank Memorial Quarterly*, 3, 317–335.

Schonberg, A. (1998). *Two basic assumptions in the psychoanalytic study of organisations*. Paper presented at the Symposium of the International Society for the Psychoanalytic Study of Organisations, 1998.

Vansina, L. (1998/90). Total Quality Control: An overall organizational improvement strategy. *National Productivity Review*, **9**, 1, 59–73.

Vansina, L. (2001). *Explorations into the impact of politics on creativity and destructiveness.* Paper presented at the Symposium of the International Society for the Psychoanalytic Study of Organizations, Paris.

Vansina, L. (2007). Misbruik en geweld in en achter goede intenties. In: S. Prins, S. Schruijer, J. Verboven & K. DeWitte (Eds), *Diversiteit en Vertrouwen in Sociale Systemen.* Leuven: Lannoocampus, 77–94.

Vincent, I. (1997). *Le travail en équipes de projet: Recherche d'une structure minimale psychologique dans une organisation flexible.* Louvain-la-Neuve: Mémoire de license UCL.

CHAPTER 9

Being in and Working with Experiences in the 'Here-and-Now'

Leopold Vansina

Observing and working with the data is an important part of the professional life of an organisation consultant, an action researcher and a manager. In the practice, however, we see quite some confusion between *modes* of being present and *frames* appropriate for one *setting* but failing in another. Each setting has its own context, task and objectives, be it coaching, group relations training, or organisational consulting, action research, managing or just accomplishing a task.

In this chapter, I don't make a distinction between the broader category of organisation consultants and the more specific group of action-researchers. The latter professionals adhere to a more specific process of helping a social system to help them-selves. Managers have a different role, but some of the activities they engage in overlap with those of a consultant. Group relations' trainers[1] have a rather well prescribed role to elucidate and interpret the underlying, unconscious dynamic processes in groups (most often temporary groups of strangers) and only seldom create structural conditions that change the dynamics of a work system; conditions that often form the ground for

---

[1] Within the Tavistock tradition they are also called consultants. I use the concept here of staff or trainer to differentiate their role from an organisation consultant.

'disturbing' behaviour (a.o. Jaques, 1995). For reasons of convenience, I will in the text refer to consultants, managers and group relations' trainers.

The *'here-and-now'* is the *space* in which a *social system* is active at any given time. Yet, it cannot be too narrowly confined to what is within a physical boundary of space and time. Objectives and tasks of a system are most often formulated by a hierarchical level above, be it a boss or the conference organisers, and members bring with them know-how, experiences, membership affiliations from within and from outside; their *past*, as well as their *expectations about the future*. More enduring groups, work systems, and organisations cannot be reduced to touchable structures, but are better conceived as streams of interwoven processes without a clear end or start in which thinking and feeling people are involved within the wider context of society. Technologies and economic realities create additional conditions in the 'here-and-now' and on the extended time dimension: past-future. What is going on in the 'here-and-now' must therefore be studied as *a part* within *a context, a history and a future*. Restricting the study of the 'here-and-now' to the formal work meetings of the social system – even within their context – deprives managers and consultants of valuable information revealed in various kinds of performance reports, customers complaints, employee grievances or in graffiti; or information shared in the bar, the cafeteria or in the lavatory. Places where the members may feel less constrained, less controlled by the existing power structure. Or where they may be either more willing to share ideas with some persons, in the absence of some others, or where they can exchange information, considered not important enough for the formal sessions, or not fitting with the 'preferred or idealised' conceptions of oneself, of the system or both. There may be even more reasons, but one doesn't know.

Managers and consultants should study *the 'here-and-now' in its context and time dimension*. Otherwise one only works with snapshots of what is in fact a stream of processes, often under changing conditions. The analogy is more *making sense of a movie with visible and invisible actors at various times and conditions*. Taking the organisational conditions, the external pressures and time dimension into account, does not simply mean 'accepting' them. On the contrary, they may become the ground for surprise and inquiry. The more limited one's knowledge of the client's history and context, the more likely it is that understanding becomes based on what is present and on one's own context, or pet ideas.

The limits of explorations into the context and history of the client cannot unfortunately be defined beforehand. One's inquiry becomes largely guided by the client's behaviour and the context, the past/future that emerge in the 'here-and-now'. Here again, I must make a distinction between the past of the system/organisation and the personal past of an individual member. As managers and consultants the organisational past is of critical importance and can rightfully be explored. The personal past of a member (his/her childhood) however cannot *rightfully* (ethically sound) and *meaningfully* (relevant for the client) be delved into. Managing and consulting should not be confused or mixed with psychotherapy or individual coaching. Nothing is more scaring and disruptive than the blending of 'giving personal feedback' or 'individual coaching' with working on a normal organisational task. One should keep clear boundaries between the tasks of coaching, managing or consulting. Furthermore, there is now ample evidence that one does not need to dig into the *personal past* of individuals to do serious and lasting work as an organisation consultant. In general, one may say that the past can be re-worked in one's work relations in the present (Vansina-Cobbaert, 2005; Vansina, 2004).

Being in the 'here-and-now' is an investment of the person in the situation. Managers and consultants are neither blank screens, nor objective detached observers. The self is the medium through which appreciative judgement shapes the selection of *mental modes, frames*, and *perspectives*; guides the choosing of intervention and methods. The making of a judgement is never confined to finding the facts only. It always includes the appreciation of the data, their relative importance, not only what we take as 'noise' or information, 'figure' or 'ground', but also their social, ethical and political implications (Vickers, 1995). That human capacity to make appreciative judgements should *be cultivated* with care in order to make more refined, less absolute or categorical judgements, with an explicit recognition that all judging activities are *culturally and contextually bound*. Yet, one may not be aware of the influences of the social context (Bargh, 2007). Judging has most often acquired a negative connotation in the social sciences – particular amongst clinical psychologists and group relations' trainers – because it is often subjectively experienced as the rejection of the whole person. It is talked about as something bad that should be avoided. This is a judgement too. We human beings simply cannot refrain from making judgements, even if we want to. This was clearly expressed in a slogan someone wrote on a blackboard during the students' uprising in Paris in 1968: "Il est interdit d'interdire!": It is forbidden to forbid!!

The social sciences have for a long time believed that they were *value free*, much like the exact sciences. This illusion was shredded in the 1960s. Around this period, Rogers (1951) put an emphasis on the unconditional acceptance of the client which inspired a lot of social scientist practitioners. *Unconditional acceptance* didn't mean that all undesirable behaviour of the client should be approved of, but that the therapist should refrain from *condemning* the client as a person because of his/her behaviour. In fact, the unconditional acceptance of the client was seen as a fundamental therapeutic condition for his/her development. It largely rested on the belief that the client could eventually outgrow the unwanted behaviour if s/he came to understand its meaning (hidden reasons) within his/her particular context. The task of the non-directive counsellor was then to help the client in his/her efforts to understand him/herself, not only in a cognitive way, but also, and most importantly, in his/her emotional experiences of becoming a person. Judging the client or his behaviour meant not only that one imposed one's own values on the client, but also that it would seriously hinder the further explorations of meaning, feelings, reasons for and the context of the dissatisfying behaviour.

Later, when we came to recognise the limitations of unconditional acceptance, Harold Bridger talked about 'suspending judgement'. This notion referred to a conscious attempt to withhold judgement until one has gained sufficient understanding of the meaning, the intentions and context of the client before making a *professional judgement* about what could best be done to further the development of the client. Whether there is a need to set *rules* about proper behaviour in a particular situation, to draw *boundaries* about what could and could not be dwelled on. For instance, distinguishing a personal problem as a 'private task' for that person to work on outside the meetings, from the 'given task' of the group. In other instances, one may have to *re-affirm social norms* when there is pretence that they don't exist, or to correct a twisted interpretation of them to justify unethical or a-social behaviour. The essence of 'suspending judgement' is to observe and to explore *in order to understand* the person or the group in its context, while avoiding premature (based on partial knowledge) or impulsive judgements.

For a long time, we have cherished the belief that whenever people can comprehend the realities they are in, they will know what to do. Although understanding the realities we are in is of utmost importance it seems often *insufficient* to take appropriate action. Most importantly, I came to realise that the consultant plays an active part in creating that reality through his/her interventions, for example, research methods, problem definition, the in- and exclusion of stakeholders. In our professional work, judgement is the process through which our social responsibilities become actualised. Judgement mediates between our appreciation of the setting and our decision to engage or not in a project or an ongoing activity. If the objectives or means are inappropriate or unacceptable in terms of their anticipated consequences one withholds one's investment, not just without debate. And judgement continues to guide our ways to achieve objectives with social responsibility. Since goal achievement, task accomplishment and social responsibilities often generate tensions within the system, the consultant or manager must not only stand up for his/her social responsibility, but be attentive to create conditions that also others can take theirs too.

After this clarification of the meaning of the 'here-and-now' and of judgement, I would like to distinguish in this chapter between different *mental modes* of being present in the situation; how these modes of consciousness relate to the kind of work we do as managers and consultants; and how we can move in and out of these different levels of consciousness. In a second part, I'll discuss the *relevance of frames* for the purpose and nature of the project and different ways of working with data and experiences. This part is rounded off with an exploration of the possible consequences of a mismatch between mental modes and the demands of the work setting. In a third part, I'll focus on working with *experiences* in the 'here-and-now' and the importance of moving away from 'interpretations' towards 'sense making' and its various implications for the practice of professionals.

VARIOUS MENTAL MODES OF BEING PRESENT

Human beings, even before they are born, are present. Unborn babies become familiar with their environment, for example, the heartbeat of their mother and the music she regularly plays or listens to. Once born, human beings – just like animals – explore and observe their environments in which they make themselves present. They touch, taste and observe what happens. In the process they learn to give meaning to what they see, hear, smell, taste and feel. From the vast number of different impressions over the years, human beings automatically come to discard what doesn't seem to be relevant while paying closer attention to (zooming in on) what strikes them as important, or what may hurt, or endanger their lives; or what may hinder or facilitate the course of their goal-directed activities. That process only comes to an end with life itself.

As consultants or managers, we most of the time interact with other thinking and feeling human beings. The latter are then not seen as *objects* but fellow *subjects* with their own conscious and unconscious intentions, meaning attributions, emotional lives and tensions. At other times, the same manager or consultant may observe the functioning of *objects*, for example, machines or people, but now taken as *objects* to assess, for example, their capabilities for a particular job. Then, s/he may shift observations from the machines to the interactions between an employee and the machine, alternating between the person as an *object* (e.g. studying his movements, tempo) and as a *subject* (e.g. what meaning s/he appears to be given to that work). What is carefully maintained is a caring relation with the client system. Later on, one may take a pause and look back at one's experiences and observations to check the progress one is making in identifying the issue at hand and move into action. At the end of the day, one may attend a concert, sit in a comfortable seat and let the music come. At other times, one may join the familiar sailing crew on the familiar yacht and race for pleasure on the sea.

From these brief descriptions, we can see that human beings can be fully present[2] in quite different, often switching, mental modes that affect what we see, experience, and even learn. Vasilyuk's typology of functional regimes of *consciousness* (1991) stimulated my thinking about the various mental modes of being in the 'here-and-now'. Maybe it is useful to distinguish between these modes in terms of the degree of consciousness in being present to understand better the differences in the realities of the world that become thereby available to us. In a first form of heightened consciousness, the person takes a stance where "forms of apprehension are active – thought and memory – the real content" (p. 21). Human subjects are then more likely to become observed as objects than subjects. Vasilyuk calls this mode "*apprehension*": the act or power of perceiving or comprehending. It corresponds with the consultant/manager in the act of studying a situation, 'what is out there' by observation or action. One or more conceptual frames or models are used to study as an expert or a distant observer a situation, a case, a protocol or 'cold data' collected by someone else. The old school of behaviourism, and its derivatives in experimental social psychology (e.g. Bales' small group interaction frame, 1950) may be considered as typical examples for the apprehensive mode. Yet, any other frame based on psychoanalytic or any other

---

[2] Being present here does not refer to the notion within Gestalt psychology of 'a presence', which points to a particular way of being with the client: "Not only standing for and expressing certain values, attitudes, and skills, but to use these in a way to stimulate, and perhaps *evoke* from the client, action necessary for movement on the problem" (Nevis, 1987, p. 54). Being present, in this chapter simply stands for the various ways of being in the 'here-and-now'.

theory from psychology, sociology, economy or anthropology may be chosen to arrive at a kind of understanding of what is out there.

In a second form of being in the situation, the person's consciousness functions are somewhat less active, enabling experiences, incidents and feelings to emerge and to make sense in retrospect of what has been happening in the 'here-and-now'. It is called *reflection*. It corresponds with the mental presence of a person individually interrupting one's active engagement for 'reflection-in-action' (Schon, 1983), or to 'review' together with others, in a sort of organised way the activities and ways of interacting of a social system of which one was part (see: next chapter). Whereas 'reflection-in-action' is a one-sided active process of a person, the organised review is a collective process. Both are attempts to understand in *retrospect* what has happened in the 'here-and-now' as a starting point for learning and improvement actions.

In a third position, the person is present in the situation, in an even less conscious, more passive, receptive way, allowing him/herself to *experience* fully what is out there. The situation is allowed to come of its own force, spontaneously, without any effort or act of apprehension or reflection. *Experiencing* is then understood as a reflection of the objective world *in* the observer. Yet, it is not a pure mirroring of what is out there, but it is a subjective, partial reflection of the real world in *its relation* to that person. Or, as Depraz, Varela & Vermersch, (2003, p. 2) put it in their introduction: "Experience is always that which a singular subject is subjected to at any given time and place, that to which s/he has access 'in the first person'".

Bion (1988) recommended this passive/receptive stance for the group relations' trainers or psychotherapist, as most suited to let the 'here-and-now' into oneself and speak for itself. It is a weakened conscious state of 'rêverie' facilitating 'unconscious communication' between consultant/therapist and client. It echoes with Levinas' thinking (1987) that meaning and intelligibility emerge in the relationship between persons.

There is, however, a fourth way of being present, which does not fit in Vasilyuk's functional regimes of consciousness, namely being actively engaged *in participative thinking and responsive acting* with others. Managers, action-researchers and organisation consultants are often in that form of being present, where in the flow of responsive activity one ". . . simply acts – not on the basis of reasons, but blindly, in response to the requirements of our joint shared circumstances" (Shotter, 2003, p. 449). There is meaning and direction in the interactions before they are consciously processed and even talked about.

This mode of being present and engaged with others is enjoyable; one becomes part of a whole. However, in order to learn from participative thinking and responsive acting one has to take time and space for reflection and review.

The four modes of being present, each with its own degree of consciousness, are all relevant to being in the 'here-and-now'. Each mode seems to bring us in contact with a kind of reality, not just another aspect of it. *Apprehension* most often filters and moulds our observations into a learned, pre-established mental frame that overshadows the 'innocent observer' stance. One observes and studies largely what one already knows. The data or what is noticed yields meaning and understanding through the structure that is inherent to the frame in use. We are as consultants and managers involved in the application of knowledge, models, principles, tested elsewhere, or just bare experiences from the past.

Reflection results either in an individual or in a collective *reconstruction* and *understanding* of what was. As such it is very much influenced by the appreciation one made of the (intermediate) known outcomes of the preceding activities. Consequently, the understanding may be more justification and validation of dominant concepts and principles than understanding the uniqueness of the dynamic interplay between a given task, the persons involved and the fields of tension within a particular context. In other words, the real causal factors may remain unexplored resulting in learning the wrong thing. *Reflection* does create a reality based on retrospective sense making that may deviate in many ways of what really happened. Although organised, collective reflection may also lead to a social reconstruction of what happened, one can learn from the divergence of insights that become shared and compared. Individual and collective reflection yield ideas about what could be done differently to improve the performance of that system in the future. In this way it stimulates exploration of what might happen if and future apprehension to validate these ideas.

Experiencing leads the human being into a world that is not just constituted by factual, objective or even observable data. It brings the person in touch with the 'here-and-now' as it resonates *within*. As such it may result in the discovery of an 'elusive truth', something that is true at a given moment within a given setting. It is a contradiction in terms to think that the 'products' of this mental mode contain *universal truths*. As soon as one departs from that 'here-and-now' these 'old' discoveries may be true, but *one doesn't know*. These discovered dynamics or concealed meaning (in the language of images, actions and relations) couldn't be simply applied elsewhere. One has to find out over and over again. Group relations' trainers, and in particular their participants may erroneously take these interventions, for example, interpretations or discoveries as *frames for apprehension* thereby violating the basic characteristics of this mental mode that made them accessible to consciousness.

Participative thinking and responsive interactions create in the people involved real affective experiences of unity, of harmony, of togetherness without erosion of distinctiveness. Although there is a reduced awareness of distinctiveness in role or as persons while forming a whole, it may not be confused with fusion, a state of total absence of differentiation. Improving participative thinking and responsive interaction is achieved through simple adjusting actions without conscious processing. Even complex but routine tasks can be successfully performed in this mental mode. Conceptualising the underlying tacit knowledge, however, can only be achieved through a phase of reflection, or through apprehension of playbacks of recordings of the 'here-and-now'.

These four mental modes of consciousness are not clearly demarcated. Human beings can and do move from one mental mode to another – back and forth – in relation to an assumed purpose for being in the 'here-and-now' or as an automatic response to an emerging preoccupation or tension. Normally, in that process, apprehension as application may give way to reflective inquiry; experiencing too may lead into reflective inquiry; and inquiry into apprehension; and one may take time and space for reflection after periods of participative thinking and responsive interaction. An evoked preoccupation or tension may break the experiencing mode. Action-researchers, consultants and managers, however, do differ markedly in their preference for, their capacity to and the time spent in each of these mental modes. Different emphasis is then given to different kinds of reality, different quality of inquiry and different relations with the 'here-and-now' and with the client system. For example, working more as a rational, distant consultant or manager; or more as a collaborative, reflective action-researcher, consultant or manager; or as a receptive, 'experiencing', group relations' trainer.

Moving in and moving out appropriately from one mental mode into another is not always easy, since we may have become habituated to a particular role and its predominant mode. Furthermore, I think that there are also personal dispositions that lead to preferences and rationalisations for holding onto a particular mental mode.

Group trainers and process consultants are taught to keep a balance between 'moving in' (more active participation and inquiry to understand the complexities) and 'moving out' (a passive, reflective and/or experiencing mode to get, for example, a feel for the possible underlying dynamics, the emotional quality of the group, the languages from 'Atlantis'), but for organisation consultants and managers it is not at all evident what is appropriate. 'Moving in' means being more active, paying attention (*apprehension*) to more specific elements (zooming in), collecting more observable data to check an 'assumption in one's mind'. 'Moving out' into *experiencing* facilitates listening to languages from 'Atlantis', 'the music', created not just by words and intonations, but also by body language, and the use made of the given space (seating arrangements) and time (last minute issues). It makes it also easier to become aware of 'fields of tensions', of emerging images in one's mind and those 'small things' which are dropped by the client as if they do not fit, thereby revealing possible psychodynamic processes. In short, experiencing widens the consultant's range of things to be explored. Yet, without further open exploration or links to observable data or particular events, the emerging images and hunches may turn into 'wild' interpretations.

The delicate issue of moving in and out appropriately can be illustrated by a frequently observed interaction: the process consultant raises a question to the group, or shares thoughts on of what might be going on beneath the surface ('moving in'). Some group member responds immediately with an approving or disapproving answer. If the consultant/manager does not take time to reflect about what this answer/reaction could mean or reveal about the quality and/or impact of the intervention, s/he is likely to be drawn into an argument, a rational discussion or in giving another formulation of the same, as if the first had not been understood. Thereby, the consultant misses the dynamics or emotions beneath the surface. Equally inappropriate is turning into a sphinx, preparing another intervention without reference to what just happened.

Managers and organisation consultants find it difficult to leave the active mental modes of apprehension and/or the participative thinking/responsive interaction and to move into the passive stance of *experiencing*. Even reflection-in-action (Schon, 1983) does not come easily when one is passionately engaged (Vansina, 1989) and the work is progressing well. Reflection may then come during a pause, for example, a coffee break, on one's way home, or during one's 'sleep'. One may then come to some insights, some afterthoughts, or realise that one has missed something in the stories, accounts or data, or that one has not paid sufficient attention to certain elements/conditions. Such afterthoughts are worthwhile sharing with the client-system even when they come late, but hopefully not too late. As a consultant one may call the client, if it is one person, or when several persons are involved keep these afterthoughts in mind for the agenda of the next meeting. However, when one meets with the client again, one avoids pre-structuring the agenda with these afterthoughts. It is preferable to wait for the members of the client-system to bring in their material; thereby one is enabled to put the afterthoughts in their context.

In order to legitimise moving into the mental mode of *reflection* together with the members of a work system, managers and organisation consultants are encouraged to institutionalise 'time-out' and 'review sessions'. In its two forms, time and space are taken to learn retrospectively about the ways of working on the task, as a social system and subsequently build commitment for improvement action. Reviewing facilitates the integration of working on the task and learning as *an ongoing process*. Furthermore, it allows for *experiencing* how the system works on this *reviewing task* in the 'here-and-now'.

THE RELEVANCE OF WORKING WITH OR WITHOUT SPECIFIC FRAMES IN THE 'HERE-AND-NOW'

From infancy our sensing and perceiving become invested with meaning. It is a continuous learning process by which apperception becomes *intrinsically* related to perception. Consequently being present generates data that goes beyond the simple registration of a camera. Direct observations and participation in activities affect human beings and allow them to gain knowledge of what is out there. They are in other words the source of 'experiences', containing cognitive, emotional and appreciative elements that are not only the product of what happens out there, but also of the personal dispositions, history, membership and context of the person, his/her mental mode and frame of mind. These 'experiences' often become expressed in the person's interactions – even when one tries to control them – to which the 'observed' in turn reacts/responds.

Working with Specific Frames

Human beings spontaneously 'take a frame' in relation to what they like to achieve in a given situation: the frame of a hunter, an explorer, a tourist, a diagnostician, an experimental researcher, a manager or a consultant. The taking of a frame can be a deliberate choice in function of: (a) the nature of the unit under study, (b) the task and objectives of the assignment. The two combined (a plus b), I call '*the setting*'. The considered choice is, however, limited by (c) the repertoire and the capability of working with a variety of frames and models.[3]

The nature of the unit *under* study can be a temporary group of participants; a 'collaborative task system' in which different interest parties come together to work on a largely self-constructed common task, for example, the deterioration of their neighbourhood; or a more enduring work system like a production unit, an organisation or even a society.

Within the task and objectives of the assignment one can further distinguish: (i) the unit *of* study, (ii) the perspectives, and (iii) the functional value of a frame or a model. In function of the unit *of* study one can focus attention on the individual, the interactions between persons, roles or groups, the group as a whole or the interplay between the socio- and technical parts of the system. These units *of* study can furthermore be studied from different *perspectives* or disciplines. For example, one may look at a unit of study with a psychodynamic, an economic, a technology and/or even a system's perspective. Each perspective generates different data and enriching insights in the multifaceted reality of that unit.

Within the category of *functional relevance* of a frame (or model) we find: (i) a wide range of *diagnostic frames*. Some frames are more focussed on observing emerging or established structures or patterns in interactions; others give preponderance to evolving processes; and with various degrees of specificity. For example, the well specified, observation frame for interpersonal interaction by Bales (1950); the psychodynamic 'wiring' diagram of Hirschhorn (2005); process consultation of Schein (1988); and Bridger's basic model of the interactions between members of a system in relation to the primary task (Gold & Klein, 2004); (ii) models for *identifying levers* for change or development, for example, the six box model of Weisbord (1978),

---

[3] In the previous chapter, we defined a frame as that which governs our perception and representation of the situation in which we are acting (Goffman, 1986). A model is usually more elaborated than a frame. It is a description or analogy used to help visualise something that cannot be directly observed (Webster, 1988). It is generally based on a theory. Yet, a model is always a simplification of a reality. Nevertheless it helps us to grasp some complexity of that reality.

the pentagram jointly developed by Bridger and myself; and (iii) frames and models for *problem solving* and *system design* derived from social, organisational psychology, and systems theory, for example, Strategic Analysis of Organisations (Crozier, 1964), Senge's system analysis (1990), Soft Systems Methodology (Checkland, 1981).

Frames and models may be further developed and systematised in *methods* or *methodologies*, for example, Soft Systems Methodology. I have a preference for methods that invite members of the work system to participate in the data collection and processing. Space, as well as a 'raison d'être', and a vehicle is thereby provided to enable the members to bring their inner lives and creative processes into the problem solving, where they can be 'worked through'. The locus is thereby moved from the consultant or manager into the collaborative relation with the problem owners (examples of several such methods are discussed by Ramirez & Drevon, 2005).

The distinctions between frames for observing or collecting data and frames for working on a diagnosed issue can be fuzzy. Take for example, the famous Force Field Analysis of Lewin: studying the driving and restraining forces in a system to improve performance almost invites the person to take action to reduce or remove the restraining and to strengthen the driving forces. Explicit and implicit frames have a great impact on what a person notices and how they work with the data. Frames have a dual function: structuring more or less what may be important to *observe,* as well as what may be relevant to *explore* either through questioning, first-person accounts, narratives or through other forms of data collection.

It is not only useful, but also essential to alternate between frames and compare the findings.

Whenever we study a unit with a frame or a model we move into the mental mode of apprehension, and work with focussed attention. The more a frame is specific and defined the more likely that one's presence in the 'here-and-now' becomes structured by that frame. One concentrates on what should be noticed or registered, while becoming unaware of all the other things that are going on but fall outside the frame. In order to reduce these risks, experienced managers and consultants start with a rather open frame, for example, how a work system in a given context is working on its task, while paying attention to (a) *'task work'*: what appropriate activities are carried out and which ones are absent, and how these are carried out to achieve task accomplishment;

(b) *'team-work'*: how the system members work together to achieve task completion, and (c) to the *fields of tensions* created either by the 'task-work' or the 'teamwork' and their *inter-relatedness*. Then, when an issue or an improvement opportunity is identified, they select a more specific, relevant frame or model to either obtain more evidence, and/or to explore what can be done to further goal accomplishment and development. Interventions may range from creating facilitating, and/or supportive process structures, and/or conditions that improve the dynamics of the system itself.

A rich repertoire and capability of working with different frames is a valuable asset. Specialist in one frame may achieve an outstanding reputation within a discipline or a particular school, but managers and organisation consultants are there to see that complex problems can be resolved and that a system can function better in a sustainable way. This demands a rich repertoire of frames and agility in taking alternative perspectives. Consequently, their role cannot be restricted to advancing a discipline or a professional school of thought. The most serious problems are created by persons who have a restricted repertoire, or hold on to one frame only – maybe proper to a particular setting, for example, an engineering frame for systems design, a psychoanalytic frame for group relations conference – to observe and work within settings of a vastly different nature. The deplorable consequence is that the study of 'task-work' within an organisational setting and its specific tensions becomes neglected in favour of 'teamwork' and its field of tensions, or vice versa. In both instances one thereby excludes the exploration of the interactions between 'task-work' and 'teamwork'.

Some familiarity with the tasks in a given setting facilitates the selection of appropriate frames to observe and work with. Yet, familiarity with the setting has its pros and cons. The better one's understanding of the nature of the work, for example, task-work, the more one is likely to see what is and isn't appropriate or efficient for goal attainment, and the more one is sensitive to the tensions generated by the work and their impact on the members in the system. It becomes easier to observe what there is to be seen, and to spot deviations from the 'normal', but it often narrows the field of what one notices. One may become blind for certain data, or take them for granted. It then leads to a reduction of the richness of the realities studied that can only be broken by 'an innocent observer' or someone with a different frame.

When we now turn to the way managers/consultants work with these data in the 'here-and- now' we observe major differences that can be grouped into three distinctive categories: (a) the data remains private: either triggering spontaneous reactions or privately processed for taking considered action; (b) the data is used for 'giving feedback' and/or (c) as a point of departure for reflective inquiry.

Privately processed with or without conscious deliberation. Often our actions are monitored spontaneously by what we see and experience. Conscious processing may be totally absent, resulting roughly in either emotional re-actions of dissent, agreement or confrontation; or in participative thinking and responsive interactions, for example, spontaneously taking up a missing role. We talk about *considered action taking* whenever alternative actions and their anticipated consequences are deliberated or explored in the virtual world: for example, suggesting a method, a facilitating or supportive process structure, a technique for further investigation, for problem solving or decision making; or taking on a needed role, providing a missing resource to further task and goal accomplishment. All these ways of working with and in the 'here-and-now' can be most appropriate under conditions of time constraints, or in order to set a learning process in motion. But, the members of the system don't learn much about the dynamics of the system unless the manager or consultant explains posterior the reasoning behind the actions taken. Even then, the learning may become more rational than experiential. In general, one should be careful with 'being helpful'. Helping may be an automatic response to the client's helplessness and foreclose inquiry. Indeed, actions to help often forego the basic question *why* the system under study is unaware, unable, or unwilling to fill that need or provide that missing resource. The exploration of the 'why' may lead into reflective inquiry into the dynamics underneath: the benefits of 'not doing anything', the need to conceal certain parts, an anxiety grounded in fantasy, or a reality-based fear, a learned response, or just an absence of know-how. Inquiry into these underlying dynamics may lead to a reality check: balancing the benefits against the costs; is the fear still warranted or are there more effective ways for working with particular tensions, or filling the know-how gap.

Working with experiences and observations in the 'here-and-now' taking the form of 'giving feedback'. Managers and organisational consultants may have learned from week-ends on personal growth, outdoor exercises, group relations and coaching to share data of *factual* observations, or of more *subjective* experiences with the client and apply this 'technique' as part and parcel of their practices as managers, and consultants. The technique of 'giving feedback' is based on a mechanistic conception of human beings and social systems. One assumes that there is an automatic connecting loop between knowing and change or development. Knowing is considered to be sufficient to enable the individual and social systems to grapple and work through the underlying dynamics and tensions on their own. From experience we know that this is most often not the case. Until the reasons beneath the surface are dealt with and the conditions are changed nothing sustainable is likely to happen. 'Feedback' may stimulate validation of an observation but it is certainly insufficient to help an *embedded* work system to change.

Another risk inherent in giving factual feedback of information – from observations, personal inventories or questionnaires – is that it may lead to labelling that stagnates development. It may result in: 'That's what I am or what we are!' or motivate the recipient to change 'how s/he appears' so that the 'impression' on others becomes more favourable. '*Appearing*' then becomes more important than '*being*'.

Using data and experiences as a basis for reflective inquiry. A more effective way of working in and with the 'here-and-now' is to share experiences and observations as a basis for *reflective inquiry* into the underlying dynamics and tensions that may increase our understanding of *why* and under what *conditions* the system under study behaves in these particular ways. 'Why don't we learn from our mistakes?' becomes an appropriate way to explore the causes, the possible benefits of not learning, the anxieties contained in shared fantasies about what would happen if one started to hold onto mistakes in order to learn from them, and/or what would become disclosed in those learning activities that must remain concealed. In this joint search process, we may find time and space to bring our 'inner' and 'outer' worlds closer together so that we can commit ourselves to considered *actions* for improvement. This way of using data to gain an *understanding* of the dynamics behind or beneath the system within given *conditions* is much more delicate and complex and cannot be reduced to 'giving feedback'. It is a guided, reflective, *psychodynamic inquiry*. It requires a move from apprehension into reflection about the 'why' and under which 'conditions'.

Getting at the 'why' is not easy. We may question but the answers need to be carefully processed. People tend to give an answer, even when they don't know, either because they never gave it serious thought, or because the reasons may be unconscious, or socially suppressed and may expose what should remain concealed. The 'why' moves then into the back of the inquirer's mind and plausible answers may emerge during the course of the project; hopefully before its ending so that they can be explored and dealt with in an appropriate way – which does not mean that the possible answers should always be discussed or brought to awareness. Selective changes in particular conditions often do the job. Yet, without such efforts good intentions and constructive actions are likely to fade with the re-emerging tensions of the situation.

Working Without a Specific Frame

Being present with an open mind is best achieved in the mental mode of *experiencing*. Such a mode is essential, if one deems it necessary to work with and on the underlying psychodynamic processes, which cannot be directly expressed in words because of social repression and other unconscious processes. Experiencing requires a *passive receptive stance* without a focus on *what should be noticed*. In view of the growing popularity of the *application* of psychoanalytic theory over psychodynamic *inquiry*, it is important to take time to understand the implications of that *passive receptive stance*.

This stance allows: (1) what is out there to become *reflected or resonate in* the consultant; (2) images, metaphors, thoughts and feelings to *emerge;* but it also allows for (3) experiences to become *evoked* or *induced* in the consultant. Bion (1988) pointed to four important conditions proper to such a way of being present. These conditions were already addressed in Part One, but it may be worthwhile going over them once more.

(a) *'Without desire'*: One is present without a need to be helpful, to improve, to cure, or relieve suffering from, for example, pain, stress, discomfort. Whenever these needs come to dominate, one risks becoming selective in one's interventions. For example, in order to *reassure* the client one may say that s/he may not be alone in the group with such fearful or painful experiences, in the absence of real data that this *is* the case. Or, one becomes more interested in helping, than truthfully revealing what one assumes to be going on.

(b) *'Without memory'*: The consultant refrains from trying to recall what happened in the past in order to get an idea about what is happening in the 'here-and-now'. If, however, some memories emerge while noticing what is going on in the 'here-and-now', they may be relevant to explore with the client.

(c) *'Without understanding'*: 'Not knowing' means that one keeps one's mind free of theoretical concepts or notions in order to avoid these notions becoming filters of what is really going on and stopping experiencing or inquiry. For example, a client could have problems with authority but that doesn't mean s/he has or had an issue with his parents, and vice versa. Because the client had a difficult relation with his/her parents he or she does not necessarily have a problem with authority or with the consultant! In some instances it may well be true, *but one doesn't know*. One has to find out! This 'cultivated ignorance' (Menzies-Lyth, 1989) or 'negative capability'– first coined by the poet John Keats in 1817 and later used by Bion (1988) – is a way of being present. It contains an active component of 'creating space' for finding out, as well as a passive element to allow things to emerge and to feel the resonance (French & Simpson, 1999). One tries to remain receptive and attentive to the reflection *within oneself* of the 'here-and-now' in its *wider context*.

(d) One is present with an *evenly divided attention* to both levels of psychic functioning: the manifest (what is observable) and to the latent (what resonates within oneself). The latter follows logically from the fact that what is socially suppressed or unconscious *cannot* be directly expressed, but becomes *revealed indirectly* in images, associations, succession of themes, interruptions; the contrast between what is said and the overt behaviour; in what is not talked about, but logically related; and in the various ways the client-system takes actions, relates, and makes use of time and space.

Actualising these four conditions is not an easy task since it presupposes that one is free from any preoccupation. In my experience, it is something that can to quite an extent be learned. However, on occasion we may find it too difficult to contain: (a) the fear of missing data, when trying to keep one's attention evenly divided over the manifest and the latent; (b) the anxiety inherent to that attitude of 'not knowing', and (c) the stress in dealing with the difficult, ongoing process of 'sorting out'.

The fear of missing some relevant data by dividing one's attention may be based on the wrong idea that one has to be at the same time a focussed observer and a passive, receptive person. In fact it means that one allows the 'here-and-now' to become reflected within the consultant, so that enough observable data (not necessary verbatim, or quotable phrases) becomes available to distinguish between an 'inner' experience[4] as 'me' (mine) from 'not-me' (or not mine, but from the client-system). These considered experiences can subsequently be used to substantiate an exploration of what is going on. The use of observable data in one's attempts to understand the 'here-and-now' is of particular importance, not only to facilitate further exploration and elaboration by the client, but also to de-mystify the intervention by exposing how the consultant's mind functions (Vansina, 2000). If one has missed something of the important data, it is likely to come up later, maybe in a different form.

Besides the fear of missing or not understanding something important, one has to withstand the temptation to become absorbed – intellectually or emotionally – in a discussion, thereby losing touch with what is not said, although it would be logically linked to the issue under debate.

Consultants and managers are supposed to know. This social expectation, even insistence on getting a comprehensive answer, adds to the anxiety of 'not-knowing'. If one is able to contain it one can give oneself time until the dynamics become clearer, or one has gained some understanding of why a particular feeling or confusion has been invoked or some hunches about the why behind the insistence. Expectations are only one of the many ways through which a *relation* is constituted between client-system and the consultant or manager. Staying in touch with this developing and evolving relation is critical to keep it realistic, not illusory, so that groundwork can be done.

Allowing the 'here-and-now to become reflected in oneself, to become receptive to emerging and evoked experiences entails with it the difficult and ongoing task of '*sorting out*' what is 'me' and 'not-me' in these experiences, as mentioned above. *Sorting out* is hard work. It is a *reflective process* by which one tries to distinguish the images, thoughts, feelings and hunches that *are mine* (the 'me' in the experience) from those that are proper to the client-system, for example, *generated* by the client-system (a particular mood in the group: helplessness, optimism, despair and consequently shared by other members) or *induced* in me by the client's behaviour, ways of talking and

---

[4] An experience can be a thought, an association, an image or metaphor, or a feeling that emerges in a person while working with a client or client-system. It is important to recognise and distinguish between the cognitive and emotional elements incorporated, in various degrees within an experience.

even looking, for example, feelings of having to protect, feelings of guilt, incompetence or even omnipotence (known under the psychoanalytic notion of *projective identification*[5]).Time needs to be taken to hold on to the experience to sort it out: (a) whether it is a reflection in me of what is out there (a resonance), or (b) whether it is evoked in me because of my own sensitivities or unresolved personal issues (known as *counter-transference*), or (c) whether it is induced in me by the client-system, before it can be identified as projective identification. Sorting out is that kind of work that, at least in the beginning of one's professional work, should best be done under supervision. Yet, it is a lifelong task. Without that hard work one is at risk of putting one's own concerns and problems onto the client.

The process of sorting out can be described in logical steps one takes in the self- inquiry about the 'why' of that experience. The first question to raise is: 'Am I the only one with this particular experience of being bored, for example, or are there more persons in the group that are giving cues of the same experience?' If it is unusual for them to look bored as they do with this kind of work at this time of the day, then it may well be that my boredom is an experience generated by the client-system. The subsequent reflection is then: 'Is there some evidence that this boredom is an attempt to control aggression (e.g. fight-flight), which cannot be expressed and why?' If I am the only one with this experience of being bored, then I have to explore whether it could be related to me. In the latter case, my boredom may be part of a counter-transference reaction to what is going on.

If, on the other hand, I am alone with that feeling of not being interested and it is unusual for me to feel that way with this kind of work at this time of the day, then the feeling is "out of character" as Krantz and Gilmore (1991) called it. I have now some grounds to assume that I am the recipient of projective identification.

Schein (1988) describes the process of observation–intervention as follows. First there is an observation to which you (secondly) have an emotional reaction (for instance an appreciation) which brings you (thirdly) to judgement and maybe finally to an intervention. In many situations people don't realise the emotional reaction and come directly to a judgement or an intervention. He encourages consultants to be conscious of the phases in that process and

---

[5] The notion of projective identification, transference and counter-transference were extensively discussed in Part One.

question themselves: 'Do I get this emotional reaction because of myself or it is generated from what is happening in the group?' This is *Ed Schein's way of explaining the difficult task and process of 'sorting out'*. However, he restricts that process to reflections to personal sensitivities. Projective-identification is not considered here.

Since most consultants and managers have not gone through the lengthy process of psychoanalysis and supervision – and even if they did – one has to be careful in the way one works with the 'experiences in me'.

First, one should avoid making authoritative interpretations of the reality, or statements on qualitative data as if they are facts, or worded in such a way that they become easily perceived as a subtle appeal to change, either to please the consultant or to join his/her 'reality'.

I wish to share with you some thoughts of Bion (1988), who repeatedly emphasised the importance of reality or the truth for psychic development and mental health. Reality, in social systems, however, can never be grasped, but looked upon via activities in motion, an event. As a consequence, the truth does not lie within the domain of knowledge, it cannot be plucked from established knowledge, unless accidentally. Furthermore, the analysis of the unconscious is not the essence in psychoanalysis, but a path to, a way of 'touching' reality. Reality or truth – according to Bion – can 'become', but not be 'known'. However, the truth exists independently from the consultant (Bion, 1988, pp. 88–89).

I have always been impressed by Bion's views on reality. Staying in touch with reality is not only important for survival, but also for psychic development. As such it is not and it cannot be the prerogative of anyone person to search for and to stay in touch with reality. It is a shared task of consultant or manager with all members of the system, all human beings. Therefore, any one person or group is not allowed to *impose* his understanding of reality onto others, especially when such an interpretation cannot readily be verified. One can *share* one's understanding or sense making of the presented realities as an *invitation* to compare it with the sense making of the others in order to set off a process of reflective inquiry. Not with the aim of finding out which 'sense' holds the truth, but what light is shed on the various facets of the 'here-and-now' and what can be done to improve the performance of, and the well-being in the system within its wider context. The validity of this process of sharing and comparing can be checked against the improved ability to relate to and handle reality. This pursuit of reality is also an unending and engaging task critical in being a social responsible citizen. It enables the person or group to discover and reveal deceptions, lies and manipulation of the media, of leaders, persons in position of power or of just common people.

If the understanding of reality cannot be the prerogative of any one person holding the truth, it is logical that the sharing of one's experiences and understanding should always include an element of *doubt* ('Could it be?'), of *wonder* ('Isn't it interesting to see . . . ?'), or an element of *surprise* (which may have a touch of humour). Ideally, in such an intervention, a *likely meaning* of 'observable behaviour' is offered in relation to an *assumed* source of tension in a way that invites further inquiry. Indeed, even after an honest effort of 'sorting out' one cannot be totally sure whether one's experience is similar to what other members feel, or is a good enough reflection of what is happening in the system, or just an evoked personal response. Neither can one predict how deeply experiences are socially repressed or removed from consciousness. The only sign that a shared understanding approaches an accessible reality is to be found in the way the client system *works with it*: a reflective silence, a hesitant questioning, further inquiry and elaboration, or an increased vigilance in working on the task. This attentive 'listening' to how the client 'talks back', is also important to understand how the intervention is understood so that corrections can be made. However careful one's formulation may be, the consultant/manager has no full control over the way the intervention is received and understood. An attempt to share one's understanding of what is happening may be taken as an authoritative statement, thereby closing off comparing and finding out.

Second, the mental mode of experiencing is not always possible to hold on to, nor appropriate. Even when one has learned and mastered working from an experiencing mode, a consultant or manager find themselves most often in a role through which s/he *legitimately* becomes – even passionately – engaged in the work, taking goal-directed action and joining in participatory thinking and responsive interaction. Even if one could abruptly shift into an experiencing mode it is likely to disrupt the ongoing work, or catch the other members by surprise. Personally, I find it most inappropriate for managers – and even consultants – to make interpretations about what is going on, or point to underlying tensions in members *during work*. The structure of a work system can neither be used for coaching, nor for analysis of psychodynamic processes. What is possible and even advisable is that the manager or consultant create time and space for a distinctive structured setting for collective reflecting and experiencing, for example, time-out or review sessions. In this setting, the manager or consultant and all other members hold, temporarily, *equal roles* in retrospective learning for the future.

Third, the experiencing mode as an exclusive stance is not sufficient to work effectively as an organisation consultant or manager. Group relations' trainers, often groomed in the experiencing mode, may – when taking on organisational consulting – find themselves in unfamiliar settings. Confronted with work systems embedded in an organisational context, they often fall back on their rich experiences with temporary groups of 'strangers', either using experiencing as the only mental mode to work from, or holding onto an exclusive psychoanalytic frame. It easily leads, at best, to *partial interpretations* based on what is present in the 'here-and-now'. Without knowledge of the more or less shared organisational history and context of the embedded work system under study that reality is left out. However important the experiential learning from the dynamic processes may be, it is only a starting point for *further inquiry into what can be done* to improve the functioning of the work system in its own unique embeddedness. To become a professional organisation consultant or a manager one needs to develop agility in moving in and out of mental modes and a richer repertoire of frames than that of clinical psychologists or group relations' trainers. They need additional organisational, and societal frames, concepts and methods (a) for inquiry into the contextual conditions, for example, structures, technologies, procedures, reward and information systems that may create their own fields of tensions or that trigger or sustain dysfunctional behaviour; (b) frames for identifying levers for improvement action, and (c) methods to specify appropriate action steps for changing the dynamics of the system. It is clear that the process doesn't stop with insights in group dynamics and interpersonal relations. Understanding must lead to *action* to bring the system at a more desirable and sustainable way of functioning.

FROM INTERPRETATIONS TO SENSE MAKING

As human beings, we try to make sense of what we observe and what we experience. Sense making however has less to do with *discovery* than with the *construction of reality*. What makes sense is a social construction; it is not 'the reality' or 'the truth'. It is the product of the available data, filtered by distinguishing 'noise' from 'information' on the basis of chosen frames and perspectives (e.g. economical, technological, psycho-sociological, psychoanalytic) and a multitude of factors like membership, gender, personality that exert an influence often beyond awareness.

In this context, I consider it important to point to the difference between *interpretation* and *sense making*. As stated earlier, Bion had a special view on 'reality' and the 'truth'. He liked to emphasise that the truth is – although elusive – waiting to be *discovered*. An interpretation[6] implies a discovery of an underlying *meaning* of the client's behaviour, something the client is not aware of. Confronted with the fact that different disciplines within the social sciences and even different schools within psychoanalysis do interpret the same situation in diverse ways, it is reasonable to conclude that interpretations, at best, throw light on certain aspects of reality. As such an interpretation can only be understood as an *approximation of the truth*.

Interpretation is widely used in psychoanalysis, group relations' conferences and in various forms of psychotherapy to reveal a hidden or unconscious meaning. When introduced in the work with groups and organisations, it raised a still unresolved debate whether or not a social entity has an unconscious beyond the one created by social repression, or that only individuals have a dynamic unconscious (Ucs.) in the Freudian sense of the concept.

In practice, managers and consultants operate most of their time as involved, 'participant-observers' for whom it is not easy to carve out time and space for *reflection*, *experiencing* and *sorting out* the various influences that impinge on their sensory, thinking and feeling capabilities. Reviewing sessions and 'time-out', although relevant, are not always sufficient to clear out these factors. Even psychoanalytically-trained or informed consultants reveal in their practices, publications and correspondence that they too are often unable to contain or control these distorting influences stemming from their ethnic, national, religious or political membership.[7] The 'discovery' of an underlying meaning, drive or tension becomes then more the creation of 'a reality'.

---

[6] Charles Rycroft (1995) defines an interpretation as: "The process of elucidating and expounding the meaning of something abstruse, obscure, etc." (p. 85). In general I use the notion of interpretation as a statement by which meaning is attributed to a particular behaviour over and above, under and below the one apparently given to it by the client.

[7] It is sufficient to read through the interpretations *various members of ISPSO gave* on 'September eleven' and on the 'pro- and anti-Bush election campaign' to appreciate the influence of membership on what is taken as reality. I wish here to refer to Billig (1999) for a study on the influence of Freud's Jewish culture on his psychoanalytic interpretations.

Therefore I give preference to the notion 'sense making', because it incorporates the elements of *social construction of reality*. This is in line with Weick's thinking. "Sense making is clearly about the way people generate what they interpret . . . Sense making is less about discovery than it is about invention" (Weick, 1996, p. 13). Sense making itself starts generally in situations that are *different from what we expect them to be*. It is basically retrospective in nature. Trying to make sense means also to keep wondering, to stay open to new information because we simply don't know in advance what could be relevant. In my thinking and practice, I have moved away from 'interpreting' towards 'sense making'. Thereby, I recognise the inevitable element of *subjectivity* in the way that I make sense of what I perceive and feel what is going on in the outer- as well as in my inner-world. The data taking into account may be partial, and/or coloured by the taken frame and perspective, my group membership and/or my personal disposition. Whatever, it does lead to a 'sense' I work with. That 'sense' and its inherent subjectivity can only be opened up for exploration and modification by new information, for example, further inquiry, and/or sharing and comparing sense-making processes with *different* others. The purpose then is not to find out which sense making approximates the truth best, but *what new insights and opportunities are being offered to our understanding of that reality so that we can better relate to and handle it.*

Psychoanalytic-informed consultants may still feel uneasy with the social construction of reality. They may still cherish the illusion that the consultant can – through training and by maintaining a distance from the observed phenomena – be an *objective discoverer of reality* and *underlying dynamic processes* (group or individual). Thereby ignoring the fact that the psychoanalytic or the broader psychodynamic perspective provides a socially anchored, mental frame with a preponderant impact on sense making. Furthermore, when in the ensuing exchanges it becomes clear that the context or history of the observed phenomena was only partially or wrongly understood, or even completely left out in an interpretation, one often, but unduly, calls it denial, projection or idealisation on the part of that consultant. The illusion is thereby preserved that it is possible – if one is free of any defensive processes – to be an *objective discoverer of social realities*.

Making the distinction between a 'discovery' and an 'invention', – in the sense of a construct that facilitates understanding – is not always easy. This is particularly the case when the matter under study does not lend itself easily to empirical verification. I'll give two examples to illustrate this point. When Freud started talking about the death instinct, as a way to understand certain phenomena, he was explicitly speculative in his thinking. Yet, the audience took it wrongly as a discovery. Later, Freud himself was still speculative when he began to write about it, but gradually, in the process of writing, he himself turned an 'invention' into a 'discovery': he became more and more convinced of its existence. The death instinct was no longer a construct by which certain phenomena could be understood; it became an unconscious powerful drive. When Bion introduced alpha and beta elements in his talk for the British Psychoanalytic Society, as something that might be useful in understanding early mental developments in the baby ('an invention'), the members left the meeting discussing these elements as if they *existed* ('a discovery').[8] New notions that enable us to make sense of particular phenomena, or even the sense that we make of an experience, take on the quality of reality and truth. Maybe it is the expression of our dependency on others for finding out what is real under conditions of ambiguity.[9] This dependency may also explain why so many psychoanalytic articles and books are overloaded with citations of other writers (with standing) that fit an author's personal point of view, while much less effort is spent on collecting data to substantiate or verify interpretations. To rally support for one's theories becomes more important than collecting evidence for validation.

Sense making does not smooth the way to the truth either. A first obstacle on that path lies in the professional him/herself. Moving away from interpretations towards sense making implies that the consultant *shares* with the client, not only his/her sense making, but also the data and/or his/her experiences, reflected or evoked in him/her. Sharing the sense that we make of them entails *a process of mutual disclosure* for both consultant and client. Yet, one may be too much a prisoner of one's professional background and training, that, despite all efforts to avoid *imposing* a possible underlying meaning onto the others, one cannot open up the sense-making process in the social system.

A second obstacle resides in the social system itself: the lack of diversity in sense making. The sharing of the sense one makes is an invitation to compare it with the sense-making processes of others.

Many managers and employees are already practicing this process of sharing and comparing sense making about signs of oncoming events, and deviations

---

[8] Personal communication of Dr. Ron Markillie, who attended this meeting.
[9] Experimental social psychology has paid wide attention to conformity in perception and attitude formation under conditions of ambiguity. For a good review of these processes one may read Elliot Aronson (1992).

from the expected. This practice is particularly relevant in times of rapid changes in conditions and innovations. New signs and phenomena need to be recognised and understood in their meaning, relevance and implications for the organisation, its members and all those who are dependent on it for their businesses and their well-being. However, learning from experience through sharing, comparing and inquiry loses its richness the more the members are like-minded (sharing the same conceptual framework, theory and culture). Homogeneity in or agreement on sense making cannot be simply taken as an indicator for its reality value. It may well reveal the reification of 'the way we do things here', or established, but not verified theoretical models. The point is that reification of a 'collectivity' justifies commitment. Having become bound to interdependent action, if the persons says: "That's the way we do things in this culture, in this firm, in this family, or when women are involved," then cultures, firms, families, and gender are invoked as macro sources of micro constraints (Weick, 2001, p. 19). Without diversity in frames or perspectives, without further (critical) inquiry genuine learning and a more realistic contact with the multifaceted world becomes impoverished. One has joined another 'religious sect', or a closed group of like-minded people.

A third obstacle can be found in the dynamic interactions between the consultant and the members of the social system. People construct their reality and act on that construction. It does not matter so much whether they process an interpretation about an underlying meaning, or a sense given to a special event. When members share their own subjectivity in sense making and subsequently, but not necessarily with intent, continue to argue, searching for consensuality in a persistent way, a process starts whereby they finally consider their *constructed* reality as the *objective* reality. The intersubjectivity in the group turns subsequently into a generic subjectivity. The danger here is that such processes can lead to a kind of conviction that this generic intersubjectivity is *the* reality. The process by which that conviction was achieved may later disappear from consciousness. The more *coherent* that sense making is, the more it turns into a self-fulfilling prophecy. The group then behaves in accordance with that shared construction. Reviews at the end of the day can hardly break through this 'pseudo-reality'. As already discussed, these reviews take place when people have already some information about the outcomes of their activities, one can observe a tendency to recall those elements that *justify* their actions and make them *congruent* with their conviction. Such processes, however, are not the prerogative of sense making. Authoritative interpretations from a *dominant, pre-established theoretical model* can equally lead to the construction of a pseudo-reality within a group. The more various observations and experiences become related to one another to make *a coherent whole*, the more that interpretation or sense making becomes forceful and self-fulfilling. The identified pattern of cues may point to an unnoticed reality or an unconscious meaning, but the patterning of events and elements may also create a seductive confabulation.

Finally, the sharing and comparing process may get stuck when dependence issues are not sufficiently resolved. One listens to a chosen authority figure and there the sharing stops, as if one knows now. This kind of talking back to the sense maker is relevant data to further explore the expectations, or dependency needs. The issue, however, may be difficult to resolve, in particular when the members come with expectations to learn from the consultant, or if one uncritically believes the designated leader.

A Note on Retention

Before closing this chapter, I would like to make a note on retaining data, observations and experiences. Here again we must make a distinction between group relations' trainers and process consultants on one hand, and organisation consultants or managers on the other. I'll first share my experiences in working in and with groups that can also be of interest to managers and organisation consultants. Second, I'll point to some additional useful routines that are valuable in the practice of organisation consultants and managers.

In group work, it is impossible and not necessary to retain everything. As already mentioned earlier, what emerges in one's mind while being with the client and working in the 'here-and-now' is important to ponder. Taking notes during meetings is not helpful. In fact, note taking comes to stand between the consultant and the client. On the other hand, jotting down some typical expressions, or quantitative data may be helpful to ground interventions or bring them to life. Typical words or expressions, however, do expose individuals, and may upset the owners of that expression. Narcissistic persons in particular are very sensitive to such disclosures, and may take offence, especially if they come un-announced.

I see three ways of being present that facilitate retention: (1) An observer is interested in identifying *patterns of behaviour and interactions*: for example, repeated behaviour over time within a setting or across settings. Patterns can more easily be retained. (2) Observations and experiences *become structured* by our sense-making efforts and meaning attributions. These structures may emerge during the meetings. They may be related to a central conflict, a dominant way of thinking or a persistent way of dealing with tensions. They should be distinguished from *pre-established structures* in a particular theory, for example, phases in group development, or standard processes of ending. The latter are popular conceptual structures that may blind the observer to what is really going on.[10] The 'contextuality' of behaviour is thereby reduced to 'universal behaviour' caused by one single fact, for example, the ending of the group. All forms of behaviour become subsequently *interpreted* either as 'mourning', or in the absence of the latter as a defence against 'ending' (e.g. denial of the pending separation), or against the mourning process itself (e.g. escape in work, in happy feelings of task accomplishment, or of going home). They may all be true, but one does not know. One must inquire and obtain data from the 'here-and-now' in its proper context that reveal these unconscious, defensive processes. (3) What comes across as peculiar, strange, deviant from the normal or habitual, or incidents usually stay longer in our minds than just the normal things that don't surprise us. Behaviour that is strange or remarkable for one person may not appear that way for others. When these strange things, discrepancies or things that do not fit happen again, they are likely to pop up in your mind while working. At that time, they become relevant to be considered and further explored.

In organisational work, consultants and managers are furthermore encouraged to make notes of their reflections *after* taking part in critical meetings. These records are helpful in preparing for subsequent meetings, in particular when there are big time lapses between them. Some of these reflections can then be checked against data of a different nature to observations and experiences, for example, statistics, financial data; or serve as a basis for further explorations in the organisation.

CONCLUSIONS

Experienced managers and organisation consultants move from one mental mode into another. In their work during the day, most of them spend some time in all four modes, although large interpersonal differences can be noticed.

---

[10] Pre-established structures are included in Bion's statement: "without understanding".

Some are taken by the pressures for short-term results amidst daily uncertainties and become absorbed in action. Others have learned to take time and space for reflection and experiencing. In the apprehension mode one selects frames to deal with the challenges of the specific setting; while enacting shared frames and methods in the participative thinking and responsive interaction mode. Frames may be more or less structured, more or less focussed. They are linked to perspectives, for example, psychodynamic, economical, and organisational or system perspective, and to the unit of study. Since it appears impossible to integrate all perspectives, one should be careful in (a) selecting frames, methods, perspectives that appear relevant for understanding the unit of study and (b) be able to move to other ones that are, or emerge as more appropriate in a particular setting. In other words, one may change frames and methods to match better the evolving processes within a setting, or consciously alternate perspectives to make sense along different dimensions. The richer the repertoire of frames, models, methods and perspectives, the more one is able to see and explore the preferential frames/methods/perspectives in use by the client, or those that are totally absent. Reducing the understanding of work systems, organisations or societies to one perspective remains a grandiose simplification of reality.

In the setting of group relation conferences the frame often includes group- and intergroup processes only, but then the aim is to assist members in understanding what might be going on in groups, and secondly to support (personal) development. This understanding is claimed to assist managers/consultants in learning to handle these processes better, and so help them to create conditions and requisite organisations that will improve the dynamics of group and intergroup relations.

REFERENCES

Aronson, E. (1992). *The Social Animal.* New York: Freeman & Company (sixth edition).

Bales, R. (1950). *Interaction Process Analysis: A method for the study of small groups.* Cambridge: Addison-Wesley.

Bargh, J.A. (Ed.) (2007). *Social Psychology and the Unconscious: The Automaticity of Higher Mental Processes.* New York: The Psychology Press.

Billig, M. (1999). *Freudian Repression: Conversation creating the unconscious.* Cambridge: Cambridge University Press.

Bion, W. (1988). *Attention and Interpretation*. London: Karnac Books.

Checkland, P. (1981). *Systems Thinking, Systems Practice*. New York: John Wiley & Sons, Inc.

Crozier, M. (1963). *Le Phénomène Bureaucratique*. Paris: Editions du Seuil.

Depraz, N., Varela, F. & Vermersch, P. (Eds) (2003). *On Becoming Aware: A pragmatics of experiencing*. Amsterdam: J. Benjamins Publ.

French, R.B. & Simpson, P. (1999). *Our best work happens when we don't know what we're doing*. Paper presented at the symposium of the International Society for the Psychoanalytic Study of Organisations (ISPSO), Toronto, June 25–27.

Goffman, E. (1986). *Frame Analysis: An essay on the organization of experience*. Boston: Northeastern University Press.

Gold, S. & Klein, L. (2004). Harold Bridger: Conversations and recollections. *Organisational & Social Dynamics*, **4**, 1, 1–21; **4**, 2, 173–190.

Hirschhorn, L. (2005). The psychodynamic 'wiring' diagram. Lecture given at HEC, Jouy-en-Josas, January 28.

Jaques, E. (1995). Why the psychoanalytic approach to understanding organizations is dysfunctional. *Human Relations*, **48**, 4, 343–349.

Krantz, J. & Gilmore, T.N. (1991). Understanding the dynamics between consulting teams and client systems. In: M. Kets de Vries & Associates, *Organizations on the Couch: Clinical perspectives on organizational behavior and change*. San Francisco: Jossey Bass Publ., 307–330.

Levinas, E. (1987). Intersubjectivity: Notes on Merleau-Ponty. In: G. Johnson & M. Smith (Eds), *Ontology and Alterity in Merleau-Ponty*. Evanston, Ill.: Northwestern University Press, 1990.

Menzies-Lyth, I. (1989). *The Dynamics of the Social: Selected Essays*. London: Free Association Books.

Nevis, E.C. (1987). *Organizational Consulting: A Gestalt Approach*. London: Gardner Press.

Ramirez, R. & Drevon, C. (2005). The role and limits of methods in transitional change process. In: G. Amado & L. Vansina (Eds), *The Transitional Approach in Action*. London: Karnac, 195–226.

Rogers, C. (1951). *Client Centred Psychotherapy*. Boston: Houghton Mifflin.

Rycroft, C. (1995). *A Critical Dictionary of Psychoanalysis*. London: Penguin Books.

Schein, E. (1988). *Process Consultation: Its role in organization development. Volume I*. Reading, Mass.: Addison-Wesley (second edition).

Schon, D.A. (1983). *The Reflective Practitioner*. New York: Basic Books.

Senge, P. (1990). *The Fifth Discipline*. New York: Doubleday.

Shotter, J. (2003). 'Real Presences': Meaning as living movement in a participatory world. *Theory and Psychology*, **13**, 435–468.

Vansina, L. (1989). On consulting practice: Towards the development of better balanced educational programmes. *Consultation*, **8**, 79–99.

Vansina, L. (2000). The relevance and perversity of psychodynamic interpretations in consulting and action research. *Concepts & Transformation*, **5**, 3, 321–348.

Vansina, L. (2004). Over zin en onzin van psychodynamiek voor organisatieadviseurs. In: W. Varwijk & R. van Zijl (Eds), *Strategie moet je samen doen.* Tandem Felix, 159–178.

Vansina, L. (2005). The art of reviewing. In: G. Amado & L. Vansina (Eds), *The Transitional Approach in Action.* London: Karnac, 227–254.

Vansina-Cobbaert, M.J. (1991). L'identification projective, une tour de Babel. *Revue Belge de Psychanalyse*, **18**, 59–82.

Vansina-Cobbaert, M.J. (2005). The therapeutic community: a space for multiple transitional change. In: G. Amado & L. Vansina (Eds), *The Transitional Approach in Action.* London: Karnac, 41–70.

Vasilyuk, F. (1991). *The Psychology of Experiencing: The resolution of life's critical situations.* London: Harvester Wheatsheaf.

Vickers, G. (1995). *The Art of Judgement: A study of policy making.* London: Sage.

Webster (1988). *Webster's Ninth New Collegiate Dictionary.* Springfield, Mass.: Merriam-Webster.

Weick, K.E. (1996). *Sense Making in Organisations.* Newbury Park, CA.: Sage.

Weick, K.E. (2001). *Making Sense of the Organisation.* Oxford: Blackwell Publishing.

Weisbord, M.R. (1978). *Organizational Diagnosis: A workbook of theory and practice.* Reading, Mass.: Addison-Wesley.

CHAPTER 10

The Art of Reviewing: A Cornerstone in Organisational Learning⊗

Leopold Vansina

I had assumed that reviewing, an activity carried out by a group of people, was a normal process within the reach of any consultant or manager. That naïvety was quickly lost when we asked the members of our *International Professional Development Programme: Leading meaningful change* to carry it out, at the end of each day in the programme. The importance I attach to reviewing matches my concern to fill this gap in knowledge and skills. This chapter is an attempt to share with you my current understanding of the reviewing process and the difficulties to *institutionalise learning from experience* as one important step in the development of a learning organisation.

REVIEWING

Where Harold Bridger and many others predominantly active in Group Relations conferences make a distinction between 'task one' the given task and

⊗ Reproduced with permission from "The Art of Reviewing" in G. Amado & L. Vansina (Eds) (2005), *The Transitional Approach in Action*, 227–254. Published and copyright Karnac, London, UK.

how the team has been working on that task: 'task two'. The latter refers to reviewing or in more general terms the study of process. This distinction, although very useful in practice, lacks some conceptual clarity. Being an organisation consultant, I prefer to use the concepts of *task-work* and *team-work* on one hand, and reviewing through self-reflection after the events and the study of what is happening in the 'here-and- now' on the other hand. 'Task-work' refers to how the *activities* have been carried out to achieve task accomplishment, while 'teamwork' refers to how the people involved have been *working together* to achieve task completion. This conceptual distinction has some benefits. Indeed, it makes explicit that self-studies and reviews should cover both domains: the task-work and teamwork. Indeed, task-work with all the required task knowledge, heuristics and logistic principles is often – but wrongly – left out of the self-study in favour of teamwork when there is a preoccupation with group dynamics and a belief that all performance loss is due to "faulty process" (Kaplan, 1979). Teamwork on the other hand is likely to be skipped over when a rational-objective, and factual framework dominates. The importance of self-study of both domains is on the increase whenever people have to change their mindsets or representations of managing, organising and working; for instance, when an organisation moves from working from a hierarchical position to working in a network or in a knowledge organisation. Changes in mindsets and mental representations are made possible through regular confrontation with the enactment of these representations, expressed in observable behaviour, within a trusting and supportive group.

Reviewing a work system generates in turn another 'task-work' and 'teamwork', which may subsequently be studied or reviewed. Here, reflections on the 'here-and-now' of the reviewing process enrich learning from that process. Consequently, there is value in reviewing the review, particularly in the beginning phase of institutionalising reviews.

Reviewing can now be defined as the organised self-study of a work system on its task-work and on its teamwork, with the intent to learn for improving performance in the future. The self-study is largely based on reflection, but it may lead to collecting, analysing and using other data, that is relevant to learn from experience. As such there are two dimensions in the self-study. The first dimension contains a reflection on the past: (a) on how the *activities* have been carried out and (b) on how people have been *working together* to achieve task accomplishment. The second dimension refers to the future directedness of the self-reflection about what happened in the past. This future directedness goes beyond learning; it stretches itself to *commitment* to future actions. Without this latter dimension the self-study of the work system becomes evaluative and easily slips into blaming, finding excuses, rather than learning for the future and the active improvement of the work system.

Reviewing is a "learning platform" as Garvin (1993) would call it. Or, within the framework of Friedman, Lipshitz and Overmeer (2001) it would be classified as a "dual-purpose", "integrated" organisational learning mechanism. Dual-purpose because reviewing is carried out in conjunction with task performance. When "reflection in action" refers to an *individual* process "by which we deal with uncertainty, instability, uniqueness and value conflict" (Schön, 1983, p. 61) while carrying out the work, reviewing is a *collective and organised* process that – in Schön's terms – leads to the creation of a reflective learning community. It is integrated to the extent that members study their own and others' experience in order to improve their own performance. From the organisational learning perspective, reviewing is an important cornerstone from which storage and dissemination of learning can develop. At Microsoft Corporation for example, project teams hold post-project review sessions, and more than half of them subsequently write a report for dissemination amongst senior executives and directors of project development and testing (Cusumano & Selby, 1995).

The purpose of reviewing is twofold. First and foremost its goal is *to learn* from the study of the ways in which people have been working on the task of a work system in order to improve its future performance. "A work system is a purposeful definition of the real world in which people spend effort in more or less coherent activities for mutually influencing one another and the environment" (Hoebeke, 1993, p. 169). Boards, management teams, project teams, self-regulating work systems, a group of students in class or a working conference can be defined as work systems. They all have a given task or broad assignment to accomplish in order to achieve a set of objectives.

In the self-study, or learning from the ways the work system has been acting to achieve a set of objectives we have distinguished two domains. Task-work or learning from the work itself, from what the group is doing to achieve task-accomplishment, and teamwork or learning from the ways in which the members are doing it with one another. These domains are *interdependent*. Some of the richest learning comes exactly from exploring their interrelatedness. In some cases the 'task-work' puts high demands on the quality of 'teamwork', for example, in football; while in other cases, where problem solving is a dominant requirement, success is often a function of the brilliance of one member and the willingness of the others to implement that solution with a minimal demand on co-ordinated efforts. On the other hand, the quality of the team has a decisive impact on the conception of the task, on goal setting, and often on the implementation of co-ordinated actions.

The study of these two domains can shed light on the *relevance* of the task to achieve a set of objectives, given by the higher hierarchical level (the effectiveness of the system), the appropriateness of the ways in which the task is carried out (the efficiency and efficacy of the work system), the development, satisfaction and frustration of the persons doing the work, and of the clients of that system. In general this is referred to as the performance of the system.

Work systems are most often part of a larger system, being influenced and interacting with other systems and environments. In other words work systems within their context can be highly complex. If we don't understand the complexities of it, we easily attribute the causes of stress, frustration and failure to other persons, while the work itself, the internal and external pressures are left aside. Therefore, the self-study cannot be restricted to just what happens within the boundary of the work system under review.

The second goal of reviewing is *to maintain* the work system. Reviewing can help to *sustain* organisational change efforts and *provide support* to the people involved as well as to their attempts to improve the change. Organisational change always entails a certain degree of stress, which can be talked about to gain understanding, or to make it more bearable because it becomes shared. Furthermore, by organising review sessions, management and consultants communicate to the persons concerned their involvement and willingness to learn from the change processes themselves. Reviewing, if properly done, also *maintains or improves the cohesion* of the team. It may compensate for the lack of proper management of interpersonal processes. Under the pressures of work and the distance from colleagues (e.g. due to the layout), certain affect- and conflict management endeavours may have lacked completion, depth, or they were simply overlooked. In the review, people may release some of their pent-up frustrations and emotional responses to the work, awaiting understanding and cognitive elaboration, or the review session simply provides time and space for *reparation*. Yet, these sessions should not become a substitute for social maintenance. The latter is indeed an essential transformation process of an effective work system.

Besides these two major goals: *learning* from task and teamwork, and *maintaining* change efforts and group cohesion, the review may serve additional goals. As a derivative of learning about the effectiveness and efficacy of the work system, people in the system may well become creative and innovative in changing the task, the work methods, the action planning and the technology. Time and space are provided to do so. Learning, maintaining and engaging in creative thinking becomes enhanced when the review is conducted in a non-threatening climate.

Reviewing encompasses *reflective planning* in which the focus is on articulations of assumptions about what is likely to happen when one takes a particular action (Darling & Parry, 2001). The self-study is not limited to pure cognitive learning through articulation and exploration of assumptions, although this becomes a vital part in gaining commitment for improvements. Reviewing is largely based on learning from experience, which includes both cognitive as well as the more difficult emotional components, and unconscious processes.

WHAT COULD BE REVIEWED?

In the search of a comprehensive framework about what could be reviewed in a work system, I chose the taxonomy of team processes described by Marks, Mathieu and Zaccaro (2001). The authors define team processes as "members' interdependent acts that convert inputs to outcomes through cognitive, verbal, and behavioural activities directed toward organizing task-work to achieve collective goals" (p. 357).

Work goes in cycles. The authors distinguish three transition processes that lead to four action processes. Under the *transition processes* they identify (1) mission analysis, formulation and planning, (2) goal specification, and (3) strategy formulation.

Mission analysis, formulation, and planning comprise the interpretation and evaluation of the work system's mission, including the identification of its main task as well as the operative environmental conditions and resources available for the execution of the mission. In other words, it is the process of purposeful positioning of the work system in its wider environment and the identification of the resources required for successful task accomplishment. This is what Trist in 1987 saw as the essence of 'task two': taking stock of the work system in relation to its changing environment and learning from this so that the members can appreciate and re-assess the opportunities and constraints while paying attention to the feelings of, and conflicts among themselves. The focus is on the improvement of the work system or the organisation in its environment, and of the members contributing to this improvement, not on self-reflection on individual behaviour without reference to the task (Trist, 1987, p. xxv). In the exploration, depending on whether the review is held at the beginning or at the end of the work cycle, the following questions may be answered: *'Why are we going to do all this work? And what is the relevance of this work in relation to the changing environmental conditions?'* or *'What did we intend to achieve by doing all this work? And what is the relevance of this work system or organisation in the wider environment?'*

Goal specification is the operationalisation of the mission in 'measurable' goals and sub-goals and their subsequent prioritisation. It is the answer to: *'What criteria can we use to evaluate whether we are achieving our goals? What is the relative weight of these criteria?'* or *'How do we experience our work in the light of our pre-established criteria?'*

Strategy formulation refers to the formulation of alternative courses of action to accomplish the mission. Relevant questions vary with the systemic hierarchical level on which the work system is located. At the corporate level the question may be: *'What kind of overall organisational strategy and design is best suited to attain the corporate mission?'* or *'What does our experience tell us about the relevance of our organisational strategy and design for realising our corporate mission?'* At the organisational or business unit level the leading question is: *'What strategy is most likely to help fulfil best our business unit's mission?'* or *'How is this strategy leading us to our objectives?'* While at the production or operational level the work system explores questions like: *'What work methods, technologies, procedures, structures and resources are most appropriate to achieve the objectives?'* or *'What does our experience tell us about the appropriateness of our work methods, technologies, procedures, structure and resources?'*

Under the *action processes* the authors further identify (1) monitoring progress toward goals, (2) systems monitoring, (3) team monitoring and backup behaviour, and (4) co-ordination.

Monitoring progress toward goals includes the tracking of task and progress towards the accomplishment of the mission; interpreting systems information in terms of what is needed to reach the goals; and informing team members about the progress made. The question here is: '*How did we use the information to find out whether we are on the right track to mission and goal accomplishment?*'

Systems monitoring on the other hand refers to the monitoring of the required resources to attain the goals and mission in relation to changing conditions. It includes the internal activity of acquiring appropriate resources and information, and the scanning of environmental conditions relevant to the work system. '*To what extent are we using the proper resources, work methods and information in relation to the changes in the environmental conditions?*'

Team monitoring and backup behaviour comprises assisting members of the team to perform their tasks. It takes various forms: (a) providing coaching or feedback to a team member, (b) helping a member behaviourally in accomplishing a task or an activity, and (c) assuming and completing a task or an activity for another team member. A leading question here is: '*How did we experience the voluntary help in the team?*'

Co-ordination is orchestrating the sequence and timing of the interdependent activities in the team. '*How did we experience the co-ordination of our individual efforts and actions?*'

When a work cycle is a succession of transition and action processes, – often but not always by far – a dominant cognitive effort is followed by physical actions. When the feedback data on the performance comes in that information is mentally processed before starting a new work cycle. Interpersonal processes occur throughout the work cycle. In other words these interpersonal processes are neither linked to time, nor to the nature of transition or action processes. The authors distinguish three *interpersonal processes:* (1) conflict management, (2) motivation and confidence building, and (3) affect management.

Conflict management comprises two activities. Pre-emptive conflict management involves the creation of conditions to prevent, control, or guide conflict before it takes place. Re-active conflict management refers to the active working through of conflict and disagreements among members of the team. Questions that may lead the review may be: '*How did we handle conflicts and disagreements in this work system? What lessons can we learn from our experience for handling conflicts better in the future?*'

Motivation and confidence building points to generating and preserving a sense of collective confidence, motivation, and task relevant cohesion with regard to goal and mission accomplishment. An appropriate question may be: '*How do we feel about the way we tried to maintain or enhance our engagement and confidence in the work system?*'

Affect management refers to regulating members' emotions during the work cycle like socialising, stress, frustration, excitement and disillusion. A useful question here is: '*How do we manage emotions and their impact on this work system?*'

Any model that intends to bring conceptual clarity in a complexity of processes risks reducing the complexity of that reality. This applies also to this taxonomy of team processes.

- The distinction between 'task-work' and 'teamwork', as we pointed out earlier, may hide the rich, subtle and important interdependencies and inter-actions between these two conceptually distinguishable domains. The nature of the task, and how it evolves over time, for example, from individual problem solving to co-ordinated actions from different members of the work system, puts different demands on 'teamwork'. On the other hand, as we all know, 'teamwork' has an important impact on the conception of the given task, goal setting and strategy definition, to name a few. A misinterpretation of these interdependencies may lead to a faulty attribution of success and failure and eventually become very costly in terms of energy and time. Fur-thermore, an emphasis on *conceptual* distinctions between 'task-work' and 'teamwork' or between 'task one' and 'task two' in the tradition of Harold Bridger often impedes learning from experience. These distinctions become particularly frustrating and interruptive of learning when working on one is interpreted as defensive against the other task without any exploration of the underlying sources of tensions or distress. Therefore, a relevant question to explore the interdependencies between these domains and to maintain the wholeness of the experience could be: '*How and why did the conception of the task and its demands on the members change over time?*'

- Work systems operate in an environment consisting of other (sometimes) overlapping systems, and sub-systems, which together form a whole organisation. Or, as Jaques (1998) puts it, each organisation consists of a limited set of systemic hierarchical levels. Work systems at each hierarchical level have their own tasks: (a) their own special task, (b) the task of creating conditions so that work systems at a lower level can optimally function, and (c) a task to manage the interdependencies amongst these work systems. Work systems vary in scope and time perspective in function of the hierarchical level on which they are located. Consequently, it has to be emphasised that reviewing how one has been working to carry out the primary task to reach a set of objectives cannot just be confined to the boundaries of that work system. It should include the study of its relations with its environment, internal and/or external, and to the achievement of its own set of objectives in relation to the overall strategic objectives. For this reason, it may be wise to start with a review of the overall experience, or the 'Gestalt', the images that come first to the minds of the members, before going into a more refined study of the different team processes. In line with this, in the 1960s Dick Beckhard already used a very open question: '*What is it like to be working here e.g. in this board, team, or work system?*' It opens up the review and reveals the first impressions and the boundaries that are salient in the minds of the people involved. They may, but are not always, the most important ones. Whether they are or not can however be found out by continuing the review in a more comprehensive way.

- The proposed framework is *comprehensive.* Not all processes are of equal importance for a particular work system. Holding the framework in mind prevents us from becoming carried away by the stream of thoughts and it offers conscious choices as to what should be reviewed, for example, some critical events or processes.

- The added questions are intended as *illustrations* of what processes and domains may be relevant to include in a review. I wish to emphasise, however, that a review cannot be reduced to a questioning and answering session. It is self-reflection on the past in order to improve future actions. In that process anyone, regardless of their role as a manager, group member, action-researcher or consultant, may make any comment one feels could contribute to a better appreciation of the functioning of the work system in its environments and its performance.

In management and educational work conferences, when the task and goals may be less concrete and the members' contributions are less or not at all specified beforehand, I use another model. This model looks at the work conference as a transformation process in which participants and staff bring in respectively issues and problems to be explored, expectations, experiences, knowledge, skills, and capacities to learn from experience; the staff bring in their knowledge, skills, and interest in learning from the experience, as well as their expectations about the participants' interests and capacities to learn. To transform these inputs into desirable outputs, relevant to the work situation back home, a variety of opportunities for learning are designed beforehand or along the way: lectures discussions, learning groups, discussions of real issues, simulations, reviews, etc. The content varies from one work conference to another. To facilitate the review, it is important to list them to help the members remember. These opportunities for learning are designed to lead to desirable outcomes, or in other words to the objectives of the work conference. For example, a deeper understanding of the issues, a richer variety of approaches to handle them, a better understanding of psychodynamic processes, greater proficiency in handling them, and an increased capacity to learn from experience. After having listed the most important inputs, the transformation process to learn from the various learning-opportunities, and the desirable outputs, one can open the review. In a work conference there are always two distinctive levels to be included in the review: the relevance of the conference objectives for the back-home situation of the participants and the experienced appropriateness of the offered learning opportunities. The first level review may lead into a reformulation of the desired outputs. An opening question may be: '*How relevant is the conference for our work back home?*' While other questions may be relevant for the second level: '*How much did each of us benefit from the different learning opportunities?*' Subsequently, one can move towards the question: '*What can we do together to benefit more from these learning opportunities?*' And finally: '*What of these learning opportunities, or others, could be included in the work conference to better reach our learning objectives?*' The two last questions lead us into the near future and actions to be taken: first, what we intend to do – from now on – to benefit more from the learning opportunities; and second, a design intervention to include in the programme those activities (learning-opportunities) that are felt to enhance learning. The latter is the joint responsibility of participants and staff to adjust or complete the work conference design.

WHEN TO REVIEW AND WITH WHAT FREQUENCY?

When

Work comes in cycles, as we discussed earlier. The best timing for reviewing is at the end or the beginning of a work cycle. At the end, when the experiences are still fresh and the data about the generated outputs become available one can appreciate the effectiveness, efficiency and efficacy of the work system. At the beginning, when a group is confronted with a new task one can define mission, goals, criteria, strategy and explore action planning assumptions; alternatively, when the experiences and feedback data generated in the previous cycle are salient. In work conferences and training programmes with an emphasis on learning from experience, I have seen reviews being organised at the beginning of the day – when one has slept over the experiences – or at the end of the day. So far no comparative data as to the differential impact is available. What seems to be clear, however, is that the *transition processes*, generally speaking, offer a *normal* opportunity for organised self-study. Important is that the review leads to commitment to improve the functioning of that *ongoing work system*. Whenever the review is part of an ongoing work system (like management conferences), or as a basis for a design or re-design task, the joint reflective study has – besides the enhancement of real learning (e.g. Daudelin, 1996) – the added advantage of clarifying the shared responsibility for learning between staff and participants, or between managers and employees.

Although the work cycle is a guiding principle, it is not always possible or economical to put the review exactly at the end/start of the transition processes. The natural cycles may be too short, or too long to make a review at the end or at the beginning worthwhile; or it may never suit all the members of a work system, like for example on an assembly line or in continuous production processes. In these last instances, some people may be in a *transition process* others in an *action process* at any given moment of time. If changes in product or/and work methods are regularly made one can use the introduction of these changes as a time to review. In other words, we need to set the time for reviews in function of the practical opportunities and the dominant objectives. Furthermore, there will always be a need to balance the learning from reviews against the costs of invested time. The work cycle is a valuable indicator but not a rule.

Frequency

The frequency, like the timing, is a function of the major purpose of the review: learning or maintenance. Although one can distinguish these goals, they do overlap.

Learning from 'task-work' and 'teamwork' for the future: As a principle, the frequency will be higher when the turbulence or changes in the work system are high, either because of labour turnover, frequent changes in product or production process, or because of the turbulence in the external environment.

Maintenance of the work system: The frequency is a function of the degree of labour turnover, and the degree of stress within the work system, either because of the nature of the task, or the degree of ruptures from the past by organisational/structural changes.

For reasons of clarification we give here some examples about time and frequency.

- The work cycles in operational work systems may be too short so that one has to fall back on batches of one week or a month. In the process industries we may use the change in shifts. Sometimes I used overlap time of shifts for reviewing so that the up-coming shift can learn from the review of the departing shift.

- Although there are identifiable phases in most project teams one may opt for the golden rule, utilised by engineers, that at one-tenth of the expected project duration one needs to present a progress report based or not on a review. For example, if the projected project time is 20 months, every 2 months would be a good time to review and present a report.

- In action-research projects the different phases are more easily identifiable: the problem definition phase, the problem-solving phase, the implementation phase, the evaluation phase, and the theory building phase. At the end of each of these phases a review is most appropriate.

- In organisational change projects, one may start with a review after the first day of the implementation, and gradually scale down the frequency as the work becomes stabilised again. After the introduction of a new technology and work organisation in the baggage handling of an airport, we reviewed the experiences with the new way of working at the end of each shift and on company time. The outcomes were subsequently used to refine the organisational changes, and for planning until the work design became good enough to be formalised. Rapidly the need to review every day tapered off to a frequency that was acceptable for routine work systems.

- Similarly, in order to sustain a large-scale organisational change project (a strategic restructuring project) review sessions were first organised every month, after three reviews the frequency was reduced to every two months and later we held two more reviews with an interval of six months. If such strategic restructuring projects, at business unit level, are not completed within 18 months, they'll never become realised.

SPECIAL OR INSTITUTIONALISED REVIEWS

Amado and Sharpe (2001) sum up the advantages of institutionalised reviews for learning. They are:

- People will get accustomed to thinking about their work, whatever the pressures are.

- They will gain an understanding of the interdependencies between their jobs and those of others.

- People will feel more open to tackle personal as well as interpersonal issues.

- They have the possibility not only to express anxiety but also to share satisfactions and explore the reasons why things go well.

- Regular opportunities to acknowledge positive feelings and outcomes will make it easier to deal with more negative ones (p. 129).

Besides all these positive reasons to institutionalise reviews, there is also a risk. Like with anything institutionalised, the review may become a bureaucratic procedure people have to go through. This risk can be countered by setting the frequency right and by an audit or to be more precise, a review of the relevance of the review.

In general the advantages of institutionalised reviews outweigh the risks. Learning from experience, pleasant and/or unpleasant, becomes a cornerstone in the learning organisation. Reviewing becomes part of the agenda. Time and space is reserved for self-reflection and explorations of how the work system has been carrying out its task-work and its teamwork in that particular context. Yet, there are situations in which *special review sessions* can most appropriately be organised. For example, when a radical change in a work system or in its environment is being introduced. In an engineering department that merged with another engineering firm, we first organised a work session in which the various specialists met and explored with one another the persons and the content on which basis new work relations needed to be established. One month later, we organised in the same setting, review sessions for each specialisation to study their experiences, in particular the ways in which the tasks were carried out, and the functioning of the information flows within this new work environment. In fact, follow-up took the form of a special review.

Review sessions can also, most appropriately, be organised in instances where most, or all the members of a work system share an experience of failure, of being stuck or paralysed in frustration, or after an incident. This special kind of review I call 'time out'. The review here takes as long as needed to come to a good enough understanding of the processes or conditions that created a causal texture for the feeling of failure, blockage, or caused the incident/accident.

HOW TO REVIEW?

The conditions for learning through self-study and reflection differ markedly from the normal conditions the work system is in. Self-reflection is a different mode of learning than learning through action, as we discussed in the previous chapter. Managers are in general, more at ease in an action mode, than in the more passive mode of reflection. Furthermore, the latter is most often less structured, yet more appropriate, to learn from reflection on one's experiences. Organised reflection on experiences includes sharing and comparing of thoughts, images and metaphors. It feels like revealing more of one's self, than just doing the work. At a deeper level there may be a more profound concern. Human beings have 'whole' experiences, not analytic ones. In organised reflection, one may be afraid that those 'whole' experiences become 'expropriated' and torn apart in analysable fragments by the group, whereby the wholeness and uniqueness of the personal experience becomes lost. If the review does not offer respect and recognition for the wholeness of the individual experiences, and when future performance improvement as a goal is uni-dimensionally defined in terms of economical or technical excellence, at the exclusion of the social-, communal- or existential dimensions, people are likely to resist organised learning. The uneasiness, stress or resistance becomes expressed in the tendency to stick to a 'factual' review of what took place, thereby avoiding the more relevant sharing of one's experiences of these 'facts', that include sense making, meaning attribution and an emotional quality. Or members stick to a general global appreciation, for example, 'It was a very interesting experience!' or 'We are all familiar with that sort of work!' As if they wish to foreclose a more serious review. In other cases, members talk about what should, or could have been done differently, without verbalising what and why things went astray and without articulating the underlying assumptions. Examples like these reveal the uneasiness, and tensions stirred up by the review process; they need to be contained and redirected towards constructive sharing and comparing of experiences from which one can learn.

Learning about the functioning of the work system within its wider environment to improve performance in the future is the overriding guiding principle for conducting the review. Here, I depart from my colleagues, who within the Tavistock tradition continue to see the primary task as the 'master' to which all process observations and experiences have to be relegated. Their position seems to rest on two assumptions. First, the individual and the group are assumed to exist only for task-accomplishment, regardless of the linkages between task and purpose. Although they may argue that the definition of primary task includes purpose, I like to make that distinction explicit through reference to the taxonomy of team processes. The distinction between task and objectives is common in systems thinking (Checkland, 1981), and it is furthermore warranted because changes in the conditions of a work system (e.g. financing) lead to an often implicit change of purpose (Long, 1999) while the task may appear the same. Finally, the reduction of performance of a work system to task-accomplishment or economical returns leads to an impoverishment of the review process and eventually to an erosion of the social quality of an organisation. Human beings, indeed, wish to satisfy besides economical needs other human needs and values. Second, other social scientists assume that 'task-work' and 'teamwork' can in real life be separated from one another, and/or relegated, as if any other group of people is able to create identical work systems by simply keeping the *normative* task constant. Or, that a good functioning team is capable of taking on any kind of 'task-work'. 'Task-work' and 'teamwork' constitute one another in a specific work system, within a given environment at a particular time. In other words, *'task-work'* and *'teamwork'* – which make up the work system – and the *environment*, are all three related to one another; they interact implicitly and explicitly. Of course mental boundaries can be drawn around each of them, leading to simplifications or denial of reality. The fact that we think about the performance of a work system only in terms of one dimension – most often but not always – the economical one, reflects the implicit and often unconscious, shared assumption that work exists only for the accumulation of material benefits. This one-sided conception of performance is equally destructive as a one-sided attention to the maintenance function in the work system. The latter may take the form of 'speaking one's mind', releasing one's feelings, which indeed may serve basic human needs, but devoid of any relation to the work and the work system itself, deflects the purpose of the review. In my understanding, there is no structural frame to guarantee *in advance* the relevance of an experience for learning about the functioning of a work system. One can only explore its relevance, when in doubt, and enable people to make the implicit assumed relations explicit. The outcome is a confrontation with the necessary but delicate process of *integrating and/or balancing different goals and values.*

Since everyone is invited to share in the organised reflections about the work system, regardless of their role as manager or consultant, everyone has been and is involved.[1] There is no longer a 'neutral' figure. Everyone has become an active part in the work processes and in that capacity becomes a subject of review. Therefore, changing from a hierarchical to a non-hierarchical structure facilitates the review process, yet the members are encouraged to *reflect* on their experiences in their *respective roles*. When someone is asked to lead the review session, he or she should avoid that the reflections and answers from the other members become directed towards him/herself, as if the review is done for the 'leader' or moderator and not for the benefit of understanding and improving the work system.

In order to deal with these subtle and less conscious issues and psychodynamic processes, the review leader and the members have to pay attention to: (a) what is being reviewed about the past and taken into the future, and (b) what is happening in the 'here-and-now'. While the first includes *recollections* of observations, experiences and afterthoughts that can be explored in terms of their relevance for *taking action into the future*, the second contains the rich variety of what one can hear, feel and observe in *the present*. The 'here-and-now' comprises:

• How things are said, when and to whom they are directed.

• The selective omissions or the over-emphasis of particular transition, team-work and interpersonal processes.

---

[1] Being involved has its advantages and disadvantages. Amado (2002) sums it up extremely well: "Engaged in the complexity one runs the risk of getting lost. But, we have to add that by staying outside the complexity, one has little opportunity to understand it." (Translated from p. 363).

- The kind of reactions or non-reactions to the reflections and intentions by other members to either what is said and/or who brings it.

- The sequence in which these reflections and suggestions for improvement action come and go.

- The non-verbal behaviour of its members, and the emotional qualities evoked during the review process.

Important and enriching learning can emerge in the exploration of possible linkages between 'what is or is not being reviewed' and 'what is happening in the 'here-and-now''. When the 'what' of the review is confirmed by the noticeable behaviour of the group or some of its members 'powerful' insights become possible. Furthermore, paying attention to these two dimensions and their possible underlying connections may reveal a range of defensive be- haviour that distorts learning from the past and/or undermines commitment to future improvement actions. In other words, the purpose of observations and reflections on the 'here-and-now' and its possible relations with the review is to help explore and clarify the meaning of what is being reviewed in order to improve the quality of the ongoing review processes.

Paying even attention to the two dimensions: to listen to the manifest (what is being said), but also to the latent or the 'music behind the words' is not easy. It is a learned form of being present with an evenly divided attention to the manifest and the latent, the conscious or the explicit and the uncon- scious or the implicit. It goes together with a passive stance (mental mode of experiencing) in the sense of allowing things to come to one's mind, rather than a forceful concentration of attention (mental mode of apprehension), or being attentive with a pre-established frame of mind about what has to be brought up (Vansina, 2000). This passive stance alternates with an active one in which one participates in the discussion, sharing one's experiences, recol- lections and observations. One way of trying to clarify this particular way of being present is to compare it with moving mentally in and out of the review process, without being absent. 'Being in' is the active part, while 'being out' provides mental space for reflection, for images to come up, to be with one's feelings, for recall to happen without effort, for understanding the music and for 'hearing' what is missing.

Ample time should be provided for the review because one is never sure what will come up. Time pressure should be avoided. The first things members then cut out tend to be the more sensitive reflections. Self-reflection is best achieved when people feel secure, comfortable and 'relaxed'. Of course this is not achieved at first, but it is a condition to be realised. Comfortable chairs, away from distracting noise and physical disturbances will help. In General Motors Continental (Antwerp, 1987–88), for example, during the redesign from individual into teamwork, a special physical setting off the line was built for the work teams to hold reviews and problem-solving sessions.

Harold Bridger's golden rule is also relevant here: "Always start from where the client is". It may well be that we hear comments about unclear goals, procedures or roles, rather than their own negligence or avoidance of clarifications, or their jumping into action. This is particularly true in the beginning of a reviewing process, when negative fantasies are still salient about what is going to happen, or what might happen if one 'speaks one's mind'. It is not wise to respond with an interpretation to early comments like negative fantasies, based or not on experiences in the past. It can only scare people more, and may stir up persecutory anxieties. At the start, the person leading the review attempts to encourage further exploration of experiences, thereby facilitating sharing and comparing, and 'secret' learning. Later when the members have experienced that overcoming the initial fears is rewarded by learning, and trust has grown in the team, one can risk offering explanations at a less conscious level for further explorations, reality testing and sense making.

Facilitating trust building is a key task in the review. One cannot make persons trust one another, but one can try to establish conditions that facilitate this very process (Vansina, 1999). It may take the form of defining some 'rules of the game' with the help of the members of the work system: 'What are the rules by which we like to conduct this review?' or 'What don't we want to happen in the review?' These rules are written down and made visible so that everyone can draw attention to them when one feels someone is trespassing. Or, one may create a minimal structure via the agenda by focussing first on the task-work and later, on the teamwork. The rules and the minimal structure introduce some predictability of members' comments and reactions, thereby reducing the anxiety somewhat and allowing for trust to develop.

In the review one should pay attention to phenomena (Guba & Lincoln, 1989) that are part of any self-study through reflection.

- During the review, one should be conscious of the fact that the stories and descriptions of what went on in their experiences is not the same as how 'things really went'. They are meaningful constructions of the group. They reflect their way of making sense of what went on. In other words they are social constructions.

- The way people make sense of the situation is largely shaped by their values. A colleague of mine reviewed an outdoors exercise – inspired by K. Lewin's selection tasks – as part of an in-company management development programme. One member arriving late was excluded from the team during the entire exercise; the group simply ignored his willingness to participate. When, during the review, this obvious incident was brought to the attention of the group, the members immediately rebuffed it as 'making a mountain out of a molehill'. Later on in the programme, the trainer was told that this was a normal procedure in their consulting firm: new partners were never introduced to the sitting team!

- As can be seen from this example, "these constructions are inextricably linked to the physical, psychological, social and cultural context within which they are formed and to which they refer" (Guba & Lincoln, 1989, p. 8). In this incident, the construction was said to be part of the group's company culture. This 'delayed' insight, however, became valuable learning for their behaviour back home.

- Consensus amongst the reviewers does not simply imply a greater degree of reality. The members of the group are simply in agreement; they have come to the same social construction that has meaning for them. "What is the value of paying attention to individual members, if we make money through the individual acquisition of large projects! That's why we are successful!" What, unfortunately was left out of the review was a further exploration of the context of this 'surprising' rebuff. As one can see from this incidence, the immediate 'retreat' context appeared to be less relevant to the construction of the experience than the remote organisational context shared by the members.

- Finally, Guba and Lincoln (1989) emphasise that any review involves human beings. It should be done in a manner "respecting their dignity, their integrity and their privacy" (p. 11). Consequently, one has to explore how far one can go. As stated earlier, it may be wise to formulate with the people some preliminary rules on how to govern the review and continue to test the boundaries once in a while, since over time, people may be ready and interested in exploring more difficult issues.

The sharing of experiences and the implicit or explicit comparing of one's own with those of the other members, may lead to "happy" as well as "unhappy" learning (Ketchum & Trist, 1992). For this and other reasons, mentioned earlier, it is not surprising that the process of reviewing often confronts us with resistance, defensive routines and practices, embedded in organisational structure and culture. Dealing with these defensive behaviour and organisational routines demands some special sensitivity and skills to bring them to awareness and offer an understanding of the sources of discomfort, vulnerability, uncertainty, or stress that these defensive processes may attempt to ward off. The more the organisational defences are rooted into the system the more we may be pessimistic about the possibility of an organisational member perceiving and understanding them. It simply may require an *outsider* like a consultant, a new manager or a new employee.

Emotions and affects do indeed play a major role in learning. The recognition of discrepancies and inconsistencies between one's sense making and models on the one hand, and the data that is coming in, on the other, is most often accompanied by some emotional responses: some pleasant or some unpleasant feelings or a painful realisation. Such emotional responses are adaptive in the sense that they draw the attention and place people in a state of readiness to react (Frijda, 1988). They may also trigger – in turn – defensive responses as well as efforts to cognitively interpret and make sense of the disconfirming information. George and Jones (2001) advance the hypothesis that people are inclined, through sense making and interpretation of the information to minimise the negative and maximise the positive emotional responses. There is in other words, always a risk that too negative information may become denied, while the positive may become magnified. Furthermore, there is evidence that when members of the work system are in a positive mood, "their judgements will be more positive, they will be more prone to recall relevant positive material from memory, they will feel more self-efficacious, and they will be more likely to make self-serving attributions of successes and failures" (p. 431), and they tend to become more creative. On the other hand, research suggests that negative moods tend to make people not only "focus on potential problems and recall more negative material from memory, but also to be very systematic and comprehensive" (p. 431) in their efforts to understand and make sense of the aroused unpleasant emotional response. In short, members in a positive mood may learn less, but become creative, while the same group of people in a negative mood may learn more from their systematic and comprehensive search for understanding. Consequently, it is important to be aware of the emotional quality and mood of the group and its relation to the kind of information/experiences recalled. Either one can explicitly ask if there are opposite experiences (pleasant or unpleasant) which so far have not been reviewed. Or, one can try to bring the possible relation between the emotional state and the selective kind of recollections to the awareness of the members.

In order to face this variety of difficulties and to learn from the ways we cope with them, I like to *review the review* from time to time. Such second order reflections help to improve or to sustain the quality of the learning from sharing and comparing experiences.

CONDITIONS FOR REVIEWING

On the basis of our golden rule: 'Start from where the client is' we also come to the conclusion that organisational or cultural conditions provide another point of departure. So it is good to know beforehand what conditions support or hinder learning from experience, so that one can work towards the development of an 'ideal' learning environment.

Organisations, in which work systems lack real or perceived control and authority to carry out improvements, often come to display a kind of helplessness towards taking constructive action. The meaning of this observed helplessness can be manifold and needs further exploration. They may have learned from experience that their efforts to convince their managers of the evident underperformance of the work system, due to poor work methods, technology, resources, etc. remain without corrective action. After a few of these failed attempts people come to accept these working conditions as normal in their organisation; they give up trying. In this case we may talk about *learned helplessness*. Or, there is a selective but defensive attribution of the causes of all problems to instances and bosses outside the work system, to make it look like they are helpless, thereby avoiding responsibility for doing something about the dissatisfying situation. Or, the experienced helplessness may be part of the basic assumption mode called dependence (Bion, 1961). In these last two cases, the helplessness is defensive. An outsider (consultant, manager or employee) may find it easier to pick up the symptom, explore the possible meanings, and intervene accordingly than it is for someone who is part of the wider system. In the first meaning of helplessness one may confront management with their choice to *really* empower the work system (Ketchum &

Trist, 1992; Forrester, 2000) and to benefit from the learning from experience of its members, or to stay with the current distribution of power and authority and forget about employee initiated improvements or managerial initiatives. Indeed, work systems in which the members are confined to restrictive boundaries and power structures are not likely to continue to generate internal commitment for improvements. In the last two forms of helplessness other interventions are called for. Either one needs to explore and bring to the awareness of the people concerned why they avoid 'putting one's house in order' before pointing exclusively to the real issues outside their authority; or one brings to their attention the possible reasons and benefits from denying their own resources to do something constructive about the problems within their reach.

From prescriptive theory (Argyris & Schön, 1978,1996) and empirical studies (e.g. Friedman, Lipshitz & Overmeer, 2001) we know quite a bit about the cultural elements or the behavioural world that foster inquiry, openness, and trust, all elements that are conducive to learning. Friedman et al. (2001) group the 'ideal' conditions for learning into three categories: *contextual factors* that interact with *psychological* factors that in turn interact with typical *behavioural characteristics*. Under the *contextual factors* they list: (a) tolerance for admitting error (people will not be punished for admitting errors); (b) issue orientation as the tendency to make judgements based on substantive data, rather than on political interests, status, or personal likes or dislikes; (c) egalitarianism or the practices of power-sharing participation, and shared responsibility for performance outcomes; and (d) the commitment of the organisation to learning.

The *psychological variables* are condensed into two: (a) doubt as the psychological precondition to inquiry. Doubting is rather unpleasant in particular when it includes self-doubt. Therefore it needs to be balanced by (b) a sense of psychological safety.

These variables interact with *behaviour patterns* essential in learning: (a) transparency or access to valid information and the encouragement of others to provide full, honest disclosure; (b) inquiry or digging into a situation, asking open questions, exploring contradictions, and gaps in the information; (c) disconfirmation or the willingness to accept error, change one's view when other more sensible perspectives or interpretations emerge; and (d) accountability: holding oneself responsible for one's actions and their consequences, but also a willingness to take corrective measures and to experiment.

These are the 'ideal' conditions for organisational learning. As such they are never present at the outset, nor can they ever be achieved for a long period. These conditions fluctuate over time and space. They demand careful, attentive and sensitive work all along the way.

THE ROLE AND STANCE OF THE PERSON(S) LEADING THE REVIEW

Although the start of this article was the query whether many consultants could do a proper review, I don't want to suggest that it cannot be learned. A good enough understanding of psychodynamic processes is an asset, but it may also become a hindrance when it is not *integrated* in the person leading the review. The interventions and questions may then become too instrumental and mechanistic. Therefore, I wish to repeat that the questions I gave earlier are only illustrations of what the inquiry is about, but I want to encourage everyone to come up with their personal ones, adapted to the specific situation.

It is also true that some persons are more apt in developing a proficiency in reviewing than others. Persons who are inclined to make great distinctions between liking and disliking, correct and incorrect, good and bad, or right and wrong have much more difficulty creating that feeling of psychological safety and tend to stop the exploration when 'their' answer has surfaced. Furthermore, persons who are more able to admit/show publicly that they themselves are learning from experience, coined "leadership in learning," appear to succeed much better in creating a learning environment (Krantz, 1998, p. 101).

It is not essential that the person who has chaired the meeting or the one who is in charge of the work system also take the lead in the reviewing process. Another member who is skilled and willing could take that role; or it can become a rotating responsibility. Assigning a role, even if it is only a moderating one, tends to create a hierarchy within the group. Therefore, one should always be aware that whoever does 'lead' the review is not excluded as a subject of that review. His/her behaviour or his/her part in the functioning of the work system is a subject of the reflective study. Furthermore, one needs to avoid that the review is being done for his/her sake and not for learning from the past experiences and the improvement of the system.

The essence of the role of a moderator is to create and maintain conditions for the work system that facilitate the proper review of the important issues and processes of its work so that the members can learn from their experiences and achieve commitment on planned improvements. In practice, we can still observe wide differences in the moderators' active participation in the reflective studies. At one extreme, the moderator does not take part in the discussions, but may set the agenda; at the other end he/she takes part as any other member while facilitating the review. Personally, I recommend a stance that does not differ significantly from the other members. He or she alternates between an active participative and a reflective stance.

LIMITS TO LEARNING FROM REVIEWING

However well the review is conducted there remain some limitations to learning which are inherent to the method of self-study. Even when people are mentally prepared to be proficient and honest reviewers unconscious processes in the group like splitting, projection and projective identification can distort the learning (Amado & Sharpe, 2001). Power and hierarchical differences in the group often lead to the imposition of the views and interpretations of the more powerful onto the less powerful. The differences in scope and time perspective, proper to one's hierarchical level, are not very easy to distinguish from power impositions for self-serving purposes, which remain unconscious or become "justified" (Lee-Chai & Bargh, 2001). Justification is achieved through the selective use of words to evoke 'their realities', the repeat of 'dominant logics', and rationalisations. Furthermore, people may be afraid – justified or not – that 'negative comments', deviant opinions and making oneself vulnerable will be used against them. Something that is not uncommon in highly political organisations and bureaucracies (Crozier & Friedenberg, 1977).

Yet, there is still another limitation to self-study namely the identification of members with the team or the group from which one derives self-esteem and a social identity (Tajfel & Turner, 1979; Hogg & Hains, 1996). In this situation it becomes very difficult, if not impossible, to perceive, recognise and accept data that may devalue the status of one's group and consequently threaten the self-esteem of its members. It takes a member of another group or even another group to learn about one's own work system. The psychodynamics of identification with a group, in particular powerful, national, religious or racial groups, became evident in the aftermath of the tragic events of September 11, 2001. The inability of the Bush administration to recognise their contributions to the disaster was stunning. Even psychoanalytically-informed persons could not even consider that an 'all good nation' could be experienced as and hated for its consistent attempts to impose their self-interests onto the world. It is in situations like these that one faces unconscious defences and/or politics that a psychodynamic informed team is more equipped to recognise and work through these limitations than those who are not informed. But even a full-fledged psychoanalytic training provides no perfect guarantee for understanding and handling the largely unconscious dynamics of social identification and power.

REFERENCES

Amado, G. (2002). Implication. In J. Barus-Michel, E. Enriquez, A. Lévy et al. *Vocabulaire de psychosociologie : Références et positions*. Ramonville St-Ange: Editions Erès.

Amado, G. & Sharpe, J. (2001). Review as a necessary ingredient in transitional change. In G. Amado & A. Ambrose (Eds), *The Transitional Approach to Change*. London: Karnac, 119–136.

Argyris, C. & Schön, D.A. (1978). *Organizational Learning: A theory of action perspective*. Reading, Mass.:Addison-Wesley.

Argyris, C. & Schön, D.A. (1996). *Organizational Learning: Vol. 2. Theory, method, and practice*. Reading, Mass.: Addison-Wesley.

Bion, W.R. (1961). *Experiences in Groups, and other papers*. London: Tavistock.

Checkland, P. (1981). *Systems Thinking, Systems Practice*. New York: John Wiley & Sons, Inc.

Crozier, M. & Friedberg, E. (1977). *L'acteur et le système*. Paris: Editions du Seuil.

Cusumano, M.A. & Selby, R.W. (1995). *Microsoft Secrets*. New York: Free Press.

Darling, M.J. & Parry, C.S. (2001). After-action reviews: Linking reflection and planning in a learning practice. *Reflections*, 3, 2, 64–72.

Daudelin, M.W., 1996. Learning from experience through reflection. *Organizational Dynamics*, Winter, 36–48.

Forrester, R. (2000). Empowerment: Rejuvenating a potent idea. *Academy of Management Executive*, **14**, 3, 67–80.

Friedman, V.J., Lipshitz, R. & Overmeer, W. (2001). Creating conditions for organizational learning. In M. Dierkes, A. Berthoin Antal, J. Child & I. Nonaka (Eds), *Handbook of Organizational Learning and Knowledge*. Oxford: Oxford University Press: 757–774.

Frijda, N.H. (1988). The law of emotions. *American Psychologist.* **43**, 349–58.

Garvin, D.A. (1993). Building a learning organization. *Harvard Business Review,* **71**, 4, 78–91.

George, J.M. & Jones, G.R. (2001). Towards a process model of individual change in organizations. *Human Relations*, **54**, 4, 419–444.

Guba, E.G. & Lincoln, Y.S. (1989). *Fourth Generation Evaluation.* London: Sage.

Hoebeke, L. (1994). *Making Work Systems better: A practitioner's reflection.* Chichester: John Wiley & Sons, Ltd.

Hogg, M.A. & Hains, S.C. (1996). Intergroup relations and group solidarity : Effects of group identification and social beliefs on depersonalized attraction. In M.A. Hogg & D. Abrams (Eds), (2001). *Intergroup Relations.* Philadelpia, Pa.: Psychology Press, 110–128.

Jaques, E. (1998). *Requisite Organization.* Arlington, Va.: Cason Hall & Co.

Kaplan, R.E. (1979). The conspicuous absence of evidence that process consultation enhances task performance. *Journal Applied Behavioral Science*, 346–360.

Ketchum, L.D. & Trist, E. (1992). *All Teams are not Created Equal: How employee empowerment really works.* London: Sage.

Krantz, J. (1998). Anxiety and the new order. In E.B. Klein, F. Gabelnick & P. Herr (Eds), *The Psychodynamics of Leadership.* Madison, Conn.: Psychosocial Press: 77–108.

Lee-Chai, A. & Bargh, J.A. (Eds) (2001). *The Use and Abuse of Power: Multiple perspectives on the causes of corruption.* Philadelphia, Pa.: Psychology Press.

Long, S.D. (1999). The tyranny of the customer and the cost of consumerism: An analysis using systems and psychoanalytic approaches to groups and organizations. *Human Relations*, **52**, 723–743.

Marks, M.A., Mathieu, J.E. & Zaccaro, S.J. (2001). A temporally based framework and taxonomy of team processes. *Academy of Management Review*, **26**, 3, 356–376.

Schön, D.A. (1983). *The Reflective Practitioner.* New York: Basic Books.

Tajfel, H. & Turner, J. (1979). An integrative theory of intergroup conflict. In M.A. Hogg & D. Abrams (Eds) (2001). *Intergroup Relations.* Philadelphia, Pa.: Psychology Press: 94–109.

Trist, E. (1987). Prologue. In G.Amado and A. Ambrose (Eds) (2001). The Transitional Approach to Change. London: Karnac: xxi–xxvii.

Vansina, L. (1999). Towards a dynamic perspective on trust-building. In S. Schruijer (Ed.), *Multi-Organizational Partnerships and Cooperative Strategy.* Tilburg: Dutch University Press, 47–52.

Vansina, L. (2000). The relevance and perversity of psychodynamic interventions in consulting and action-research. *Concepts and Transformation*, **5**, 3, 321–348.

PART THREE

The Psychodynamic Approach In Consulting And Action-Research Projects

Introduction

Leopold Vansina

We have selected four consulting or Action-Research projects on quite different problem areas in diverse settings to illustrate the variety in working with a psychodynamic approach.

In a first consulting project: Understanding and working with organisational dynamics, we describe a design to foster the development of role identities in a growing European supermarket chain. The design enabled the members to *understand* the dynamics within roles and a pattern of roles, beyond interpersonal relations. Subsequently, we review our attempts to bring to life a newly amended structure of roles while providing time and space to work through the stresses of *embedding roles in the organisational structure.*

The second consulting project aimed at the *transformation of governance* in a family-owned international corporation (third generation). The project lasted for more than three years and moved from a disentanglement of the 'family shareholders', the wider 'family community' and the governance of the 'business'. A 'family council' was constituted to consult and buffer between these three entities. Subsequently, the governance structure was modified to facilitate a broader representation of the family.

The third project describes an Action-Research approach to the strategic re-structuring of a production plant. An independent party of researchers studied its outcomes for the organisation and the people working in it.

In a fourth set of consulting projects in the domain of collaboration between multiple interest groups Sandra Schruijer, and myself present first a summary of the social psychological findings about intergroup relations. Subsequently we briefly describe four ways consulting projects in this domain and ways of combining socio-psychological knowledge with a psychodynamic approach.

CHAPTER 11

Understanding and Working with Organisational Dynamics: Coping with Organisational Growth

Leopold Vansina and Gilles Amado*

Amazingly few people know how they get things done. Indeed, most of us do not even know that different people work and perform differently
Peter Drucker (1999)

Everyone is against micro management but I think macro managing is far worse; it means you're working at the big picture but you don't know the details. CEOs who adopt this approach are incapable of coming up with interesting strategies or fresh approaches because they don't know what's going on in the business at the ground level
Henry Mintzberg (2005/6)

The two statements above, made forcefully by two of the best specialists in management, highlight two major difficulties in today's management: the relative lack of knowledge of how things get done well.

The prevailing management fashion constantly focusses on leadership, and in particular its charismatic dimension, transforming the leader into a solitary

*We wish to thank Dominique Lhuilier for her co-operation on this intervention and her contribution to this chapter.

hero ("Did the CEO really do that all by himself or herself?" asks Mintzberg with irony) and managers into mere bureaucrats. This results in an emphasis on the psychological dimensions of the leader and the ways in which he or she exerts influence, notably over groups. Empathy, self-knowledge and knowledge of others and intra-group processes, usually for instrumental reasons, are constant features of training courses, to the detriment of understanding the activities involved and the context in which they take place. This remains the case despite many criticisms, including those of specialists in group dynamics (Jaques, 1995; Bridger, 1990; Amado, 1999, 2003; Vansina, 2000).

On top of this, the prescriptions given to consultants are increasingly problematic. First of all, because there is always a gap between prescription and reality, in other words between the instructions and the way those involved perform their activities. This gap is due partly to a relative lack of knowledge of the ground level by those issuing the prescriptions, and also to the inevitable, 'secret' ways in which those involved invent their own ways of doing things. Secondly, it is due to the growing complexity of socio-technical and political processes. As Edgar Schein insisted, in taking stock of his career as a consultant, the growth of technology and globalisation and indeed its growing organisational dilemmas do not allow us to really understand organisational and managerial dynamics well enough to be prescriptive about them. He perceived the field of Organisational Development as insufficiently informed by sociology and anthropology, "lapsing back to individual and small group levels" unlikely to be helpful with inter-group issues (Taplin & Carter, 2005, 78–79).

If we want to increase co-operation between the departments in a company, and within a given team, it is therefore clear that it is not enough to study interpersonal dynamics or to turn to training courses of the team-building type that create often artificial bonds. It is more appropriate to give the work itself (Lhuilier, 2006) and the activity (Clot, 1999) all the attention it deserves through a genuinely 'clinical approach'.[1] Likewise, care should be taken not to mix things up, for example, by naïvely believing that the creation of one or several teams composed of people from different departments will necessarily increase co-operation between those departments.

---

[1] The 'clinical approach' puts a great emphasis on understanding and discovery of the subjective experiences in a setting.

Our conviction, based on 'clinical' experience, on the work of anthropologists and our own research and work, is that co-operation requires a sound feeling of identity. There can be no genuine otherness without security. A security that is not necessarily "ontological", as Laing (1959) called it, but a security provided by a strong sense of belonging to the same (professional) group. This conviction converges with that of Gerard Mendel who developed a method of intervention based on a 'socio-psychoanalytical analysis', from which we drew inspiration for our design. Before entering into the details of how it was applied inside a large international company, we will present the theoretical basis of our design.

It was in late 1973 that Mendel initiated and then over the next 20 years continued to elaborate the concept of the 'power-act' in a series of interventions in several institutions (Mendel, 1992). This concept has a threefold meaning:

1. There can be no act without power over the immediate environment.

2. The subject has more or less power over his or her professional acts.

3. Depending on the amount of power, different and even opposite psychological effects can occur: pleasure or displeasure, interest or disinterest, etc.

In his thinking any professional power over one's own act is experienced as a transgression of the unconscious 'parental authority', resulting in a sort of status quo, a sort of passive dependence or counter-dependence on the 'hierarchical authority'. This is ultimately dysfunctional for the organisation as a whole and detrimental to the development of the *'psycho-social'* dimension of the personality. This dimension is that part of ourselves that can only be developed within institutions through our acts, our possibility to create. The other part of our personality is qualified as *'psycho-familial'*, the product of our childhood history, our identifications, counter-identifications and early conflicts. If Mendel had gone on as a psychoanalyst, he would probably have settled for studying the experience of transgression of authority at an essentially *psychological* level. He would then have fallen into the trap he warns against: regressing from the *political* (understood here in its broadest sense) to the psychological. For despite being foremost a psychoanalyst, Mendel rejected (often in very forthright terms) *psychoanalysis applied* (often wildly) within organisations. In his opinion, the psychological expression of conflicts in social life may be considered as a pathological symptom. This means *the absence* of the political dimension in the make-up of the psycho-social personality. The discovery of certain unconscious processes by social psychoanalysts must therefore be used essentially to increase the power of the protagonists over their acts and not merely to highlight the intra-psychological processes that are at work.

In the early 1970s, Mendel apprehended institutions through what he called "institutional classes": these are groups of people who have common interests within the institution and a specific place in the distribution of power: workers, foremen, executives, pupils, teachers, and so on. It is on the level of this class that each individual would exercise his/her social power, if they were not prevented from doing so through the capture of this 'surplus value' by the higher hierarchical level, as well as by the unconscious fears (mentioned above) of the members of the institutional class. In order to corner this surplus value of power, the institutional and political powers seek to ensure that individuals live their conflicts to the greatest extent possible in 'psycho-family' mode, in order to prevent those conflicts being played out fully. However, an organisation that is 'healthy' in human terms, according to Mendel, is an organisation in which there is democratic negotiation of conflicts between institutional classes and between different interests, and not one in which legitimate conflicts are hidden or manipulated.

In order to allow these normal situations of conflict to take place, and to provide a source of genuine democracy in the company, Mendel developed an original intervention design with the support of several teams, including his founding 'Desgenettes' group. It is based on work in homogenous groups and concerns the whole of the organisation. The homogenous groups (formerly institutional classes) are composed along the lines of the division of work and on a voluntary basis. Their task is to elaborate essentially work-related reflections and requests to be passed on in writing to the other groups, which are then obliged to reply. These groups meet for two-hour sessions, taken from their working time, at frequencies that vary from four to eight meetings a year. The minutes are taken by a secretary (on a rotating basis) and must receive the agreement of all the participants. This design is considered to be a 'third channel' alongside the managerial channel (line management) and the channel(s) of the unions, and does not overlap with them. In other words, line management (and the decisions incumbent on them) and the negotiation processes between labour organisations and management continue their activities. The third channel is a specific communication channel enabling an improvement in working conditions on all levels in a way that is both concrete and transparent. Of course, mixed groups (task forces, project groups) can operate in parallel, at the initiative of management.

Two factors are particularly crucial to this approach: the homogenous groups on the one hand and written communication on the other. Freed as they are from any direct influence of hierarchy, the homogenous groups allow open debates both on the work problems that preoccupy them as a group and their work relations with the other groups. The preparation of the requests addressed to the other groups requires, in particular, that they come to an agreement on their wording, not only so that they reflect the preoccupations of the whole of the group effectively, but also so that they can be heard and worked through by the groups they address. This intra-group work increases the feeling of professional identity and of responsibility.

The written communication, meanwhile, develops these feelings and adds an understanding of the broader context of the organisation. Each group, in turn, receives requests and responses informing it of the problems encountered by the other professional groups. Also, any disagreements there might be with the others' remarks are handled internally first, in intra-group debates in which empathy (what did they mean, why are they reacting like that?) supplants the immediate emotional reactions. The absence of face-to-face confrontation aims to focus attention on the act and on the work, enabling this concentration that is diverted or hindered in day-to-day company life by all kinds of intra- and inter-psychological phenomena that occur in 'physical' confrontations: fear of being judged or exposed, verbal domination, fascination effects, manipulation, transfers, enmities. It is this psychological 'pollution' that is therefore intentionally eliminated by this system of written exchanges, which also guarantees anonymity.

However, while such a pure design is justified in a long-term intervention, such as that conducted since 1986 in the Société des Transports Poitevins (Weiszfed, Roman & Mendel, 1992) covering the whole of the organisation, it seems to us that it cannot be applied in exactly the same way in more limited and/or one-off interventions. For this reason, we drew our inspiration from it for our work in a large company, while adapting it to the requirements of the situation.

The purpose of this chapter is to share with you the actual designs and the outcomes of a two-year intervention in an international supermarket chain (15,000 employees). The purpose of the project was to assist the company in gaining a better understanding of the internal tensions between different roles and to improve co-operation and initiative taking within the structure of roles.

The international company under study is steadily expanding through internal organic growth and acquisitions. These developments led to some experienced difficulties with overlapping roles and role boundaries, and loss of efficiency. People tended to create roles more to reduce their workloads than as part of a considered organisational strategy. After attending an external conference on group dynamics, senior management expressed an interest in setting up some similar learning experiences within the company; something like a mini-company programme, similar to the mini-society conferences designed and introduced by the Danish social scientist Gunnar Hjelholt (Higgin & Hjelholt, 1990). Without waiting for a special design they had used one of their annual meetings with the commercial director and all the store managers to take time out and reflect upon their roles and ways of working together with the commercial staff and line management. This meeting revealed an urgent need to clarify roles and relationships in order to reduce work overload and curb the tendency to select subjectively from the immense range of expected activities those that suited them best.

The original request led to a meeting of company's internal consultants, and the two authors as external consultants. Together they outlined a design to be presented and approved by the management team. Its objective was to better understand the interdependencies between three role-groups, for example, area managers, product-sales 'merchandisers', and store managers, to learn about the organisation, and to study ways of improving collaboration.[2] Particular care was taken to strip the roles from the personal features of the role holders and to make the roles visible within the existing role structure so that role tensions and overlap could more readily be studied and acted upon. A four-day residential, pilot workshop was designed with three homogeneous role-groups of six persons each without any established, hierarchical or existing interpersonal work relations. The commercial director and members of his commercial management would be invited during the last half-day to hear directly the comments and recommendations from the workshop. The workshop itself was conceived not as a decision-making body but as a reflective study for actions to be taken later on. Subsequently, the commercial management team would process the recommendations and its conclusions

---

[2] A product-sales 'merchandiser' is a role with an advisory responsibility for product knowledge and proper product display in the sales outlets. The activities are often grouped together under the label: merchandising.

would be presented to the overall management team and then be translated into the structure of work roles, later on.

In the subsequent discussion the CEO and the commercial director talked about their expectations of the project. We summarise them in the following points: (a) an increase in initiative and taking charge by the store managers; (b) an improvement in the self-confidence of the store managers and a better understanding of the differences between their key tasks and the more ambiguous parts of their role as they emerge in the concreteness of their store and in the interactions with the wider organisation; (c) an improved capability to balance the specifics of their role, with a more general appreciation of the other roles in the organisation; (d) an increase in mutual respect for the advice of the product-sales 'merchandisers' and the final decisions of the area manager; and (e) an improved capacity to work with status differences between 'merchandisers' and area managers resulting from the established promotion system. Furthermore, it became clear to us that the project – in the first instance – should be aimed at *improving* rather than *re-thinking* the structure of roles. Yet, the sponsors approved the objectives and the suggested design for the pilot workshop.

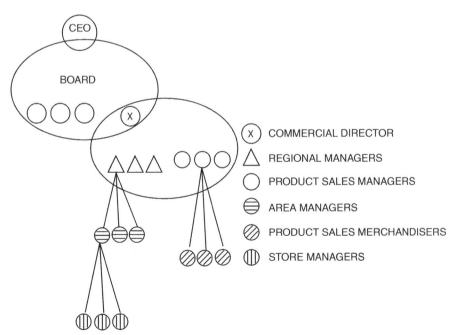

Figure 11.1 Graphic representation of role structure.

PART 1: CREATING AWARENESS AND A BASE FOR ACTION
WITHIN THE ORGANISATION

THE PILOT WORKSHOP

The Design

Within the theoretical frame inspired by G. Mendel, a design with four basic elements was developed for a four-day residential pilot workshop.

- Three *homogenous 'role-groups'* of six participants each that would work in separate rooms to define *in writing* the primary task of their roles (the basis for their professional identity), the experienced issues with the two other role-groups and their expectations about them. These homogenous role-groups would receive and process the written documents on the primary tasks, what was expected from the others, and the experienced issues with the other role-groups. After processing these data, each group would write their reactions and responses to these documents to the other two role-groups and subsequently return them to the respective senders.

- In the subsequent *'plenary sessions'* the three role-groups would meet face-to-face to further clarify roles and explore the tensions and interdependencies, which are part of effective collaboration at work within that structure of roles.

- Three *'mixed role-groups'* would be formed containing two members of each role-group to prepare the groundwork for effective inter-role collaboration. Thereafter, they would work with and through the acquired additional information on concerns and issues in their original *homogeneous role-groups*.

- The *'plenary sessions'* had two major objectives. First, to position the co-operation between these three role-groups in the organisational context of the company and its environment. In this light, the CEO, the commercial director, a product-sales manager and a regional, commercial manager (encompassing a region with its several area managers) were invited to share their concerns and ideas with all members of the workshop.[3] Second, to

---

[3] At that time, the roles within the commercial team had not been clarified. Everyone in the management team called him/herself a director. However, to facilitate comprehension we have here already filled in the roles as they became clarified later on in the project.

gain commitment on the proposed action-ideas, to check their relevance for the company and to review the workshop as a whole.

Each role-group and each mixed role-group would have an internal and an external consultant to assist their work on the respective tasks and to learn from the experiences. All consultants would take part in the plenary sessions and remained present throughout the overall workshop.

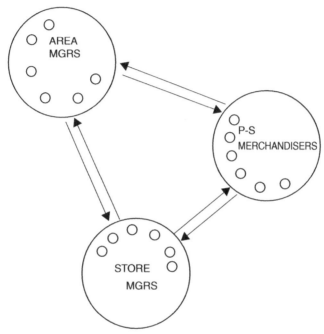

Figure 11.2 Graphic representation of written communications in the pilot workshop.

Reflections on the Pilot Workshop

The pilot workshop turned out to be quite successful. The members had been highly engaged in clarifying their respective roles and suggesting some improvements in the ways they could work together. They appeared hard working and dedicated to make the company successful. Yet, one might expect that besides the organisational and work requirements, many other more personal elements would be built into the self-conceived roles. This became evident in the design. The homogenous groups enabled the members to hear and see how they had built themselves roles that fitted themselves, since their roles had never been formally prescribed nor described. Some parts of the roles occupied a central position in some members' conception, while others emphasised other parts, which together made up the role of the respective store managers, 'merchandisers' or area managers. Slots of work had been filled in according to personal preferences and/or upon instigation from someone higher up in the hierarchy, or just by delegation of a chunk of work. Some slots were only partly filled and large overlaps in roles became visible through the exchange of written core role definitions. These facts became evident first in the *written comments* of the other role-groups, and again in the *mixed groups* where they became the subject of discussion in a face-to-face setting. The written comments often stirred up some emotions while they reflected some authority issues. Sometimes the comments didn't leave anything in doubt when, for example, it read clearly in red ink 'à refaire!' (To be redone). The tensions between the role-groups became even more visible in the *plenary sessions* due to heightened inter-group dynamics.

The original homogeneous role-groups became the home base for working through the experienced confrontations and comments, and for finalising their role definition. They became the basis for developing role identity.

Most striking however was a tendency for the area managers to take over the role of the store managers, from one higher hierarchical level. At the same time, the area managers tended to use the product-sales 'merchandisers' as inspectors to keep them informed about what was going on in the stores. In turn the area managers seemed to conceive themselves as (legitimate) relay stations to the regional, commercial managers. The store managers were said to be totally responsible for everything that happened in their stores. Yet, they complained that others, for example, area managers and product-sales 'merchandisers' were impinging on their responsibilities and that they often felt overruled.

The product-sales 'merchandisers' on the other hand didn't appear to be a homogeneous group since they seemed to receive different instructions from their bosses (later distinguished as product-sales managers). In general their role was conceived more as inspectors than consultant-educators.

As a logical consequence of unclear and personalised roles, the members of the pilot workshop could not and did not have insight into the criteria-in-use to appreciate their role performance. The area managers, for example, came up with a variety of vague criteria against which they thought they would be appreciated by their bosses, namely: being positive in discussions; whether or not there was a good climate in the stores; their personal honesty in reporting everything they had noticed; and the profitability of their stores.[4] Only in the last criterion one could recognise an *indirect* evaluation of their role performance, to the extent that the area managers were responsible for creating appropriate conditions (e.g. financial means, human resources) for the store managers to achieve their own results. All the other cited criteria referred either to a personality factor or to the evaluation of the store managers.

Furthermore, there seemed to be quite some confusion over the boundaries of control. Who was supposed to control what domain of activities and outcomes: the CEO, the commercial director, his regional managers, the product-sales managers, the product-sales 'merchandisers', the area manager, or the store manager? The function of control was equally ambiguous. Did control refer to 'to bring under control' in the Anglo-Saxon sense of the notion, or did it refer to 'inspection'? The distinction between 'inspection' and 'audit' was not made, neither had the respective objectives of 'inspection' and 'audit' in the organisation been defined. The resulting confusion was exacerbated by the established way of senior management (directors and managers) to visit the stores on a regular basis, 'in order to stay in touch with operations, while the organisation kept expanding'. These direct personal contacts (and personal control) allowed for the development of confidence in persons, but not in the system that senior management had and was setting up to manage the business. Sales per square metre was the only mentioned impersonal control criteria/system.

Yet, these visits and the requested reports and notes from the area managers and the 'merchandisers' were not felt to be sufficient to reassure senior management. Finally, and to our surprise, we came across some negative consequences of the climate of openness that had been installed and valued for so many years. With the growth of the company the unsystematic information flowed across boundaries and the unavoidable gossiping seemed to contribute to a lot of suffering (e.g. how to restore a negative image based on one visit),

---

[4] With the emphasis on *their* stores we wish to underline the feeling of most area managers that *they* were responsible for the performance of the stores, not the store managers. The latter were conceived more as their extended arms.

even suspicion about the real intent of the broad range of questions and observations of the visiting managers.

A more general need emerged: the absence of an appropriate vocabulary to communicate about role ambiguities and tensions between roles. In particular around 'responsibilities' which could be delegated and 'accountabilities' which could not; between 'inspection' and 'auditing' (Hoebeke, 1990) and the rich meaning of 'recognition', 'authority and freedom'. These concepts were picked up and clarified in short lectures by the staff.

Review and Discussions with the Sponsors

These observations left consultants and participants with some critical questions that could only be answered formally by management. At the first opportunity, a meeting was arranged with the sponsors to review and discuss the most pressing questions and observations. Their answers to questions on the organisational strategy had great implications for defining the roles and the work relations within the existing role structure. Of utmost importance was the location of the function of *integrating* the local commercial policy with the technical inputs of the three product-sales 'merchandisers' and the organisational conditions, human resources, competences and means provided by the area manager to his/her store manager. Do we wish to locate the integrative function with the store manager, or with his/her boss: the area manager? This location has different consequences for (a) the product-sales manager fresh meat, and other product-sales 'merchandisers', (b) the relations between the area manager and the 'merchandisers', and (c) the need to distinguish and adjust the roles of the regional managers and the product-sales managers within the commercial management team. We also discussed the need to arrive at a formal agreement on the role definitions within the commercial management team and all the other roles around the team: area manager, product-sales 'merchandisers' and the store managers. In other words it appeared desirable to extend the structure of roles under study.

The pilot workshop had generated a lot of observations and suggestions but as consultants we could only explore what seemed appropriate from the position of the current organisation, but we needed to know more about the strategic direction in which the organisation wanted to grow and develop.

From the discussions with senior management we retained the following points:

- The sponsors were encouraged to continue this kind of workshop. They thought that the next step in the project should be another workshop with a similar design but with an extra role-group namely the commercial management team composed of the commercial director and his regional commercial managers and the product-sales managers.

- They wanted to continue our careful approach to further clarify roles within the pattern of roles and the inherent role tensions.

- They intended to make the store managers responsible for the integration of the advice of the product-sales 'merchandisers', with one qualifier, namely that the personal competences of the store managers should be carefully considered. Furthermore, they informed us that in some geographical areas they had already started to experiment with giving more responsibility to the store managers.

THE SECOND WORKSHOP

The Adjusted Design

About two months later, Workshop Two was organised with the same objectives, but this time they could be formulated more explicitly:

- To explore the conditions necessary to improve the effectiveness and efficiency of working together from different roles and hierarchical positions;

- To gain a better understanding of co-operation at work and the entailing tensions and gratifications; and

- To arrive at a better understanding of the functioning of the organisation, and what could be done to improve its effectiveness, efficiency, and pleasure at work.

The design was adjusted so as to accommodate four role-groups. By reducing the number of plenary sessions, we could cut the duration of the workshop to three full days. The fourth group or the commercial management team received in advance some preparatory instructions to formulate personally and in writing what they: (1) considered the essence of their roles and (2) the issues they encountered with other role-groups in working together. This individual preparation was needed to speed up the work in the workshop.

The three basic design elements from the pilot workshop were retained:

1. *Homogeneous role-groups*: eight store managers, eight 'merchandisers', eight area managers and the commercial management team. Each role-group would define its major tasks, the experienced problems, and their expectations about the other role-groups.

   The so-called 'fourth' role-group or the commercial management team was not a homogenous role-group. It consisted of three different roles: the commercial director, three regional commercial and three product-sales managers. When the management team met, the consultant divided them in two sub-groups: regional commercial managers and product-sales managers and one person, the commercial director, to process their written notes on the two tasks given to them a couple of days in advance. Having done this processing they came together as a commercial management team and worked these issues through. Then they dealt with question three: their experienced work-issues and expectations about the other three homogeneous role-groups in the workshop. Here we allowed for differences between the regional commercial managers and the product-sales managers.

   The other three role-groups would be asked to: (a) clarify their role and send a copy to the commercial management team and to each of the two other role-groups, and (b) to describe the experienced issues with and expectations of the commercial management team (by preference they could differentiate between the two kinds of managers), and with the two other role-groups. Copies of this last list were given to the commercial management team and the two other role-groups.

   The three regional commercial managers and the three product-sales managers would send their respective documents to each of the three role-groups: 'merchandisers', area managers and store managers. The commercial management team were to keep two documents *for internal use*: one from the three regional commercial managers and one from the product-sales managers. The commercial management team would receive three documents respectively from the store managers, the area managers and the 'merchandisers'. Each of the latter three role-groups would receive four documents.

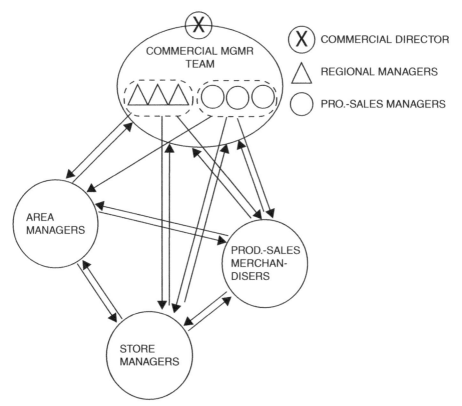

Figure 11.3 Graphic representation of written communications: Second Workshop.

2. The *mixed groups* would now contain members of the other 'four' role-groups. They were designed to prepare the groundwork for further clarification of roles and effective, inter-role-group co-operation.[5]

3. The *plenary sessions* would provide an opportunity to further clarify roles, explore the interdependencies and role tensions within the structure of roles, suggest ideas to facilitate co-operation within the daily realities of the company, and finally to review the working conference as a whole. Some

[5] Since the commercial management team had only seven members, we would form four mixed groups (three of eight and one of seven): two merchandisers, two store managers, two area managers, one regional commercial manager, one product-sales manager and in one mixed group the commercial director. After this mixed role-group session, they would return to their original, homogeneous role-groups.

short lectures were also given in plenary to cope with issues identified by the participants, for example, the difference between responsibility and accountability, inspection and audit.

A Brief Outline of this Second Workshop

The first day was reserved for discussions and work within the role-groups and the commercial management team. All interactions across groups were done in writing, with the exception of the plenary sessions in the evening. During this session the commercial management team and the three role-groups met to review the work done so far, and to gain a better understanding of the dynamic processes impacting upon their exchanges.

The second day was designed to re-think one's role and work-issues in mixed groups in the light of all the exchanges which had taken place between homogeneous role-groups and the face-to-face interactions in the plenary. Subsequently an exploration of the conditions for more effective and efficient forms of co-operation took place. Some short lecture-discussions were organised around issues or concepts that needed further elucidation in plenary. In the evening, another plenary session was organised to: (a) search for agreement on role definitions and minimal conditions for effective co-operation; (b) to explore tensions between roles within the structure of roles; and (c) to review how we had been working together in the conference and what needed to be done to improve its effectiveness.

The third day was opened with some lecture-discussions on critical concepts/issues. Subsequently, we moved into mixed groups to re-think the work done in the light of the plenary session. Then, the original homogeneous role-groups formulated action proposals to achieve role clarity and to create conditions facilitating co-operation at work. During this period, the commercial management team defined its joint tasks,[6] before thinking about appropriate action proposals to facilitate co-operation.

---

[6] Not all the work could be accomplished within the set time. Consequently, the commercial management team organised an additional one-day workshop to complete their work, for example, what should be integrated at their level in order to set objectives.

In the last plenary meeting the primary task of the commercial management team and the action proposals of the three role-groups were reviewed and integrated in the presence of the CEO. Rounding off, we reviewed the work done and explored how best to share our experiences of the conference with the colleagues back home in the organisation.

Reflections on Workshop Two

Although the full presence of the commercial management team could have turned the workshop into a decision-making working conference, the discussions were still kept at the level of clarifying roles, recognising role tensions and exploring ways to handle them more effectively so that co-operation could be improved.

The presence of the 'fourth' group, the commercial management team, revealed the organisational dynamics more clearly.

Within the *homogeneous group*, the regional commercial and product-sales managers had defined their roles in terms of key tasks. However, in the *mixed groups* and the *plenary* sessions the emerging role pattern shed light on the role-tensions present in the workshop. As a direct consequence, the *regional commercial managers* could see their core responsibility as: (1) to optimise the *objectives* of the different product-sales managers with their *own regional* commercial policy in relation to the overall company objectives and strategy and the available resources (e.g. space, financial and human resources); and (2) to translate these integrated objectives and policy into *guidelines* for their area and product-sales managers.

The *product-sales managers* could see their core tasks as: (1) to manage the demanded product flow from purchasing to the customer in accordance with high quality standards and low integral costs; and (2) to provide technical and sales support with the delivered products to guarantee customer satisfaction.

During the workshop it became apparent that the commercial management team lacked a good understanding of the daily realities and opportunities in the stores. They heard the store managers' direct and indirect complaints about not getting any information from the management team about what was done with their suggestions and information passed on to the product-sales 'merchandisers' and the area managers. In fact the commercial management team didn't exist for the store managers; they had their dealings with their area manager and product-sales 'merchandisers'. This pattern of role-tensions, partly revealed already in the first workshop, pointed to the tendency of (a) the members of the management team to take over the roles of their area managers, who they perceived as either doing nothing or taking the decisions themselves without consultation or feedback; and (b) the area managers to take over the role of the store managers. These two tendencies could only be curbed when the commercial management team became *the platform* to *integrate* product-sales objectives, regional strategies and available means. Along the same lines, one could understand the request from the commercial management team for more information from the area managers about the stores and more detailed written reports of the product-sales 'merchandisers'. Likewise, one could understand the area managers' efforts to use the 'merchandisers' as their 'informers' and to take decisions that could more appropriately be taken by the store managers. We assume that the wide-open communication system, expressed by sending copies of one's reports of store visits to one's respective boss, had pushed decision making up one level too high.

In the homogeneous groups one observed some deviant conceptions of roles within that 'fourth' group. It had resulted in a separate line of command by which some product-sales managers passed on their objectives to their 'merchandisers', who in turn interfered in the responsibilities of the store manager. The latter had to integrate various product-sales objectives with his/her store objectives within the given space and allocated means. These difficulties for the store managers were even more outspoken for the 'merchandisers: fresh meat'. They directly passed on their instructions and demands to the butchery section in the stores, thereby bypassing the store manager. It exposed the tensions between the current role-taking and the new *intended management* role of the store manager.

Finally, it became evident that in the history of the company, role tensions and ambiguities were predominantly dealt with by improving interpersonal relations, thereby *side-stepping the power issues*. The workshop design, however, had eliminated these interpersonal relations and deals, enabling the participants to rethink the roles and activities within the structure of roles and gain awareness of the power issues, and to take into account the *willed* functioning of the hierarchy in the business organisation: integration and management of interdependencies; objective setting; creating appropriate conditions and follow-up or evaluation of achievements.

The three other role-groups present showed the same difficulties as in the pilot workshop. This time, however, the structure of roles – extended by the presence of the commercial management team – shed new light on the organisational dynamics, leading to a better understanding of the total picture by most participants. The members were so committed to the suggested ways of improving collaboration at work that they even wanted to apply their insights in their own area of competence right away.

After Workshop Two, the consultants reviewed again with the sponsors the experiences, findings and suggestions. The sponsors concluded that a one-day seminar was to be organised with the commercial management team to further clarify roles, tasks and work relations and that another role-group should be invited to Workshop Three, namely the so-called 'chiefs' of butchers.[7] We would again have four role-groups together in the next workshop, yet, without the commercial management team, but with the same objectives and basically the same design. Workshop Three, however, would be extended by an extra half day.

THE THIRD WORKSHOP

The Fourth Role-group: 'Chiefs' of Butchers

The fourth group, '*chiefs of the butchers*', had again a great impact on the dynamics of the workshop, although some of the reactions and dynamics might be explained by the fact that too much attention was drawn to them in the opening session.

The butchers formed a special clan, different from the other role-groups. Within the clan they seemed to find self-esteem and a professional identity. Outside the clan, in society at large and within the company, they felt that their professional image was unduly unfavourable, that it should be enhanced, and that they lacked recognition from the company as a whole, for example, their

---

[7] The heads of the butchers' departments were called 'chiefs', while the others had the title of head of a department.

career opportunities stopped at the level of 'merchandiser'. Furthermore, they felt that they could *only* receive instructions from a colleague butcher (like their 'merchandiser: fresh meat' because of legal accountabilities), who they most often considered to be their 'super chief'. Neither the store, nor the area managers were considered their boss.

During the workshop, the role-group made a remarkable recovery and started to suggest ways of correcting their unfavourable image in society and within the company. They wished to change the name from 'chief of the butchers' to 'manager of the butchery' (i.e. the place where the meat is prepared for sale); they repeated their wish for an equal hierarchical status level with their store manager (for example, why shouldn't they get a company car like the store managers?). The role-group also suggested ways to open up the role boundaries of the butchers for multiple skills, and additional training in commercial and personnel affairs.

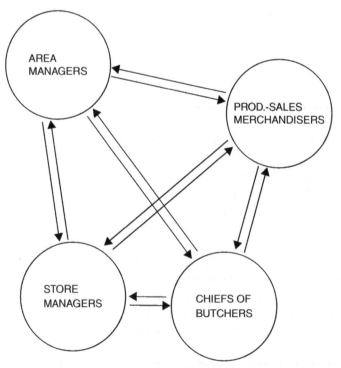

Figure 11.4 Graphic representation of written communications: Third Workshop.

The experiences in the *mixed groups* and later in the *plenary* sessions had a positive impact on the chiefs. Some of them realised that the felt lack of recognition only seemed to emerge *within* the conference. This may be partly explained by the salience of the other groups in the company (they were not invited to the two previous workshops). Then there were rumours that they might be put under the authority of the store manager in the future. We, the consultants, had a feeling that the other role-groups present had a tendency to see the butchers as 'different from them'. Indeed, they were different in terms of legal accountabilities, distinct rules and regulations for matters of hygiene, wearing white coats, working in a separated, *cooled* space and they had a clear professional identity. Furthermore, they were dealt with differently by the organisation, for example, no multi-skilling and limited career opportunities. These real differences and the clan-like behaviour were recognised and responded to by the area managers, and the 'merchandisers: fresh meat'. Indeed, the area managers tended to talk, during their visits, only with the store managers, not with the 'chief of butchers' and vice versa. Thereby, a *parallel system* of the 'chiefs of butchers', and their fresh meat 'merchandisers' was strengthened (a shared professional identity), next to the system of heads of the other departments, their 'merchandisers', and the store and area managers. It had become a trade organisation within the stores. These developments had to be dealt with because it might have led to paying less attention to the *shared responsibilities* of the 'chief of butchers' and the store manager and possibly to the exclusion of the first group from the mainstream of the company.

The Product-sales 'Merchandisers' within the Structure of Roles

In the third workshop, the *homogeneous* role-group of the product-sales 'mer-chandisers' was a special group. At least three members were about to retire and so therefore maybe talked more freely about their experiences. The three others had only limited experience. In that respect, it was not a homogeneous group. The differences between the dominant fresh meat 'merchandisers' (now finding in this workshop a natural professional alliance with the 'chiefs of butchers') and the other product-sales 'merchandisers' were striking.

From the start in the *mixed groups* of this workshop an observable tension emerged between all 'merchandisers' and the role-group of area managers. The product-sales 'merchandisers' saw the area managers as machos. They became even more upset when they noticed that the area managers as a role-group had not defined their own role like all the other role-groups. Furthermore, they did not address the 'merchandisers' as *distinctive* from the other role-groups. Neither did the area managers state their expectations about the product-sales 'merchandisers'. What they did write about them revealed that they were only conceived as an extension of themselves and a source of information for what went on in the stores.

The tension between these two role-groups led, first, to an affirmation and redefinition of their role as product-sales 'merchandisers' (with the exception of one fresh meat 'merchandiser' who did not agree) in which they crossed out with a red marker the 'requested' *inspection activities*. Second, they demanded in plenary and with anger that the area managers should define their role like any other role-group. Third, some aggressive feelings lasted till the very end of the workshop. On a non-conscious level, these tensions may well be seen as an expression of the readiness of the homogeneous role-groups to work through some power relations considered illegitimate.

It was difficult to discuss and come to some insights into the complexity of the tensions inherent to the role of the 'merchandisers'. Only in the last homogeneous role-group meeting, one came a little bit closer to an understanding of their proper role problems, when the 'merchandisers' started to talk about their ambivalent relations with the area managers. On the one hand, frequent contacts enabled them to *share* in the hierarchical power of the area manager, who could influence their promotion opportunities. On the other hand, they resented being seen as their *extended arms*. Maybe this very behaviour reinforced their feelings of being inferior to them (lower salary). This was very likely since they insisted with vigour on being drawn to the same hierarchical level as the area managers. Their anger found further ground when they realised that the area managers engaged in sales promotional activities (e.g. encouraging barbeques on the parking lot), that clearly belonged to their newly claimed responsibility to manage commercial, product-sales projects. They resented these role infringements. Furthermore, training, educating and consulting those responsible for a department – without taking away their responsibilities and undermining the 'new' attempts to empower the store manager and his department heads – was considered part of their newly re-thought role. In their view, the area managers should restrict themselves to *coaching* the store managers. Another field of tension was found within themselves, namely in finding a balance between the stated requests from the store managers and the 'chiefs of butchers' to visit them more frequently –

despite their already loaded agenda – and the fact that they themselves benefited financially from working overtime.

The stated need by store managers and 'chiefs of butchers' to be visited more
frequently may have had different meanings, which could not be seriously
explored in the workshop, although they may be critical for the further development of the organisation (in terms of empowerment, recruitment of more
'merchandisers', and costs). For example, were these visits an attempt to
maintain contact through the 'merchandisers' with the rest of the organisation? Or, a way not to feel forgotten or *left alone*? Or, was it a wish to reduce
the *risks in decision taking* by hearing *what* the others in the company were
doing? Or, was it a complex mixture of all these? One more question was
left unanswered: why didn't the product-sales managers emerge as playing
a salient role in the minds of the 'merchandisers'? Was this due to their absence at the conference – only role-groups present are worth discussing – or
did it reflect a reality in the operations? One thing was emphasised: some
'merchandisers' just filled in reports for one of the product-sales managers to
please him, while in fact they had stopped working in his preferred 'inspector's
way'.

The product-sales 'merchandisers' were eventually ready to formulate how
they wanted to deal with the tensions in taking their role:

- The core objective of the product sale 'merchandisers' was to help those
  responsible for a department in a store.

- 'merchandisers' often became seduced into taking over from those responsible in the store in order to avoid customers becoming dissatisfied. The latter
  was recognised as not only satisfying the customer while being around, but
  also gratifying oneself by the feeling of doing something worthwhile. The
  pleasure of fire-fighting was felt to be more rewarding than the slow process
  of educating those responsible, which would benefit all clients.

- Confidentiality was required to explore problems in depth. However this
  was felt as incompatible with the formal request of some product-sales
  managers to write evaluative reports to persons who could affect the careers
  of the persons concerned.

- The 'merchandisers' conceived it to be their task to help the head of a
  department take promotional actions. They could support their initiatives

by helping them to calculate and explore the likely consequences of those promotional activities.

- Instead of simply passing on, imposing or reinforcing the commercial objectives coming down from the product sale managers, the 'merchandisers' expressed a wish to engage with the area and store manager and his/her department heads in a process of setting objectives. Subsequently follow-up was to be organised so that all could learn from their efforts.

- A distinction was made between the inspection of hygiene and safety regulations and education on product-sales technical matters.

- The 'merchandisers' became aware that in order to be effective in carrying out their new roles they needed to maintain a relative autonomy in relation to the other role-holders, in particular to the area managers (the power dimension).

Let us now review the tensions experienced by the product-sales 'merchandisers' within the structure of roles:

Tensions between 'merchandisers' and area managers and product-sales managers:

- These three roles, in the experience of the role occupants, largely overlapped due to a lack of distinctive definition and training. Some persons enjoyed the promotion but continued to work from their old role conception (either as store manager or as 'merchandiser'), *but* from a higher level. This could go on unnoticed for a long time, because there were no distinctive criteria to appreciate role performance. Yet, 'Trees planted too close to one another cannot grow!'

- The 'merchandisers' complained that some area managers and product-sales managers gave them instructions as if the 'merchandisers' were the bosses of the department heads or of the 'chiefs of butchers'. In fact they had a combination of tasks, predominantly consultative and educative, and only for hygiene and safety matters did they carry out real inspections.

- The area managers showed off with the successes that the 'merchandisers' helped to realise. This feeling may have reflected the tendency of the area managers to take the role of a *super* store manager, and/or it may point to some personal abuse of a power position.

- The area managers didn't talk to the 'chiefs of butchers'. Although they were responsible for the allocation of means, they didn't have information about the butchers available in one region to stand in for manpower shortages in other butcheries in nearby stores. Consequently, the 'merchandiser: fresh meat' took over this task.[8]

Tensions between 'merchandisers' and store managers:

- We are dissatisfied, said the 'merchandisers', because the store managers don't show interest in our work, although eventually they have to decide on what actions to take in their departments. This raised some questions, first, whether the department heads had a formal and empowered role in the stores; and second, whether the store manager needed to know the ins and outs of every department. They were in particular ignorant about their butcheries. Nevertheless they were also accountable for their achievements. Yet, if the store manager needed more time to manage his/her resources than s/he should be allowed to delegate some responsibilities while remaining accountable.

- Along the same lines, it was felt that some store managers considered the time spent with the 'merchandisers' as a loss of productive time.

Tensions between 'merchandisers' and 'chiefs of butchers':

- The fresh meat 'merchandisers' had the technical knowledge, while the 'chiefs of butchers' lacked knowledge and skills in managing their shop.

- The 'chiefs' had no information about other butcher shops to compare achievements.

- Whether one liked it or not, the 'merchandisers: fresh meat' were perceived as the bosses of the 'chiefs' of the butcher shops. This confusion may be due to the fact that the area managers didn't manage the 'chiefs', nor help them out when they faced a shortage of appropriate personnel. This complaint

---

[8] It should be remembered that this role-group of product-sales 'merchandisers' was particularly angry with the area managers – with whom they didn't have any interpersonal work relations – because even in this workshop, they didn't do their work.

might also reflect an annoyance about the lack of promotion opportunities for the 'merchandisers: fresh meat'.

The store managers didn't take a dominant position in the plenary sessions. They affirmed being all responsible for their store, and for the final decision taking regarding advice from the 'merchandisers'. In the face-to-face inter-actions, however, they remained more in the background, as if they saw it as their task to reconcile and absorb tensions and differences between the other role-groups. At the end of the workshop, they became very alive discussing the 'discovered' differences in freedom and practices of store managers in the different regions.

THE RELEVANCE OF THE DESIGN

The value of the design is expressed in (a) its potency to *create awareness* of one's subjective creation of roles to deal with inherent role-tensions and fields of tensions within the existing structure of roles, and to *stimulate action taking*; (b) its potential to enable a more *congruent integration* of the various pleasant and unpleasant tasks within organisational roles and to *clarify* roles to facilitate co-operation within the structure of roles; and (c) in the *generation of information* amongst the many internal stakeholders about organisational issues that need to be dealt with in a systemic way. These three elements play an important part in the building of role identities within a structure of roles.

The Design's Potency for Creating Awareness and for Action Taking

So far, we have regularly referred to emerging insights by the participants about their efforts to form their roles as a function of their own personality and their boss's perceived instructions. Here we want to summarise the most striking examples:

• Tensions proper to a specific role emerged in the *homogeneous* groups as different accents put on specific tasks by different people within that role. For example, some 'merchandisers' conceived their key task as *inspecting*, while others put the emphasis on giving *technical advice, educating or coaching*.

Within the role-group these tensions became visible, while they were not necessarily recognised (any longer) by all individual role occupants.

- In the *mixed* groups and *plenary* sessions one could notice how the role ambiguity between roles was maintained (as well as a possible psychic pay-off) by holding on to one's old role after promotion (e.g. area managers and 'merchandiser' as store manager), rather than learning to take the role proper to that hierarchical level. Furthermore, the absence of an accepted distinction between the roles of regional commercial and product-sales manager led to situations in which the 'merchandisers' and/or the area manager were guided, instructed or appreciated for the wrong *role performance*.

- Simply following the instructions of the boss, whether or not appropriate to one's role, or leaving the boss with the illusion that one is still doing what he wants, tended to become a more common practice in order to avoid inter-role stress and conflict.

- The fear of taking authority within one's role became expressed in the inter-group interactions in plenary. The preferred cover was: 'we are all concerned with the same interests of the company' or 'we are all working for the same objectives' with the implied message that any role differentiation was not necessary and every role occupant could share in the real overall success of the company, while not making a specific role contribution. Furthermore, one thereby ignores the power differentials between roles. This over-identification with the company and its goals reflects also the inclination to hold on to the old performance criteria – when the company was still small – while in the actual situation it became a convenient way of taking a ride on the company's continued commercial success.

- The fear to be held accountable by one's boss tended to turn role occupants into controllers of the employees in the stores, thereby eroding the ownership and responsibilities of the store manager. Some regional and product-sales managers had prescribed in rules and procedures such controlling behaviour. The roles of 'merchandisers' and area managers became thereby simplified: checking whether things were in order. Observed deviations in the stores became translated into new rules, while a *simple open personal talk* with the persons concerned would have been sufficient. These practices by some managers eroded learning about consulting and managing, leading inevitable to a shortage of future needed candidate managers/leaders for the expanding organisation.

- The design exposed a *defensive tendency* to deal with role-tensions and issues of co-operation through simple 'human relations' approaches, for example, having more frequent meetings, calling for more trust in one another, sending a person to a personal growth workshop or expressing the belief that if we would just get to know one another better we could also co-operate better.

- The plenary session also revealed that roles had been created in an organic way, more to help cope with work overload than on the basis of an organisational strategy to deal with the needs in an expanding organisation. Consequently, overlapping roles and/or redundant tasks became exposed.

- At this stage, action taking was confined to confrontations and recommendations in the workshops with the intent to influence/change the current structure of roles.

The Design's Potential to Integrate Various Tasks, Clarify Roles and Build Role Identity

We point here to the potential of the design. During the workshops it became evident that the consultants played an important role in enabling the members to integrate various tasks within their roles. The consultants' familiarity with group dynamics and processes of splitting was sufficient. Yet, the clarification of roles within the structure of roles called upon the *sensitivity* of the consultants for the *strategic implications of role clarification*. In the first pilot workshop, we realised that genuine organisational role definitions would only be possible if the legitimate strategic elements were brought into the workshop. In response to this felt absence, the commercial management team was included in the second workshop. In the third workshop this strategic element was carried by the consultants and checked with members of the management team in the last sessions. Without this sensitivity for the strategic implications and a good enough understanding of organisation theory, role clarifications may have led more to simply maximising role satisfaction rather than *organisational effectiveness and efficiency*. In the clarification of roles (e.g. the 'merchandisers' in the third workshop), we can see how many role occupants gained insight into the various fields of tensions and suggested more appropriate ways of dealing with them. This is also reflected in the enthusiasm with which one of the product-sales managers wrote about some of his conclusions after the second workshop:

- "We should make a distinction between, on one hand, hygiene and safety regulations, and product-sales procedures on the other. The first call for 'inspection' with zero tolerance, while product-sales regulations call for a regular 'audit' about the whys of possible deviations, which may reveal new and better ways of displaying the products in the department or a lack of product-sales understanding demanding further training.

- The distinction between responsibility (that can be delegated) and account-ability (that cannot) is useful to deal with the frequently heard complaints about 'too much work'."

Yet, he also spotted some *unrest* in the role-groups of the area managers and 'merchandisers' when the core tasks in their roles became re-defined. They seemed to experience this as impinging on their freedom to fit their roles to their own choosing. However, after the discussion they could see the benefits of a clearer defined pattern of roles. He felt so much commitment amongst the members of the workshop that he *wished* everyone to implement immediately in his/her own work domain their insights and redefinition of roles.

Generating Information for Organisational Diagnosis

Together with our comments on the workshop we discussed our diagnostic observations. Here, we bring them together as a report. Much more could be said, but due to confidentiality reasons and respect for the international corporation, we decided to limit our diagnostic review to understanding the various subjective role experiences (identities) within the pattern of roles on the basis of the material collected by our design.

Professional identities and inter-role co-operation

The store managers

They tended to define themselves as the heart of the firm and took particular pleasure in playing the role of interface between the firm, their personnel and the customers, regulating tensions and constantly mediating between different, and sometimes diverging imperatives and opportunities. Two pitfalls awaited them: on the one hand, an increasingly bureaucratic role and growing pressure to focus on managing, which they appreciated only moderately, or at least less than the role of field leadership and super sales person for which they felt a certain amount of nostalgia; on the other hand, there was the solitude they felt when faced with tensions in labour relations. Admittedly, they benefited from precious support in the person of the department head, but they did not have a genuine supervisory team. The implicit specialisation of the department heads did not necessarily facilitate cohesion within the organisation, since they considered the 'merchandisers' to be their real bosses. The store managers' relations with the 'merchandisers' were therefore naturally very ambivalent: were they partners or a force of opposition?

The store manager was and remains the focal figure in the history and culture of the store, fulfilling all the functions with the utmost concern for customers' satisfaction and sales. Today, it would seem that the product/region tension that existed between the managers had penetrated the level of the store managers via the tension between the 'merchandisers' and area managers.

The store managers liked freedom 'with support', because their responsibilities were increasing and were leading them from the role of super sales people to that of managers. They did not have a clear vision of the results that were expected of them, and often felt they were the victims of sudden changes that remained unexplained by the managers whose decisions rained down on them without their meaning or legitimacy being really understood. The means granted did not always correspond to the targets that were set, they received more and more orders from above, and relations became increasingly impersonal.

Any additional active co-operation with the various levels in the company seemed to them to represent an extra workload.

The area managers

What the area managers seemed to have understood or learned during the workshops is the following. Their empathy with the store managers had developed to the detriment of their manager role. A role they tried to strengthen by establishing close ties with the 'merchandisers', who they wanted to play an inspection role in the departments. They were submerged by memos and, like the 'merchandisers', were faced with the question of the nature of the help they could provide. In our opinion, it was no coincidence that they were unable to formulate the core tasks in their role. It was because they had discovered to a certain extent the complexity of the other roles, and even their problematic sides (e.g. the 'merchandisers' as 'law enforcers') that they hesitated and preferred, on the whole, to place the emphasis on projects (e.g. regional project) to give their role a healthy, creative dimension. The development of greater store autonomy could have helped them to do so. The dissemination of learning from the action taken in other stores in the area was not yet considered as a significant task. Neither was objective setting.

The 'merchandisers'

Their function was to a certain extent in contradiction with the corporate culture of polyvalence. As specialised, functional employees without a clear position in the line management (although in formal terms, they were the employees of the product managers), they would have liked to be acknowledged as advisors, but they very often operated as inspectors. When they took the time to think it over together, they clearly felt they were faced with a paradox: how to help a department by creating relations of trust, while reporting as extensively as possible on any shortcomings that they observed. From this point of view, their reports on their visits were an obstacle. These notes were sent to the department head, store manager and area manager. They inspired wariness, while only going part of the way towards satisfying the area managers, who admitted that they did not have time to read everything (hence their focus on problems rather than on successes). In the end, the question was raised for whom were the 'merchandisers' working? Without any secretarial support and constantly on the road, they could have orientated their role towards that of trainers, provided that they focussed their action on improving a department and reduced their role as inspectors to the domain of hygiene and safety. Such a shift would have required this new activity to be understood by the area managers and their respective product-sales managers. The question was to determine the basis on which their actions were to be assessed/appreciated. Hence the proposals to create a platform for consultative integration between 'merchandiser', store manager, and area managers in each store.

Another difficulty was revealed, namely in order to be promoted to area managers (and not all wanted to be) certain 'merchandisers' felt obliged to demonstrate their authority as inspectors.

The 'chiefs of butchers'

They were the only producers and the only specialists with a 'real trade', an identity and the skills that go with it. But this identity was seen as being in decline outside as well as within the firm: the Meat Director was the head of the 'merchandisers: fresh meat', not of the butchers. They were satisfied with the resources allocated by the firm to ensure good-quality work.

Their role had become more complex, however, with the increase in the size of the butchery and the increase in personnel management activities, the risks inherent to product quality and the vigilance of the customers. The stigmatised image of the profession (death, dirt and brutality) set them apart, just as they were set apart in the store where they formed a separate entity that received few visits from the other employees or even from the store manager who seemed happy to accept the existence of this enclave. Signs of this mere state of co-existence were the fact that contacts with other staff were limited to distant relations in the canteen and merely saying hello in the morning. Was it that people were afraid of them, or envied them? The latter was probably the case, as well as the obvious exasperation that their 'specificity' aroused because they represented, in some ways, a symptom of the structural tension between polyvalence and the shift towards greater specialisation.

As they worked under licences issued in their individual names, they were also ultimately legally liable, which may have contributed to justifying a higher status and level of recognition.

Who did they work for? The area manager? The 'merchandiser: fresh meat'? The store manager? At all events, although they agreed to co-operate with the store, they did not want to find themselves under the formal authority of the store manager, and the store manager demanded no such authority anyway.

We may round off this part with one general, but important observation. People who don't sufficiently understand the dynamics in and between roles tend to explain experienced difficulties in collaboration in terms of personal and/or interpersonal attributions.

PART 2: WORKING THROUGH THE DRAFT BLUEPRINT

The commercial director organised several meetings with the internal consultants to discuss the reports and the observations in the three workshops, before writing a first blueprint of the new roles within the structure of roles. In the meantime and parallel to our project, some other projects had been initiated to set up a management by objectives system – including the Balanced Score Card – and a new feedback report system to improve the existing management information system. These projects were complementary to our project and expressed the intention of the CEO to introduce management systems more appropriate for managing the large corporation. Three issues emerged regularly in these discussions. First, the pros and cons of establishing a separate hierarchy for the product group 'fresh meat' in order to make full use of the competences of the 'merchandisers' and to honour the trade identity of the butchers. They needed a boss who was a professional butcher him/herself. Second, the search for a balance between the established top-down management of the stores and the departments through the intermediates of area managers and 'merchandisers', and on the other hand the bottom-up approach by which the store manager became a fully fledged manager of the store and not simply a site manager. Three, the experienced difficulties of maintaining a clear-cut distinction between regional commercial managers and product-sales managers was repeatedly raised. Eventually, the commercial director sent out a confidential note to be discussed first in the commercial management team and subsequently with the area managers and the 'merchandisers'. A second draft of the blueprint was then sent to the CEO for comments on the proposed changes. This lengthy document included besides the clarified roles some important new elements: (a) the product group 'fresh meat' became a parallel line with their own area managers, (with some 'merchandisers') and a 'chief of butchers' in each store; (b) a balance was struck between the store manager as a site manager including the butchery; and (c) three levels of integration and objective setting were introduced: one between the regional and the product-sales managers, the second between the area managers and the product-sales 'merchandisers' in each region, and a third platform for integration at the level of each store.

The project sponsors chose not to deliver a finalised blueprint of the re-thought structure of roles, but a draft blueprint to be discussed with the role-groups concerned. They could even suggest some adaptations so that the blueprint would really fit the large organisation. The project leader, an internal consultant, was asked to set up a series of workshops to facilitate the working-through process with the help of an external consultant (the first author). Together the project leader and the external consultants made a new design to facilitate the implementation.

THE SIX TWO-DAY WORKSHOPS

The Design

The design was developed largely within the theoretical framework and its three basic elements. Yet, in contrast to the three original workshops in which we had only role-groups *without* established work relations between the various role occupants, we wanted now to have the *role holders and their work relations in the same workshop*. Because of the size, each region was divided in two subunits of around 60 employees in various roles but with direct work relations. Since not all the store managers and 'chiefs of butchers' had participated in the original workshops, it was decided to spend one half day with these two role-groups in a mini-workshop, before the other employees – with different roles – would join in.

The mini-workshops were kept pretty simple. With the help of a graphic picture, the 'new' and 'old' comers were introduced to the history of the project, its objectives and its various phases over the past year. Homogeneous role-groups were formed (two groups of 'chiefs of butchers' and three groups of store managers each assisted by a consultant) to explore:

- What are in my experience the most important activities proper to my role?; and

- To make an inventory of those activities they liked best and those they liked the least.

From these explorations they were subsequently asked to write down the essence of their roles in *five verbs*.

In the subsequent session, five *homogeneous* groups were re-composed to provide for an exchange between different homogeneous role-subgroups about their definition of the essence of their role, so that the store managers and the 'chiefs' could each speak with one voice. The conclusions about the essence of their role were put on paper to be subsequently explored in *mixed* groups of 'chiefs of butchers' and store managers. In the mixed groups of existing real work duos, one store manager and his 'chief' of butchers, the essence of their role definitions was discussed and where needed, amended to improve effective collaboration. In the first mini-workshop, we handed out the most recent draft blueprint of the commercial director on the new structure of roles. In the five subsequent workshops, this blueprint was sent to them in advance so that they could read and reflect on it.

From the very beginning these implementation workshops were focussed on *existing work relations* – inclusive interpersonal relations – and *experiences* with the aim of setting in motion a process of worrying and working through the possible consequences of the pending changes for themselves and significant others, while working towards the objectives of the overall workshop.

The objectives of the implementation workshops were to a large extent complementary to those of the original three workshops. Taken together they made the structure of roles become fully expressive of the organisational dynamics in the organisation: roles, real work-relations, objective setting, information flows and the accountabilities to the hierarchy. At the same time, we wished to create conditions for the employees to work through the proposed changes while still consulting them on remaining issues and questions. In other words, we tried to create a *transitional space* for the role occupants in the proposed role structure.

We formulated the general objectives for the six workshops as:

1. To become familiar with the new roles and work-relations; and to validate one's own role within the new structure of roles (*new roles and work relations*)

2. To explore the key activities and information flows necessary to achieve the agreed objectives within the organisation (*responsibilities for key activities, information flows and criteria for role performance appreciation*)

3. To explore the core tasks and objectives of the integrating level proper to one's role, the next higher level and their inter-relations (*objective setting and achieving agreement on objectives*).

These overall objectives were further specified for each of the composing blocks of the workshop while *facilitating structures* fostering task achievement and *supportive process structures* were offered throughout the design.

During the lunch break the commercial manager in charge of that region, the product-sales managers, the area managers, the area manager of butchers (a new role to manage the 'merchandisers: fresh meat') and the product-sales 'merchandisers' joined the workshop. The group was welcomed, and introduced to the network of roles and the graphic representation of the overall project. The first task given to the now five homogeneous role-groups (e.g. area managers, area manager 'fresh meat'; product-sales 'merchandisers', store managers and the 'chiefs of butchers' were: to formulate the five core activities in verbs (core task they are responsible for) and indicate where they differed from the past. Time was reserved to raise remaining questions pertaining to the new role structure. Each role-group was to appoint a spokesperson to present their work in the subsequent plenary session, attended by the three product-sales managers and the commercial manager in charge of that region.

In this plenary session the five role-groups presented their deliberations, which were compared with the newly proposed roles and role structure in the draft

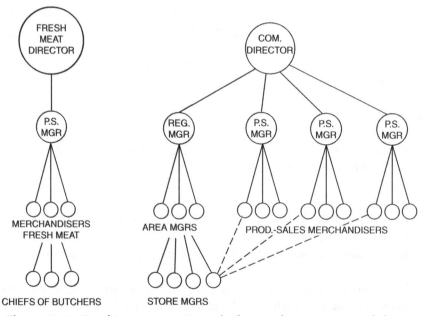

Figure 11.5 Graphic representation of roles: Implementation workshops.

blueprint. Deviations from the proposed roles were noted on a flipchart. All presentations were opened up for clarification and comments. This session was rounded off with short lectures about the basic differences between 'being responsible and being accountable', 'between inspection and auditing' and between 'work information and steering information'. These lectures were a repeat of old concepts for some, while being new for others. Eventually, everyone could work with the same vocabulary on the subsequent tasks.

All role-groups, including the regional commercial manager and the product-sales managers were subsequently asked to explore the necessary *information flows*, either generated by doing their core activities, or needed to carry out their role. Furthermore, they were asked to distinguish the domains of work that required an *audit* from those domains that demanded *inspection*. And finally, the role-groups had to think about the *performance criteria* they would respectively use to appreciate their co-workers or would like to see used in their own performance appreciation. To facilitate this task achievement cards on which they could write their answers were distributed to all the role-groups.[9]

- Three *white* cards for the three most important *information* domains on which they wanted to be informed and/or three others for the domains for which they should inform the other role-groups;

- Three *yellow* cards for the three most important domains on which they either wanted to be *audited* and/or three other cards for the domains they thought they should audit in the other role-groups;

- Three *blue* cards for the three most important domains on which they either wanted their *performance* to be evaluated and/or three other blue cards on which they should write the performance evaluation criteria for the other role-groups.

Each role group was instructed to write these cards to their immediate role-partners, depending on their position in the role structure. The *store managers* wrote and sent cards to their area managers, to the 'chiefs of butchers' and to their three product-sales 'merchandisers'. The *area managers of butchers* wrote and sent their cards to their 'chiefs of butchers' and to the store managers. The *area managers* wrote and sent their cards to their regional

---

[9] Homogeneous role-groups that were too big for effective work were split up into smaller ones.

commercial manager, their store managers, the 'merchandisers' and the 'chiefs of butchers'. The '*chiefs of butchers*' wrote and sent their cards to their area manager of butchers, to the area managers, and to their product-sales manager. Finally, the '*merchandisers*' wrote and sent their cards to their product-sales manager, to the area managers, to the store managers and the department heads (since the latter group was not present the cards were handed over to the store managers).

The second day of the workshop focussed on three major tasks:

1. Bringing into line the first explorations of the most important information flows, domains of auditing and performance evaluation criteria to and from the different role-groups;

2. A first clarification of the core tasks and objectives of the three new integration levels and their inter-relations; and

3. The exploration of meetings that would become redundant in the new structure of roles.

In the first morning sessions, the homogeneous role-groups distributed their coloured cards to the designated role-groups for sharing and comparing their contents. Once the cards were distributed, each role-group had a chance to compare the sent information with the needed information; the wished audits with the intended audits, and the preferred performance evaluation criteria with the intended criteria. Each role-group could then deliberate and write their comments on the received cards to be further discussed in a specially structured plenary. Finally, each role-group was asked to appoint a presenter who would be seated around the table with the other representatives of the other role-groups.

The subsequent morning session was organised in this particular setting. In the middle of a big room a 'round' table was set with chairs for each representative of each role-group and for the external consultant, plus one empty chair. All the other employees were to sit in a fishbowl setting around that table with their representatives. Members of the outer circle (including the internal consultants) could take the empty chair to make extra comments to the representatives and/or the consultant about issues of direct concern. Only the persons sitting around the table were allowed to talk. In sequence the representatives presented all cards of a role-group in focus. Where necessary they were corrected by the others, or the consultant, or the person taking a seat on the empty chair. After making his/her comments the person left the empty chair so that someone else could take it. The consultant had an explicit role to chair the fishbowl and to comment on the deliberations only from the perspective of organisational theory in order to maintain congruency in principles used to send and receive information, to identify auditing domains, distinguish responsibilities from accountabilities and evaluate role performance. This fishbowl-like plenary session became most lively and effective in eliminating or correcting role and authority relations (e.g. information flows, audits, accountabilities and performance evaluation criteria) within the new role structure. All cards per role-group, with the corrections made, had to be carefully kept to be typed and preserved for the real work in the back-home situation.

In the afternoon, we tried to clarify the tasks and relations between the integration levels. In a first session the natural duos of store managers and the 'chiefs of butchers' met. Area managers, 'merchandisers' and area managers of butchers formed a separate group to formulate what they saw to be the core tasks of the integrating levels one and two. Subsequently, they shared and compared their findings in plenary.

In a final session the relations between these two integrating levels were discussed in terms of who decides on the allocation of means and underwrites the action plans to achieve the agreed objectives. With what frequency do they meet and for what purpose? Finally they looked at the existing meetings and indicated which of them had become redundant in the new role structure.

The subsequent workshops had the same design as the one described above but the tasks were formulated in a slightly different way. More emphasis was put on comparing the past with the future role responsibilities and work relations and on discussing possible changes in the present blueprint. Furthermore, the short lectures on respectively: (a) the differences between responsibility and accountability; (b) the differences between inspection and auditing; and (c) the differences between steering and work information had become more articulated.

Reflections on the Implementation Workshops

The six workshops were organised in such a way that all employees had real work relations with one another: collegial, functional and hierarchical. Consequently, role-group and inter-role-group tasks were all given to people who knew one another from working together. More care was taken to provide appropriate facilitating and process structures to enable the employees to engage in transitional change processes. This was achieved: First by making the impending changes in role structure more salient, for example, studying the draft blueprint of the commercial director *before* coming to the workshop and by an emphasis in the workshop on *comparing* roles experienced as vital with the roles roughly described in the blueprint. Remaining questions were noted on a flipchart. *Past and future* were thereby brought into the *present*. Second, by gradually bringing in the *day-to-day work relations* between roles and role-groups. From 'final' role clarification in direct interaction with other role-groups, we proceeded towards the *inter-role-groups* study of information flows, auditing and role performance evaluation, and finally to the *integration levels* and *inter-level interactions*.

In this trajectory, participants experienced gradually more and more difficulties with the given tasks. Not that they were in any way protesting. They had rather difficulties in articulating the implications of the re-defined roles in terms of giving and receiving information, formulating performance evaluation criteria, and domains for auditing. Once again it exposed the overruling identification with the company as a whole (selling as the dominant purpose) overshadowing the identification with one's role-group (contributing to making selling possible). Logically, they also had difficulties in distinguishing between the different time-spans and scopes proper to their roles in a given structure of roles (Jaques, 1989) and between the three integration levels. Whether this was an indication that the process of working through the changes in the structure of roles was not yet sufficiently achieved, or that we were confronted here with deeply ingrained elements of the company's culture could not be verified. Probably the two were so intertwined that they formed a whole to be transformed within oneself and externally (in relation to the structure of roles). Later on we learned that this identification with 'selling' was even reinforced by some 'personal growth sessions' organised by the company, in which one talked with admiration about an exercise in which one product-sales manager was seen walking across the room expressing repeatedly his identity-task as "I sell electronics. I sell electronics. I sell . . .".

Exploring core tasks and purpose of the three integration levels was the most difficult assignment. It was not only new in the structure of roles, but it was also a hesitant departure from a tradition in which objective setting was done top-down by the commercial director. The members of the commercial management team cherished the belief in their effective power to manipulate known success factors leading to the expected results in the stores. Consequently, one struggled with top-down objective setting through which each integration level added some objectives or increased the ones already set by a higher level versus an iterative process of bottom-up and top-down exchanges.

As we worked through each of these six workshops the realities of the proposed changes in the structure of roles could not be sidestepped. Attempts to minimise their impact through statements like: 'We'll only be working as we used to do, but with better defined roles' no longer made sense. Changes in the structure of roles and in work gained a quality of: this is for real. The original intent to improve role definitions had ended up in rethinking roles, relations and the structure of roles.

For some persons the working through processes along with this sequence of tasks became too much or confusing. Rather than going through the hard work of integrating their role and the structure of roles with their working experiences they said they were willing to work with the blueprint of the commercial director as it was presented.

UNDERSTANDING AND WORKING WITH ORGANISATIONAL DYNAMICS: DISCUSSION

Although the design has potentials for understanding and working with organisational dynamics in organisations other than those coping with organic growth, we would like first to discuss some of our findings in this particular expanding company.

With rapid organic growth, managers gradually lose contact with the daily realities of what is going on in their organisation which they once knew so well. But, do they still need to know the ins and outs of the daily activities in the company, or is it sufficient for managers to know how the system is working to manage the business? The ambivalence towards developing a system that allows them to manage a growing organisation can often be traced to experienced difficulties with the power dimension. This may be particularly true for organisations that see the looming spectre of bureaucracy behind any organisational structure that creates a distance from the top manager. That distance created by an extra layer in the hierarchy or dividing the work is perceived as a loss of power directly derived from affiliation with the manager in charge; while the manager may doubt his influence and presence in the organisation when s/he becomes removed from reassuring, regular face-to-face contacts with his employees. The commercial management team was a typical example of sidestepping, even denying the actual changes that had – because of the size – occurred in the authority structure. All its members still enjoyed *the same title* of 'director' like their boss and their roles remained *undifferentiated.*[10] They were all considered equals while in fact all power was located in the commercial director; a man with an excellent flair for the business. The exclusive emphasis on human relations, at the expense of organisational differentiation of work-roles, can indeed be seen as a defence against the recognition of differentials in power and the knowing and understanding of the requisite tasks of an employee at that level. The renamed regional commercial managers, the product-sales managers, and the next layer of area managers and 'merchandisers', became in fact extended arms. The whole project with its specific designs, helped management to transform its *awareness* of the difficulties resulting from vaguely defined roles into a blueprint of a rethought *structure of roles* more adapted to the size and organisational strategy of the company.

The over-identification with the founders and the overall company had produced a highly committed workforce and a largely shared perspective on the business and hence an expectation of agreement, neither provoked by, nor arousing feelings of dependence. Yet, at a cost of not developing differentiated work-role identities and hence diversity in perspectives with the likelihood that conflicts, constructive or not become perceived as interpersonal issues rather than task-related conflicts. Within organisations there is a structural element of power in most role structures (most visible in hierarchical role structures), based on a mutual agreement of what is best to manage and to make the company successful. Power relations either derived from social or structural power are based on reciprocity (Isaac, 1992). In other words, power as a structural property of a particular way of dividing the work can only be effective to the degree and the extent that this is considered a good-enough way to achieve the company's objectives, from all internal and external stakeholders of the organisation. Whether that structure of roles – and power – is appropriate is therefore context bound.

---

[10] This state of undifferentiated roles may reflect a belief in an assumptive reality that not much was changed in the team by the organic growth of the company; a belief reminiscent of Bion's basic assumptions (1961).

Differentiating roles (e.g. in regional and/or product-sales responsibilities) and delegating responsibilities are ways of dealing with increasing workloads in rapidly expanding companies. In general, these work-roles become defined by norms structured by management. In themselves they cannot become role-identities that form a balance with the dominant identification with the overall company and/or the founders. In order to achieve that, they need to become internalised and transformed into role-identities.[11] Core activities in roles probably don't constitute a role-identity either, but a *shared role experience* does, and so does a *shared project* to amend roles and the structure of roles of which one is a part.[12] The amendments to and affirmation of one's role also contained a *political claim* to be recognised as such by the others in the structure of roles. In other words, in role-identities one needs not only *self-definition* but also the *other role-groups* must come to recognise and relate to that role in a more or less consistent way. The store managers wanted to be seen as fully-fledged managers and so did the 'chiefs of butchers' in their claims to operate as professionals on an equal level with the store managers. This was a political claim that other role-groups must come to perceive them in such a way. Likewise, the 'merchandisers' wanted to be recognised as product-sales *consultants* and not as extended arms of the area managers or product-sales managers and so on. It is a *social and political construction process* by which role-groups construct the structure of roles, which in turn constructs their role-identities.

People in organisations carry a plurality of identities in which they find sources of meaning and experience (Calhoen, 1994). Not only role-identities, but also ethnic and demographic identities interact and may overlap with what is called 'organisational group identities' in the embedded inter-group relations theory (Alderfer & Smith, 1982). Role-identities can be conceived as a kind of organisational group identity. Since individuals belong to a plurality of groups, for example, the company, a department, a team and one's own role-group, they are likely to develop a plurality of identities. The hierarchy in the structure of roles and the inclusiveness of these groups (teams or functions are part of the wider organisation) together create a *hierarchy of identities*. Some become salient, while others remain dormant or implicit depending on

---

[11] But the internalisation process should be a voluntary one, i.e. not one created through manipulative or unconscious influences.

[12] The original workshops were – for the area managers and the store managers – not sufficient to create role-group identities for the whole group. Only about 10 % of them had been able to attend one of the three original workshops.

the changing context. In other words, the relative importance of an identity within this hierarchy varies over time in relation to the context one is in. The salient identity renders priority to a particular source of meaning for thinking and action. This diversity of role-identities within the same social system impacts upon the social interactions at work in positive and negative ways. Positive to the extent that it brings variety in perspective into problem solving, decision making and action taking needed in getting the work done. Negative to the extent that role-identities take precedence over the common organisational identity, hampering co-operation (Nkomo & Cox, 1996). Yet, it is precisely the ability of the individual to move back and forth between one's role-identity and one's organisational identity that allows an employee to be influenced (leading to consensus), rather than to being dominated (leading to conflictual power) by the hierarchy in the structure of roles (Simon & Oakes, 2006). The more the organisation operates as networks, and/or with multidisciplinary or multifunctional taskforces (or project groups) the more important role- and professional identities become for *effective* collaboration.

When talking about collective identity formation, Manuel Castells (1997) always raises four questions: how, from what, by whom and for what? Before we comment on the relevance of the design elements in the project, we would like to briefly answer Castells' four questions. *How?* By bringing together homogeneous social categories of role occupants as a group to clarify their role within a structure of roles. This process facilitates *self-categorisation* whereby the various ways of taking a specific work-role can become part of the self. A social identity can then be formed that gives meaning to experiences and guides thoughts and action.*From what?* We started from a collection of existing similar roles and experiences within a structure of roles. *By whom?* It was largely achieved by the role occupants through a process of self-categorisation within a given design, and later to be formalised by the commercial director. *For what?* There was no clear threat present that could coalesce resistance and role holders, except by the product-sales 'merchandisers' and the butchers. Role occupants were brought together to clarify their roles in order to operate more effectively and efficiently within a structure of roles appropriate to manage an expanding organisation.

The h*omogeneous* and *re-composed homogeneous role-groups* contributed not only to the clarifications of roles, but also to the development of a role-identity based on experienced similarities in key role activities and claims to be recognised in a specific role within the structure of roles. The *mixed groups* were clearly *new* groups in which different members could – in a more intimate constellation of a face-to-face small group – discuss their reactions to the earlier written comments and confrontations in order to adjust role definitions and distinguish roles to facilitate co-operation at work. Co-operation was now based more on role differentiation than on just working for the same company. The *sequence* of working in homogeneous role-groups and mixed groups and back into homogeneous groups further strengthened role-identity and the knowledge of shared issues within the role-group and with the other roles in the structure. In the project, we can find evidence that identity forms the basis for action taking and that a strong sense of job identity allows for more openness and real interdependency. The 'chiefs of butchers' and the 'merchandisers: fresh meat' who shared an already established identity were the first to make the most powerful claim in the original workshops, followed by the store managers and 'merchandisers'.

The interactions between role-groups in *plenary sessions* created foremost conditions to reinforce role-group identification – partly encouraged by the explicit inter-group constellation – while making the organisational dynamics and tensions within the overall structure of roles visible and discussable. This was even more evident when the physical conditions of the meeting room allowed us to seat each homogeneous role-group around a separate table. They also brought the identity of the company forwards in the form of the structure of roles of the commercial function. The identification with the overall company existed and was earlier expressed in identification with 'selling', but now it emerged as a hierarchical or super identity on top of refined role-identities. The hierarchy of the structure of roles became particularly evident in the fishbowl sessions.

The *fishbowl sessions* became a powerful element in the design. Representatives of all role-groups communicated with one another in a face-to-face setting, while other members could join in the discussions by means of the 'empty chair'. The role-groups at the bottom in the hierarchy of roles gained power through the sheer size of their groups to discuss and argue with those in power, power derived from their role position in the structure. All role-groups were equal as a similar task was assigned to them, and equal for the outside consultant who intervened from an organisation theoretical perspective to maintain organisational congruency in the principles used to define information flows, auditing domains and role performance criteria. The fishbowl sessions served three major functions. First, to work through the power relations: *power over* (e.g. role performance evaluation) and *power to* (e.g. information flows and auditing) while searching for agreement between role-groups.

The awareness and acceptance of the hierarchical and the power correlates inherent in the structure of roles were of particular importance – and could never have been achieved without strong role-identities – to differentiate role activities within the general strong dedication of the employees to selling: the commercial function and core of the business. Second, the fishbowl sessions served also as a *validation and reinforcement device* of the appropriateness of the role conceptions alive in the minds of the role occupants. On the one hand, all these role formulations made *organisational sense*, for example, made a workable coherent whole of the structure of roles. On the other hand, these roles became sufficiently *part of the work-selves* of the role holders when they engage and relate to the hierarchical structure. Thirdly, the psychic struggles in the fishbowl *confirmed* most of the elements in our earlier organisational diagnosis, which we had discussed with the sponsors during the course of the first three workshops.

The explorations of *the integration levels* introduced new platforms for co-operation: objective setting and follow-up. It was by far the most difficult part in the design of the implementation workshops. The integration levels were not only new in the organisation, they were also not yet thought through by management who had to let go part of their authority to set objectives for *all* levels in the commercial function *without* much *distinction*. Furthermore, it was a different and new form of co-operation. Not just working together ad hoc, but working together on a shared task (objective setting) – with changing authority relations – that led to binding commitments for a given time, for all parties concerned. In one setting the area manager is in a hierarchical position and role in relation to the store manager, while in the lowest integration level during the upward phase, s/he is just an advisor to the store manager's platform. Yet at another time, in the *iterative process* s/he seeks agreement on the objectives that finally come top-down. Letting some *prerogatives go* and *learning to work with and in different authority relations* had started but was far from complete. Yet, the integration levels are a vital element in managing the expanding organisation.

The *short lectures* were introduced to help develop a shared vocabulary to facilitate the study of the role realities and to help the conceptualisation of findings and experiences. They also appeared to support self-reflection and working through.

The *implementation workshops* were designed with even more focus on creating conditions that would enable transitional change processes to emerge:

'worrying' and 'working through'. Consequently, they appeared also *more stressful* than the original ones. From the start, tasks were given that drew attention to activities proper to their roles that they liked or disliked, activities to be continued or discontinued in the new structure of roles.

The store managers were the first to realise and express a regret that being the best salesperson was no longer the core in their management role. Also the area managers had to work through the anticipation of becoming more a manager of a group of store managers within an area with specific market requirements/opportunities than just enjoying the successes of the stores. The product-sales 'merchandisers' struggled with becoming more of a technical-commercial consultant than a simple inspector. While working on the blueprint, the commercial management team had probably worked through some of the changes, yet some of them still had a hard time holding on to their newly distinguished roles as regional and product-sales managers. A few persons didn't like to translate in their own terms the proposed changes, and expressed a wish to just accept the draft blueprint as *the* new way of working. The uncertainty that goes with fitting prescribed roles and their individual interpretations with past experiences was too much. They preferred to receive clear-cut role descriptions from their bosses, and live with that. By far the majority found the workshops worthwhile but difficult and they appreciated having been consulted before a new role structure became introduced.

The design, through the 'third' channel, facilitates this major step in managing, in a more appropriate way, the expanding company. Role-identities can be developed within a structure of roles, without losing the overall identification with the values and goals of the company. The way these organisational changes were introduced made them not only acceptable but generated new commitments. Not one person resigned, nor applied for a transfer outside the commercial function. This does not mean that problems will always be resolved in such a way but the intervention design can provide a meaningful tool for continuous problem-solving situations.

REFERENCES

Alderfer, C.P. & Smith, K.K. (1982). Studying intergroup relations embedded in organizations. *Administrative Science Quarterly*, **27**, 35–65.

Amado, G. (1999). Groupes opérationnels et processus inconscients. *Revue Française de Psychanalyse*, Vol. LXIII, **3**, 905–916.

Amado, G. (2003). Le charisme contre le travail. *Informations Sociales*, **105**, 116–123.

Bion, W.R. (1961). *Experiences in Groups*. London: Tavistock Publications.

Bridger, H. (1990). Courses and working conferences as transitional learning institutions. In: E. Trist & H. Murray (Eds), *The social engagement of social science, a Tavistock anthology*, Vol. I: The sociopsychological perspective. Philadelphia: The University of Pennsylvania Press, 221–245.

Calhoen, C. (Ed.) (1994). *Social Theory and the Politics of Identity*. Oxford: Blackwell Publishing.

Castells, M. (1997). *The Power of Identity: The information age: economy, society and culture*, Vol. II. Oxford: Blackwell Publishing.

Clot, Y. (1999). *La fonction psychologique du travail*, Paris: PUF.

Higgin, G. & Hjelholt, G. (1990). Action-research in minisocieties. In: E. Trist, & H. Murray (Eds.). *The Social Engagement of Social Science. Vol. 1, The Socio-Psychological Perspective*. Philadelphia: University of Pennsylvania Press. 246–258.

Hoebeke, L. (1990). Measuring in organisations. *Journal of Applied Systems Analysis*, **4**, 79–90.

Isaac, J.C. (1992). Beyond the three faces of power: a realist critique. In: T.E. Wartenberg (Ed.), *Rethinking Power*. Albany: State University of New York Press, 32–55.

Jaques, E. (1989). *Requisite Organization: A total system for effective managerial, organization and managerial leadership for the 21st century*. Arlington, VA.: Cason Hall & Co.

Jaques, E. (1995). Why the psychoanalytical approach to understanding organizations is dysfunctional. *Human Relations*, **48**, 4, 343–349.

Laing, R.D. (1959). *The Divided Self*. London: Tavistock Publications.

Lhuilier, D. (2006) *Cliniques du travail*, Paris, Erès.

Mendel, G. (1992). *La société n'est pas une famille*. Paris: La Découverte.

Mendel, G. (1998). *L'acte est une aventure*, Paris: La Découverte.

Nkomo, S.M. & Cox, T. (1996). Diverse identities in organizations. In: S. Clegg, C. Hardy & W. Nord (Eds), *Handbook of Organization Studies*. London: Sage, 338–356.

Simon, B. & Oakes, P. (2006). Beyond dependence: An identity approach to social power and domination. *Human Relations*, **59**, 1, 105–140.

Taplin, L.J. & Carter, M. (2005). Catching up with … Edgar Schein. *Organization Development Journal*, **23**, 2, 78–82.

Vansina, L. (2000). The relevance and perversity of psychodynamic interventions in consulting and action-research. *Concepts and Transformation*, **5**, 3, 321–348.

CHAPTER 12

Transformation: Hope , Illusions and Reality. Transformations within a Family-Owned International Corporation

Leopold Vansina and Marie-Jeanne Vansina-Cobbaert

The concept 'transformation' has a special appeal. It borders on magic, peaks of alchemy in the very old days, and has become associated with spiritualism. It contains a promise of creative development, a better life, a more human organisation, even a better society. Not surprisingly, the social sciences often use the notion in propagating new concepts: 'transformational leadership' (Burns, 1978; Bass, 1985) and 'transformational change' (Kilmann et al., 1988). In the 1980s, for example, one used the metaphor of a caterpillar turning into a butterfly to express the intended transformation of the 'old' organisations into new, modern and more humane businesses and organisations (Ackoff, 1981; Vansina, 1989). In most instances, the new concepts were built on hope, inspiring and empowering others, stimulating creative and rational thinking to realise organisational transformations. The latter were defined in terms of a *desired output*: a work system that appeared different, felt different and functioned differently. The empirical findings, however, are sobering. Total system changes failed like most of the process re-engineering projects. At the macro-level, greed became a socially accepted economical driving force, to replace the older concept of continuous improvement in quality, cost efficiency and development. Human beings became resources to be coerced or manipulated into a flexible – even disposable – workforce. Management's talks revealed an increasing distance between what they really thought and what they said.

Words were carefully chosen to mask their intentions in order to engage people in courses of unjust or insane actions. Yet, there are laudable exceptions. In particular family businesses appear not only to perform better in the market, but also turn out to be more humane employers and better citizens in society.

In the psychoanalytic literature, however, the notion of transformation refers to *mental processes*. The outcomes are left open. With the interest in Bion's work, his notion of 'transformation' became the subject of discussion in the International Psychoanalytic Association at the beginning of this century, before the International Society for the Psychoanalytic Study of Organisations (ISPSO) decided to hold a symposium on the subject (2004).

By bringing the two streams of thought together, the desired output thinking of Organisation Development and the psychoanalytic thinking about mental processes, we may be able to see better the *challenge* for organisation consultants or managers. In essence it lies in creating conditions to enable the persons concerned to realise desirable and sustainable outputs through mental processes that also support psychic development. At this point, I refer here briefly to mental processes of (a) gaining understanding, not just cognitive but also emotional; (b) transitional processes; and (c) learning processes based on exploring, testing and accepting realities. All these processes are intrinsically linked to the pursuit of truth and justice in changing times. In this way, organisational improvements may transform the *very being* of persons and thereby enrich their capacities to relate, accept and deal with the wholeness of the realities within and around him/her, and restore or strengthen his/her social relatedness. The *task of a psychodynamic consultant* is then not just to add to the volumes of speculative, interpretive understanding *after the facts* without any previous interaction with the client, but to generate knowledge that has implementation validity, for example, knowledge leading to action for improvement and which is testable on its relevance in practice. Or, in Chris Argyris' words: social knowledge that is useful, not just for the specialist but also for the layman (Crossan, 2003).

We have structured the chapter as follows. In the first part, we will discuss the consulting project in a family-owned international corporation operating in Europe. This part is lengthy because we would like to bring alive the work in the project as it evolved over more than two years so that the reader can become engaged, while we try to make sense of the processes and of some key concepts and assumptions in our practice. In the much shorter, second part, we first explore to what extent these processes could be clarified by existing notions in the psychoanalytic literature. Second, we will use the project experiences to advance our thinking about transformations in organisations. In other words, what can be learned from these consulting experiences that has implementation validity.

PART ONE: THE CONSULTING PROJECT

We start with a description of the request and the situation of the sponsor, so that the reader can begin to play with his own ideas of how s/he as a consultant would engage in the project. Since the project lasted more than two years, it was an impossible task to describe the various interactions and developments in a chronological way. We finally decided to present the project: First in terms of the actors, namely (a) the consultants and project manager, (b) the family membership and (c) how they (consultants, project manager and members) evolved during the project. Second, the time and space provided for creating a platform for the 'Family Community'. Under this heading, we will further specify the *facilitating and supportive process structures* that we as consultants tried to create: time, space and a means to facilitate the processes of exploration and transitional change and their outcomes. Third, the time and space provided for clarifying the *power structure* in the family business and the enactment of the *transformations* that came out of the work. Fourth, we will present a chronological review of the emerging behavioural transformations and the *interplay between* the platform of the 'Family Community', the 'Family Shareholders' and the 'Business', and the later, created 'Family Council' (for a graphic representation, see Figure 12.1). Doing things differently is taken as an indicator of possible transformations to be subsequently explored whether or not, and to what extent, they reveal a change in object relations with the family, the business and its governance.

The Request

The Board of a family business that developed during its third generation into a European-based International Corporation of more than 10,000 employees (spread over several parts of Europe) wanted to rethink its current family-structured ownership in the light of the expanding family. Three years

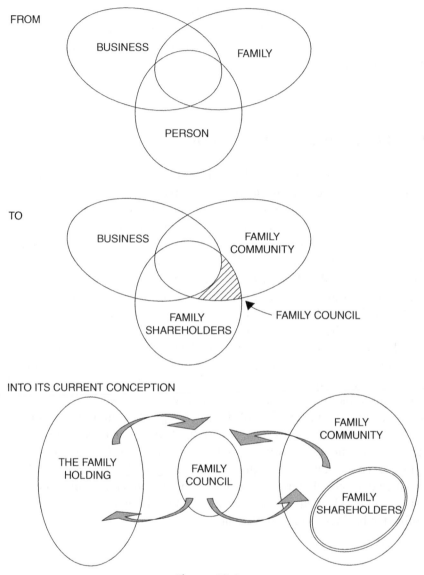

Figure 12.1

before the start of the project, we[1] had had some talks with the new president (designated successor of the previous one) and the members of the Board, all members of the family. This time (early Spring), the Board felt that it was time to face the need to clarify and disentangle the complex interactions between the family and the family business in view of the oncoming, fourth generation. We listened to their concerns about the complex structure of the financial ownership – designed by the previous president to hold the family shares together in the family business – and to their accounts of the leadership transitions. David provided a rudimentary model to disentangle the complex relations within a classic family business and illustrated it with some of his experiences elsewhere. Out of the discussions emerged a commitment to bring all family members together – between 50 and 60 persons in the second and third generation[2] – in a series of residential weekend meetings to discuss: (a) the current needs and challenges in the family, (b) their expectations and relations to the business and (c) to initiate a process and a structure to explore ways to meet identified needs. The project manager and the consultants would design a programme and the intention was to finish the work before the end of the year.

We left that meeting with some major questions: What minimal structure would be appropriate to start such a delicate process? How would we handle the language problem since many family members talked only French and not English?

THE ACTORS WITHIN THE SYSTEM

The Consultants and the Internal Project Manager

David was an external consultant to this family organisation and a stranger in its socio-cultural environment. In order to get to know the situation and establish some working relations, initial meetings with each family member

---

[1] The 'we' stands here for the internal project manager and member of the family, and two external consultants: David, an American OD consultant with international experience in working with family businesses and myself (the first author). I had known the previous president when he took over from his 'founding' father and turned a small ailing local company into a successful business.

[2] The remaining family members and their partners represented the second generation. Only blood-related family members in the third generation were invited.

of the second generation were arranged, with the possibility of talking to him again. Sequential translations were going to be taken care of by some of the family members. But each member was encouraged to talk either in French or English during the meetings.

David had a more training-oriented approach to consulting. He had a standard programme of questionnaires and a sequence of tasks to work on. His rudimentary model distinguished the 'family', the 'business' and the 'person'; a revised version of his questionnaire on the health of family businesses, and the discussion of the family legacy seemed to be good enough for starting the process. My background was different.[3] I had only directly worked with the family business 25 years ago, but I had a rich experience of working with a wide variety of international corporations in many different countries within and outside Europe. As a consultant, I like to start 'from where the client is', work on 'the agenda in the middle', generated by all persons concerned, and with the emerging dynamic processes. Consequently, I was more used to working with minimal structures to enable exploration of expectations, concerns, needs and tensions, and with providing conditions for transitional change.

The *internal* project manager had an important role in the project. Not only did she have direct access to (a) some afterthoughts of family members, and (b) developments within both the family and the business; (c) she could also arrange meetings for the consultants with the sponsor, while (d) being in an excellent position to clarify certain sensitivities and dynamics. It was also a difficult role, being at the same time a member of the family and a member of the consultants' team. She had – like some other family members – taken part in psychodynamic programmes for consultants and managers, of various kinds and durations. As such she too had a proficiency in working with psychodynamics and minimally structured work settings.

The Membership

Fifty to sixty family members and partners of the second generation, board members and the president attended the meetings. Several of them had taken part in programmes in group dynamics and/or personal development. So there was a group within the family that recognised the importance of the *inner*

---

[3] Refers to the first author of this chapter.

world and of tolerance for *ambiguity*, as a *necessary condition* for genuine development and change. From the initial personal talks of the second generation with David, we learned about the diversity within the family shareholders in terms of their relation to the business and ownership, their expectations about the project, and about their appreciation of the achieved business successes. Also some sensitive issues of employment of members in the family business, balancing personal needs and family business obligations were revealed.

All members were invited for the first meeting by the president, who also opened the meeting explaining the context and his intentions with the project.

How the Actors, their Objectives and Frames Evolved Over Time

The objectives of the project remained largely the same over the years, but they gained clarity and depth. However, other expectations, needs and opportunities surfaced – or became better recognised – as the community of family members gained more trust in sharing, comparing and exploring their experiences, prospects and engagement in the family business. It was a process similar to writing an article. One starts with some basic ideas, which become refined and modified along the way. For example, the membership became recognised as more diversified, for example, family branches, individuals and different roles. Different conceptions of a family business and intentions with their capital became expressed, while one was becoming aware – emotionally and conceptually – of the changed realities and meaning of *the family business* over the generations: its changing environments, relevant to a small, local family firm into an international, diversified business and a family financial holding company and the nature itself of the family community.[4]

During the project, the president and the members of the board gained credit from the family. The members became able to tell the president: "you are not responsible for keeping the family community together. This responsibility is a shared one". The meaning of this statement was further discussed and revealed not only the explicit distinction between his role in the business and in the family, but also the shared responsibilities of the members to keep the family together regardless of the business.

---

[4] In the second part, we'll come back to the mental processes, assumed to underlie these transformations in the family and the business.

Also the consultants were affected by the work. Their conceptions of *family* and *family business,* and their ways of *framing* and *mapping* the interactions and processes within the family community gradually displayed major differences between them. Three of these differences may be worth noting. First, we discussed the difference in conception: *one cohesive family* with one identity versus a *family union* consisting of (possibly) different families and personal identities. Second, the disentanglement between the *business,* the *family shareholders* (blood stream) and the *wider, extended family* including partners. Third, the family that *runs* the family business (operational management) versus the *family shareholders* that *appoint* the board and *express* their expectations about the family business for themselves and for its place in the international community. In other words, the appointed board takes on the role of *governance* of the business within *that frame* of expectations and values.

These differences emerged also in the membership where they became an *appropriate subject* for exploration and discussion. As consultants we had to be careful not to favour one conception over another in designing a minimal structure for the family community, neither could we take these issues away from them where they had to be dealt with.

The sequential translations distinguished our roles as consultants in terms of how and what we could contribute. The translations into French were a repetition for those who understood English and a pause (a space) for the others, while the translations into English took place – in a low voice – between one or two members and David. Consequently, David could hardly take part in emotional engaging or small group discussions. Furthermore, it made interventions on the spot difficult or impossible. His contributions mostly took the form of short talks and the display of some prepared slides with encouraging or inspiring statements. Drawing attention to and making sense of the evolving psychodynamic processes were largely left to the members and myself.

'MINIMAL STRUCTURES' AND 'TIME AND SPACE'

Within OD, one talks about 'minimal structures' (e.g. Barrett, 1998), while in the psychoanalytic-inspired literature we prefer to talk about 'facilitating and supportive process structures'. We use the notion of 'facilitating structures' to clarify goals, assist people in setting their own agenda (also called the 'agenda in the middle') and to enable them to achieve task accomplishment. This agenda in the middle may and does evolve over time. It is kept open for changes in content and/or in timing, as long as these suggestions become part of joint review and shared decision making. We also suggest or create 'supportive process structures', for example, 'time and space' to enable healthy mental processes to take their own course. We don't think we can be more prescriptive. It would confine one's creative use of being in touch with the whole. In *being in touch*, many variables are taken into account, for example, the purpose of the meeting, the agenda, the state of the client system, including the consultants and the context. Furthermore, these variables and their interactions do change overtime. So what are apparently good enough minimal structures are *judgements* made by the consultant, based on understanding of the context and anticipated processes, and on the consultant's professional integrity.

The Minimal Structures for the First Two-Day Residential Weekend at Foresthill

Purpose, location, time, space and available means

At the meeting the *overall objectives of the total project* were formulated on flipcharts as follows:

- To develop a well-functioning platform that will support core values, culture and harmony within the family community, and to promote family goals and business success;

- To increase communication, trust and conflict resolution processes between family members; and

- To set the stage for family and business sustainability in the transition from the third to the fourth generation.

All residential meetings were held at Foresthill, a small, modest conference centre in the countryside. All the 'Family Community' meetings to discuss and explore issues directly related to the family, the relations between the family and the business, and the first 'Family Council' were held at Foresthill. A rough timetable for the two-day meeting with a sequence of tasks was sent out before arrival. A large room was set up with chairs in a wide circle, some flipcharts up front, and an overhead projector in a corner for possible use. Smaller breakout rooms were available.

The *'facilitating structure'* comprised: (a) a sequence of tasks: discussion of the outcomes of a previously collected questionnaire on health in family businesses, sharing and working through their expectations about the project, sharing and exploring the family legacy and building the agenda for the following meeting; (b) a flipchart for the 'running agenda' on which items could be put that could not appropriately be handled at that time, and (c) possible work settings: plenary meetings, meetings within the family branches (which they called "nests") and in small mixed groups. Furthermore, (d) a rudimentary model was presented to distinguish the 'family' from the 'business' and the 'person'. (e) Sets of cards were made available on which individuals could privately express their views or items for the agenda, along with sets of stickers that each member could use to express his/her personal view on the relative importance of an item, or a cluster of items. All members of the family, regardless of their position, received an equal amount of stickers: *one person, one vote.*

Context, processes and outcome

A couple of days before the first weekend, a business journal had written an article on the family business. At the start of the meeting, the president rephrased the purpose of coming together and made a passing comment to this article. Thereby, he brought the business realities into the meeting. Then, the consultants introduced themselves and roughly described their roles. The members said a few words about themselves and wrote their first name on a name tent and put it on the floor in front of their chairs. David, the OD consultant, presented his rough model and discussed the outcomes of the questionnaire, which showed that the family business was in a healthy state. Subsequently, every member had the opportunity to talk about his/her expectations and concerns ('hopes and fears') about the overall project. Since every statement was written down on a flipchart, summarised and translated into English for David, unintentionally it created a 'time-space' for reflection.

The expectations and concerns focused mostly on the *family,* less on the *business* and the *person,* and expressed quite a few *concerns* about the future interaction processes in the large family meeting. Expectations about the *fam-*

ily centred around: (a) understanding and coming to terms with the history of the family in relation to the business, the legacy, what and how to pass it on to the next generation and/or share it with one's partner; (b) having enough freedom and choice to be different within the family and/or different in one's relation to the business; and (c) a wish to maintain the family bond over the generations as valuable in its own right, regardless of the business. The expectations about the *business* were largely restricted to: (a) a better understanding of the power- and financial structure of the holding and the business; and (b) a better understanding of the specific values of a family business for management, employees and for the wider society. The expectations in the category '*person*' clustered on working through identity issues related to being rich, living with a legacy and being just different within the family or the nest. Then, there was a diverse list of expectations that could not be classified under the three entities within that rudimentary model. Most of them were really concerns and hopes that the discussions would be open and honest, allowing sensitive issues and experienced crisis to be opened up and worked through, and that the decision-making processes would be transparent and fair. There was a hope that the platform would relieve some of the pressures on their managers and a concern that these family community meetings might generate feelings of exclusion in their partners. The most valuable outcome of this first inquiry was: (a) the 'abstract painting' of a background of concerns, fears and expectations against which issues could be voiced and discussed, and (b) a careful, vague introduction of some *delicate issues*.

We all looked at the flipcharts and discussed what sense we could make out of this and how it felt to work together in this way. The discussion took more time than estimated so we adjusted the timetable.

Later that afternoon, we embarked upon an exploration of the legacy of the family. The translation of 'legacy' in French ('l'héritage') left some ambiguities. Legacy didn't mean only money or shares, but most importantly the values and principles that were passed on within the respective branches from the parents to the children. When this was clarified, the (remaining) members of the second generation told their *stories, their recollections, views on life and principles*. This time, we didn't write anything on a flipchart. Some of us took notes. These stories or accounts were again summarised and translated into English.

The *ambiguity* in the meaning of the notion 'legacy' and the *time-space created* by the translations enabled each member to bring in whatever came to their minds, triggered or not by what had been said by the preceding member: the second generation, their brother or sister, nephew or niece. Old memories emerged; forgotten experiences were brought back to awareness, at times so vividly that a deceased parent or another family member came back to life, as it were. The distinction between the values and principles within the person and those still out there as 'instructions' faded into a whole: 'my life'. There was recognition within the wider family, sometimes underlined by a good laugh. Yet, not every part of the legacy could be put in words; some found their expression in tears, a call for attention or for forgiveness and acceptance back into the nest.[5]

The whole legacy was for many members a source of *ambivalent feelings* (e.g. appreciating certain values which were part of their upbringing while sometimes wanting to get them out of their system in order to simply enjoy life; feeling grateful for the donated shares/money, but being unable to enjoy that wealth freely; gratefulness that was accompanied by a feeling of having to contribute to the business, without knowing how to do that. In the process, *some identity issues* emerged as well (e.g. 'I am rich because of other family member's achievements, but who am I?').

After this exchange in plenary, the members came together in their respective family 'nests' to further discuss the legacy and sort out the values and princi- ples they wanted to preserve and pass on to the next generation, versus those that they did not want to pass on, either because they had served their time, lost their relevance or were simply not appreciated in hindsight (e.g. too much personal free choice, when one was not yet ready to take that responsibility). Subsequently the core values and principles were written down on cards to be displayed and grouped together by the whole family in the plenary room. It was hard work first to *integrate and cluster* – through comparing and infor- mal clarifications – all those cards brought in by the different family branches, and second to *decide what values/principles they wished to retain or to leave aside*. Since this sub-task was done in the large room, everyone could see members moving around, discussing 'cards' in changing sub-groupings.

---

[5] Although the words reparation or forgiveness were never used, the process was present and worked through around some central persons who had gone too far out of the family tradition. It was expressed in compassionate listening followed by a visible embrace or a gentle slap on the back in or outside the big room. We draw the attention to this process of reparation, first, because it is of such importance in community development; and second, because it is psychologically different from 'working through' and the popular notion of 'healing'.

When that work was completed, members sat down and exchanged what sense they could or could not make out of that process. It became very clear that the family appreciated making a list of its shared core values, but were opposed to turning them into a *code of conduct.* Subsequently, small coloured stickers were handed out to enable each member to express the relative importance of the list of values/principles for themselves and thereby reduce the long list to *core values of general importance.* In this way, some parts of the legacy became condensed in a list of values: austerity; freedom and respect for choice; honesty; staying in touch with the family; reliability; being responsible; trusting; striving for justice; openness and transcendental aspirations. Other parts, maybe the most important ones, were revived and somewhat re-worked in the process, underlining the importance of the 'nests', the bonding within the family branches and the mutual recognition of their special quality within the overall family community. Yet, at another level, the lengthy process provided enough freedom and space to enable the individual member to emerge as a person in his/her own right, and as a member in different groupings (generations, gender, employee, manager or being non-active in the family business). It appeared that sufficient reparation and trust became established to make their personal expectations and concerns now more explicit in terms of what should be discussed and worked on as the agenda for the project.[6]

Building the 'agenda in the middle' could, however, not be done directly without further talks within the family nests. The individual talks with David, previous to the first weekend, had initiated some discussions within the family branches. Yet, more explorations were needed for various reasons: absent members, too sensitive issues, or not all branches having taken that opportunity. So the branches met separately and discussed their concerns and questions for the overall agenda of the project. They noted them down on flipcharts to be displayed in the large room. Their review and clarifying comments *revealed* a number of sore experiences, questions, unresolved conflicts and diverse interests. The tension went up and ebbed down when it became clear that all those concerns appeared *acceptable and legitimate.* Not one item was moved under the carpet.

After a break, all members were given the opportunity to compose the agenda for the future by writing their individual items, one on each of the distributed cards. Within this context, each member had optimum freedom to voice his/her

---

[6] It is a good example of how the 'agenda in the middle' evolves and changes over time with new insights and under more supportive conditions.

personal interest. Some items contained or revealed the original concerns, stated at the beginning, others were new. All cards were hung up on one big wall, and the members were asked to *cluster* them in rough categories. Several of the categories had already been used during the reporting back of the deliberations in the branches. This time, they were written statements (without names) to be put into categories. The cards, which could be taken off the wall and stuck on another place, became a vehicle in a further process of *comparing* and *finding out* similarities, differences and sensitivities. A rule rapidly emerged that no one could move or modify a card without the consent of the owner. Anonymity was no longer a concern. However, the comparing and exploring still enabled some to express 'secretly' their concerns, or to clarify the *attributed* similarities and differences in their points of interests. It seemed that this clustering of personal cards had created time, space and a means of working through partially similar or different concerns: 'In one way you can see that as similar, yet, I mean something different . . . but now, yes, I can have my card there (under that category)'. All these discussions in freely, changing constellations of members, and the moving of cards from one cluster into another was visible to everyone. A process had begun to sort out and to differentiate: the individual from the family branches, interests in and concerns about the family versus the business, differences between generations, gender or between members with and without a role in the business. Then 'stickers' (coloured dots) were distributed to express the relative importance of the clustered agenda items. The outcome was their *'agenda in the middle'*: a ranked order of subjects (categories), specified by a number of cards. These cards were carefully preserved. They contained the personal wordings and related emotional experiences.

A workgroup of family members, representing the branches, was asked to prepare the following one-day meeting together with the internal project manager and the consultants. The workgroup took the agenda items and the clustered cards and had them typed up and circulated.

The Minimal Structures for the Subsequent Meetings at Foresthill

The 'agenda in the middle' contained about 10 major clusters of items. In order of their ranking: (a) the history of the family in relation to the business; (b) the family's expectations about the future of the family business; (c) the financial and power structure of the family holding; (d) specific questions within the family branches; (e) personal issues: practical or urgent questions; (f) information about selling and buying shares of the holding; (g) expectations about the overall family; (h) new developments in the business; and (i) the platform itself. The workgroup took these items and sorted out which of them could best be discussed in which of the existing bodies (several legal bodies within business, for example, the Holding Board, the Boards of the various companies in the group, the General Assembly; or formally established bodies like the Junior Board) or in the platform of the Family Community. Working on the most important agenda item, they invited the second generation to a brief meeting at Baritone (the headquarters) in order to clarify the expectations of the Family Community and to encourage them to prepare and tell their stories and recollections of their family history *with the business* in the next one-day meeting at Foresthill. In a subsequent meeting, at Baritone, the financial and power structure of the family holding would be openly explained with the assistance of a financial expert, along with the existing procedures for buying or selling shares.

Time, Space and Means

Sitting in a wide circle, the second generation told their stories about *the family histories with the business*. The members didn't use any papers; they just told about their experiences and recollections, which were partly known, partly forgotten or told in another context, from another perspective and consequently, differently understood. The presence of their partners encouraged them to speak up. Additional details, painful emotional episodes or recollections were added which led to corrections, further elaboration or questions. The stories were more delicate than the accounts of the legacy. They contained a rich variety of experiences: being excluded, being left alone with all the responsibilities for the business, putting one's private possessions on the block, the joy of succeeding in the business, or the pain of being left alone and not really being a part of the developments, choices and decisions made which in hindsight were less beneficial in terms of personal advantages; some resentments, unfair treatment within the family, etc. No one felt a need to take notes on the flipcharts. One listened, allowing the past to become alive again and some recognised the past in the present and in the items on the 'agenda in the middle' leading to various futures.

Besides the relief linked to having had a chance to talk about it, the stories had three major impacts on the project. First, a new reality, that had been present all the time, emerged and became conceptualised with and without the assistance of the consultants. For example, two persons from two different generations were experienced as founders of the family business. Some of the second generation took their father and uncles as the founders; others took one of his sons as the founder, since he transformed a small, local business into a corporation. Linked to these experienced realities were marked differences in emotional attachment to the family business, which had been reinforced by the creation of a family holding. Some members had a firm interest in the inherited *capital* that had been invested in one major company. A large group of the third generation though held strong emotional ties to the *activities* of that major company, one of the core businesses in the international corporation. Only a few members were engaged in the family holding, the oncoming business to be managed. Second, the stories created a context against which the various items (the cards) behind the agenda in the middle could become more fully understood *within a historical perspective and in their emotional depth.* Third, members of the second generation started to feel that they had done their work, their presence was no longer necessary in the family community. Time had come for the next generations to take over. They were, however, willing to participate in the following meetings in support of the younger generation.

This second meeting ended with a clarification of the various formally existing bodies (e.g. boards, general assembly) and what issues on the agenda should be discussed in those specific settings. First on the agenda was the structure of the family holding.

Baritone, Time and Space to Discuss the Business

Baritone became the location to organise the meetings to discuss all issues proper to the 'family business'. From the very beginning of the project a clear distinction was maintained between Foresthill and Baritone. The first was a temporary, informal platform to explore, work through and decide important issues pertaining to the family as a whole, or to its members without having a direct relation to *the running of the family business.* If the discussions turned into or revealed a business issue it was put on 'the running agenda' and referred to the Baritone location, the headquarters. The opposite took place during the Baritone meetings. The boundary between family and business had to be kept clear. Certain implicit rules were made explicit or fine-tuned as we progressed in the project, for example, one voice, one vote in all meetings of Family Community, the Family Shareholders, the Family Council, but one share, one vote in the General Assembly.

The structure of the meetings at Baritone was also different. Presentations and explanations were given from behind a desk and the other family members took seats behind conference tables. Experts in finance or legal matters were brought in whenever deemed necessary or helpful. I was the only external consultant present to help them work with the dynamic processes, for example, keeping the boundaries of the issues clear, clarifying processes that interfered with task accomplishment.

The interactions between the developments in the Family Community or Foresthill meetings and the business meetings at Baritone – and vice versa – were of utmost importance in realising the project. At Foresthill, not only were the conditions for effective work on the business created, for example, trust, openness, context and historical perspective, but also the complexity of the realities became visible to the total family. What bonded the members together became gradually differentiated in the various fluid subgroups, depending on the issues under discussion. These evolving differentiations and the ways one related to them became expressed before everyone's eyes. Something that members may have assumed or known in a special way, now could become conceptualised. Thereby they lost something of their '*exceptional*' or even '*deviant*' quality, so that one could work with them. These developments offered new insights and opportunities, which were picked up by the president and board members to further *imagine* and *explore* alternative structures and procedures for the holding, the governance of the International Corporation and for taking better calculated risks.

In this Baritone meeting the financial and power structure of the family holding and their current procedures (e.g. selling and buying of shares) were explained and discussed, so that everyone had a good understanding of the *actual situation and the reasoning* behind its creation. Placing the founding of the holding in its *historical context*, opened perspectives on possible adaptations. Subsequently, the annual report and the legal requirements of the business were studied. Only a couple of times, did we need to raise the question of whether or not a particular subject would be more appropriately discussed at Foresthill. After lunch in the cafeteria, members moved around, continued their discussions for a while and then took off for the rest of the weekend.

The Interactions between Foresthill and Baritone: The Transition of 'Knowing and Valuing' into 'Actions'

This meeting at Baritone had created a mild urgency. Important business decisions had to be taken. The meeting had clarified the established power and financial structure of the family business and had raised the need to create a 'Family Council' to mediate between the business and the members of the family. Yet, a variety of questions remained unanswered, for example, about the investment interest of the family, about the members' values for and concerns in the family business. When, after the summer holidays the family community met for a two-day meeting at Foresthill the focus was on three major issues: (1) Where are we with the urgent issues on the 'agenda in the middle'? (2) Where did we come from? and (3) Building a Family Council to mediate between the emerging, distinguishable groups within the large family and the business.

The most urgent issue – not explicitly on the 'agenda in the middle' – was a new business venture to be decided on within a couple of months and linked to the future of the family business. The president informed the family community about the history and prospects of that venture. The ensuing discussion provided grounds for embarking on the next item on the 'agenda in the middle' namely the family expectations about the future of the family business. These expectations were explored in terms of the intentions of the family owners with their capital and their expectations/values for the family business. An overwhelming majority wanted the family business to remain *leading* in social responsibility, while *balancing* it against ecological soundness and profits. But, there were also members with different investment interests and values. Also, a meaningful percentage of family capital was found for the new venture initiated by the board of the family holding.

The review of where we came from – which included a summary of the legacy statements – became the ground against which the 'known' differentiation within the membership could become further conceptualised. The crude model for the disentanglement was refined. The 'Business' was more than the original small, local family firm turned into an international corporation with a number of spin-off companies. The *family holding* gradually became recognised as *the* family business, although most of the emotional ties were still with the original business. Yet, the holding became recognised as the power centre from which the different values of the family had to become disseminated in the businesses under its governance.[7] The current family community at Foresthill was now perceived and recognised as largely corresponding with the actual *family shareholders* that needed to be distinguished from the future 'extended' family or *new family community*. The latter should also include the partners so that both parents could raise the children with knowledge of the family business and within the context of the family legacy. Although one was aware of the necessity to extend the membership, it was not without serious concerns, as we will see later. The 'Family Council' to be created had to serve as an entity to relate, advise, filter and amplify between these three bodies: the 'Business', or better now the *'Holding'*, the *'Family Shareholders'* and the *'Family Community'* to be extended in the near future.

The desirability of and necessity to create the 'Family Council' had become the item on the 'agenda in the middle'. Small groups met to discuss and list the major tasks (some pressing agenda items were often included as tasks) for the Family Council, and to suggest some guiding principles for its composition. From the discussions of their various suggestions, the community concluded: (a) for the first year, only blood-related members should be eligible; (b) members could hold a job in the family business, but not a managerial role; and (c) members of the council should be paid for their time and expenses.

The second day was reserved for the composition of the Family Council. One of the consultants suggested taking the seven major interests in the business – which had been extensively discussed the previous day – as the basis for the formation of seven groups that would then select and propose a representative for the council. In that way the guidelines could be followed and the Family Council would represent the various interests of the family shareholders in the business. The suggestion was accepted. After time for consideration, members opted to join one of the seven interest groups. Within each group, one deliberated and eventually selected a nominee. Then, the nominees met – in the centre of the large room – to explore whether they could work together as a group. In this discussion, it became clear – to their regret – that not all family branches were represented. However, they thought they could live with that decision till they had written *themselves* the protocol for the Family Council to be elected within a year.

---

[7] Gradually one became aware of the need to move from operational management to governance of the corporation through the family holding.

After lunch, the Family Council met alone to prepare their agenda. The other members took a walk in the woods. When they came back in the large room, the Council summarised their work agenda and informed everyone that they were going to organise – with the project manager and one of the consultants – part of the next meeting at Foresthill. This last session of the two-day meeting, was rounded off with the handing out of symbolic presents to the Family Council. Presents the other family members had picked up from the forest. Everyone said some words of encouragement, or expressed a wish. We did not comment on the symbolic meaning of this ritual. Such an intervention would only have disrupted the process.

The Subsequent Disentanglements within the Extended 'Family Community': The 'Family Shareholders', the 'Family Council' and the 'Family Holding' and Work on the Interdependencies

The Family Council spent a lot of time distilling information from the Family Shareholders regarding the new venture and transforming it into an advice to the Holding Board. In that process they learned a lot about working as a team with differences between the family branches and amongst themselves. One of their meetings was devoted to the preparation of the next one-day gathering at Foresthill. The agenda was quite clear, but designing a facilitating structure for the different items demanded more attention from everyone, including the project manager and the consultants.

The next one-day meeting at Foresthill, after the summer, started with a welcome and an attempt at 'bridging the gap' between the last gatherings of the family community and the present. Then the Family Council gave a report on their work and the work in progress. Subsequently, the president informed the membership about the launching of the new venture and the composition of its Board. Furthermore, he encouraged the organisation of educational programmes in business and finance and in handling possible business crises for interested family members. This business-like opening served as a basis for clarifying and strengthening the *dynamic interplay between identity and boundary management* of the existing legal business entities: Boards, General Assembly, and the formal bodies: the Family Council, the Family Shareholders and the still virtual *extended* Family Community. In order to facilitate this process, all family members of the different boards were asked to take a chair on one side of the large room, the Family Council seated itself in the centre, the Board members sat at one end and all the other members at the opposite end of the room. When this disentanglement was completed, the family members without a formal role were invited to think about questions they would like to put to either the 'Business' or to the Family Council. This process was visualised by moving their chair near the addressed entity. Then, one by one these individual questions were raised and responded to, if judged appropriate by that entity. If not, they were asked to move their chair again and address the appropriate body. During this process members started to distinguish the different identities of these critical bodies, practiced boundary management and even learned that it was legitimate not to answer questions *on the spot* but to claim time before giving an honest, valid reply. Understanding the different functions of the various entities was felt to be less difficult than controlling one's affiliations and habitual ways of obtaining an answer.

Subsequently, flipcharts – each one with one named, legal or formal entity – were used on which all the remaining questions of the members became listed. It allowed further differentiations and it made visible *what* important issues still needed to be dealt with by *which entity*.

The next issue was extending the family community of Foresthill. A number of small mixed (different branches and generations) groups explored subsequently three major questions: (1) what kind of Family Community do we want to be (major characteristics)? (2) What wishes and concerns do we have about extending the community with the partners? and (3) how to integrate the oncoming fourth generation? The first question was almost a repeat of values, which had been discussed earlier. However, it opened up again the discussion of needing or not needing a 'mission statement', and some related issue of the distinction between the extended Family Community and the more restricted group of Family Shareholders. The deliberation on the second questions revealed how sensitive and difficult the inclusion of the partners in the Family Community really was. Although most members could see the advantage of the partners taking part in the community for educating the children in the spirit of the legacy and developing an interest in the family business, their inclusion did raise a variety of concerns. The experienced trust, openness and intimacy of the family might get lost. The community of the family as a family may become eroded by the importance given to business issues. Some partners had already said that they did not want to have anything to do with the family business; they wanted to keep it evident that they married their partner out of love and not for their wealth. Others would like to share their responsibility for their capital investments with their partners, or at least talk with them about the business, weight the decisions and see all the confidentiality boundaries between them removed. The partner would then be better prepared to raise the children especially when something happened to them. But what would happen if the partners separated? Others were afraid to have a partner that might become too interested in the business and the pressures that might bring onto them for a position in the business. Would that generate doubts about the real reasons for their marriage? Even if one made a boundary between the Family Community and the Family Shareholders, what minimal information needed to be shared with the partners to achieve the wished benefits? Or should the sharing of business information be left to the discretion of each person? The explorations continued for a long time, quietly but with visible emotional intensity. The second generation listened with empathy, but their grown-up children had to deal with these very issues. Their generation had not inherited much wealth; it was gradually acquired: facing crisis, working hard, taking risks and trusting others, sometimes without a real choice.

The integration of the fourth generation was felt as a necessity too. The questions were: when and at what age? First one needed an agreed family protocol, then the invitation of the partners and subsequently the inclusion of the fourth generation.

The Family Council took these three issues onto their agenda. The president in turn brought the new or restated list of agenda items for the Business down to three questions to be thought through. First, what do we, as family shareholders in our holding, wish to achieve on the economical, the social and the ecological dimension through capital investments in different (business) ventures? Second, to what extent are we committed to live with the consequences of our choices? For example, accepting reduced return on investment (economical dimension) for realising our social and ecological objectives. Achieving high social and ecological objectives implies that we, as a family, obtain and maintain a majority ownership. Third, who wants to commit – and to what degree – his/her capital to such business ventures: totally, partly (with a safety net) or not at all? These crucial questions had to be discussed in each family nest. Subsequently, the Board would visit them to collect their considered answers. On his side, the president and his board members should organise a meeting at Baritone to discuss with all the family shareholders possible changes in and amendments to the constitution of the holding. By this intervention, he pointed to the *interdependencies* between the distinguished legal and formal bodies.

It had been a day of hard work. Several members and myself had difficulty sleeping that night. The next day, many sought the company of another member to continue the discussion and find support. In hindsight, this meeting at Foresthill had been a confrontation with *multiple transitions*, which were not only taking place in the virtual world, but also in the 'here-and-now' and the foreseeable future.

- In the *first Foresthill meetings*, the major thrust was on recalling the past. It allowed the members to notice differences amongst themselves, to hear about some unresolved conflicts and issues, form an agenda, while largely accentuating what was held in common, either as a family, or within one's nest. After a first, but *careful* confrontation with individual differences in objectives for the business, there was still that joint creation of the Family Council, a promise for the future. In *this* meeting, however, one was repeatedly drawn to recognise that the present was changing: a new business venture was launched and there had even been a physical confrontation in the 'here-and-now' with the different legal or formal entities, their boundaries and the consequences for everyone involved. Furthermore, the issue of extending the family community with partners and the oncoming fourth generation threatened to disrupt – what was called – the cosy, intimate togetherness of the family. The future was clearly not an extension of the past.

- Attempts to escape from the demands of the changing realities into the formulation of a mission statement, either for the Family Community, or for the Family Shareholders, had not succeeded. Instead, they were confronted with: (a) their own list of unresolved issues to be dealt with either by the Business, the Family Council and/or the Community; and (b) the personal work of most members with their partners, and one's personal choice of capital investment. *Knowing and valuing had to be turned in actions:* real decisions with implications for each shareholder and for the family business.

Over a period of two months, the family branches met separately and with the visiting Board members to deliberate their respective capital investment strategies. Two months later, a General Assembly of shareholders was organised at Baritone in which the Board of the family holding made concrete proposals on possible changes in the constitution, based on the collected data, in order to allow investors to make explicit value choices. At the end of that year, in a *special* General Assembly, the new constitution and a new procedure to allow for selling and buying of shares were approved. The governance of the holding had been opened up for shareholders from other branches of the family.

Approximately one year later, we had our last two-day meeting at Foresthill. The Family Council had written a protocol, defined the principles for its election, and organised some educational programmes. In their work, the members had repeatedly been confronted with the necessity to distinguish the family community *with the partners* from the Family Shareholders. Formulating the boundaries between the two was delicate. Indeed, in the past meetings the partners of the second generation had always been invited. It had allowed for some reparation for their exclusion in the past during a critical decision-making process. No one wanted to create another painful situation in the present, nor for the future. Despite these difficulties the Family Council did succeed in making a clear distinction in membership in the proposed family protocol.

The Family Council, the internal project manager and one of the consultants had jointly prepared this last meeting.[8] Special attention was given to maintaining clarity in the role boundaries between the 'project team', comprising the internal manager and the consultant, the 'sponsor' (the Board), and the 'Family Council'. This was done, by spending enough time on 'bridging the gap' or a review of how the project started; what had been done in the meantime, and where did we want to go. Drawings were made to illustrate the successive differentiations that were made within the membership and the transitions (also emotional) from the successive 'founders' and their 'businesses' towards the 'new founder' of the 'new' family business: the Family Holding. Then the Family Council presented their written protocol, defining the membership requirements, purposes, boundaries and functions of the differentiated formal entities and the working and election procedures of the Family Council. After a first hearing, the written text was handed out with the request to turn in all suggestions for modification before the end of the day. That night, the Family Council deliberated the suggestions and modified or corrected the protocol. The final text was approved the next day.

The whole afternoon was reserved for the expression and adjustments of expectations about and individual contributions to the Holding Board and

---

[8] The project had come to rely more on small group discussions and direct interactions, without additional means, the translation into English became a burden. Consequently, David's contributions diminished. By mutual agreement, it was decided that he would no longer attend these meetings.

the Family Shareholders. Before starting this cumbersome process, a brief talk was given by the external consultant to clarify some confusion that had emerged in the meaning of 'reality' and 'justice'.[9] The clarifications were well received and used in further discussions.

Coloured cards were handed out as a 'process structure' for expressing, sharing and comparing their expectations and contributions; a stepwise approach was suggested to facilitate task accomplishment. First, board members and directors were grouped together and asked to write down individually on separate cards: (a) their three major *expectations* about the Family Shareholders; and (b) what do *I* (each director) *want to be for them* (the Family Shareholders). The non-directors formed three small groups. Likewise they were asked to write down individually on cards: (a) their three major, personal *expectations* about the Holding Board, and (b) what each of them wanted *to be for the Board*. Second, each group would internally review, compare and further explore their personal expectations and contributions. Similar cards would then be stapled together, while different personal expectations and contributions were kept separate for further discussion with either the directors or with a small group of shareholders. Three, the directors copied their processed cards and in pairs they went to visit the small groups of non-directors but family shareholders to review, compare and explore expectations and contributions. Whenever a match could be achieved, it was written down on a yellow card, to be displayed in the large room. Cards on which no agreement could be achieved were kept separate to be displayed. Fourth, the whole membership was given an opportunity to review the process and discuss the outcomes.

The ensuing discussion lasted until dinnertime. The Board felt supported and encouraged by the experienced reciprocity in expectations, contributions and values. The shareholders predominantly wanted to be reliable, long-term investors. The directors made it clear that they welcomed business initiatives from the shareholders in return for open and frank communication, and reasonable achievement on all three dimensions: R.O.I., social responsibility and ecology. The shareholders did not expect the president to be responsible for

---

[9] 'Justice or righteousness' could refer to treating everyone equally, or to equitable treatment or even according to the person's needs. They decided to use 'equally' to be appropriate for working either in the Family Community or the Family Shareholders group. 'Equitable' was to be used in the General Assembly and according to personal needs was experienced as proper in the family.

keeping the family together, but they wished to see a greater distinction in the composition of the different boards (e.g. holding, companies within the group).

The next morning, we spent an hour reviewing and processing afterthoughts. One key issue emerged: the difficulty in choosing between internal, conflicting expectations about the Board, when choosing made a difference to themselves and to the management of the business. There was a growing awareness of a tendency amongst some of them to saddle the Board with different, even conflicting expectations, so that the Board had to make the choices, rather than the individual shareholder.

The rest of the day was taken by the Family Council, setting the agenda for the year to come, collecting information about the interests of the partners in the Family Community and its activities, and how to strengthen the interest of the fourth generation in the family business before they reached the age for joining the Family Shareholders group and the extended Family Community. Then, new criteria for the election of the Family Council – giving more weight to the branches – were jointly defined, followed by the election of the second Family Council.

Six months later, the Family Council organised a Family Community meeting, not at Foresthill, but at Greenfield, another location, to which the partners were invited and informed about the long travelled road up to the present day and the prospects of integrating the fourth generation. With that one-day meeting at Greenfield, my work on that project ended. The project itself goes on. A chronological overview of the meetings at Foresthill and Baritone is presented in Figure 12.2, p. 348.

PART 2: MAKING SENSE OF THE WORK

TRANSFORMATIONS

Our work certainly led to various developments and changes. But not all changes are transformations. In *organisational* terms, we speak of transformations when an organisation or a work system not only appears as changed, but also functions and feels different from what it was in the past. Under this heading, we will briefly review some major, manifest transformations as organisational outcomes of the project. Subsequently, we'll explore whether these organisational transformations can also be taken as manifestations of *transformations at another psychic level* and through which underlying mental processes they can be explained.

As manifest *transformations in organisational terms* we note: (1) the disentanglement of the family community in distinctive legal and formal bodies, for example, the Family Council with a mediating and advisory role between the business and the extended family community.[10] (2) The changes in the power structure of the holding, allowing new family members to join the Board. The investment in new ventures, initiated not only by family members but also by outsiders; and its diversification in businesses with varying emphasis on either return on investment, or ecology while remaining leading in social responsibility. (3) The transition from operational management of different companies into the governance of the international corporation. All these manifest transformations went together with profound changes in emotional relations to the founders and the current president, the original business activities and the governance of the businesses.

Transformations as psychological processes occur at the level of 'being', not at the level of 'doing'. Such transformations, however, may and often do lead to a different way of doing. The behavioural change is then an expression of a psychological transformation that took place. Donald Winnicott (1958) contrasts 'being' from 'doing'. 'Being' has to do with the inner world, appeals more to the female part in the human being and allows for some early, basic, mental processes (primary processes) making *transitional changes* possible. 'Doing', on the other hand, is taking action in the outer world. It has been associated more with the male parts in us and is more mind-dominated, or guided by logical thinking (secondary processes). Transformation[11] comes about from the interactions between the inner and outer worlds. It touches the deeper levels of human reality and conditions. Change is more rational and even more superficial, at least in its conception. Transformation takes place in the 'here-and-now', including different steps over a period of time through which a previous state of being develops in a future state of being. For example, an infant moving from a state of complete dependence with

---

[10] A graphic display of the evolving differentiation can be found in Figure 12.1 p. 324.
[11] Note that Winnicott did not use the notion of transformation. Transitional change, however, can be seen as an essential process leading to psychic transformations: being-doing.

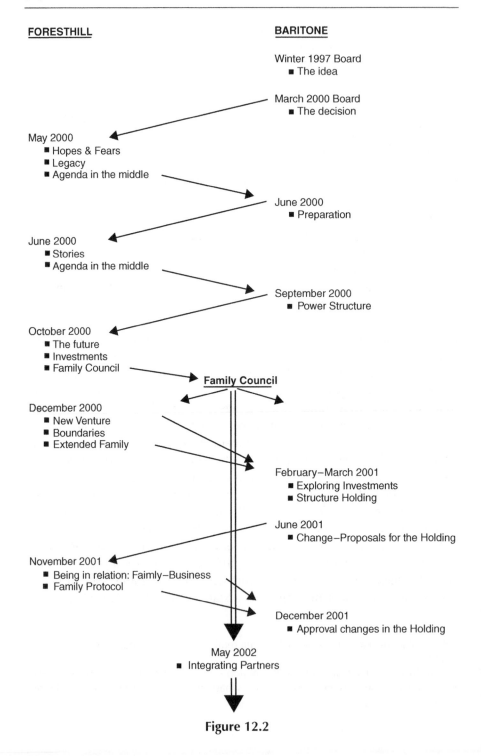

Figure 12.2

illusions of omnipotence (creating its world), to one of experienced dependence (working through the disillusionment of its omnipotence) and later on to interdependence. As such transformations, in the psychological sense, include a component of *psychic development*, not confined to childhood, but as part of psychic development throughout life. A transformation starts – in psychoanalytic theory – from a 'not-knowing gap' emerging from experiences in the 'here-and-now', which is eternally new and evolving. Bion's theory (and speculations) on transformations are described in his basic model of 'thinking' (1962), and further elaborated in thinking and transformation in 'knowledge' (1963) and in thinking and transformations in 'O' (1965).[12] His abstract theoretical thinking, based on his rich experiences as a practicing psychoanalyst, is not easy to understand. Nevertheless, we wish first to briefly summarise the essence of his work and subsequently illustrate it in simple words with some manifestations of transformations in the course of the project.

Influenced by Freud and M. Klein, Bion advances that *thinking* starts from an unconscious and continuous mental processing of sensory data that are transformed in impressions (sensations which are more than sensory perceptions) with a budding psychic nature. These impressions are linked in a spontaneous, associative process, resulting in more complex and abstract elements, and contained in pre-existing patterns or pre-conceptions. This automatic, associative process is not yet thinking. Thinking emerges when these elements are used to represent something that is not present: a thought for a 'no-thing' as Bion puts it. Thoughts are there before thinking. A thinking process needs an environment to help bear the affects and to provide thoughts to contain them (Vermote writing about Bion, 2005, p. 53). Later Bion adds a new dimension to this model of thinking by presenting it as a process of transformation of elements of manifestation of psychic functioning that can be located in his Grid. Transformations are seen as "A spontaneous dialectic movement between a mental state in which the inner and the outer reality are perceived as phenomena without cohesion into a mental state in which some order and relatedness between phenomena emerge" (Vermote, 2005, p. 53). This movement is not a cognitive but an emotional experience in which an emerging image in a person (a patient) becomes the elusive truth for both that person and another person with whom one is interacting in a rather intimate way (a patient and his/her analyst).

---

[12] 'O' refers in Bion's work to 'the elusive truth'.

In plain language, transformation, in Bion's thinking, is a movement from a basic experience (an impression) – that cannot yet be put into words – to an image ('dream-thought') that allows for conceptualisation (a thought) and later on for logical elaboration (thinking). In our project for example, the listener to a story about the legacy hears a family member say, for example, "... We drank tap water, not bottled water!" and some image(s) emerge of what that story is all about. The image may be vague; a kind of what we may call a pre-metaphor, that still lacks a thought through similarity. For example, a 'glimpse' of a reprimanding father, or of someone collecting pennies, but not drinking tap water *is* like collecting pennies. The latter would already be a metaphor. When the listener in turn tries to put that image into words (which entails a loss of the original richness of the story) and talks about it (a new loss, since not everything in the image or 'glimpse' can be put into words that do justice to the intended message), it can create transformations in the storyteller, or another listener who in turn associates, thereby starting a new spiral. At the end it may converge into being careful about spending money, even when one is well off. Transformations are likely to take place when people communicate with 'rich' words and symbols and allow images to emerge in their minds, for example, 'our nest', 'laying one's egg'. Transformations can also be triggered by the use of, for example, simple common objects in a symbolic way like leaves and fruits taken from the woods as symbols to express the handing over of authority to the younger generation. Primary mental processes, characterised by displacement, condensation and symbolisation are expressed in images, unconscious fantasy, myths, pre-conceptions and conceptions at the level of dream-life. Logical or rational associations and interpretations block these primary processes. Important transformations can also occur independently from insight or whatever form of interpretation of unconscious anxieties, through well-chosen activities.

Three examples from the project may clarify as well as illustrate these mental processes. One, the stories about the legacy and their histories allowed the members to express their inner worlds (thoughts, memories, feelings and values), to listen – allowing for images and memories to come to their minds – and to get a better hold on their lives by making new linkages between their inner and outer worlds. The cards facilitated the expression of personal experiences, values and principles, while the process of clustering enabled them to get deeper in touch with and share and compare their inner worlds that they wanted to express in their own words. The time spent as a family community in a big circle and the trust and openness that grew in the interactions between the various persons (holding also different roles in the business) reduced possible unconscious anxieties about destructive tendencies in the family and/or partic-ular members without the need for those anxieties to become conscious. This in turn allowed the Board to better recognise their interdependencies with the family shareholders and propose changes in the power structure of the holding.

When psychic transformations come about – to a large extent – through those primary thinking processes and affective experiences, they don't exclude con-scious, rational thinking. The images put into words, the things one knew at a certain level (the 'un-thought known' as Bollas, 1987 calls it) may become visible in the evolving sub-grouping of the family community allowing for conceptualisation (e.g. mapping the disentanglement; the different capital in-vestment interests) and further elaboration (e.g. diversification of the business with specific purposes).

In the Anglo-Saxon psychoanalytic literature, the original French concept of 'mentalisation' is frequently used to describe a form of transformation, com-plementary to Bion's notion. Of particular interest are the studies by Fonagy and colleagues, which are largely based on attachment research and devel-opmental psychology. Within the mentalisation theory of Fonagy (Fonagy, Gergely et al., 2002) they introduced the concept of *interpretive interpersonal function* referring to a neural system for affect-regulating psychic processing and reflective functioning. It has a dual function: one is affective regulation similar to empathy, while the second is cognitive. This latter function was earlier described by their concept of *reflective functioning* (Fonagy & Target, 1998), which denotes the interpretation of relational experiences, namely the capacity to perceive one's own and other's behaviour in terms of mental states such as feelings, beliefs, wishes, intentions. It implies a more refined way of self-reflection than just interpreting the other's behaviour as 'liking or dislik-ing me'. The other can be seen as a separate, intentional human being with a more or less rich internal world. The capacity for reflective functioning can be developed through reflections on the mental states of a person, compared and differentiated from one's own and from those of other persons with whom one is interacting.

The theories of Bion and Fonagy on transformations are complementary and overlapping in certain aspects. Bion, influenced by M. Klein, stresses the unconscious and pre-conscious side of psychic functioning where feel-ings and thinking are interwoven with unconscious fantasies, pre-concepts, to more conscious thoughts and theories. Fonagy is more of an ego-psychologist, putting the emphasis more on cognitive processing of interpersonal interactions (Vermote, 2005). Looking back at the interactions within the project and the illustrations presented above one can without too much effort identify elements of both.

Exploring all the organisational transformations to identify assumed psychic transformation processes, however, would lead us too far. We have only pointed to some obvious ones. An interested reader can dig further into the project as it has been described rather in detail. The enumeration of some manifest transformations and our explorations into some underlying psychic transformations seem sufficient to conclude that it is possible for organisation consultants to create conditions that enable both kinds of transformations to take place.

WHAT CAN BE LEARNED FROM THE CONSULTING EXPERIENCE AND CONCEPTUAL CLARIFICATIONS FOR ADVANCING THE PRACTICES OF ORGANISATION CONSULTANTS AND MANAGERS?

How can minimal 'supportive process structures' be provided to enable psychic transformations to occur, and how can subsequently the logical elaborations also be directed through minimal 'facilitating structures' to an outcome that is useful and relevant for organising an organisation?

Ideas and insights from the literature on mentalisation and transitional change: Transitional change (Amado & Ambrose, 2002; Amado & Vansina, 2005) and the discussed notions on transformation and mentalisation are interrelated (Vansina-Cobbaert, 2005; Vermote & Vansina-Cobbaert, 1998). Transitional change concepts describe the minimal conditions to enable mental processes like transformation and mentalisation to develop. In the paragraph above, through some illustrations we displayed the relatedness of supportive process structures and transformational processes. Now, we would like to briefly describe some major ideas and insights from the literature that may be useful in the practices of consultants and managers.

1. A primary condition for transitional change is that the outcome is relatively undetermined or open-ended at the start of the process. The same is true for

mental transformations/mentalisation. One starts from a need or a wish that has to be explored and that evokes an emotional involvement of the people concerned. From this experience the process gets on its way. Within the provided, transitional space, experiences become shared and discerned. They may belong to the past, to the 'here-and-now' as well as to vague anticipations of a future. The past (history) can be important, not to be interpreted, but to see *how we got where we are*, to understand possible influences of past experiences, realities, hopes and illusions on the actual situation and our relatedness to and views on possible futures.

2. Transformations and transitional change both require conditions and relationships that make us feel safe, contained. While consultants and/or managers play a central role in providing an environment of safety, one may not diminish the role of other participants in the system who through their affective relations create a heaven of togetherness and mutuality. Furthermore, these persons provide a continuity that external consultants cannot.

3. One can change oneself, but one cannot transform oneself or someone else (groups, organisations, society). One can only create conditions, for example, containment, 'time–space', and make some means available for transformations to happen. These conditions include:

   • Creating ways of enabling the inner worlds to become expressed, and worked on through processes of sharing, comparing and finding out. Personal expressions on cards, in drawings, in three-dimensional figures and subsequently clustering them are useful means to initiate such processes of sharing, comparing, discerning, finding out and working on the interplay between the inner and outer world.

   • Since transformations involve a level of functioning that is not, or at least not fully accessible to rational, secondary process thinking, one should facilitate and legitimise the expression of images, metaphors, stories, pictures and other creative expressions in, for example, collages, in moulding clay. This may appear very difficult in business situations in which facts and figures, rational argumentation and logical thinking has become overriding. Yet, it is worth trying.

   • The provision of realities that can be explored and given meaning from diverse angles: not only intra-personal, but also from the organisational context and its environment. In the project, for example, the subsequent explorations of one's attachment to family shares, one's intentions with them and one's expectations of personal capital investments.

4. As pointed out earlier, transformations can occur independently from interpretations or insights. Indeed, interpretations often create obstacles to the very psychological processes that lead to genuine transformations. Bringing processes to the level of consciousness may interrupt; even stop the constructive work at the non-conscious level. As many transformations are the results of alternating processes of 'worrying through', 'working through' (Amado & Vansina, 2005) and 'acting through' (Vansina-Cobbaert, 1993), we should not restrict these mental processes to conscious, rational processing of data. *Doing* 'meaningful' things in relation to an external object can be extremely important. We have learned that from observing children's play with their transitional objects, for example, a teddy bear or a rabbit. That object does not have to be tangible. It can be an idea, an image, a card or a statement – as long as it comes from the outside – which people play with in their minds, or it can be an innocuous activity (e.g. arranging the meeting room, cooking, cleaning).

5. Transformations ultimately give rise to the acknowledgement of reality, to the acceptance of the unchangeable and to recognition of what can be done about the rest. A critical transition is moving from 'knowing and valuing' to taking action. It implies a mental process of imagining – in the safety of the virtual world – the action, the future before and after taking action and a realistic exploration of its consequences for oneself and for meaningful others, now and in the future. In groups, commitment to action taking on the basis of knowing and valuing is supported by the perceived degree of consensus about its desirability. Important in this process is openness, honesty and integrity of the persons involved, and even more so of the consultant or manager who must be willing to explore openly their influence in and on the work.

Some learning from the work on the project:

1. Even within large groups of 50 to 60 members, it is possible to provide minimal conditions for the members to feel safe. We cannot tell which of the following were most helpful, taken separately or in combination: seating members in a circle, giving them shared control over their 'agenda in the middle', for example, through reviewing, establishing affective relations with consultants who are willing to work from within the client-system.

Clearly, one does not need a rigid time and programme structure, advanced by many Group Relations consultants, to create a containing environment. The affective relations within the system and with the consultants, however, require continuous attention to one's way of being in and working with the 'here-and-now'. Putting the locus of psychic and organisational development with the members of the system largely compensates possible, missed opportunities to understand some deeper unconscious dynamic processes.

2. It appears that working in and with the 'here-and-now' does not seem to require, as an absolute necessity, a conscious understanding of the influence of individual's past experiences on present behaviour. Furthermore, what we witnessed was the importance of moving from emotional experience to images to words, enabling 'thinking about' and constructive work to be accomplished *without an emphasis on the interpretation of defensive processes* against task, and/or group-related tensions. Instead of focussing on interpretation of underlying processes, it was important to invent and provide conditions, for example, supportive process and facilitating structures to enable *psychic developmental processes and task accomplishment.* In this respect, it appeared particularly relevant to initiate 'repeats in explorations' from a slightly different angle – over a certain period of time – to come to terms emotionally and rationally with the evolving perspectives and meaning of legacies, personal histories, critical items on the 'agenda in the middle' and planned actions.

3. As a team of consultants, we also endured the tensions evoked by the unknown and the 'un-thought' in both the client-system and in us. This carrying over of tensions and emotions appears to be an unavoidable consequence of staying in touch with and close to the emotional life of the client-systems: 'working from within'. These tensions became a rich source for understanding of what seemed to be required to enable the client-system to work constructively.

4. Learning from experience is not confined to learning about the evolving dynamics through interpretations and 'feedback'. In fact inner learning may be more enhanced by the provision of conditions (e.g. minimal structures) to enable the client-system to gain access to 'un-thought known'. Indeed, much of the legacy, the histories, the different relations to and expectations about the business and some of the tensions within the family community, were present at a more or less vague, pre-conceptual level. Yet, as such

they were not fully accessible to conceptualisation. At present it looks much more that the transitional space in which (a) spontaneously recalled stories of legacies and personal histories were told and elaborated; (b) the inner worlds of members became shared and compared; (c) the playing with images and futures and (d) the evolving experiences in the 'here-and-now' made room for 'mentalised affectivity', thoughts and thinking, and exploring actions in the virtual world. At these moments in the two-year project the client-system could become fruitfully engaged in conceptualisation. These were also the occasions in which the consultants' understanding and familiarity with organisational and theoretical concepts were needed in building a sound conceptual base for the client-system to take considered action. This latter process of learning could be called 'learning about' in contrast to previously described processes of 'inner learning', or more accurately psychic development. The alternating business meetings at Baritone and the family community meetings at Foresthill facilitated the interplay between these two forms of learning. Some explored actions in the community meetings were subsequently taken in the real world of the business (Baritone) and further worked through in the family community (Foresthill). They enriched one another, thereby strengthening psychic and organisational development.

REFERENCES

Ackoff, R. (1981). *Creating the corporate future.* New York: John Wiley & Sons, Inc.
Amado, G. & Ambrose, T. (Eds) (2002). *The Transitional Approach to Change.* London: Karnac.
Amado, G. & Vansina, L. (Eds) (2005). *The Transitional Approach in Action.* London: Karnac.
Barrett, F. (1998). Creativity and improvisation in jazz and organisations: Implications for organisational learning. *Organisational Science,* **9**, 5, 605–622.
Bass, B.M. (1985). *Leadership and performance beyond expectations.* New York: Free Press.
Bion, W. R. (1962). *Learning from Experience.* London: William Heinemann Medical Books.
Bion, W. (1963). *Elements of psychoanalysis.* London: Karnac.
Bion, W. (1965). *Transformations.* London : Karnac (reprinted 1984).
Bollas, C. (1987). *The shadow of the object: Psychoanalysis of the unthought known.* London: Free Association Books.
Burns, J.M. (1978). *Leadership.* New York: Harper & Row.

Crossan, M. (2003). Altering theories of learning and action: An interview with Chris Argyris. *Academy of Management Executive*, **17**, 2, 40–46.

Fonagy, P. & Target, M. (1998). Mentalization and the changing aims of child. *Psychoanalysis Psychoanalytical Dialogues*, **8**, 87–114.

Fonagy, P., Gergely, G. et al. (2002). *Affect regulation, mentalization, and the development of the self*. New York: Other Press.

Kilman, R.H., Covin, T.J. et al. (Eds) (1988). *Corporate transformation: Revitalizing organisations for a competitive world*. San Francisco: Jossey-Bass.

Vansina, L. (1989). *On tap dancing elephants: Transformational change in management and organisations*. Unpublished paper presented at the international conference on organisation development, Austria.

Vansina-Cobbaert, M.J. (1993). Per-agir. *Revue Belge de Psychanalyse*, **23**, 13–32.

Vansina-Cobbaert, M.J. (2005). A therapeutic community: a space for multiple transitional change. In: G. Amado & L. Vansina (Eds), *The Transitional Approach in Action*. London: Karnac, 41–70.

Vermote, R. & Vansina-Cobbaert, M.J. (1998). A psychoanalytic hospital unit for people with severe personality disorders. In: J. Pestalozzi, S. Frisch, R.D. Hinselwood & D. Houzel (Eds), *Psychoanalytic psychotherapy in institutional settings*. London: Karnac, 75–94.

Vermote, R. (2005). *Touching inner change*. Doctoral Dissertation, Catholic University of Leuven.

Winnicott, D.W. (1958). *Collected papers: From paediatrics to psychoanalysis*. London: Tavistock Publications.

CHAPTER 13

Participative Redesign: Action-Research into the Strategic Restructuring of a Plant

Leopold Vansina

Action-research is a loosely defined method to learn from our actions and to further theory building. Although action-research has been with us for a long time – Lewin (1946) is often cited as being the first to launch this notion – its many forms are still the subject of debate. This looseness may actually serve to stimulate creativity and flexibility in designing approaches for taking action in complex situations, and for exploring outcomes and data for subsequent theory building. So we can continue to invent and learn, while adapting the general methodology to the specificity of the situation and respecting the minimal criteria for generating valid knowledge.

In this project: 'The restructuring of a plant', we have defined action-research as an approach in which the client-system and the consultant engage together in problem solving and generating action to improve the functioning of a specific organisation in a sustainable way. At the same time, the consultants and the organisational members involved take time out to learn from the responses and outcomes as they go along. This definition is not complete but it was good enough to explain to the members of the organisation the particular way of working of a psychodynamic action-researcher. As you may have noticed, the explanation of our approach includes the essence of what Eden and Huxham understand by the notion of action-research:

> ... the term to embody research which, broadly, results from an involvement by the researcher with members of an organisation over a matter which is of genuine concern to them and in which there is an intent by the organisation members to take action based on the intervention (1996, p. 526).

There are, however, some noticeable differences. First, we place emphasis not just on action taken by the members, but that the action taken leads to a sustainable improvement. Second, the consultant's involvement with the organisational members appears to be more intense. There is a difference in role and kind of knowledge but we work together.

The project started from an awareness of the need for change by the general manager and the personnel manager that grew over time into a genuine concern over the viability of the organisation. The consultant proposed an intervention methodology that engages the members and is likely to trigger their interest in learning from the generated actions. The short-term outcomes of the strategic restructuring project were so interesting that two researchers from the University of Amsterdam undertook an extensive follow-up study. They investigated (a) the results of the intervention on several dimensions: financial, internal business process, learning and innovations, and customer satisfaction, and (b) the change process itself. These research findings and the notes of the consultant/author could then be explored for further theory development.

The purpose of this chapter is to present a realised, participative redesign of a small company as evidence that: (a) people are able to face the realities of the business situation they are in, however painful that may be; (b) they are furthermore willing to search for and implement agreed solutions. In other words, the reader will be able to appreciate a more humane way of restructuring an organisation under unfavourable economic conditions.

In the first part, I will describe the project itself: the history and context of the organisation; the intentions and role of the consultant and author; his methodology and the structuring of the change efforts introduced over time. I will develop this part more extensively to encourage the reader to explore different interpretations of what went on and to enable him/her later on to formulate alternative 'theories'. In the second part, I will review the outcomes of the intervention, and the major findings from the follow-up study. Finally, I will explore the learning from the action-research itself for theory building.

PART 1: THE PROJECT

HISTORY AND CONTEXT

The plant, located on the outskirts of a small town in Belgium, belonged to a company founded in 1897 to produce yeast and alcohol. In 1968 the plant was transformed to make other industrial products without major changes to the existing installations. In the mid-eighties, the company was in trouble and it was sold to a much larger Dutch biochemical corporation. New products were introduced but they turned out not to be that successful. The plant was again reorganised in 1989 to reduce costs through a reduction of personnel by early retirement, but nothing changed fundamentally. In 1992, the plant became part of a new division in industrial enzymes, but failed to generate the expected profits. After about two years, headquarters were convinced that new changes were necessary to reduce costs, change the prevailing culture and become more market-oriented. Nevertheless, a large investment was made to manufacture a new product. In October 1993 the corporation appointed a Dutch Human Resource Manager and six months later, a Dutch General Manager from the mother company. Both had participated actively in a 'corporate-culture-change' project before they moved to Belgium. Their assignments could be seen, on the one hand as a sign of headquarters' determination to change the situation, and on the other hand, as an expression of their inability to appoint locals to these positions. In April 1994 headquarters ordered an audit. When the results were presented in July, the General Manager was given the formal assignment of making the company competitive. The General Manager and the HR Manager produced a blueprint for cost cutting. The planned reductions were clearly insufficient: the more the plant produced, the more it lost money. In November they formed a change team, called C2. Their task was to make another blueprint of cost reductions. A financial consulting firm was appointed to help them. One month later, the General Manager moved his existing management team aside in favour of the change team C2. By that time, the OD consultant to the corporation had already introduced two local trainers to the Dutch managers, but they did not click. Now it was my turn to stand the test.

When I met the General Manager and the HR Manager, I was struck with the following impressions, which I discussed with them, and put down in writing. First, the various change efforts over the years had been sporadic and without satisfactory results. The current efforts looked too slow to gain momentum and focussed largely on cutting labour costs. Each functional manager in his domain was doing this. Consequently, the inefficiencies in the interfaces were left undisclosed. Second, there was a strong bias towards introducing organisational change through training: 'changing the management style'. The local company culture was seen as too much dominated by hierarchical concerns (suspected as being typical for a Belgian situation). Third, in order to become competitive they had to reduce their costs by at least 20%. Personnel reductions and outsourcing appeared insufficient to make the company competitive. Furthermore, these actions were not likely to create confidence in the new organisation without a new strategy and a new way of working together. Fourth, management was concerned that their cost-cutting plan would inevitably lead to social unrest instigated by the local militant unions. Fifth, there was an absence of direction for the company as a whole, within the corporation and within their markets. On the basis of all this, I suggested rethinking the organisation and its production processes, with all the key people concerned, in order to create minimal conditions for organisational success. The required 20% reduction in costs was not a strategy. It was to be taken as an indicator for the effectiveness of our efforts in enabling the employees to organise the work to better serve the customers in an optimal way. Training, if needed, was to follow the organisational change.

MY ROLE, APPROACH AND INTENTIONS

Originally, they expected me to take the role of a trainer. I had a good understanding of the local culture. Their expectations changed subsequently into the role of consultant. By linking their concerns about cultural change and social unrest to the urgent need to jointly re-think the organisation in order to realise a long-term strategy, the sponsors came to see the relevance of a participative redesign approach.

My role became defined as: to help the organisation in its efforts to redesign the company, to realise an agreed strategy and to learn from our experiences and activities to improve our performance in working together. I was to bring in, at appropriate times, questions and methods useful to rethinking and re-designing the company, and assist them in the implementation. The sponsors, for example, the General Manager and the HR Manager agreed to hold on to their respective positions until the end of the implementation phase and to have regular reviews of the way we were working together on the project. The existing C2 team became the steering group for the duration of the redesign.

The collaborative approach was to become the cornerstone of the project. The sponsors and I would try to engage as much as possible the people concerned in joint problem solving, in generating design proposals and action alternatives to realise an agreed strategy. Not only would we together try to learn from our experiences, findings, outcomes and responses to our actions, but by engaging people in the redesign of their own organisation we would create an ideal opportunity to study the members' 'theories-in-use' and their ways of coping with the emerging psychodynamic processes. In fact, participative redesign would create an action-learning situation for all of us: managers, employees and consultant(s) alike. The strategic objectives had to be set at the highest level of the company, while the work and organisation had to be designed bottom-up. Consequently, we would start our explorations with the change team C2 of which the sponsors were members. Based on our experience, a project like this had to be completed within 18 months. All major changes should by then be implemented, while fine-tuning and continual improvement would have started. The approach intended to facilitate the development of a capacity within the organisation to continue to learn and change independently from the consultant.

The approach – it can hardly be called a method – was based on Ack-off's thinking about recreating the corporation (1974, 1981); socio-technical systems design (a.o. Trist & Bamford, 1951; Herbst, 1974; Emery, 1982); designing high involvement organisations (a.o. Hanna, 1988; Mohrman, Cohen & Mohrman, 1995); psychoanalytic studies on organizations (a.o. Janis & Mann, 1977; Menzies-Lyth, 1960; Miller, 1993), and action-learning (Revans, 1980). Since I had been working with these ideas for several years and in different settings and having read abundantly about redesign issues, the learning has turned into an approach of my own. An approach that comprises the experiences and notions of many more colleagues, social scientists and engineers than this brief enumeration gives credit to.

It is suggested that action-researchers should commit themselves to the temporary suppression of pre-understanding in order to make space for drawing out new theory (Gummesson, 1991). Personally, I find such a suppression of existing knowledge very difficult when I have a commitment and a 'passion' to help the system improve itself (survive), while learning from the process and the various 'theories-in-use'. In my practice, most new insights seem therefore to come from a confrontation with the facts that 'some knowledge does not work here!' This in turn triggers a reflection on the actions undertaken, the current conditions, theoretical underpinnings or emerging processes. When taking time out to study the dynamic processes, however, I fall back on a stance of 'not knowing'. Later, at the end of the project, in reviewing the practice with peers or in writing about the action-research project, additional, new insights emerged retrospectively that have led to some theorising.

As a psychodynamic consultant, my first commitment is to the client-system, to assist them in creating a system that functions better while developing a capability for self-management and enabling personal development (Vansina, 1989). On top of these primary responsibilities the consultant may have some particular interests in knowledge generation. In this particular project, I had some specific interests that crystallised along the way into the following.

From earlier work, I realised that combining modern design principles with the existing knowledge and experience of the people concerned leads to more responsive organisations, and improved performance. These results were obtained from restructuring projects in different organisations (e.g. General Motors, Monsanto, Unilever, etc.) but always under the condition that the employment and salaries of the employees were guaranteed, although changes in role and career perspective were most likely to take place. In this case, it was clear from the start that such guarantees were impossible. On the contrary major lay-offs seemed inevitable. Yet, participative redesign would be initiated, despite the obvious differences in objectives between employees and managers, as well as within each person. Vroom's theory (Vroom & Yetton, 1973; Vroom & Jago, 1988), dictating that conflicting objectives amongst the members is a counter-indication for participative decision making, would in other words be challenged. We had argued earlier that more humane and equally effective alternatives to the then popular 'Business Process Re-engineering' existed (Vansina & Taillieu, 1996a), but these were largely neglected because they called upon different competencies and values that did not appeal to macho managers or consultants. Now we had a project in which first, an alternative could be tested and second, the benefits of conflicting objectives could be appreciated in the quality of the restructuring.

1. I started from the belief that a collaborative approach to re-thinking and restructuring one's own organisation would provide ideal conditions for developing a capability in the organisation for managing the learning and change processes independently from the consultant. In the process of checking 'where we are as an organisation' with its current management and work practices, against 'where we want to be' (strategy) and 'what we need to do to get there', people become confronted with their various 'theories-in-use', their relevance and validity in changing conditions. These confrontations generate real behaviour. Indeed, the members worked on: (a) real tasks, (b) affecting everyone highly, and (c) exploring and creating a socio-technical system that is capable of performing at a higher level (the future). As such, people became involved in action-learning in which one learns about the task as well as about oneself in relation to the task. We had three questions of interest: first, does involvement in the project enable people to learn about management; second, do they continue these learning and change processes when the consultant has left the organisation. Third, what can we learn from the processes that go on in the workgroups when people study their daily realities of work and engage in free thinking about redesigning their organisation.

2. Participative redesign invites the members (or a large part of them) to design an organisation that is new both to those who traditionally have the power and to those at lower levels, and to (re)formulate the purpose or reason for existence of the company in society. The members are as such participating in all critical dimensions: identifying problems, generating alternative solutions, selecting specific solutions, planning their implementation and evaluating the outcomes. The higher levels of participating, proper to redesigning, would as advocated by Pasmore and Fagans (1992) foster ego-development. Affirming oneself by expressing where one stands, by advancing creative ideas, while encouraging others to do likewise is

in itself self-enhancing. From these arguments, we assumed that the participative redesign incorporated minimal conditions for personal growth: expressing oneself, facing up to and coping with the realities of working life over which one has only partial control. The suggested methodology would confront the people involved with the necessities and consequences of organisational change, thereby creating conditions that provide space for transitional processes.

With these three broad domains of interest and without specifying how to measure possible outcomes, we started the project.

PHASE ONE: EXPLORING THE COMPANY IN ITS ENVIRONMENT

As an introduction to the C2 members' team meeting, I described my role and repeated what objectives we (the sponsors and myself) had with the participative redesign. They listened, but only a few questions for clarification were asked. All of them seemed to be aware that some radical change was needed after so many failed change efforts in the past. So I continued with a brief talk about recent design principles, in contrast with traditional thinking about organisations and the problems of unlearning what one has practised for years. Then I went on to clarify the importance of involvement for gaining confidence in and ownership of the new organisation, and for working through the psychological consequences of organisational change. I ended with a note on how I expected to work with them. After a discussion and some small talk, we sat down to find answers to the following questions.

a. What are we: a business unit or a production plant?

b. If we are a production plant within a business unit, what is its strategy in which we have to fit?

c. Who are our actual and potential customers? What do they expect from us?

d. What are then the most important characteristics of the production plant to be able to contribute to the business strategy? And what are then the required output criteria to satisfy our customers?

I summarised the outcomes of this first meeting in a short report:

a. We are a production plant receiving instructions from four different business units.

b. The most important business unit of the four wants to grow in market share in sector x by:

- A radical improvement of cost-effectiveness;

- An improved innovation performance through co-development of products,

- While maintaining responsiveness to niches.
  Gaining market share meant that one should become a preferential supplier to big international corporations, while keeping the existing small customers.

c. The most important characteristics and/or expectations about the plant to contribute to the business unit's strategy are:

- Integration of a new technology to simplify the production processes;

- Cost competitiveness;

- Reliable quality;

- Speedy and reliable delivery.

These characteristics were subsequently checked against the registered customers' complaints and their highest expectations. Then the C2 team and I searched for a way to organise the production processes in an optimal flow. In this process, the C2 members were encouraged to consult as many employees as they deemed necessary to appreciate the following alternatives:

- Organise the production lines to serve groups of customers with similar requirements ('focussed product lines');

- Utilise the new technology to develop two production lines for the 16 products: a dedicated line (for bulk product) and a multipurpose line (for specialities);

- Utilise the existing technology to produce in-flows with the planning of products in batches.

Each alternative way of streamlining the production processes was discussed in the C2 team and appreciated against the most important characteristics of the plant to contribute to the business unit's strategies, and the minimal, fixed cost reduction of 20%. None of these alternatives in their pure form met the expectations but we learned a lot about the organisation, its quality issues, waste and ways of keeping the plant operating at full capacity, without much consideration for efficiency. After some debate, we opted for the development of two production lines: one dedicated to bulk products and a multipurpose line for specialities. The next step was now to discuss and develop this alternative in detail with a larger segment of the organisation and to set up a working party to make a capital investment proposal for the new technology.

The way of reviewing this phase may give the impression that it was all a rational process and just a planning problem. This is far from the truth. There was a lot of uncertainty and struggle with incomplete, ambiguous information about market developments and production capabilities. The question: 'who are our customers and why do they buy from us?' stirred up wide embarrassment, for example. One just could not answer the question. The idea to build two product lines was a radical departure from the existing situation in which three groups of customers (big multinationals, small customers needing technical assistance, and tolling) were all being served by a two-step functional production process. Discussions of ideas like these heightened tensions, raised hopes and expectations, created disappointment and some curiosity about the other ways of looking at organisations. In the process of developing these alternative strategies for the plant, the members of the C2 team became aware that the functional organisation was not capable of meeting the basic requirements. This conclusion meant that at least two of the nine members would minimally have to give up their current position. In several meetings we had to 'suspend business' to pay attention to what was affecting the members and to recognise the legitimacy of the depressed mood of some of them. But the team as such behaved in a very supportive way towards their colleagues, and remained hopeful of transforming the plant into a viable production system within the community. Whenever experiences like these became visible we took 'time out' to talk about it and comment on the likelihood that they may reappear in some form while redesigning the plant with their co-workers.

PHASE TWO: ENGAGING THE EMPLOYEES TO REDESIGN THE OPERATIONS TO MEET THE NEW PRODUCTION STRATEGY

The work so far had allowed for the development of confidence and trust among the members and the consultants. The new production strategy, although radically different, looked so much more efficient, for example through the reduction of the turnaround times, that we wanted to develop it further with a larger group of employees. About 16 employees (supervisors, engineers, planners, operators and process specialists) amongst whom some local union representatives, were called together for a meeting with the C2 team and myself. The General Manager opened with an explanation of the business situation they were in (exposing the need for change); the purpose of being here, namely to redesign the plant to make it competitive and viable. The C2 team had taken an option, which it wanted to develop further with them, namely to set up a dedicated and a multipurpose line to produce in uninterrupted flows. The discussion became emotional and serious with a seemingly rhetorical question by one of the employees: "Are you asking us to build our own coffin?" Management seemed to be caught and searched for some reassuring statements. At that point, I felt that I had to keep the discussion real. So I replied: "It will be impossible to make the plant competitive without any loss of jobs. Taking part in the design teams is no guarantee of securing your own job. The key issue here is that the plant is not competitive and we invite you to rethink and redesign the organisation to give it a future." The straightforward intervention worked, and we could proceed, discussing the brief and the planning of the two study groups: one on designing the dedicated line and the other on designing the multipurpose line. Everyone was given time to think about it before volunteering for one of the study groups. Almost everyone invited eventually signed up. To facilitate the work, the internal consultant from the corporation and myself each joined one of the groups.

Each study group made a flow analysis. With each transformation process they answered four standard questions: (1) What can go wrong in the transformation? (2) Who can detect or see this deviation first? (3) What can be done to correct it? and (4) What can be done to prevent it from happening again? Then, they appreciated the design in terms of the most important production characteristics and output criteria. One or two members subsequently presented the reports to the C2 team. The team then integrated their ideas into one primary process, checking back and forth, when needed, with the other members of the study groups. Flow or stream thinking had indeed produced remarkable savings in production time and costs, at least on paper.

The work in the study groups and in the C2 team created opportunities for the members to explore ideas on how to produce in a different and competitive way while gaining a deeper understanding of the existing and expected quality issues. At the same time pictures emerged of possible future ways of working and how they differed from the past. For example, they experienced that they could work together across functional and hierarchical differences in the here-and-now of the study groups. But they also became aware that less people were needed to do the work and that the remaining work would demand different skills and attitudes. In other words, the members came to see an emerging reality that was liked and feared at the same time, of which they were part as someone whose role was changed, made uncertain or painfully disappeared from the scene. Pictures that they emotionally did not want to accept but rationally made sense. Splitting the emotional from the rational, to project the rational part onto management, could not be sustained because it was also their idea and made sense to them too. Yet, the concern of keeping one's job or one's employment was there too. Yet, no change at all was not an alternative. In the long run it would lead to more severe consequences.

Once the primary process with two production lines was designed, we took the next step to rethink the technical support functions. The design objective was to integrate those support activities into the primary process that would allow the operators to better control and own the production processes. The production teams would thereby have the necessary resources to become self-regulating and be responsible for their outcomes, minimally specified in terms of quantity, quality, time and costs. For this purpose new study groups were created with on the one hand operators, laboratory and process specialists, and on the other hand, operators, engineering and maintenance people. Three alternative ways of improvement were explored: (1) integration of activities that could be better done by the operators themselves (integrated and increasing polyvalence); (2) employees from these support functions to be assigned to the production teams (they work in a production team to maximise the benefits of their expertise); and (3) employees to be dedicated to work by preference for a particular production team or an installation (to make optimal use of their experiences in a specific domain). In each instance, the respective departmental manager was part of the study group that he chaired. The internal consultant and I participated in most of these meetings. A third study group on logistics was set up likewise by one of my colleagues, an engineer. At the first meeting of each study group, each consultant held a briefing, which resulted in a written document. For example, the Engineering & Maintenance (E&M) study group eventually received the following brief:

1. Assignment: Design work systems that will guarantee that the installations are always in operating condition. The new work systems must lead to: (a) a reduction of total costs; (b) guaranteed reliability of quality and service; and (c) improved flexibility through the reduction of shutdowns and turn-around-time.

2. Work method: Keep thinking about an uninterrupted flow of production processes.

(a) Make an inventory of recurrent maintenance tasks, the most frequent unplanned repair jobs and all preventive maintenance tasks.

(b) Review and assign these tasks/activities to one of the following categories:

  • Integrate into production teams (can be done during operations and/or during standstill);

  • Should be done by E&M in all shifts;

  • Should be done in the day-shift only;

  • Can best be outsourced?

(c) Explore the training needs and time required for the transfer of tasks:

  • Knowledge and skills available;

  • Needing training;

  • Rough organisation of the training.

(d) List all new assignments/tasks for Engineering and Maintenance: like *Preventive* maintenance, continual improvement, maintenance audits and managing the outsourcing.

(e) Briefly describe the new ways of working together.

In the process of discussing how to make the best use of the support functions, a number of current practices came under critical review. To illustrate, the following inefficient practices were identified in the Lab-Process Development team:

- Suppliers and instrumentation were not reliable; consequently more lab tests were made than would normally be required.

- A number of lab studies were made to identify causes for what went wrong. Their findings were seldom used to prevent quality problems.

- Measurements introduced with a specific purpose in a specific project became frequently standard practices.

- The distinction between tests to determine the effectiveness of a new process or tests to steer a production process had largely disappeared, leading to more and more elaborated tests.

Before reporting back to the C2 team, the study groups that I took part in made a first estimation about the qualifications and number of persons needed to make the system work effectively and efficiently. Their findings were then presented, integrated and appreciated against the most important required characteristics of the total plant and our output criteria. While this work was going on, the business unit, our plant inclusive, was sold to an American international corporation.

Before moving on to the next phase, it may be useful to briefly review the principles (and values) that had guided the design efforts so far.

- Design an uninterrupted flow of transformation processes as expressed in two production streams; steps in the process are performed in a logical order avoiding going back and forth; no re-factoring; 'go-go' procedures to enable the process to continue unless there is information to stop. Reduction of downtime, turn-around time and cycle time.

- Employees take decisions at the level where the activities take place and the required information is generated.

- Several activities are combined to form a whole task with a meaningful output that can minimally be specified in terms of quantity, quality, time and costs. These whole tasks call upon a variety of skills and competencies and provide ground for work-identity. The focus of control and performance measurements shifts from activities done to results achieved (e.g. desired output, and/or objectives set). Self-control and learning replaces external controls. Design feedback- and feed forward information systems and instrumentation to support learning and control. Work is performed where it makes most sense, for example, quality checks and lab tests are where possible done on line to speed up corrective steering. Spare time is used to carry out relevant activities that do not distract attention from the process.

- Organisational structures are flattened. Functional departments are transformed into respectively self-regulating teams (at the operational level) and project teams to solve issues that require diverse perspectives and /or functional expertise.

- Managers' role changes from scorekeepers to leaders that provide meaning, inspire and coach. One of their key tasks is to create and provide the proper conditions for their workers to do good work. They see to it that all people understand the objectives, the output specifications and the relevant contextual information. Value change from protecting one's turf and image towards caring for results that come from well-trained and engaged people. Managers were encouraged to organise regular audits to verify of the system was still valid and followed.

- Staff specialists have a responsibility to maintain an updated body of knowledge to be transferred to those who can use it directly to improve the work.

In order to facilitate the joint optimisation between the social and the technical requirements at the group and the individual level, we moved from an emphasis on job description towards specification of the desired output. In the first period of the implementation, more people than required were provided to facilitate adequate training. Finally, some employees were offered some choice of roles and polyvalence. The latter was introduced, gradually.

PHASE THREE: CHANGE IN OWNERSHIP AND IMPLEMENTATION

When we had almost finished with the redesign, we learned about the sale of the plant. It ran like a shock wave through the C2 team and the organisation. No one knew anything about the new owners, their intentions, their management philosophy, nor about the product markets they wanted to be in. Rather than wasting our time in guesswork, the team decided that the best way of securing a meaningful future was to continue the participative redesign work, to be ready to present a 'blueprint' to the new management, at the first opportunity. It was noted, however, that at this point in time we could only prepare scenarios. They could be altered or fine-tuned when the takeover was finalised and we had a clear view on what, how and for whom to manufacture. Some team members were assigned to inform the new owners about our approach and its first outcomes. The new senior management agreed and the work continued.

By the time the American manager in charge of Europe arrived (six weeks later), the renewal plan was completed. Nevertheless, a couple of events affected the organisational change process and content.

First, the American manager was invited to take part in the C2 team. To the great relief of the team, the whole 'blueprint', including the capital investment in the new technology, was accepted. In the ensuing joint work some further changes were introduced. The portfolio of products was to be reduced so that the distinction between a dedicated and a multipurpose line could be lifted. In the future, the two production streams were to produce planned programmes (campaigns or batches) of products. Experience with the new technology in the USA told us that production lines could be operated with two persons less than we had estimated. In the self-regulating teams, each member was to be trained to take four different roles; in one of them he had to be a specialist. The specialists from all the shifts formed a 'ring team' to continually improve the work. Finally, they did not want to have R&D activities in the plant. The integration into the new corporation thereby increased the number of jobs lost from 40% to about 50%. In other words from the current 290 employees only 143 could continue to work in the plant. However, the acceptance of the plan, backed up by a significant capital investment, increased our confidence.

Second, the change of ownership resulted in a leadership gap. The General Manager, who had been on a foreign assignment, was without his consent transferred – to put it mildly – to the new owners. Finding enthusiasm in a 'reduced' role of a plant manager, with the American manager on site, and under conditions experienced as de-motivating, proved to be an impossible task. Consequently, the C2 team became largely self-regulating. Even when the American manager no longer participated in the C2 meetings, he was consulted on critical issues as a direct representative of American headquarters. Ten months after the takeover, the General Manager left the organisation.

Third, as soon as the sale was announced the internal consultant departed from the project. However, he maintained an interest in the developments, as is expressed in his subsequent follow-up study.

From the start, the C2 team had been informed about the three key tasks that compete for the attention of managers during radical organisational change: restructuring the existing organisation (with or without downsizing), running the ongoing business and engaging the members in realising the new strategy (revitalising) (Vansina & Taillieu, 1996b). Once the 'blueprint' was sufficiently clear, we needed to confront the difficult tasks to staff the new organisation, decide on which persons to be made redundant and around what time. First, we discussed some notions of the psychological consequences of radical organisational change for the individual employee. These notions became linked to the experiences in the study groups of losing one's role, even one's job, the experiences of surviving the downsizing and getting into a new role. Then we moved on to talk about the notion of social justice and revitalisation with its implications for the selection of redundancy criteria, compensation packages and re-establishing self-confidence, new, internal and external work relations.

Social justice is commonly distinguished between *procedural and distributive justice*. The former refers to the legitimacy and objectivity of the decision making, the dignity and respect for people expressed in carrying out the redundancy process. The latter, distributive justice, refers to the perceived fairness of the extra-legal compensations and support (e.g. outplacement, training) given to those who lose their employment.

The process of restructuring the plant in open participation with a large number of persons meant that gradually no one came to doubt the necessity for a major turnaround. Consistent with the stated purpose, we departed from the common downsizing practices. Instead of using, the so-called 'objective' criteria like age, last in first out, to select the ones to be made redundant, we specified the competencies and attitudes of the employees needed to make the new production strategy successful. The HR Manager prepared such a list of criteria for the various functions, which was then reviewed and finalised by C2 to be used by each member. Their ratings and rankings were subsequently presented to the C2 team, enlarged with people from the personnel department. Whenever there was doubt about the qualifications of an employee, the whole record was reviewed and a group consensus decision was searched. Each manager was to have an individual discussion about the future possibilities of each of his co-workers as soon as the unions had accepted the whole social plan. In this way, we wanted to take care of the *procedural justice*.

It was the task of the HR Manager to work out a well-considered 'social plan' since he had the key role in the negotiations with the unions. The 'social plan' included compensation and a support plan, offering some choices to the employees. For example, people above 57 years of age could opt for early retirement; some others had choices between jobs, if they qualified for several. The social plan was designed to take care of the *distributive part* of social justice. The negotiations with the unions took their time but ended in an agreement without one single day of strike (January 1996).

Another key element in the successful implementation is the shared confidence of the 'survivors' that through personal efforts they can make the new production strategy work and bring about a desirable future. That confidence grew from the work in the design teams and was later strengthened by the acceptance of the 'blueprint' by the new owners.

Once all the individual talks had been finished, our efforts concentrated on re-establishing new, internal and external, working relations and the clarifications of the new ways of working together. The C2 team was transformed into the management team. Two valued members were put on early retirement. However they stayed on for some time to help with the instalment of the new technology.

Before the summer of the subsequent year, the new technology was installed. The departure of the General Manager had led to some further changes in the management team. The production manager was promoted to General Manager, while new local persons became responsible for Production, Quality and the Laboratory. During the summer, the new organisation was gradually introduced, while the redundant employees started leaving in waves, according to plan. Under American initiative a workshop for the new managers was organised to continue the work on four retained values from their company programme: empowerment, teamwork, open communication and integrity. Before the completion of these workshops, my contribution to the organisation came to an end.

Part 2: Organisational results and research findings

The internal consultant kept an interest in the project, despite his premature withdrawal as a consultant. Together with some colleagues from the

University of Amsterdam, he researched the results and the process of the participative redesign, six months after its implementation (Schuiling et al., 1997). Since no data was available about the starting conditions, they compared the survey results with a Dutch reference group. This group left somewhat to be desired, since it was taken from the banking sector and it had not been restructured recently. It was, however, the only one available, at that time.

RESULTS FROM THE PARTICIPATIVE REDESIGN

From the *financial standpoint*, the organisational change was quite successful. As you will remember we had set a minimum reduction of 20% of the fixed costs, not as a goal, but as an *indicator* for successful rethinking. In reality, the restructuring resulted in an overall, cost improvement of 47%, without any decrease in production volume. It is, however, impossible to sort out the relative impact of the redesign approach, the introduction of a new technology, or the changes in the organisation of the work. The customer satisfaction (measured in terms of complaints), which was already low, remained unchanged (Schuiling & Jansen, 1998).

A questionnaire was designed to measure *employee satisfaction* in relation to their work and management. These results were compared with the Dutch reference group. The employees of the restructured plant scored statistically significant higher on: (a) the importance and meaningfulness of their work; (b) clarity of role, working together and ease of the information flows; and (c) inspiring leadership. There are indications that the employees gained confidence in management and in the organisation, and increased their *self- and collective efficacy* (Bandura, 1997). The restructuring had strengthened their belief in their personal and collective capacity to change things of importance in the organisation. But they also reported increased work pressure. The latter was more outspoken amongst the managers (Schuiling & Jansen, 1998).

No statistical significant correlation was found between *direct participation* in the redesign groups and personal development. The latter, was measured in terms of subjective perception of power, initiating change, risk taking and knowledge of results; not in terms of being more in touch with the daily realities of life and with their relative influence over events that shaped their future.

THE PROCESS OF SUCCESSFUL ORGANISATIONAL CHANGE

Schuiling and Jansen (1998) compared in retrospect the features of the process of the particular redesign approach with the five success criteria of organisational transformations of Pettigrew (1997).

First criterion, *a sustained commitment from top management.* The improvement of the cost-effectiveness of the plant was a major part of the assignment of the General Manager. The corporation, as well as the General and the Human Resource Managers had made various efforts in the past such as reduction of personnel cost and other cost savings (with the assistance of an external consulting firm). It could be said that they were committed to cost savings but that they did not have a firm idea about how to turn the company around.

Second criterion, *linking pressures from the top with operational concerns at lower levels.* The assignment from corporate to make the plant cost-competitive became linked to the concerns to survive and improve the poor relations at work through participation.

Third criterion, the *level or intensity of participation in the rethinking of the organisation.* Once the strategic issues and performance criteria were sufficiently clear, more people from different levels (managerial and operational) and disciplines took part in various study groups.

Fourth criterion, *inclusive change teams.* Those persons who directly took part in the change teams *had been invited.* Some even spent a couple of sleepless nights deliberating their decision before eventually taking part (Schuiling & Jansen, 1998). The broad invitation, however, made the search for resolving the issues more open-ended.

Fifth criterion, *the use of operational indicators* to enable the members to appreciate their ideas and efforts. In this case they took the form of strategic objectives and output requirements, as mentioned earlier.

The researchers concluded that the process criteria of Pettigrew had been 'spontaneously' included in the approach (Schuiling & Jansen, 1998). In addition, more time and energy had been invested in creating conditions to enable the members to work through the psychological implications of radical organisational change.

LEARNING FROM THE ACTION-RESEARCH ITSELF

Conflict of Interests and Participation

Diversity of interests, even conflicting objectives of the people involved is not a counter-indication for participation. Indeed, the outcomes of the total restructuring show an overall reduction of fixed costs with 47%. The relative ease and speed by which the changes have been implemented, the improved work relations and increased self- and collective efficacy all point to a successful radical, organisational change. Yet, diversity of interest and objectives, existed. Some people wanted to just reduce labour costs, while others wished to save their job. Some aimed to produce in the most economical way, while others wished to maximise customer satisfaction. Others saw the economical results as overruling all other considerations, while still others wanted to create a situation in which it was good to work. Consequently, something fundamental must have been left out in Vroom's theory when he concludes that conflicting interests are a counter-indication for participative decision making.

Vroom's thinking seems to start from the assumption that managers' interests equal the interests of the organisation. Managers know what is best, although they may lack operational information. People with assumed conflicting objectives may misuse their information to make managers take decisions that are, at least, not beneficial to the organisation. Therefore, these employees must be prevented from taking decisions. They can only be consulted. In other words, everything is interpreted in reference to the manager's perception of the tasks to achieve the manager's objectives (which are seen as sacrosanct). Vroom's model may well apply to issues which are rather trivial compared to redesigning an organisation to make it viable, or issues which do not so much require a diversity of perspectives to resolve them, nor generate much ambiguity and uncertainty.

In participative redesign the diversity of perspectives and objectives is a requirement. It brings multiple perspectives into the deliberations from which awareness grows that cost reduction as such is not a strategy. Cost reduction is a form of simplified management, working directly on improving the financial results, rather than on the improvement of the *productive processes*. As we all know, it often leads to only temporary success, followed by a steady decline (Cameron, Freeman & Mishra, 1993). In this sense diversity of interests and objectives in organisational redesign enriches the quality of the thinking.

It helps to clarify different possible and real perspectives and enhances our understanding of the multi-dimensionality of organisational life itself. Organisations are not just economic machines but social systems in which technological sophistication, economic success, belonging, learning and transcendental aspirations compete for priority (a.o. Vaill, 1989; Pfeffer, 1998).

From the experience with participative design, overcoming resistance to change takes on a clearer meaning. Resistance to change is seldom directed against change itself, but at the perceived, anticipated, negative consequences of change for oneself and/or significant others, for example, colleagues, family, community. 'Resistance' processes therefore need to be distinguished in (a) attempts to include different dimensions, perspectives and values into the change efforts, thereby enhancing their effectiveness and/or eliminating, alleviating and/or reducing the negative consequences for oneself and meaningful others; (b) attempts to gain psychological control over those negative consequences. The latter can be seen as a 'working through' process of the anticipated, painful and/or fear arousing consequences of a modification of the status quo. 'Overcoming resistance to change' therefore cannot mean preventing or overruling resistance, since these endeavours risk to impoverish the variety of perspectives, and to eliminate the working through process.

This distinction is not just 'playing' with words. It calls for other ways of relating to people who are 'resisting' than providing more information about the relevance of the envisaged change to convince them, trading favours or just listening to their 'objections'. Conditions are to be created to (a) enable people to understand fully the situation so that they themselves may become aware of the need for change; (b) to legitimise the balancing, optimising and integration of various perspectives to achieve a sustainable, high performing social system; and (c) to enable individuals, groups and social categories to work through the anticipated consequences of the envisaged changes for themselves, their work and for their family and social life (e.g. working hours, days and location).

Bringing diversity into the redesign groups by *inviting employees* from different functional, hierarchical, and educational levels proved to be sound. In this way, one obtains a sample of the existing 'organisational community'. Furthermore, inviting people offers them a choice to have a say and to take responsibility for it, or to turn down that opportunity. Although some felt the invitation to be a recognition of their value for the business, it was later not used as a causal explanation for either promotion or being asked to stay. One union representative remarked later on: "Because participation was voluntary, I felt I could bring in my union background. I felt that they were honest in their redesign efforts" (Schuiling, 1997). Inviting people may have had three important effects. First, being invited to help management does strengthen the institutional identification of the employees and their confidence in the design, as is pointed out by Rijsman (1999) on the basis of his experimental work on attitude change. Second, *inviting* people creates freedom of the mind. Since the consultant wished to see more employees becoming involved, he encouraged the study group members to consult others outside the group on critical issues. Unfortunately, there is no systematic data on what went on outside these study groups or in between the scheduled meetings. Thirdly, it may account for the improved 'psychological contract' of the employees with management (Rousseau, 1995), expressed here in more trusting relations and solidarity. This brings me to the next reflections on action-learning.

Participative Redesigns as Action-Learning

In the course of the project it became evident that the employees were learning a lot about their own theories-in-use, new ways of organising the work and of working together. Flow thinking, output specified and self-regulating design principles gradually replaced their traditional, functional, hierarchical and Taylorian way of thinking. The split between 'management is responsible for the economic results' and 'we, rank and file, are responsible for doing the work' had disappeared. Consequently, one can hypothesise that the *experience of* jointly designing one's own organisation from a multi-dimensional perspective fosters psychological ownership. Supportive evidence is found in the interview data (Schuiling, 1997), where several persons, at different levels and in different roles, expressed their concern: "Will *we* be able to generate the demanded productivity standards *fast enough?*"

The experience in the here-and-now setting of the study groups, the C2 team and subsequent informal discussions, of working together with a consultant, across hierarchical, functional and status boundaries, gives a sense of reality to rather abstract principles and individual insights of how work can be done differently. The consultant, however, cannot be seen as working with a uni-dimensional interest or as a simple representative of the sponsor. S/he should (a) contain the tensions proper to a multi-dimensional view on organisational life, and (b) stimulate 'finding out' across boundaries, whether or not these new forms of working will generate the expected results. These experiences can hardly be generated by teaching or training because of the ingrained split between theory and practice; a split whereby the consultant would likely become excluded as not being one of them.

People changed during the course of the project. By redesigning, they created a new organisational reality: a virtual reality that gradually – by checking back and forth – gains the quality of a new social reality. That transformed social reality in turn transforms the members themselves. In other words, by creating and responding to that reality the members themselves become transformed.

The used participative methodology created conditions in which people came to see that the past had become impossible, that drastic changes were necessary and to see an emerging new design as a possible solution. Combined with a supportive group climate it enabled transitional processes to take their course.

If participative redesign is a form of action-learning we should find evidence that learning and change become a self-generated process. Indeed, when the new design was implemented many of the C2 team members took the initiative to set up their own informal training sessions with their new groups of employees. When we reviewed the design principles during the implementation phase we only had to list their citations from their training programme.

Some unexpected learning surfaced that demanded attention. People who directly participated in the redesign not only expected to be recognised for their contributions, but also developed higher expectations about the quality of management. The way of working together during the participative redesign resulted in high expectations about the future.

Managers of a company in trouble may be willing to give more responsibility and attention to their people because they too are in trouble. The overall ambiguity and uncertainty is high. Consequently, managers too look for assistance, which is partly expressed in the hiring of a consultant. Once the transformation has been completed, they may wrongly assume that they can fall back on their 'normal' way of managing. Other managers may have noticed an alternative management practice at work during the redesign, but they are just not capable of putting it into practice right away. It takes time and extra effort. Consequently, they are likely to experience more stress during that learning period.

The structural (and geographical) separation of production units from market-ing and sales within a business unit favours the development of an unfortunate mindset. The production unit comes to be seen as a controllable machine, while Marketing and Sales are seen as constantly struggling with the outside turbu-lence, hence less or not controllable. The consequence of this mental split is twofold. First, the production unit has to absorb all the variance in the market, while being held accountable against the standards of the best benchmark. Second, stream thinking is easily stopped short at the boundary of the produc-tion unit. Both lead to a sub-optimising, and a feeling in the production unit of having to carry the whole burden and the strain. Transfer pricing may further blur the understanding of the relation between efforts and financial results. In-deed, as a function of the country's taxation system, profits are, through trans-fer pricing, being shifted to the most favourable location, blurring the need for change in that location and unduly raising the tensions/stress in the other.

Surprisingly, there was not much information about what the employees learned from the severe reduction of personnel. They did not appear to be surprised. Downsizing had already taken place in their company and in neigh-bouring ones. Yet, it remains a painful break. Despite the proper preparation of a social plan, the timely information about their future, within or outside the company, there is clear evidence that the ceremony or its absence on their last day at the plant leaves a markedly strong imprint on the total experience. The longer people have worked for the company, the higher these expectations are about that last day, by those who left and by those who stayed.

Finally, while one may feel quite confident about the quality of the redesign, of the social plan and the people, the consultant has to be present at the various debriefings during the implementation phase. First, the many adjustments, the way of parting from old friends, the efforts invested in fine-tuning do provide a rich variety of information about what people have learned and continue to learn from the ongoing experiences and from the quality of the redesign. In this case, a more visible presence would also have created stronger continuity in social support, while the management team was in transition.

Do People Grow as Persons in Participative Redesign?

The distinction between 'learning' and 'personal development' may be de-batable. Learning here means that the person becomes at least familiar, on the cognitive level, with new principles of managing and organising work activities. Growing as a person refers then to the fact that the person becomes more capable of experiencing and relating to the changing realities of life, even when that person may not be able to verbalise why s/he behaves differently. Personal development implies an adjustment of the inner self.

In this action-research project I have kept the definition of personal development very open. Neither did we try to isolate the factor participation from its context: working together through an experienced organisational crisis. Those two factors are inseparably linked in this project.

Participation therefore takes on different psychological qualities. Participation as the act of expressing oneself in relation to an important issue, which as such may have a positive impact on *self-affirmation*. Participation or interaction is also an essential condition for *group formation*. The group then becomes a forum in which members, through a process of sharing and comparing, arrive at an appreciation of reality, fairness and of one's influence or control over one's destiny. Under certain conditions of openness, trust and honesty, the group becomes a supportive context in which members can start 'worrying' and 'working through' their anticipated and real, painful experiences. This is what actually happened in the C2 team and the various study groups in which I took part. The group came to serve many more functions than just a place in which members participated in a redesign. Often these potentials of the group to appreciate reality, to sort out fairness, and to grow from the confrontation with one's own influence over and above simple participation, has not been recognised enough. Let us now explore what observed personal changes could be related to these processes.

In the interview data, collected about six months after the completion of the implementation phase, we find *a well-balanced appreciation of the evolving situation*. There is the recognition that the plant is still in transition and a lot of fine-tuning will be needed. There is a justified concern that one may not be able to meet the productivity standards fast enough, and that the shareholders may become unhappy with the plant. They realise that the workload has increased but that this will come down as they learn to cope with multiple tasks, peaks, urgencies, thinking and doing, and the new way of working together which is not translated in procedures, etc. But this wasn't true for all employees. Some attributed the increased workload only to a shortage of personnel. From such a qualitative interpretation we may say that most persons were able to face the realities at work in a mature way.

In an organisational crisis, people become confronted with the limitations of their influence over important events that affect their lives. In this case, the corporate decision to sell the business unit and the competitors' use of more cost-effective production processes were largely out of their control, but not completely. People do have some influence on the course of events. One could have exerted some pressure on management to invest in new technologies, or one could have done more to make the plant perform. Thoughts like these are painful whenever they pop up. They trigger a variety of uncomfortable feelings like guilt, shame and regret. By making senior management wholly responsible for the crisis, by blaming exclusively, external factors, or by creating a dreamlike unrealistic future, or by holding on to reassuring, omnipotent thoughts, one can avoid this confrontation. During the redesign we noticed how people *gradually gave up these escape mechanisms and came to terms with the limited influence they really have. Then they started using whatever that influence was in a constructive way.* Their courage to risk and to invest in creating a transformed plant, over which they had no full control, was first expressed in their decision to carry on with the redesign without knowing the new owner's intentions. The absence of dysfunctional behaviour during the negotiations with the unions and after the announcement, also points to a controlled and realistic appreciation of where their power could be used constructively. That capacity to accept and work constructively with whatever influence one has over complex, evolving events that shape our destiny, characterises a mature person. However, we don't know whether that observed capacity was strong enough to stay alive, outside the study groups. These aspects of personal growth were unfortunately not included in the follow-up study.

At that time of the follow-up study a lot of fine-tuning was still taking place. For some individuals the study may have come too early in their 'working through' process (they were still down), for others the timing may have been right (they saw themselves in an upward curve).

Exploring the data further, it revealed that persons differed markedly in their responses to the whole restructuring experience while these differences did not coincide with *direct participation*. Therefore it appears to reflect a person-related variable. Three categories of persons emerged: (1) The 'indifferent': people who do not feel affected by the changes and events in the organisation. They don't show any signs of modified behaviour. (2) The 'shell-shocked': people who have not yet recovered from the radical change. They long for more support and structure. They remain rather passive and dependent. (3) The 'revivers': the break from the past offers them new oppor-tunities for growth. They are active, self-confident and initiate adjustments to make the new system work. Since the self- and collective efficacy was found to be much higher than in the reference group (Schuiling & Jansen, 1998), one might assume that the 'revivers' constitute the largest group. If so, then we have indications that participative redesigns facilitate the development of a capacity for *self-generation of learning and change processes.*

However much one might like another follow-up study, it most probably will not produce more conclusive evidence since corporate decisions have led to further changes (without participation). Some managers have left the organ-isation and changing economic conditions continue to affect the plant. Con-sequently, it may be difficult to sort out the impact of personal involvement, redesign and group work on personal growth.

CONCLUSIONS

1. Participative redesign works. A follow-up study indicates that significant improvements have been realised on several dimensions: financial, satisfac-tion at work, and increased self-efficacy. Diversity in the redesign groups is not an obstacle. On the contrary it is a necessary condition to (a) provide a positive experience of working across hierarchical, functional and status boundaries in the here-and-now; and (b) to guarantee that the renewal of the organisation is thought through not only on economic, but also on several other dimensions.

2. Vroom's model for participative decision making does not seem to apply to participative redesign of an organisation in crisis. His model is most likely developed on the basis of empirical data generated in a macro con-text of 'dominant logics' that the manager is the sole representative for what is good for the organisation. I believe that the time has come to drop the notion of participation in favour of collaboration. The latter concept seems to provide a much richer perspective to gain an understanding of organisational and community realities, nowadays. Indeed, organisations are becoming more and more changing constellations of different inter-est groups having their own perspectives like subcontractors, co-makers, preferential suppliers, employees of different kinds (core-, employable and peripheral employees), temporary workers, professionals of all sorts, and

key customers. At the same time the pyramid of authority is losing its relevance for thinking in terms of systemic hierarchical levels (Jaques, 1976, 1998). The introduction of project work, self-regulating teams and empowerment is eroding the traditional barriers of authority, while exposing the need of the people involved to be able to think in at least two different *recursive levels*. Consequently, it is conceptually sounder to call this approach collaborative redesign.

3. More prominence should be given to the group in collaborative redesign. Here the psychodynamic consultant has a double role. One, to help establish the *ground rules* for collaborative redesign: broad, voluntary involvement and a collaborative search for new ways of thinking about the organisation of work. Two, to *foster* a climate of openness, honesty and trust that enable transitional processes to occur, while assisting the members in learning from their group processes. Most of the redesign work is indeed done in groups: gaining awareness of the situation, strategy definition, re-thinking, creating, deciding on alternatives, planning, working through, implementation, and evaluation. The group often acquires the characteristics of a transitional space: a space in which the realities of daily working life and free, creative thinking about the future overlap; where there is a time dimension and a purpose to move from one state of existence to another. Where people in the here-and-now feel supported to face the realities and tensions between the known past and an emerging future; where people are encouraged to explore ideas and to think out loud without fear of sanctions. The group fulfils, indeed, different functions: reality testing, working though, creating and transforming. The sharing and comparing of experiences and data that takes place consciously or unconsciously, enables the members to come to a better appreciation of the situation they are in, of the meaning of fairness, of the feasibility of the redesign and their influence or control over events that shape their future. The group is also a place where members can start working through the anticipated consequences of the organisational change, so that they are better prepared to face the hard realities later on. In the group a new organisation is being created (acquiring a social reality) to which the members start responding in new ways. In other words, it is the group that enables the members to transform the organisation by which they become transformed as well. In that process they acquire ownership over the new design and less energy needs to be invested in gaining their commitment.

4. Collaborative redesign is still an approach and probably will remain so. The consultant as a person plays an important role in working with the

group and psychodynamic processes as they emerge. His/her work cannot be reduced to a set of things to do in a chronological way. What can be done is to identify and objectify some of the essential conditions that make the approach effective. For example, it appears that the emphasis is wrongly placed on participation as such, at the expense of the group in which most of the redesign work takes place. But by working on and with the dynamics of redesign the consultant becomes engaged as a person with his/her values and beliefs. Divorced from these human elements, like respect for the personal relation to one's work and without regard for the group processes, participation becomes a managerial tool to extract needed information and/or to overcome resistance to change.

5. Collaborative redesign is a form of action-learning. The direct confrontation with outcomes, other ways of thinking and behaving, leads to a questioning of one's 'theories-in-use'. This in turn opens space to explore the relevance of new designs and management principles, more adapted to the changing conditions of organisational life. Most managers learned from the initiation and 'management' of organisational change and integrated these experiences in their daily practice. They established better working relations, perceived as more trusting and inspiring. Unfortunately, as the organisation develops, new management will come in that has not been part of this transformation. It needs to be seen to what extent their theories, espoused in standard workshops, are congruent with their 'theories-in-use', and how long the learning in those who transformed the plant will stand in changing weather conditions.

REFERENCES

Ackoff, R.L. (1974). *Redesigning the future: A systems approach to societal problems.* New York: John Wiley & Sons, Inc.

Ackoff, R.L. (1981). *Creating the corporate future.* New York: John Wiley & Sons, Inc.

Bandura, A. (1997*). Self-efficacy: The exercise of control.* New York: Freeman & Co.

Cameron, K.S., Freeman, S.J. & Mishra, A.K. (1993). Downsizing and redesigning organisations. In: G.P. Huber & W.H. Glick (Eds), *Organizational change and redesign.* Oxford: Oxford University Press, 19–63.

Eden, C. & Huxham, C. (1996). Action research for the study of organizations. In: S.R. Clegg, C. Hardy & W.R. North (Eds), *Handbook of organization studies.* London: Sage, 526–542.

Emery, F. (1982). Socio-technical foundations for a new social order. *Human Relations*, **35**, 1095–1982.

Gummesson, E. (1991). *Qualitative methods in management research*. London: Sage.

Hanna, D.P. (1988). *Designing organizations for high performance*. Reading, Mass.: Addison-Wesley.

Herbst, P.G. (1974). *Socio-technical design: Strategies in multidisciplinary research*. London: Tavistock Publications.

Janis, I.L. & Mann, L. (1977). *Decision making: A psychological analysis of conflict, choice, and commitment*. New York: Free Press.

Jaques, E. (1976). *A general theory of bureaucracy*. London: Heinemann.

Jaques, E. (1998). *Requisite organizations*. Arlington, VA.: Cason & Hall.

Lewin, K. (1946). Action research and minority problems. *Journal of Social Issues*, **2**, 34–46.

Menzies-Lyth, I. (1960). The functioning of social systems as a defense against anxiety. *Human Relations*, **13**, 95–121.

Miller, E. (1993). *From dependency to autonomy: Studies in organization and change*. London: Free Association Books.

Mohrman, S.A., Cohen, S.G. & Mohrman, A.M. (1995). *Designing team-based organizations: New forms for knowledge work*. San Francisco: Jossey-Bass.

Pasmore, W.A. & Fagans, M.R. (1992). Participation, individual development and organization change: A review and synthesis. *Journal of Management*, **18**, 375–397.

Pettigrew, A.M. (1997). Slagen en falen bij transformatie van ondernemingen. *Nijenrode Management Review*, March–April.

Pfeffer, J. (1998). *The human equation: Building profits by putting people first*. Boston: Harvard Business School Press.

Revans, R. (1980). *Action learning*. London: Blond & Briggs.

Rijsman, J.B. (1999). Role playing and attitude change: How helping your boss can change the meaning of work. *European Journal for Work and Organizational Psychology*.

Rousseau, D.M. (1995). *Psychological contracts in organizations*. London: Sage.

Schuiling, G.J. et al. (1997). Assessment van de organisatie ontwikkeling. *Internal Report*.

Schuiling, G.J. (2001). *Persoonlijike ontwikkeling door organisatie ontwikkeling*. Deventer: Kluwer.

Vaill, P.B. (1989). *Managing as a performing art: New ideas for a world in chaotic change*. San Francisco: Jossey-Bass.

Vansina, L. (1989). On consulting practice: Toward the development of better balanced educational programmes. *Consultation*, **2**, 79–99.

Vansina, & Taillieu, T. (1996a). Business process reengineering or socio-technical system design in new clothes? In: R.W. Woodman & W.A. Pasmore (Eds), *Research in organizational change and development*, **9**, 81–100.

Vansina, L. & Taillieu, T. (1996b). Revitalisering: Een essentieel proces bij strategische herpositionering. In: R. Bouwen, et al. (Eds), *Organiseren en veranderen.* Leuven: Garant.

Vroom, V.H. & Yetton, P.W. (1973). *Leadership and decision-making.* Pittsburgh: University of Pittsburgh Press.

Vroom, V.H. & Jago, A.G. (1988). *The new leadership: Managing participation in organizations.* New York: Prentice Hall.

CHAPTER 14

Working Across Organisational Boundaries: Understanding and Working with Intergroup Dynamics

Sandra G.L. Schruijer and Leopold Vansina

INTRODUCTION

'Diversity', 'collaboration' and 'partnership' are popular discourse in the 21st century. Being able to work across organisational boundaries has become increasingly important in a world where organisations and institutions are more intertwined and interdependent than ever before as reflected, for example, in the existence of joint ventures and organisational networks. They need one another to meet their own goals as well as to be able to tackle societal issues. Simultaneously, organisations and institutions themselves consist in many instances of large conglomerates, where working across the boundaries of business units, subsidiaries, departments, hierarchical levels and disciplines, has become a key challenge. Indeed, senior managers see collaboration between organisations as inevitable, desirable and feasible (Schruijer, 2006a).

However, professing the need to collaborate does not guarantee the ability to collaborate successfully, as can be inferred from anecdotal evidence and recent studies. Involved parties speak of the difficulties of developing and sustaining trust, and of the need to counteract power games and negative stereotyping. Obstacles that are most strongly experienced as hindering successful collaboration are distrust between parties, an absence of open communication, power games, poor leadership, conflicting personalities, egos of the representatives and lack of a shared vision (Schruijer, 2006a). Since the difficulties mostly pertain to social and psychological factors, a psychodynamic approach seems called for. The latter may help in understanding the dynamics yet also in assisting the parties to cope with their various interests, identities, perspectives, power positions in other words, their diversity. Social psychologists study the determinants and dynamics of conflict between groups and organisations extensively, using surveys and doing experiments. More than simply an absence of conflict is needed, however, to achieve successful collaboration. Moreover, in order to understand the complexities of collaboration that involves multiple parties, one has to engage with the parties themselves, very much in line with the thinking of Kurt Lewin who spoke the famous words, "if one wants to understand something, try to change it". An action-research approach seems called for.

Below, the social and psychological difficulties of interorganisational interactions are outlined first. The dynamics described are based on a simulation specially developed to gain insight into underlying tensions and processes. Then four projects of the first author are briefly described so as to be able to provide examples of how consultants and action-researchers can assist organisations to work with diversity. The chapter ends with describing some generic dynamics that need to be faced when working across organisational boundaries and some practices and principles to deal with these within a psychodynamic approach.

PART 1: THE PSYCHOLOGICAL DIFFICULTIES OF WORKING ACROSS ORGANISATIONAL BOUNDARIES

THE MEANING OF COLLABORATION

The term multiparty collaboration was introduced by Gray (1989) to describe the process through which multiple groups or organisations meet and explore whether it is beneficial to work together so as to realise own objectives as well as joint objectives. More formally, multiparty collaboration can be defined as "... the characteristic of an emerging or developing work system of people who, because of their membership in other groups, institutions or social categories, come to work together on a largely self-constructed task or problem domain" (Vansina, Taillieu & Schruijer, 1998, p. 162).

Three elements of this definition are worth noting. First of all, parties come together because they are different. A party becomes interested in working with others since these others may have access to different resources, may adopt different perspectives and have different skills or competences that the former party may need. Rather than developing such resources or competences oneself, collaborating seems desirable, based on the principle of interdependence. In successful collaboration the diversity in interests, identities, perspectives, resources, etc., that different parties bring to the table is explored and capitalised on.

Second, collaboration usually starts when no shared problem definition exists yet. At the very beginning, parties may have some notion that collaboration might be fruitful to address a problem, a concern or an opportunity. Individual problem definitions are likely to exist but these are not likely to be shared by the different parties at the start. The danger is to assume that other parties, who may use similar language in explaining why they were motivated to come to the table, share one's own problem definition. This is unlikely to be the case. Likewise, no joint aim has been formulated and accepted at such. Problem definitions and aims need to be developed together. Working towards a shared problem definition and shared goal is part and parcel of the collaboration process.

Thirdly, collaboration is an emergent process. At the start the work system is under-organised as there are no ground rules yet, no agreements, no working practices, no trust, no shared problem definitions. These need to be developed by the participating parties themselves. As a consequence, the work system becomes organised (Gray, 1989). While collaborating, parties retaining their (legal or structural) independence or autonomy (Vansina et al., 1998). It implies that members become conscious of these differences and subsequently come to accept that they need to construct jointly a good enough problem definition and desirable outcomes rather than trying to impose one's own wishes on the others. Ideally differences in resources, competences, etc. are constructively dealt with, as a function of the jointly defined goals, so as to be able to develop strategies that will solve the joint problem or opportunity (Gray, 1989). The involved parties share a responsibility for dealing with the defined issues and for the collaboration process. An eventual agreement is not the end of the collaboration process – the agreement has to be implemented and overseen by the parties themselves or by their jointly designed monitoring system.

THE YACHT CLUB

In order to study the dynamics of interorganisational relationships more closely, we developed a simulation, entitled 'The Yacht Club' (Vansina, Taillieu & Schruijer, 1999). The simulation helps people to gain insight into the complexity of conflict and collaboration between multiple organisations (Vansina & Taillieu, 1997; Vansina, Taillieu & Schruijer, 1998; Schruijer, 2002). Besides an instrument for experiential learning about interorganisational collaboration, 'The Yacht Club' generates important insights on how individuals, groups and organisations deal with one another in a situation that is characterised by many problems, interests and interdependencies.

The simulation is based on a real issue that emerged in and around the island of Kotlin, Russia, in the Gulf of Finland as a consequence of the political developments involving the dismantling of the Soviet Union. Unemployment loomed large after the Russian marine stopped maintaining and expanding their fleet. Orders to the shipyards located on the island waned. Seven organisations take part in the simulation. They can attempt to deal with the problems by ignoring each other, competing, forming alliances or otherwise. Besides the shipyards there are three yacht clubs, domestic and foreign, a bank, a group of young rich entrepreneurs and the local authorities of the island. Parties can meet freely as long as no more than three parties (or their representatives) gather simultaneously. During approximately half of the available time for the simulation, collective meetings may be held. During such meetings organisations send a representative to the discussion table, while constituencies take their place behind him or her. Constituencies can contact their representatives through written messages.

The simulation lasts for some 13 hours. We, members of staff, do not intervene in the dynamics. After the simulation is finished we spend a full day reflecting on the dynamics, together with the participants. We try to understand why the events happened as they happened, explore what could have been done differently under what conditions, and try to prepare the participants for future 'real' collaboration. We do so first by allowing each party to reflect on their own learning and then engage in a plenary review for the rest of the day. In the case of in-company workshops we allow time for the participants to reflect on the way the characteristics of the company proper may have influenced the dynamics in the simulation and how the learning from the simulation can be applied to the back-home situation.

The dynamics vary each run, as the people are different, as early events may have an impact on later events, and as the dynamics of in-company sessions are different from those of open programmes. However, there are general behavioural patterns and phenomena that we observe most of the time. This is not surprising as the dilemmas and issues concerned remain similar: How to relate to other parties? How to develop trust? How do we arrive at a joint problem definition? How will leadership be exerted? Will we all have a part to play? Will I be listened to? How can we achieve our aims when it is not clear what the others want, when we do not even know them? Such questions are especially difficult to answer as the problem situation is characterised by ambiguity, unknown facts, fields of tensions and, not least of all, relationships that still need to be built.

Generally, very quickly a win–lose climate emerges, in which information is withheld, other parties are met with suspicion, negative stereotypes are maintained, and positional (or competitive) bargaining is enacted. From the moment participants and their parties start preparing in their separate rooms and before any interaction occurs, they assume a zero-sum situation in which one's gain is the other's loss, without checking this assumption. Rather than testing assumptions and attempting to slowly develop trust, the distrust continues or even gets worse. Parties flag their presumed power position and play hard to get. Often the fear of being dependent upon other parties is as strong as the fear of becoming excluded. They quickly search for that aspect in their identity that may be of use to others and present it as their strength. Other parties react with presenting their strengths and alleged unique capabilities. It seems to be hard to explore underlying interests and interdependencies. Time is rarely spent on developing a joint problem definition. As a consequence the simulation often ends in a power game – who is the strongest and most independent?

Meanwhile, with all this posturing, the real problems, as depicted in the scenarios, are not dealt with. In the beginning parties sometimes show glimpses of a vision and derive goals from these – towards the end of the simulation the goals seem forgotten and the whole purpose becomes striking a deal, even when this means departing from the realities. Feasibility and reality checks get avoided in favour of closing a deal, as if one prefers to maintain an illusion of success rather than developing reality-based work relationships. Note that the simulation does not require them to reach a solution! We make clear that it totally depends on them how to spend the time together (real time that is, a minute being a minute, unlike many business games). It is striking that parties opt for bilateral agreements, not using the possibilities of the collective meetings to explore all interdependencies first. Rather than making an informed choice, it seems as if a fear of exclusion makes parties form coalitions swiftly. Although 50% of the time during which the simulation is played is available for joint meetings with all the representatives, this time is almost never used in full. As if the discussions during collective meetings do not have anything worthwhile in store. Indeed deals are struck away from the table, despite initial calls to keep everyone informed and 'collaborate' (the rhetoric of collaboration being conspicuously present during the simulation).

A final observation that we like to share here concerns leadership. It is the public authorities that almost always assume a leadership role, in their words 'to facilitate collaboration' and 'to help parties arrive at a joint goal'. Although they present themselves as a neutral party, they often act as the central manager or even judge. Due to their dominating and partial style they lose credibility over time. They may choose such a style so as to safeguard their power position, or to portray an image of a public authority in a situation of ambiguity, lack of information but full of tension. They may do so out of lack of experience or insight what successful collaborative leaders do, but they also become victims of a 'seduction cycle': at the beginning of the simulation parties, confronted with the complexities and ambiguities that are inherent to multiparty problems, expect the public authorities to take a leading role and provide the contours of some sort of master plan that spells out which activities are allowed and prohibited on the island.

The simulation shows us how difficult the development of collaborative interorganisational relationships can be. 'The Yacht Club' is on the one hand a simplification of more complex real-life processes while simultaneously it is sufficiently complex and lasts long enough to experience the emerging dynamic processes. Survey research and in-depth interviews confirm much of the findings derived from running the simulation (e.g. Huxham & Vangen, 2005; Schruijer, 2006a). The question we wish to discuss now is of course, what can be done to either prevent or work with these all too frequent dynamics so that constructive collaboration becomes possible.

PART 2: HELPING GROUPS AND ORGANISATIONS IN DEVELOPING SUCCESSFUL COLLABORATION

Social psychology has traditionally dealt with understanding the nature of inter-group conflict and has suggested various ways to reduce conflict, for example, through developing a common identity, through establishing contact under specific conditions and through introducing superordinate goals (see Schruijer, 2008a). The snag is, however, that absence of conflict, of distrust or of negative stereotyping do not make people trust each other or help them to proactively collaborate! Developing trust is an active process and so is collaboration. Both must be achieved and maintained. It is not surprising that no trust exists the first time parties come together. Unlike institutional trust, interpersonal trust, that is, trust that is put in other persons rather than institutions, needs nurturing and time. Further, the psychological dynamics prevent parties from starting to develop a common goal – the introduction of a superordinate goal cannot therefore be automatically and instantly successful. Moreover, joint goals are not a given and need to be developed by the autonomous parties themselves, in view of a commonly defined problem or opportunity. Nevertheless, senior managers are convinced that trust, clear goals, a shared problem definition and good relationships need to be present at the very start for successful collaboration to emerge (Schruijer, 2006a). It is as if people, in the words of Harold Bridger, want to be there without making the effort! A crucial need then is to gain insight into how to develop a common problem definition and a shared goal. And for consultants, what supportive process and facilitating structures can we create to enable collaboration?

Below some basic practices, conditions and principles are presented to assist groups and organisations in working with diversity. First several projects are sketched out in which the first author has been a consultant or action-researcher. These projects form the knowledge and experience base, for formulating concrete, minimal conditions and principles supported by the insights from a psychodynamic perspective, Organisational Development literature, and the social psychology of inter-group relations.

SHELLFISHERIES: CONFLICTS OF INTEREST BETWEEN NATURE AND ECONOMY

The first project addressed a complex policy issue in the Netherlands, namely the future existence of mechanical cockle fisheries. Balancing nature and fishing has been on the Dutch political agenda for many years. The long-standing controversy between the interests of the fishing industry on the one hand and concerns of nature conservation organisations on the other recently heated up again. During that episode a two-day workshop was organised in which all stakeholders were invited to take part. This workshop was intended to bring the stakeholders together (knowledge institutions, government organisations, industry and nature conservation organisations) in a depoliticised climate and to stimulate creativity so as to find new ideas for shellfish fisheries within ecological boundaries. A colleague, a sociologist, and Sandra herself observed the dynamics of this workshop (Neven & Schruijer, 2005) and fed these back to the facilitators, who organised a subsequent workshop afterwards, taking our observations into account.

COLLABORATION IN THE BUILDING SECTOR

In a second project the possibilities of working across organisational boundaries in the building industry were explored. The project was initiated to find an alternative way of realising large building projects, called 'conceptual building' (Huijbregts, 2006), in which from the very beginning collaboration between organisations in the building sector around a particular building project is organised. It is intended as an alternative on the one hand to the traditional, totally custom-made approach, in which the different building organisations execute their specific contribution to the building in sequence, leading to many delays and costs, and mass production on the other, where individual choices by the client are ruled out. Representatives of approximately 20 organisations took part in the project, supported by a process co-ordinator and led by an expert on innovation and collaboration in the building industry. Three heterogeneously composed workgroups were formed, each around a common theme. They had their separate meetings and they met as subgroups together. Sandra was a consultant for several of their collective and workgroup meetings, provided insights on collaboration, and conducted a small evaluation study.

ORGANISATIONAL CHANGE OF A NURSING HOME

This third project concerned an organisational change process in and of a nursing home that was part of a larger health care organisation with various homes throughout the country (Schruijer, 2006b). A governmental inspection body had negatively evaluated the home where Sandra was called in as consultant. The diagnostic interviews revealed that interdepartmental hostilities and distrust between hierarchical levels existed, related to a competition for scarce resources. Further, a culture of non-confrontation and a well-developed grapevine flourished. These problems needed to be situated within the problems of the larger organisation and the health care sector in general. After an extensive round of interviewing the consultant designed and facilitated four conferences in which representatives of all stakeholder groups of the nursing home participated (with 50% of the total number of employees present). During these conferences the present was analysed, based on the interview data, relationships across departments and hierarchies were built through working on a variety of tasks and reviewing the dynamics, problems were jointly defined, goals were set and action plans developed. Projects were defined and executed between conferences and reported upon during following conferences.

MEDICAL CALL CENTRE

The fourth project, a medical call centre with 80 employees suffered from internal difficulties such as dissatisfaction, labour conflicts, poor relations between hierarchical levels, between departments, and between staff and line. The call centre had just been through a turbulent period with lots of changes in top management and key personnel. Sandra, the consultant was called in to study the problems in depth and work the findings through with the total organisation. The consultant distributed a questionnaire, conducted 25 interviews criss-cross through the organisation, and observed half a day in the call centre. The findings of the questionnaire and the interviews displayed shattered trust in top-management, partly as a result of many personnel changes. Incidents from the past were still in people's minds although they had never been formally discussed. Combined with the turnover of key personnel and the stress of the job, it had become difficult to establish and maintain good working relations, especially between the interdependent departments. To this end Sandra subsequently organised four sessions to which all employees were invited so as to be able to voice the concerns, openly discuss them, and work through the difficulties.

The four projects differed in multiple ways. Some were explicitly focused on organising collaboration or solving conflict (shellfisheries, building industry), while others were initiated to organise change (nursing home, call centre). Some involved relationships between legally independent organisations while the two projects in the care sector concerned relationships between departments and hierarchical levels within organisations. Yet diversity was an important element in all and needed to be worked with in order to design and implement change and collaboration. Below we will use examples from these projects to illustrate the dynamics, the minimal conditions, practices and principles, relevant for establishing fruitful intergroup and interorganisational relationships.

PART 3: DYNAMICS, PRACTICES AND PRINCIPLES

WORKING WITH THE WHOLE SYSTEM

Involving all stakeholders: In all projects an underlying principle was to work with the whole system, with the diversity and the interdependencies. It implied working with all potentially relevant stakeholders, namely those parties who are likely to have a stake in the envisaged collaboration process and outcomes: those who can influence it and who are influenced by it (cf. Cummings & Worley, 1997). It is very important to bring the relevant parties together and to proactively legitimise the presence of all parties, including those that are small or relatively powerless. When deciding whom to invite for the very first meeting, it is more advisable to invite too broad rather than too narrow. Those who are wrongly omitted will feel excluded; those who were wrongly invited will withdraw as they cannot see how the joint work will further their goals. Neglected or uninvited yet relevant parties may block the process of change. In the shellfisheries workshop one relatively extreme nature conservation party was not invited. As a consequence all nature conservation parties decided not to participate. It needed a second workshop to involve at least some of them (Neven & Schruijer, 2005). In the nursing home project a lot of effort was spent making sure all stakeholders were included. Still a mistake was made: when it was decided to experiment with cooking and eating in small units rather than deploying the food centrally prepared, it appeared that the technical-maintenance staff, asked to build a kitchen, was not included in the change project. It was an unintended omission and sincere apologies were made. Subsequent attempts to involve them were successful – in this case the mistake could fortunately be repaired (Schruijer, 2006b).

Working in the here-and-now through large group meetings: In all projects it was deemed important to have all stakeholders meet face-to-face while addressing real issues (a.o. Weisbord, 2004). It implies designing and organising large group meetings (Bunker & Alban, 1997). During such meetings, tasks are defined with the stakeholders and discussed or worked through in homogeneous or heterogeneous subgroups and in plenum. Heterogeneous groups are preferred when the differences are largely known but need to be worked through within smaller groups. Subsequently, they report back in plenum offering opportunities to compare and discuss observed differences in outcomes and processes to achieve them. Homogeneous groups are mostly used when the existing differences are largely unknown, but assumed. They have the benefits of exposing in plenary their respective identities and group views, thereby providing a platform for interaction and understanding underlying dynamic processes.

An important principle in designing large group meetings is compatibility by which is meant that the design and processes during the intervention should be compatible with the kind of organisation or system (e.g. climate, structure, voice) that one wants to realise (cf. Cherns, 1987). Furthermore a design principle concerns an allowance for maximum exchange of information, knowledge, opinions and feelings within and between groups or organisations, creating the possibilities of experiencing interdependence between parties and seeing the whole system, and establishing a situation in which the responsibility for process and outcomes can be shared. Systemic thinking is encouraged through exploring the interdependencies. Important to address is the transfer of the organisation-as-manifested-in-the-interaction (which is intended to consist of a representative slice of the organisation) to the standing organisation and also to discuss that interface. This includes the confrontation of one's self-constructed pictures of the whole system (the 'organisation-in-mind') with one's observations of the system in action before one's eyes (the 'organisation-in-action') (Vansina, 2000).

In each of the nursing home conferences 125 people participated, representing the various hierarchical levels, the staff departments and the clients. Key managerial and care staff took part in all conferences while the remainder of the personnel rotated. This way everyone could at least participate once. The first conference started with scepticism among the employees. In order to be able to start developing relationships between hierarchical levels and functions, openness was enacted through providing the interview data uncensored to everyone beforehand. Also, ground rules were put forward, for example,

having respectful and open interactions, intended to provide a minimal structure for participants to cling to. Although psychological equality among all
participants was emphasised, real differences in roles and tasks were not denied. Participants were asked to work on the tasks and activities from their
role perspective. For example, if ideas were developed the implementation
of which was beyond a realistic budget, the sponsor, who was also present,
would state that such ideas were unfeasible from a financial perspective.

The conferences, despite the initial scepticism, proved to be energising to the
participants present. The tasks and activities scheduled for the four conferences (working through the meaning of the interview data, coming to a shared
problem definition, defining a joint vision, working on a plan to move from
the present to the desired future, reporting on the activities and experiments
that were carried out in between the conferences) were enthusiastically em-
braced and were continued even though Sandra's involvement had ended (see
Schruijer, 2006b). A major concern while conducting the four conferences
was how to involve those who were not present. Partly this was alleviated by
the rotation system. Participants were moreover invited to be ambassadors and
inform those absent. In practice this was not easy as the work pressure was
very high and not much spare time existed. Newsletters were attempted but in
hindsight not proactively enough. A major lesson learned was the need to continuously and consistently bridge the gap between those present and those not.

Note that large group meetings are not a trick or panacea (bringing parties
together is a necessary yet insufficient condition for developing collaboration)
– it can backfire if it is used as a kind of illusory participation tool that does
not deal with the underlying dynamic processes but only goes through the
motions at the surface level. A large group intervention may thereby turn into
an excellent platform for boycotting the envisaged change process (Schruijer,
2001).

*Working with the complexity at the interorganisational and interpersonal lev-
els*: Collaboration between parties means relating to the different representatives and developing interpersonal trust, while simultaneously representing
one's own party and its interests. Although collaboration may be the intent, its experiences, anticipated or not, consciously or unconsciously may
feel like a threat to one's own identity or a breach in one's loyalty to one's
group. Both experiences are anxiety-provoking. Multiparty collaboration involves developing an interpersonal relationship and an intergroup relationship
(Stephenson, 1984). If the emphasis is too strongly placed on the interorgan-

isational relationships and representing the interests of one's party, it may become more difficult to develop interpersonal relationships. If on the other hand good interpersonal relationships are built at the expense of representing one's constituency, success is not likely either.

Reducing complexity can also be done through simplifying the problems or the solution, ignoring stakeholders in the problem definition or in the solution, over-structuring the process, or, by 'psychologisation', that is, attributing experienced difficulties, that are caused by the underlying intergroup relationship, to individuals (for instance the egos of the representatives, see the survey findings referred to above) or their relationships (Schruijer & Vansina, 2006). The shellfishery workshop, for example, was presented to the participants as an interpersonal session. They were explicitly asked to be themselves and to forget about their constituencies ... An impossible task. And insofar as it seems to work, the newly built interpersonal relationships can only bear fruit if these are subsequently related to the underlying interorganisational relationships. It is imperative to think in system terms when engaging in interorganisational interactions and to continually sort out whether what is said or done is to be explained at what systemic level (individual, interpersonal, group, intergroup or interorganisational relations, situational) and at what systemic level(s) interventions have to be directed.

WORKING WITH THE PSYCHODYNAMICS OF CONFLICT AND COLLABORATION

Relational conflict and task conflict: In all the projects the relationships between groups, departments and organisations were full of tension. The diversity of interests and identities was large. The relationships between parties were mostly of a conflictual nature, characterised by distrust and stereotyping. For example, the different workgroups in the building project, the different departments in the nursing home and in the medical call centre, with a few exceptions, exhibited so-called group serving biases in which their own group was put in a more positive light as compared to the other groups or departments.

Individuals need guidance sometimes in accepting that the reality may be constructed and/or interpreted differently depending upon one's perspective or, in this case, one's group membership. Further, help can be offered to understand the situation from the others' point of view, using for example various existing conflict management interventions or techniques (French, Bell & Zawacki, 1999). Furthermore, making a distinction between acts and utterances as an individual and as a group member is important. This might require a cognitive intervention, illustrated with some examples exhibited during the interactions. Especially since participants are being asked to communicate and behave within one's role. Further, one may reduce tension by making it intelligible and helping parties to accept that trust is unlikely to be present when individuals meet for the first time – that it is something to be developed. And, that it is quite understandable not to have clear goals from the beginning, but that these need to be constructed together and that the initial frustration is a natural part of any starting collaboration process.

In order to work at the quality of the relationships and create conditions for collaboration, multiparty interactions need to be facilitated. The establishment of shared ground rules helps in agreeing on some minimal principles that guide the interactions, such as interacting respectfully, accepting psychological equality despite role inequality, etc. Ground rules like this, jointly formulated, provide security and make behaviour more predictable. When people stick to the ground rules they can be a basis for trust development. Other conditions for trust to develop pertain to not avoiding difficult issues yet helping the parties to explore these together. If such issues cannot be dealt with in the here-and-now, separate appointments need to be made to address them. Further, it is important to pay attention to (perceived) fairness and equity and to conduct face-to-face meetings as much as possible (Gray, 1989; Schruijer & Vansina, 2004; Vansina, 1999).

Working constructively with differences, by the way, does not imply an absence of conflict. Task conflict is most desirable by which is meant a confrontation of differences in perspectives, ideas, resources, goals, identities, etc. It is only when these differences surface that ways forward can be found. It may be a frustrating process though. Generally people like to be with others and work with others who think like them, have the same values, etc. Collaboration, however, is not working with similarities but working with differences. Although a natural tendency appears to exist to suppress differences (e.g. by exercising power, or by conforming), or to ignore them through glossing over real differences, an honest confrontation of real differences is called for. That may not be done at the very first meeting. But over time, as trust develops, there will be more space to work with the differences and to find strategies to incorporate and even capitalise on them. Task conflict is the basis of creativity and innovation, unlike relational conflict where beating the other person or other group is the main goal.

Collusion: Participants of the simulation often have the feeling that they have been collaborating well – a feeling that may continue into the reviewing phase. The paradox is that while they do engage in stereotyping and power play, direct confrontations are not all that common. Besides, assumptions and 'facts' often go unchecked allowing fantasies to flourish, fantasies that serve one's aims. Thus an illusion of harmony is sustained. Since necessary task conflict is avoided, the climate is collusive rather than collaborative. In a collusive relationship parties work together in serving an implicit and often not conscious goal. It is aimed at satisfying hidden needs such as a need for attention, to be needed, to be included, to develop and reinforce a positive self-concept, etc. Also, a shared interest in avoiding a confrontation with a threatening reality may exist. As a consequence parties deny the diversity in interests and identities and reach a premature and often false consensus. A different perspective on reality may destroy the collusion. It can be introduced by an outsider, who typically recognises collusion earlier than insiders, or by a deviant from within the social system – someone who has been able to retain his or her psychological independence (Schruijer, 2008b). Important in avoiding collusion is to create conditions so that deviants can be tolerated. A climate in which diversity is valued and that is experienced as safe is essential as a sudden confrontation with reality can result in feelings of shame and loss of face.

The importance of reviewing: Reviewing the sessions and the interactions is an important part of helping groups or organisations to collaborate. It will help them share the responsibility for working with the dynamics of conflict and collusion. In such retrospective study things may come to awareness: interactions and experiences that in the heat of the exchanges could have remained suppressed. These dispersed, sporadic references can be linked to be explored together and worked through to further the task. Or they could lead to a discussion about what can be done to improve working on the task in sessions to follow. Further, it is essential to work with the here-and-now, that is, with the dynamics as they are expressed in the moment or as they are evolving during the meeting. This can be done by sharing observations and exploring why, possibly making an intervention that could be further worked with. It may have as a consequence that the activities for the joint session may diverge from the original plan but such flexibility is imperative if one really wants to start from where the client is. If too many issues pop up, at least more than can sufficiently be dealt with at the time, a running agenda can be created which helps remind the group of what needs further discussing and at the end of the session, if these have not been addressed, find space and time to do so.

Allowing for play and creativity: Thus far we have talked about sessions in which participants discuss, share opinions, and engage in cognitive tasks. Engaging in creative play, either by role-playing, playing with an idea or engaging in a creative exercise may help participants to express concerns, fears or ideas in a different way, possibly because they are more difficult to express in words (at least for some). Play and playfulness (not being completely serious) can contribute to the emergence of transitional processes to work through difficult aspects of change. In the nursing home, for example, Sandra asked the participants in one of the sessions to construct a home in which they thought it was good to work and live, using clay, paper, glue, etc. They did so in heterogeneous groups in which ideas could be discussed; ideas partly related to the creative construction, and partly related to how they wished and expected the future work setting to be. Afterwards they explored each other's creation by asking questions and making sense of what they saw and knew about one another. The homes were exhibited in the actual nursing home. Visitors to the home as well as staff who did not take part in the exercise questioned the meaning of this display of paper homes. As a consequence the display got expanded with texts containing explanations, photographs, and poetic statements revealing their processes of working through the new, displayed social architecture of the nursing home and their internal worlds.

LEADING COLLABORATION

Above we have described how attempts at leading collaboration in the simulation failed. Chrislip and Larson (1994) introduced the concept of the 'collaborative leader'; a person who is neutral, works at the process of collaboration yet has no stake in its content, convenes the parties and facilitates their interaction, and minimises power and status differences between the parties in the collaboration process. He or she does not have a formal authority or power position and does not aspire to one. Described in such terms, the leadership role is a facilitative one, rather than a stereotypical managerial one that is based on power. Attributing those activities to a person called a collaborative leader is not meant to take all responsibility away from members when it concerns leadership activities. If the designated leader does not fulfil these activities or does so inappropriately, other representatives present can step in and, among others, can help discuss which ground rules need to be adopted, point attention to process issues that need discussing, etc. Representatives might not be neutral but even that can be accepted temporarily, as long as it can be discussed by those involved. Leadership, rather than a role, can evolve into a function that can be shared.

Leading collaborative processes cannot be invested in everyone. The person must be able to face a lot of ambiguity, uncertainty and tensions without falling into a position of judging others: making black-and-white distinctions or good and bad categories. Such reactions divide the world instead of seeing overlapping interests, spotting complementarities and ambiguities that signal a changing position.

Leading collaboration involves creating conditions for the different parties to come to a common problem definition and a strategy to deal with it (Schruijer, Taillieu & Vansina, 1998). Sponsors, managers, other employees and the consultants all play a role in leading collaboration. The sponsors are making time, space and resources available. The extent to which their expectations are realistic, they are willing to take part as an actor in the process, and are capable of 'not-knowing', is determining the success of any intervention. In the nursing home the sponsors were willing 'not to know' and agreed with a very open-ended and participatory approach. They were capable of staying in role while being able to build relationships with employees, being sincere and caring in their behaviour, and being able to show their concerns with respect to experienced difficulties within the nursing home.

The consultant helps by creating the time and space and other supportive process and facilitating structures for working at collaboration and by designing an intervention, enabling parties to deal with emerging dynamics, from a position in which the whole client-system can benefit. He or she does so together with the sponsors and with other members of the participating parties or organisations who may have joined steering groups or support groups yet who also may take up leadership activities during the intervention, for example, by drawing attention to here-and-now dynamics or by calling for new ground rules to be established or simply by contributing to getting the task done.

EXPLORING THE 'WHY?'

Some generic dilemmas and issues have been enumerated and discussed. The underlying dynamic processes and the ways they are dealt with vary with (a) the mix and nature of the groups involved (e.g. organised or unorganised aggregates, established groups, legal, independent entities), (b) the kind of problem domain concerned and (c) the wider context in which collaborative efforts take place. In this wider context, one finds other groups, organisations and institutions that cannot be called 'stakeholders' but who may not remain neutral or passive in the face of collaborative efforts around a given problem. Latent concerns or interests may become salient by leaked information about how the problem domain is being dealt with, its anticipated outcomes and the likely changes in the socio-economic and political fabric of inter-related institutions and groups. This has two major consequences. First, the attention to the 'why' of what is going on cannot be restricted to the parties trying to work together. It must also include or cover the institutions in the wider context that become secretly or openly active in exerting influence on the collaborative processes, either directly or indirectly through the media or through third parties. Second, the answers to the 'why' questions, or the generated understanding of the processes beneath the surface, tend to be specific for each case.

The uncertainty, the ambiguity and the lack of valid information increase tensions within the collaborative work system and create a breeding ground for unchecked assumptions, stereotypes and defensive moves. All together they provide good reasons for managers and consultants to try to understand and get a grasp of the underlying processes. Yet, not all processes need to be brought to awareness, in order to work them through constructively as we have seen in the project of the nursing home. Transitional processes, self-reflection and facilitating structures may do the work. However, there are some processes that if not dealt with consciously will continue to create some barriers to genuine collaboration and task accomplishment. We think here about systematic attempts to distort valid information and/or unconscious escapes from the realities into fantasy, hidden manoeuvres to exclude or isolate a party, dominant leadership coupled with the pursuit of self interests, enduring stereotyping as the outcome of splitting and projection of the good parts in one party (positive stereotyping, idealising), or projection of the bad parts into another (negative stereotyping, scapegoat, demonising). In both instances part of the whole reality is denied. The most difficult of them all, is when a group or party becomes the object of projective identification. Fortunately, that only happens rarely.

Many, if not most of the 'why' questions may not be aimed at understanding unconscious underlying processes, but at exploring reasons, concerns and fears behind the positions taken in discussion, bargaining and conflict situations. Getting such 'undisclosed' information on the table enriches the database and enables the parties to focus on the major interests, concerns and fears. Furthermore, this kind of questioning may serve as a model to enable negotiators to move from positional or competitive into interest bargaining.

CONCLUDING REMARKS

While managers tend to become overactive to get control over the collaborative processes to achieve tangible results, consultants too often see their role exclusively in terms of process facilitation. They underestimate the importance of creating facilitating and process support structures that enable development of trust, collaborative relations and task accomplishment. Trust and collaboration cannot be designed, they come through hard work. Obstacles are gradually removed to achieve a shared problem definition and a jointly constructed common goal in which the parties can recognise some of their own advantages. Much of this work is achieved through processes one is often not aware of.

A lot of intuitive understanding and creativity help us to create these supportive process and facilitating structures, while encouraging other participants to venture their own (Vansina, 2007). A standard facilitating structure is to collect information, prior to the meeting, by a neutral third party and to present the raw data in a subsequent first meeting of the stakeholders. The data becomes then the ground for various interpretations and sense-making processes that can be checked against the raw data and respective 'experiences'. Thereby a process may start of an internal 'dialogue' between the outer and inner world of the participating parties.

Ambiguity is an important feature in collaborative work systems. Minimal structures may help people to better focus their interactions, reduce some of the chaos and tensions, but they may not eliminate ambiguity to the point that one is left with only one choice: either to accept or reject a proposal or position. Some ambiguity is a necessary condition for creativity and change. One must allow for slight shifts in position, that do not express so much inconsistency, but may reveal a phase in changing one's point of view. Yet, when one has arrived at searching for final agreement all ambiguity needs to be gradually removed, so that all parties involved can check its feasibility and know what they are committing themselves to.

An important ground rule that we would like to become established is the right to formulate deviant points of view and a commitment to pay attention to individual observations, afterthoughts or reflections. They need to be explored for their potential value either for clarifying underlying tensions or for bringing the group back to reality and the task they came together to accomplish.

REFERENCES

Bunker, B. & Alban, B. (1997). *Large group interventions. Engaging the whole system for rapid change*. San Francisco: Jossey-Bass.

Cherns, A. (1987). Principles of socio-technical design revisited. *Human Relations*, **40**, 153–162.

Chrislip, D. & Larson, C. (1994). *Collaborative leadership*. San Francisco: Jossey-Bass.

Cummings, T. & Worley, C. (1997). *Organisation development and change*. St Paul, MN.: West Publishing Company.

French, W., Bell, C. & Zawacki, R. (1999). *Organisation Development and transformation: Managing effective change*. Boston, MA.: McGraw-Hill.

Gray, B. (1989). *Collaborating: Finding common ground for multiparty problems*. San Francisco: Jossey-Bass.

Huijbregts, P. (2006). *Conceptueel bouwen: Denken in doelgroepen*. SBR Rotterdam: Giethoorn ten Brink.

Huxham, C. & Vangen, S. (2005). *Managing to collaborate: The theory and practice of collaborative advantage*. London: Routledge.

Neven, I. & Schruijer, S. (2005). Creativity and conflict in shellfish fisheries: Assessment of a short intervention. In: T. Goessling, R. Jansen & L. Oerlemans (Eds), *Coalitions and collisions*. Nijmegen: Wolf Publishers, 197–206.

Schruijer, S. (2001). "Bringing the whole system in a room": A participant's perspective. In: B. Boog, H. Coenen & L. Keune (Eds), *Action research: Empowerment and reflection*. Tilburg: Dutch University Press, 175–184.

Schruijer, S. (2002). *Delen en helen: Over conflict en samenwerking tussen groepen*. Inaugural address, Tilburg University.

Schruijer, S. (2006a). Leadership and interorganisational collaboration as perceived by directors and managers. In: N. Gould (Ed.), *Engagement*. Exeter: Short Run Press, 271–280.

Schruijer, S. (2006b). Research on collaboration in action. *International Journal of Action Research*, **2** (2), 222–242.

Schruijer, S. (2008a). The psychology of interorganisational relations. In: S. Cropper, M. Ebers, C. Huxham & P. Smith Ring (Eds), *Handbook of interorganisational relations*. Oxford: Oxford University Press (forthcoming).

Schruijer, S. (2008b). *Samenwerking, collusie en de rol van devianten*. Inaugural address, University of Utrecht.

Schruijer, S., Taillieu, T. & Vansina, L. (1998). *'Leadership' in collaborative task-systems*. Paper presented at the Fifth International Conference on Multi-Organisational Partnerships and Cooperative Strategy, Oxford, 6–8 July.

Schruijer, S. & Vansina, L. (2004). Multiparty collaboration and leadership. In: T. Camps, P. Diederen, G.-J. Hofstede & B. Vos (Eds), *The emerging world of chains and networks: Bridging theory and practice*. The Hague: Reed Business Information, 219–234.

Schruijer, S. & Vansina, L. (2006). The meaning of 'social' in interpersonal conflict and its resolution. In: P. Herrman (Ed.), *Blackwell handbook of mediation and conflict resolution: Tools for working with interpersonal problems*. Malden MA.: Blackwell, 326–343.

Stephenson, G. (1984). Intergroup and interpersonal dimensions of bargaining and negotiation. In: H. Tajfel (Ed.), *The social dimension: European developments in social psychology (Vol. 2)*. Cambridge: Cambridge University Press.

Vansina, L. (1999). Towards a dynamic perspective on trust-building. In: S. Schruijer (Ed.), *Multi-organisational partnerships and cooperative strategy*. Tilburg: Dutch University Press, 47–52.

Vansina, L. (2000). The relevance and perversity of psychodynamic interventions in consulting and action-research. *Concepts and Transformation*, 5, 321–348.

Vansina, L. (2007). *How could one lead without being the leader?* Paper presented at the MOPAN conference: Learning for Interdependence, Leuven, June 28–29.

Vansina, L., & Taillieu, T. (1997). Diversity in collaborative task-systems. *European Journal of Work and Organisational Psychology*, 6, 183–199.

Vansina, L., Taillieu, T. & Schruijer, S. (1998). 'Managing' multiparty issues: Learning from experience. In: W. Pasmore & R. Woodman (Eds), *Research in Organisational Change and Development (Vol. 10)*. Greenwich, CT: JAI Press, 159–181.

Vansina, L., Taillieu, T. & Schruijer, S. (1999). *The Yacht Club: A simulation of multigroup processes*. Korbeek-Lo: Professional Development Institute.

Weisbord, M. (2004). *Productive workplaces revisited: Dignity, meaning and community in the 21st century*. San Francisco: Jossey-Bass.

Glossary

Accountability   refers to being answerable for one's indirect actions like the outcomes of delegated responsibilities. Accountability in contrast to **responsibility** can't be delegated.

Action-Research   a research model that encourages broad participation of the people concerned in the research process and supports actions leading to a more just and satisfying situation for the stakeholders, while generating learning from these transformations.

Affect regulation   refers to the capacity to monitor, evaluate and modify the intensity and form of expression of affect in the pursuit of goals.

Anxiety   (in psychoanalytic thinking) is an emotional response of the unconscious as a dynamic system (Ucs.) to vague dangers emanating from the inner or the external world. Fear is a basic emotional reaction to specific situations or objects that are recognised as dangerous.

Apprehension   refers to the mental mode of heightened consciousness to perceive and comprehend what is out there.

Audit   a methodical review of prescribed norms/ standards and procedures with the current practices, followed by an organised inquiry into the reasons behind observed deviations. Depending on the diagnosis and understanding of the system under audit, special action needs to be taken e.g. additional training, adjustment of outdated procedures. Audit information must be relevant to the purpose of the system and valid.

Authority   the legitimate power to act upon others to achieve a given outcome.

Basic assumptions   are modes of group behaviour, in which members act as if they are working hard on the given task while in fact – and often visible for outsiders – they seem to share and work with unrealistic and unconscious assumptions about the group, its task and leadership. Basic assumption functioning occurs in small groups (8 to 15 members), whose task is experienced as dangerous, while group members are interdependent for the successful completion of it. Some authors use the thinking of basic assumptions more freely, beyond these small group conditions, to explain behaviour in organisations.

Boundaries   (a) mental boundaries are the outcomes of a mental frame that separates and relates what is within from what is outside a system.
(b) social boundaries refer to groupings of persons who are bonding together and/or who derive their social identity from their membership within that group. In sociology one distinguishes symbolic from social boundaries. The first refer to conceptual distinctions to categorise objects, people, practices and even space and time. Social boundaries are objectified forms of social differences manifested in unequal access to and unequal distribution of resources.
(c) system boundaries are not an objective given; they always refer to a purpose and to intentions by those who define them.

Boundary management   the management of transactions with the external world in order to maintain a dynamic equilibrium of the social system with its environment. The dynamic equilibrium is experienced as tensions between opposing forces to maintain and to create, between continuity and discontinuity in the system.

Boundary role   refers to a psychological and structural location an individual occupies in which s/he carries dual roles (or membership), one in his sentient group of constituents and one with 'outsiders' (or task group).

Client-system the system that holds the problem and whose members will become engaged in the change efforts either as actors and/or subjects. They may or may not benefit or suffer from the change outcomes.

Clinical sciences or 'les sciences cliniques' refers to an action-research approach, which puts more emphasis on understanding than on mastering or control, more on discovery than on giving evidence, more on generating in-depth understanding than on formulating universal laws.

Collaborative task system is a work system in which legally independent, interested parties (or their representatives) come together to work on a largely self-constructed task or problem.

Consultative approach an approach by which consultant/manager and client search together to gain a better understanding of the situation one is in so as to take effective action.

Disillusionment the shattering of an illusion whereby people are brought back into contact with reality.

Displacement one of the primary processes by which a person shifts his interest from a specific object or activity to another in such a way that the second becomes a substitute for the first. It is one of the important processes in dream construction.

Dominant logics are social constructions of reality like one-liners or statements of common wisdom that through their rational and logical appeal block further critical investigation and creative search for alternative courses of action.

Dream life a notion indicating that dream-like processes not only belong to sleep, but go on as well all through waking life. In this way of thinking dreams become 'the internal space where meaning is generated'.

Dream thoughts is the notion that Bion introduced to refer to the first mental products that result from the processing, the 'digestion', of raw sense data.

Effectiveness refers to the extent that a work system is achieving its objectives.

Efficacy   refers to the extent that a work system is using the most appropriate means (work methods, technology) to achieve task accomplishment.

Efficiency   refers to the degree to which a work system is achieving its objectives without wasting resources (time, money, energy, space, people and material).

Enlarged unconscious   consists of elements human beings are not aware of like: (a) material that has been socially suppressed through interactions, (b) social defences embedded in work systems, (c) defensive strategies and routines. They may become revealed in actions, words, imageries and relations.

Experiencing   as a mental mode refers to a less conscious, more passive receptive state to allow the 'here-and-now' to come into the person of its own force. The real world becomes reflected within the person but in its relation to that person. It is a subjective, partial reflection of what is out there.

Facilitating structure   is any device (a method, a technique, a rearrangement of the composition of the group, or its conditions) that facilitates task accomplishment either through organising information processing or physical efforts, and/or through the reduction of stress within the work system without determining the outcome of the task.

Fantasy   is a fully conscious, multi-functional mental process, which may be influenced by phantasies.

Fear   see Anxiety.

Flow analysis   a methodical study of the successive transformation processes in a work system to produce a desired output. The purpose of a flow analysis is to improve the functioning of the work system by aligning the successive transformation processes and the removal of repetitive delays, stoppages and quality problems.

Frame   is any kind of structure that organises a person's experiences perceived as outside or inside oneself and renders them meaningful. A frame facilitates people to locate, perceive, identify and label phenomena. Frames are implied in the responses of people to occurrences. Frames become part of the human being and are socially embedded.

Fusion   a formation of parts into a whole, through conscious or unconscious processes, wherein the parts can only be distinguished with difficulty, or not at all.

Groupthink   a situation in which the members of a group abandon their individual capabilities to think independently in favour of thinking like the group seems to be thinking.

Happy learning   is learning by accumulating or adding more things to what one already knows, extending and/or refining one's repertoire in a particular domain. This kind of learning is experienced as enriching.

Here-and-now   is the space in which a social system is active at any given time. It refers to what is happening or not happening in the interactions and what is emerging in relations and images within a social system that is engaged in a task.

Id, ego, super-ego   in Freud's structural theory, these are the three entities that constitute the adult mental system and its functioning. Developmentally the id is the original part of the mental system (called 'apparatus' in Freud's original terminology). It contains the psychic expression of everything that is present in the constitution at birth. Later on it will also contain whatever becomes repressed. As it conforms to primary process functioning, it is directed at immediate satisfaction of all needs. Through demands of reality and under parental influence, part of the id develops into the ego, which conforms to secondary process functioning and is therefore better adapted to external reality. One of its basic tasks is to compromise between internal needs and external demands, often through postponement of satisfaction and often mostly in order to avoid punishment. The super-ego (a combination of ideal-ego and conscience) develops at the end of the Oedipal relationship, out of that part of the ego that introjects the values and norms of the parent towards whom the child felt ambivalent. Later on, it may become more complex through personal choices and through the assimilation of ideals and norms of respected or admired others.

Identification   (a) in psychoanalytic literature it refers to a largely unconscious mental process whereby a person assimilates a quality of another person and makes it part of his or her own constitution. It can be based on a wish to be like that other person, or on anxiety, like in the identification with the aggressor.

(b) In social psychology it means a process that occurs when an individual accepts influence because s/he wants to establish or maintain a satisfying self-defining relationship with another person or group.

Inner world   a mental space wherein personal representations of the external world (persons and objects) 'live' and interact with each other.

Inspection   a systematic, most often un-announced, follow-up to see if procedures, machines, tools, processes, inputs and outputs are in fact still meeting the prescribed specifications.

Internalisation   (a) in the psychoanalytic literature it refers to a mental process by which elements of the external world acquire permanent mental representation in the inner world.
(b) In social psychology it refers to a process whereby an individual accepts influence because the content of the induced behaviour (e.g. the ideas and actions) is intrinsically rewarding.

Interpretation   is the process of elucidating the meaning and background of a way of feeling, experiencing, thinking, acting, behaving or organising over and above, under and below the one consciously given to it by the client. It is a process of tentatively adding, rephrasing, introducing links as those become indirectly expressed in an actual situation. Worthwhile interpretations are only possible in the context of an ongoing relationship characterised by a sufficient level of basic trust and an agreement that whatever is brought up or occurs in the here-and-now, can be thought and talked about. Such interpretations are the result of explorative, associative interactions, while the final conclusion resides with the client (system), never with the consultant. If a client (system) accepts an interpretation on the basis of the high reputation of his consultant, without the gut feeling that it makes sense, that 'something falls into place', that it 'opens new perspectives', even although initially it created some anxiety, be sure: this interpretation is worthless. It will never induce needed changes; at best it may be used (sometimes mockingly) for a while as an interesting explanation of an existing reality.

Intersubjectivity   denotes the shared experiences that occur between interacting human beings (and groups) with reciprocity and mutual influence. Intersubjectivity theory is a field theory that seeks to understand psychological phenomena not as products of isolated intra psychic mechanisms, but as forming at the interface of reciprocally interacting worlds of experience.

Learning group is a small, temporary group (up to 15 members and a specially trained consultant) formed to learn from the various ways a group and its members can work on a given, minimally structured task and from the emerging psychodynamic processes.

Mental capability or work capacity a person's ability to work (the exercise of judgement and discretion in making decisions in carrying out goal-directed activities) which is a function of his/her cognitive capability. Mental capabilities can be measured in the way an individual collects and processes information from the outside world.

Mental modes refer to different levels of consciousness in being present whereby different realities come into being.

Mentalisation is a psychic process by which a person manages to keep together within him/herself the bits and pieces of his/her sensory experiences, link them up with their emotional counterparts, stand the pain and anxiety that may accompany this process, and then use the whole to think and maybe talk about, rather than throw the different elements around in the external world.

Non-conscious a state of mind in which human beings behave without being fully aware of their actions, images and relations which have been conscious, but which are no longer directly available to awareness. They have either been replaced by an automatic response to a situation, or have been suppressed through social interaction. Their access through reflection and confrontation is however much easier than when they are unconscious.

Object relations theory is a psychoanalytic theory in which the person's need to relate to other persons and objects occupies a central position. This is in contrast to instinct theory, which centres on the person's need to reduce tension.

Oedipal relation vs. Oedipus complex is (in Freudian theory) the normal phase between infantile autoerotic and adult sexuality. It occurs between the ages of three and five and is characterised by the desire/wish to possess the parent of the opposite sex for one's self, which necessitates the elimination of the parent of the same sex towards whom the child feels ambivalent: as parent, s/he is loved, as rival s/he is hated. It is often said that according to M. Klein the Oedipal phase starts already in the first year of life. Yet, what

M. Klein talked about is not quite the same. At this early age complicated experiences such as ambivalence do not yet occur. The only thing possible at that time would be that one parent is seen as all good and loved, the other as all bad and hated. In fact, what Klein stresses is that triangular relations start much earlier in life than Freud thought, and that the course taken by the first one will influence the course of the second one. In normal development the Oedipal relation will be solved – outgrown – around the age of seven. It might resurface shortly during puberty, and finally be worked through. At least in our western civilisation, Oedipal relationships are a normal part of growing-up. An Oedipus complex however is not. It occurs only when the Oedipal relations get repressed instead of resolved. This important distinction seems to be lost in contemporary literature, where the notion of Oedipal relationships has disappeared in favour of Oedipal complex.

Participative thinking and responsive acting   as a mental state refers to being present and engaged in joint activities, without reasoning, but in response to the requirements of circumstances shared with others. There is meaning and direction in the interactions before they are consciously processed and even talked about.

Phantasy   (today sometimes referred to as phantasm) is a technical notion, originating in the field of kleinian psychoanalysis. It is an unconscious process of sense making that seems to start even before we are born and then goes on all through life. As such it belongs to the realm of the dynamic unconscious processes, and it may have an influence on all sorts of conscious mental activities and on their behavioural consequences.

Pre-conception   is (in Bion's thinking) an innate disposition, a kind of adapted expectation, about the objects that are right for the satisfaction of needs. Once such a connection is established, the pre-conception can develop into conceptions. Put into a broader kleinian perspective, one could say that conceptions belong to the domain of phantasies. As such, pre-conceptions can give rise to several quite different conceptions while the notion 'concept' (which belongs in the field of secondary process thinking) is fixed.

Primary process thinking   is the way of thinking typical for the unconscious as a system. It is characterised by condensation (a process by which different images combine into one, or a word is simultaneously used in different meanings), displacement (a process whereby attention is transferred from an important element to a more neutral or less scary one) and an elementary form of symbolisation based on the combination of images. Primary process thinking forms the basis for dream building, while need satisfaction can be obtained in an imaginary way.

Problem setting   is an existing situation with all its aspects (social, technical, physical, economic) in which at least some persons are dissatisfied; other possibilities are therefore considered worth investigating.

Psychodynamics   refers to the study and the body of knowledge of the psychic forces and associated processes operative within a social system.

Psychodynamic approach   an approach through which it is endeavoured to gain a good enough understanding of the conscious and unconscious reasons, rational and irrational for what is happening or not happening, but supposed to in a social system. This understanding forms the basis for taking action to improve the functioning of that system in a more lasting way, while offering opportunities for psychic development of the people in it.

Psycho-familial dimension of personality   is that part of the human being that is the product of our childhood history, our identifications, counter-identifications and early conflicts. It is distinct from the **Psycho-social dimension of personality** which is that part of the human being that can be developed within institutions through our acts, our possibility to create.

Real (intergroup) Conflict   or realistic group conflict arises when groups have to compete to obtain the scarce resources necessary to achieve their interests as their respective goals are incompatible. **Social Identity Conflict** on the other hand is the conflict that results from either the attempts of groups to increase their social esteem by gaining membership in a higher status group which denies access, or from efforts to ward off attempts to reduce the social standing of one's group identity. Underlying these attempts are the dynamics of categorisation, identification and comparison.

Reality acceptance   refers to the willingness and capability to accept and adapt to changing realities one either cannot change or one does not want to change.

Reality exploration   is the activated capacity to be fully present and to listen and compare observable behaviour with what is being said with an interest in finding out what is happening in or with a system in its context.

Reality object   an object that exists in the external world. Such an object e.g. a figure, a method, a facilitating structure, a 'raison d'être' can be taken as a cover around which transitional processes can emerge.

Reality testing   is the active capacity to withhold acting upon one's impressions, assumptions or understanding of people, social systems or the external world until they have been sufficiently explored and validated.

Reflection   as a mental mode refers to a somewhat less active state of consciousness enabling the making sense in retrospect of emerging experiences, incidents and feelings from what happened in the 'here-and-now'.

Reflective planning   reflections are focussed on the articulations of assumptions one makes about what is likely to happen when one takes a particular action, for example in strategic planning.

Reparation or making good   is a healthy mental process together with its behavioural counterparts by which people try to repair whatever damage they may, intentionally or not, real or imagined, consciously or unconsciously have done to other people or to things that are dear to them. Reparation helps to control destructiveness by love and care and to increase trust in the positive qualities of one's love.

Paranoid-schizoid and depressive positions   are the notions that M. Klein introduced to refer to phases in psychic development. M. Klein prefers the notion 'position' because it is more encompassing than 'phase', which often indicates only a passing developmental level of a specific drive while the term 'position' refers to a specific combination of object relations, anxieties and defence mechanisms which persist throughout life, although most of the time one position dominates over the other. As such, the **paranoid-schizoid position**, which is the starting one, is characterised by the fact that infants do not perceive persons as complex entities, but seem to equate individuals (called 'part-objects) with each different function that people perform for them. The dominant anxiety, which belongs to that position, is of a paranoid nature, and splitting mechanisms are preferred defences. The **depressive position** is marked by the recognition of whole persons – persons that one recognises as performing different functions in different ways at different moments. This supposes the activity of integrative functions, and introduces feelings of ambivalence, depressive anxiety and guilt about the anger and hate one might feel towards loved ones. At all times people may oscillate between the two positions.

Secondary gains   benefits derived indirectly from one or another form of overt suffering whereby the status quo is maintained.

Secondary process thinking   (the counter part of primary process thinking) is a form of thinking which is adapted to reality and follows the rules of logic, rational, scientific thought processes; it tries to reduce the tensions created by unsatisfied needs through adaptation to the exigencies of reality, which may only mean: avoiding punishment.

Sense making   is an active process by which pieces of data are brought together into a congruent whole that draws light and gives new meaning to what may appear unrelated. It is more an invention than a discovery of a concealed meaning and it always includes a 'fragrance' of doubt.

Sentient group   the group on which a member depends for emotional gratification (e.g. recognition, rewards) as distinct from a **Task group** in which members derive frustration and emotional gratification from working on the task.

Social Architecture   refers to the knowledge and experiences in the behavioural sciences pertinent to the theory and practice of building viable institutions

Sorting out   a reflective process by which one tries to distinguish what experiences are proper to oneself from those that are either generated or induced by another person, a group or a situation.

Splitting   is one of the original, primitive defence mechanisms. It is a phantasmatic process by which good qualities/characteristics of objects/ people are separated from bad ones, thereby avoiding ambivalent feelings and creating the illusion that some things may be all good while others are totally bad. Splitting is always related to denial (of the good parts in the bad ones and vice versa), and often provides the basis for idealisation.

Steering information   information needed for corrective, regulative action by the actors in a work system. The corrective feedback information must point to a statistically significant deviation from the set standard or norm to avoid over-steering and oscillation of the work system.

Supportive process structures   are conditions created (e.g. 'holding', 'containing', 'time and space') to enable constructive mental processes to take their own course: 'psychic development', 'transitional processes' and 'reparation'.

Task work   refers to all the activities, appropriate or not, that are carried out to achieve task accomplishment.

Team-work   points to the various ways members work together to achieve task completion.

The setting   refers at the same time to the nature of the unit under study (in its context) as well as to its task and objectives.

Transformation   (a) In psychoanalytic literature it refers to a fundamental change in mental processes whereby a person not only behaves differently but is also changed at the level of 'being'; his/her inner world has changed. (b) In Organisational Development it means a genuine change from an old organisation into a new organisation that feels differently, functions differently and in a more humane way.
(c) In systems theory it refers to a conversion of some input into some output.

Transitional change   points to the provision of enabling conditions to help human beings to work through the tensions of moving from the past to a future that is only partly known and largely imagined.

Transitional object   is an object e.g. a toy, a tune, a reality object that bridges and makes contact possible between the individual psyche and the external reality; that gives room for the process of becoming able to accept differences and similarities.

Transitional space   a neutral, intermediate space between the inner and the outer world that allows for transition from a subjective state to a more objective state of experiencing the world, allowing the individual to distinguish fantasy from facts, inner reality from external objects. Within the context of **transitional change** it refers not to an internal space of experience, but to external conditions of time, space and sanction to allow transitional processes to emerge.

Unconscious (a) system-wise (Ucs.) refers to our primary, original way of mental functioning that is, over a period of about 15 years, slowly and almost completely, supplanted by different forms of conceptual, rational, scientific thinking. Yet, this original way of mental functioning stays active. During sleep it produces dreams and it may have an important influence on whatever we experience or do during our waking hours. This is why one can refer to it as 'dynamic'. It expresses itself through what we called "the languages of images, actions and relationships". It becomes visible also by the way of defensive mechanisms, processes and structures.
(b) content-wise, and apart from our original ways of explaining experiences, it also contains whatever disappeared from consciousness through repression and suppression. The repressed parts can give rise to symptom formation as an aspect of psychological problems.

Unhappy learning is disconfirming learning, it involves a reorganisation of the values, beliefs, axioms, theories and models that together make up one's personal paradigm, which has been built up through one's life experiences. It often entails 'unlearning' and it may even lead to changes in one's identity.

Unthought known a kind of knowing that can't yet be shared, since one has not been able to conceptualise it.

Work information information needed for doing the work properly and/or information generated by doing the work that another person needs to do good work.

Work system There are many definitions possible in function of one's purpose. In most general terms a work system is conceived as a purposeful system consisting of a system of activities and a system of human beings by which input is transformed in a desired output.

Working through is a healthy mental process of integrating new or painful experiences e.g. a troubling insight, a loss of something valuable, real or imagined (an illusion) into a new, accepted state of being.

Worrying through a mental process of elaborating upon the anticipated positive and negative consequences of particular courses of action before committing oneself to one or another action or decision.

. . . And in this complex world,

the only one we have,

we carry on

working, worrying, loving, trying to find out

and creating new ways into the future,

a socially desirable and sustainable future.

Index

Note: Page references in **bold** refer to the Glossary

Printed and bound by CPI Group (UK) Ltd, Croydon, CR0 4YY

16/04/2025

14658543-0005